Constructing Foucault's ethics

Manchester University Press

Constructing Foucault's ethics

A poststructuralist moral theory for the twenty-first century

Mark Olssen

MANCHESTER UNIVERSITY PRESS

Copyright © Mark Olssen 2021

The right of Mark Olssen to be identified as the author of this work has been asserted by him in accordance with the Copyright, Designs and Patents Act 1988.

Published by Manchester University Press
Oxford Road, Manchester M13 9PL

www.manchesteruniversitypress.co.uk

British Library Cataloguing-in-Publication Data
A catalogue record for this book is available from the British Library

ISBN 978 1 5261 5660 0 hardback
ISBN 978 1 5261 7627 1 paperback

First published 2021

The publisher has no responsibility for the persistence or accuracy of URLs for any external or third-party internet websites referred to in this book, and does not guarantee that any content on such websites is, or will remain, accurate or appropriate.

Typeset by
Servis Filmsetting Ltd, Stockport, Cheshire

This book is dedicated to the memory of
David McKenzie
Barbara Calvert
John Codd
James D. Marshall
Peter Jarvis
and
Judith McFarlane

When today we see the meaning, or rather the almost total absence of meaning, given to some nonetheless very familiar expressions which continue to permeate our discourse – like getting back to oneself, freeing oneself, being oneself, being authentic, etcetera ... I think we may have to suspect that we find it impossible today to constitute an ethic of the self, even though it may be an urgent, fundamental, and politically indispensable task, if it is true after all that there is no first or final point of resistance to political power other than the relationship one has to oneself.

Michel Foucault

Foucault allies himself with the critical tradition, but will anyone extend him a welcoming hand?

Judith Butler

Success is not final, failure is not fatal, it is the courage to continue that counts.

Winston Churchill

Contents

Preface	viii
Introduction	1
1 Foucault and normativity	31
2 Life and error: Foucault, Canguilhem, Jacob	56
3 Nietzsche's life philosophy: naturalism, will to power, normativity	85
4 Continuance ethics, objectivity, Kant	116
5 Foucault, Hegel, Marx	157
6 Hobbes, God, and modern social contract theory	187
7 A politics of pluralism	220
8 Democracy, education, global ethics	243
9 Ethical comportment	262
Appendix 1: A reading list for Foucault's ethics	292
Appendix 2: The Anglo-American and Continental traditions on Nietzsche scholarship, a note	295
References	298
Index	329

Preface

Writing this book has been somewhat experimental, an approach I justify with reference to Foucault and Nietzsche, who saw experimentalism as methodologically central to ethics in a world as uncertain as the one we live in. Although I have read Foucault for some thirty years and have already published two books where his name warrants a place in the title (Olssen, 1999; 2006; 2009), I had become increasingly dissatisfied at the lack of an explicit normative perspective on his work. This book is my attempt to correct that lacuna. Although it doesn't pretend to be a work in advancing Foucault scholarship, and in this sense does not claim to be an exegesis of his *oeuvre* or any of his central concepts, it does seek to construct a normative theory, complete with a perspective on ethics and morality, that is consistent with the core principles that have guided Foucault's approach. It therefore seeks to elaborate an ethics that is not explicitly stated, or even implicitly embodied, in Foucault's work, but is consistent with his approach overall. It starts from the acknowledgement that Foucault didn't develop an ethics, and hence this book is my attempt to construct one for him. This is my effort to render Foucault as normative.

It is experimental in another sense; in the sense that it has meaning for me, and assists in helping me to resolve some of the 'nagging doubts' that I have had in adhering to Foucault's approach over thirty odd years. This, however, can also be justified with reference to Foucault: As he says:

> [I]t would probably not be worth the trouble of making books if they failed to teach the author something he hadn't known before, if

they didn't lead to unforeseen places, and if they didn't dispense one toward a strange new relation with himself. This pain and pleasure of the book is to be an experience. (1984a: 339)

These 'nagging doubts' led me to formulate a basis for making normative sense that, even before I attempted to think the issues through in any coherent way, was of assistance in justifying the types of normative claims that one unwittingly makes. The types of formulas and answers I adopted developed quite independently of writers such as Badiou, who was also influenced by Foucault and who has also written on ethics. I have read Badiou only recently, and his insights and views have subsequently provided a rich source of inspiration and encouragement. In my own views, I have tried to utilize Foucault's approach as a *dispositif* in a way that links him with Nietzsche and Heidegger to provide an approach to ethics that is novel and quite different to existing models on offer in the Anglophone world – Kantianism, Hegel or Marx, Bentham, Aristotle, alterity, multiculturalism/difference, or identity. I try as best I can to relate these ideas to my own in order to show how they can work to arbitrate ethical dilemmas.

This book is also an extension of my previous one, *Toward a Global Thin Community* (2009), in that it constitutes part of a series rather than standing alone. In that book I first introduced the concept of life continuance to express a normative orientation to the future in terms of the quest for survival and well-being, giving rise to irreducible normative values as part of the discursive order of events (Olssen, 2009: esp. ch. 6). This book seeks to develop that conception further and, in this sense, it is a continuation of my writing. Given that, as stated, I am not primarily concerned to advance a faithful summary or compendium of Foucault scholarship, I have decided not to reference citations in both English and French, in the way that some authors have done in recent years (see O'Leary, 2002; Eldon, 2016). In this book, I will reference using the English translations, or English originals where the text was first published in English.

The section of the introduction on complexity builds on analyses in my essays 'Foucault as Complexity Theorist: Overcoming the Problems of Classical Philosophical Analysis', in Mark

Mason (ed.), *Complexity Theory and the Philosophy of Education* (Oxford: Wiley–Blackwell, 2008), pp. 91–111, and 'Ascertaining the Normative Implications of Complexity Thinking for Politics: Beyond Agent-Based Modeling', in Emilian Kavalski (ed.), *World Politics at the Edge of Chaos: Reflections on Complexity and Global Life* (Albany, NY: SUNY Press, 2015), pp. 139–66. Part of the analysis of Foucault on structural linguistics is drawn from my earlier book, *Michel Foucault: Materialism and Education* (London: Bergin and Garvey, 1999). Parts of the introduction and Chapter 5 draw on material from M. Olssen and W. Mace, 'British Idealism, Complexity Theory and Society: The Political Usefulness of T. H. Green in a Revised Conception of Social Democracy', *Linguistic and Philosophical Investigations*, 20.1 (2021), pp. 7–34. Chapters 3, 4, and 5 draw in part on material from my article, 'The Rehabilitation of the Concept of Public Good: Reappraising the Attacks from Liberalism and Neo-Liberalism from a Poststructuralist Perspective', *Review of Contemporary Philosophy*, 20 (2021), pp. 7–52. Chapter 5 draws on my responses in R. Raaper and M. Olssen, 'In Conversation with Mark Olssen: On Foucault with Marx and Hegel', *Open Review of Educational Research*, 4.1 (2017), pp. 96–117. Chapter 7 draws in part on material in 'Foucault and Neoliberalism: A Response to Critics and a New Resolution', *Materiali Foucaultiani*, V.12–13 (2019), pp. 28–55. Parts of the introduction and Chapter 8 draw on material in 'Complexity and Learning: Implications for Teacher Education', in Michael A. Peters, Bronwen Cowie, and Ian Mentor (eds), *A Companion to Research in Teacher Education* (Singapore: Springer Nature, 2017). The editors and publishers of these works, and my co-authors, are thanked for the use of this material.

As with any book such as this, various friends and colleagues have assisted or supported me, even if only to ask how it was coming along. Among those that I would like to acknowledge are my mentors and referees, and the staff at Manchester University Press, who have been extremely supportive, especially Alun Richards, Emma Brennan, and Caroline Wintersgill. Evangelia Sembou and Hugh Lauder kindly read over a final version of the manuscript in the months preceding its submission and I am very grateful for the invaluable suggestions and comments that they

Preface

made. I would also like to thank my colleagues at the University of Surrey, as well as those from New Zealand and throughout the world, including Marie Breen-Smyth, Chris Flood, Martyn Barrett, John Eade, Alex Brimson, Tom Dyson, Susan Breau, Theofanis Exadaktylos, Malte Kaeding, Jack Holland, Ipshita Basu, Tereza Capelos, Richard Benny, Regina Rauxloh, Rosina Marquez-Reiter, Nesta Devine, Georgina Stewart, Andrew Gibbons, Lynette Reid, Janita Craw, Jane Gilbert, Leon Benade, Adrian Schoone, Alison Smith, Jyoti Jhagroo, Megan Lourie, Toni Ingram, Chris Jenkin, Howard Youngs, Neil Boland, Ruth Boyask, Sue Sutherland, Jennie Billot, Jocelyn Jesson, Richard Watermeyer, Rille Raaper, Michael Peters, Richard Heraud, George Lazaroiu, Henriëtt Graafland, John Bennett, Stephan Ball, Michael Apple, Gary McCulloch, Amelia Hempel-Jorgensen, Janet Soler, Terri Kim, Bhikhu Parekh, Gary Gutting, Roberto Serpieri, Mitja Sardoc, Petar Jandric, Joseph Zajda, Shelina Thawer, Andrew Gibbons, Will Mace, Rajani Naidoo, Roger Dale, Susan Robertson, Martin Thrupp, Stuart Mundy MacPherson, Vivienne Duffy, Keun Im, Jamba Tolkien, Annie Waqar, Anne Bostanci, John Morss, Jim Flynn, Graeme Christie, Peter Rich, Dot Scott, Christine Gardener, Dan McKerracher, Shirley Gillett, Grant Gillett, John Barsby, John Dawson, Howard Lee, Clare Olssen, and Anne-Marie O'Neill, as well as all my students, past and present. Lastly, I thank my family – Jabez, Bridget, Clare, Chike, Ursula, Tochi, Arlo, Sabe, Ella, Kirstin, and Chidu. Without their support I doubt whether I would have finished this book.

Mark Olssen
Guildford
September 2020

Introduction

General aim of the study

Michel Foucault never undertook a serious study in normative political or moral philosophy. Scholars sometimes speak of an 'ethical turn' in his work, occurring in the second and third volumes of *The History of Sexuality* (1985a; 1986a), and many of his essays and lectures contain important ideas about ethical comportment and self-fashioning,[1] but nowhere does he provide a normative ethics that could lead to prescriptive studies in law, morality, ethics, politics, education, or the policy sciences. Indeed, he steadfastly opposed such prescriptive approaches. Nonetheless, I believe it fruitful to extend his approach in this direction, because I consider it a weakness of the Foucauldian approach as popularly understood. In this, I confess that my approach to Foucault is one of rendering him coherent in terms of ontological, epistemological, and normative commitments. The seeds of such an approach are, I believe, located in Foucault's later work, especially his forays into life philosophy, as for example in the introduction he wrote to George Canguilhem's book, *The Normal and the Pathological* (Foucault, 1985b), as well as his final lecture course at the College de France, *The Courage of Truth* (2011a).

While I will not claim that Foucault's writing on the concept of life in his introduction to Canguilhem's book represented an intentional attempt to resolve issues of normativity in his work, to me it is suggestive. Foucault was certainly aware of the normative role that the concept of life played in relation to Canguilhem's writing, as well as in the philosophies of Nietzsche and Heidegger. He was also aware of the criticisms regarding the absence of normative underpinning that could ward off charges of epistemological and moral relativism in his work, made by Habermas and others during the 1980s. While not having sufficient evidence to support my claims as to whether Foucault was actively seeking to sketch out some initial possible answers to resolve the issue of normativity in his project, there is an important sense in which I do not feel the need to support such a contention. For irrespective of Foucault's intentions, I have been tempted by the fact that the concept of life could offer a way out of the difficulties that Foucault was facing and still faces from, as Paul Patton has put it, 'the problem of the lack of normative criteria in [his] work' (1998: 70). As Patton expresses it, '[Foucault's] descriptive analysis of power provide us with no criteria for judgment' (1998: 64). Further, 'he offers no alternative ideal, no conception either of human being or of human society freed from the bonds of power' (1998: 64). Patton seems to think that this situation could not have been otherwise and that Foucault 'cannot provide such criteria' (1998: 70). If Patton means here that it is *not possible* to provide normative grounding to Foucault's project, I disagree; I believe that adequate criteria can be constructed.

As for Foucault's view on the matter, although he seemed decidedly hesitant to consider the issue, there appears to be no final determination as to his ultimate view as to what was or was not possible. No doubt he was aware of the difficulties such an undertaking would present, as well as the risks involved. A decade earlier, Foucault had sounded decidedly provisional in *The Archaeology of Knowledge* when he said that 'for the moment, and as far ahead as I can see, my discourse, far from determining the locus in which it speaks, is avoiding the ground on which it could find support' (1972: 205). Nothing should be read into such a statement, but Foucault was clearly aware of this lacuna within his project. Maybe the fact of writing the introduction to Canguilhem's book relatively late in his career, only a few years before his death, produced a 'moment' when a consideration of normative concepts could be entertained. But irrespective of whether Foucault was conscious of the normative possibilities inherent in the concepts of life and error, that such concepts suggest a possible way out of some of the difficulties he faced in this regard, and relatedly open up new domains of possibility for Foucauldian studies, has motivated me at least to undertake to extend the idea on Foucault's behalf.

Not everyone will welcome a book that seeks to render Foucault as normative and to construct a macro-ethical framework for his approach. Did not Foucault oppose universal rule type moralities? My response will be that the meta-principle established will do no violence to any of Foucault's ideas or concepts, will not derail or interfere with his genealogical approach, and will not seek to develop or impose a universal rule type morality, at least not of the sort that Kant developed. The question becomes, in effect, whether a concept can be developed that can support a normative principle that is consistent with Foucault's central concepts and principles, including the principle of historicity, even that of a historicity of concepts. The advantages of succeeding are considerable in that it will make possible a great deal more by opening up new, 'prescriptive' domains of Foucauldian studies – in ethics, morality, politics, law, and a whole range of policy sciences. Such a normative principle must also appear as both social and historical yet provide an architecture that is not relativistic in any trivial sense, and that builds from the foundation of Foucault's major philosophical teachers and those who influenced his thought. In that the task of constructing a 'normative Foucault' goes well beyond Foucault himself, my treatment will be faithful to the 'Foucauldian spirit', as well as attempting to be faithful to his philosophical project overall in terms of its central precepts and insights. In this sense, my project can be represented as 'neo-Foucauldian'.

I could not even attempt such a project if I did not take some liberties. As Foucault himself appeared resolutely committed to not being normative at certain times, an issue that will be taken up more fully in Chapter 1, the very fact that I believe this to be an omission within his project constitutes one instance of my taking liberties. Another is the fact that in some chapters I write *as a Foucauldian*, rather than with reference to Foucault. The chapter on Kant is a good example. While Foucault is barely cited, I am confident that my critique of Kant would square with both Foucault's and Nietzsche's views, although, of course, I cannot be sure they would agree with everything I say. In this sense, my task is to construct a normativity *for* Foucault rather than to study or represent Foucault. I cannot claim either to be completing Foucault. Although I have noted his later foray into 'life philosophy', I am not advancing any view that Foucault was working or thinking along these lines, or that had he lived longer, he would have developed his project in these ways. The thesis I advance here is solely my own. I claim only that such a work prepares the way for an 'applied Foucauldianism' and that the construction advanced is broadly compatible with his project overall. In a sense, it provides a poststructuralist ethic, in which Foucault is the central exemplar for the purposes of defining poststructuralism. The term I give to this ethic is 'life continuance'. As my task is to construct a normativity, I am also not beyond making editorial revisions if needed. In relation to Foucault, bar the fact of rendering him normative in the first place, I do not believe that there are any significant points of disagreement. In relation to Nietzsche, however, there are several, and these will be commented upon further when it is pertinent to do so.[2] Nietzsche's personal attitudes on social and political issues constitute the general domain in which these disagreements occur. In all cases, however, the areas of disagreement are over beliefs that are tangential to Nietzsche's core philosophy, or, at least, the core aspects that I require for my purposes, as well as to my own task of construction.

On constructing ethics

I am not the first to be interested in Foucault's writing from the standpoint of moral philosophy, although I believe that the approach that I develop in this book is original. Like most new work, however, it builds upon fragments that already exist within current literature, not least in Foucault's own work, especially his later work. Here, also, I acknowledge other scholars who have done serious work in relation to Foucault and ethics, even from the standpoint of moral philosophy, such as Judith Butler[3] and work inspired by her (see Carver and Chambers, 2008; Thiem, 2008), as well as some of Foucault's friends, colleagues, or acquaintances, such as Paul Veyne (1997; 2010) or, more recently, Frédéric Gros.[4] Although this book starts with and seeks an answer to Socrates' question, 'How should one live?', and will seek to formulate an answer to this question that is faithful to Foucault, my own understanding as to what Foucault was trying to achieve philosophically requires some initial explanation. In this context, let me repeat that this book does not attempt to provide an exegesis of Foucault's writings on ethics that aims or claims to extend Foucault scholarship in the sense of being definitive, final, or faithful to his writings; others have done or are doing this. My aim is to take Foucault's distinctive philosophical approach and ask whether it is possible to formulate a distinctive approach to ethics and moral philosophy based on Foucault's work, and if so, what would this look like? Foucault himself would not have appreciated an exegetical study of his writings from someone whose original language was not French. Besides, he preferred people to use his ideas and insights for creative purposes, and it is in this spirit that this study has taken root.

In utilizing Foucault as a source of inspiration on ethics, while also going beyond Foucault, a central theoretical interest is to create an ethics that provides an alternative to other positions currently on offer. At the outset I should state that my view of Foucault on ethics is not faithful to one widespread interpretation of his position, relating to narcissism or 'dandyism'. Although Foucault, in a later essay (Foucault, 1984c), references Baudelaire's figure of the 'dandy', a figure who seeks to turn his life into a 'work of art', celebrating 'style' over deeper moral or ethical commitments, which is one reading that can be taken from Foucault in reference to 'asceticism', I reject such an analysis. If dandyism is viewed as representing a priority of 'style' over 'substance', or of the 'superficial' over the 'serious', or, indeed, if it is seen as embodying the 'strength' of Nietzsche's Superman in the way that Nietzsche's Superman has been interpreted in both popular and academic cultures of the West, then I also reject the argument that Foucault was proselytizing for such a view. Foucault invokes Baudelaire's dandy, quite legitimately and quite seriously, as a 'counter-figure' to the hegemony of oppressive heterosexual norms in Western societies. This has turned out to be a very serious and accurate claim. But in no sense should it be interpreted as arguing for a merely stylistic, or even merely artistic portrayal of an ethical self. Foucault is not advocating any sort of avant-garde (bourgeois or bohemian) ideology that the fashionable thing to do is to give style to one's existence.

At the same time, I do not consider that Foucault was advocating or accepting that *any* style of life will do. In this sense, Foucault is not represented as a thinker who relativizes all moral values and maintains – incoherently – that any style of life is as acceptable as any other. As an extension of this, a Foucauldian ethic is being developed in part because it does not represent ethics as an 'ethics of cultural difference' which claims to be tolerant and accepting of all manner of divergent group values. Similarly, it will be claimed that Foucault is not an advocate of multiculturalism where every social group's practices are necessarily accorded the same degree of respect. Just as Foucault would reject the universalist ethics of Kant, or of Rawls, or Habermas, so he would not countenance an ethics of difference or of alterity. Foucault's ethics would also not involve a return to the Ancients, based upon identifying any predefined teleological conception of the Good, or, whether ancient or modern, as based upon happiness, pleasure, or any other conception of utility. With rights theory, too, although rights are important for Foucault, they are not primordial and cannot ground ethics, as they did for Locke.

Foucault's ethics would also resist basing ethics on a recognition of the other. As we will see, his opposition to many of the fundamental precepts of Hegel's philosophy makes the ethics or politics of (mis)recognition a poor candidate for locating Foucault. As Foucault makes clear in many of his interviews, it is not that the other is not integral to the self and its development, as in the models of the self studied in Greek and Roman antiquity;[5] however, despite this historical observation, the other would not be seen as central to a discourse of ethics in any primordial or foundational sense, at least not in the sense in which Levinas (2004) and many others (Derrida, 1997; Irigaray, 1991; Spivak, 1996) represent the ethical encounter with the Other.[6] In Levinas, the Other is posited, as Peter Hallward says in his introduction to Badiou's *Ethics*, as 'a pure or absolute value to a realm beyond all conceptual distinction' (Hallward, 2001: xxiii). The other also warrants a place in Hegel as the source of recognition, and thus identity. Foucault's ethics must resist association with any 'ethics of identity' based upon alterity, no matter how it is formulated.

My working assumption in this book is that Foucault's interest in Nietzsche and Heidegger offers the best clue to constructing an apparatus of ethics within his project. Nietzsche and Heidegger offered a way of thinking that was quite distinctive within the Western philosophical tradition. This is today clearly accepted by all those who write on Foucault, as well as all those who take him seriously. Nietzsche and Heidegger offered Foucault a way to 'circumnavigate' Hegel and Marx, to avoid phenomenology, and to reject humanism and essentialism, which had not only constituted the dominant representations of philosophy since Plato, but also, as far as modernist representations of science, determinism, causation, and so on, were concerned, since Newton.[7] He viewed these 'categories' and 'key figures' as problematic in terms of distorting our capacities to understand history in a way that was adequate to our present conjuncture, including our capacity to understand the future, existing representations of 'normality', 'sexuality', or, indeed, what it means to be human. His efforts to 'evacuate', 'modify', or 'transform' these categories led him to embark upon a profound critique of the present, and of the discourses and practices of humanism, and of the technologies that have constructed us as the subjects that we are. To understand how subjects are constructed socially and historically in terms of power, and how they act through power on others and on themselves, but not to see this as a purely random process or activity where 'anything goes', or conversely, portray ethical actions in terms of fixed rules or specified teleological ends will constitute my objective. What a normative Foucault can offer us, I will claim, is a critical ethics of the present that is well and truly beyond Kant, Hegel, and Marx, and that can guide action and conduct for the twenty-first century.

Foucault, ontology, complexity

Centrally important to such a task is Foucault's historical ontology. I have represented this before in several papers on complexity science as the complex ontological-historical approach that best describes Foucault's *oeuvre* overall. Although complexity research takes its origins from its applications in physics, chemistry, and the 'hard' sciences, undergoing its formative development in the early and mid-twentieth century, during the second half of the century it has exerted an effect on the social sciences as well. Over the past half century, complexity research has generated a 'quiet revolution' in both the physical and social sciences.[8] Today there exists a multitude of different research centres and approaches.[9] Edgar Morin (2007) distinguishes 'restricted' and 'general' approaches. While both endorse the ontological postulates of non-linearity and the relational nature of complex systems, restricted approaches seek to reintegrate complexity insights to reductionist, methodologically individualistic conceptions of science, while general approaches speak to a new language beyond dominant positivistic representations that have characterized standard approaches to Enlightenment knowledge. It is to general complexity that Foucault's innovative research programme leads us.

Central to general complexity is the rejection of an exclusive emphasis on either reductionism or holism. Whole and parts must be represented in interaction. The compositional rules are neither Aristotelian (in terms of substances) nor Cartesian (in terms of an additive or compositional model). Neither description nor explanation can therefore be achieved exclusively in terms of either parts or wholes but must be grasped as a system in process. The system comprises both linear and non-linear interactions. In postulating non-linear interactions, it is accepted that wholes are, in certain instances, more than the sum of the parts, in that collective entities can act differently to the parts and exert forces independent of the parts (downward causation).[10] Complexity theory presents a new relational holism that avoids the unifying and dialectical connotations of classical holism. Classical holism was deficient in terms of its blindness to the parts as well as in its ignorance of complex processes of change and order.

In my article 'Foucault as Complexity Theorist' (2008), I establish the claim for complexity for Foucault as well as for Nietzsche and Heidegger, the two thinkers who had the major influence upon his thought. Central to representing the world as a complex dynamical system is a series of core postulates that include openness, infinite possibility, indeterminism, non-predictability, uncertainty, chance, novelty, uniqueness, non-linearity, and the rejection of traditional early modern conceptions of science premised upon the idea of the world as a closed universe and its correlates of linear determinism, predictability, certainty, and time reversibility. Although Foucault did not articulate a concept of system or complexity as such, representing knowledge in terms of complexity aptly expresses the onto-epistemological principles that subtend the approach he pursued throughout his career. I will argue with respect to Foucault that it is towards a new historical form of systems thinking constitutive of a nominalist form of historical materialism that complexity directs us. Although historical materialism has been traditionally associated with Marxism, the classical stereotype of the economy as a determining foundation, as well as a lack of attention to other forms of power differentials (racism, sexism, etc.) rendered Marxism problematic as a vehicle for comprehending systems complexity for Foucault.[11] In the sense that complexity can be described as a form of historical materialism, then, it is as a non-foundational approach, which, in the language of complexity theory, is characterized by 'self-organization', 'time irreversibility', 'contextual contingency', and 'discursive mediation'. In Foucault's conception, the topographical model of base and superstructure with its central foundational role of the economy is absent. In such a complexity view, history is reconceptualized, altering both our epistemological and ontological frameworks in relation to the way we understand and represent our world.[12]

At its most general level, as Frederick Turner points out, what complexity does is 'place [...] within our grasp a set of very powerful tools – concepts to think with' (1997: xii). What complexity enables is an approach that prioritizes axioms about *indeterminacy, non-predictability, uncertainty, emergence, contingency* and *historicity, limited* or *partial knowledge,* as well as *insufficiency* or *interdependency,* and *systems ontology,* as basic postulates. It offers a way of understanding the role of structural factors in change, including non-predictability and its consequences, the delayed, unintended, or indirect effects of actions, and the importance of 'uncertainty', 'noise', 'accident', and 'emotion'. Complexity theory asserts, in short, that linear models of science cannot on their own reveal the dynamics of complexity in systems. In addition, contextual contingency defeats the possibility of laws of behaviour or development as being decisive. As with developments in fields such as thermodynamics, chemistry, biology, and across the sciences, complexity theory has shifted understanding of science and the world in a way that also has application to the social sciences and history. For people working on writers such as Foucault and Deleuze, complexity insights have assisted in resolving issues of determinism and indeterminism, structure and agency, nature and nurture, system and part, as they have calamitously played out in the philosophies of writers such as Marx and Hegel in relation to determinism.

In a range of publications, Ilya Prigogine has developed a complexity formulation relevant to both the physical and social sciences. In works such as *Order Out of Chaos* (1984), written with Isabelle Stengers, and *Exploring Complexity* (1989), written with Grégoire Nicolis, it is claimed that complexity theory offers a bold, new, and more accurate conception of science and the universe. This new conceptualization is superseding standard models including classical and quantum mechanics, which came to prominence at the beginning of the twentieth century as 'corrections to classical mechanics' (Nicolis and Prigogine, 1989: 2). The departure from the classical model of physics was made possible by a number of factors, including Planck's constant,[13] as well as Einstein's *Annus mirabilis* papers of 1905.[14] The research of Henri Poincaré was also to be highly significant in the subsequent development of chaos theory.[15] Prigogine's innovation was to criticize Newtonian mechanics and quantum theory, which represented time as reversible, meaning that it was irrelevant to the adequacy of laws, supplementing physics with a new conception of time irreversibility.[16] Complexity theory builds on and intensifies the '"temporal" turn' introduced by these 'corrections' (Nicolis and Prigogine, 1989: 2). Prigogine places central importance on time as real and irreversible. With Newton, say Prigogine and Stengers, the universe is represented as closed and predictable. Its fundamental laws are deterministic and reversible. Temporality is held to be irrelevant to the truth and operation of the laws. As Prigogine and Stengers say, 'time ... is reduced to a parameter, and future and past become equivalent' (1984: 11).

If time is irreversible the future never simply repeats the past. Prigogine's revolution in response to the classical and quantum paradigms in formal terms was to challenge the *principle of ergodicity*[17] which resulted in Poincaré's recurrence.[18] This was the principle that held, in conformity with the law of the conservation of energy, that system interactions in physics would eventually reproduce a state or states almost identical to earlier initial states of the system at some point in the future.[19] It was on the basis of such an approach that time reversibility had been defined as real, and time irreversibility as an illusion. Prigogine challenged the relevance and applicability of these assumptions to classical or quantum measurement. If systems are never isolated or independent from their surroundings, then in theory even small perturbations or changes in the surroundings could influence the system's functioning or trajectory. Even *very* small perturbations could cause *major* changes.[20]

As the physicist Alastair Rae notes, '[t]he consequences of this way of thinking are profound', for they replace assumptions of reversibility with irreversibility, and introduce notions of indeterminism into physics (2009: 114, 113).[21] Another consequence explains how the individual subject can be both historically and socially constituted, yet unique. While each subject lacks an essence or substance (*ousia*), in Aristotle's sense, ontological uniqueness is constituted in terms of differential effects of the environment in relation to the differential effects exacted as a consequence of specificity of space/time location, demonstrating time irreversibility. Such a view will be of major significance for understanding Foucault.

In introducing a complexity perspective, Prigogine's innovation was to introduce a different way of understanding order. Because complex systems are holistic in the sense that the whole is more than the sum of its parts, new entities *emerge* from the interactions between part and part, and part(s) and whole. Prigogine's contribution was to postulate that systems could also develop in states of non-equilibrium where, through a process of emergence, new features of the system develop in ways that are both practically and theoretically unpredictable.[22]

Such a model of development also can explain *chance*. When a system enters 'far-from-equilibrium' conditions, its structure may be threatened, and a 'critical condition', or what Prigogine and Stengers call a 'bifurcation point', is entered. At the bifurcation point, system contingencies may operate to determine outcomes in a way not causally linked to previous linear path trajectories. Deleuze drew on writers such as Prigogine in order to conceptualize indeterminacy at the level of philosophy.[23] For Deleuze (1994a), as Protevi (2006: 22) summarizes him, 'a singularity in the [topological structure of the] manifold indicates a bifurcator'. The trajectory is not therefore seen as determined in one particular pathway. Although this is *not* to claim an absence of antecedent causes, it is to say, says Prigogine, that 'nothing in the macroscopic equations justifies the preferences for any one solution' (1997: 5). Or again, from *Exploring Complexity*, '[n]othing in the description of the experimental set up permits the observer to assign beforehand the state that will be chosen; only chance will decide, through the dynamics of fluctuations' (Nicolis and Prigogine, 1989: 72). There is no way, even in theory, to tell what the future will be. Once the system 'chooses', '[it] becomes an historical object in the sense that its subsequent evolution depends on its critical choice' (1989: 72). In this description, 'we have succeeded in formulating, in abstract terms, the remarkable interplay of chance and constraint' (1989: 73). As such, 'bifurcation is the source of innovation and diversification, since it endows the system with new solutions' (1989: 74).

A schematic diagram of *bifurcation* appears in Figure 1, reproduced from Nicolis and Prigogine (1989: 73). They make the following comment on the model:

> A ball moves in a valley [a], which at a particular point becomes branched and leads to either of two valleys, branches b1 and b2 separated by a hill. Although it is too early for apologies and extrapolations ... it is thought provoking to imagine for a moment that instead of the ball in Figure [1] we could have a dinosaur sitting there prior to the end of the Mesozoic era, or a group of our ancestors about to settle on either the ideographic or the symbolic mode of writing. (1989: 73)

Although, due to system perturbations and fluctuations, it is impossible to precisely ascertain causes in advance, retrospectively we find the 'cause' there in the events that led up to an event, in the sense that we look backwards and point to plausible antecedent factors that contributed to its occurrence. While therefore not undetermined by prior causes, the dislocation of linear deterministic trajectories

Introduction 13

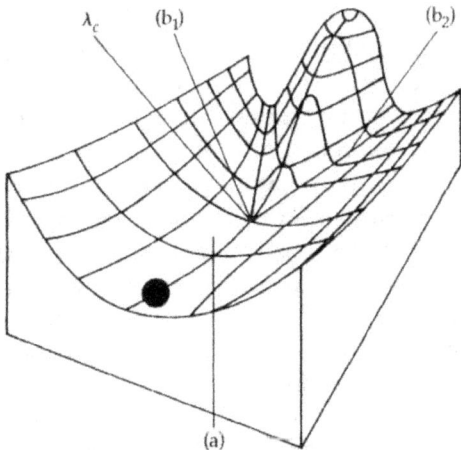

Figure 1 Mechanical illustration of the phenomenon of bifurcation (from Nicolis and Prigogine, 1989: 73. Reprinted by permission of Henry Holt and Co.)

and the opening-up of alternative possible pathways that cannot be *pre-ascertained* in open environments is what Prigogine means by 'chance'. In thermodynamics, Nicolis and Prigogine give the examples of thermal convection, the evolution of the universe itself, as well as climate and all physical processes. They were also aware, however, that their conclusions extended across all open systems to the social and human sciences, embracing life, all biological organisms, as well as social and political processes, as illustrations of non-equilibrium developments. In this context, the future is not simply *unknown*, but *unknowable*.

Two key ideas of complexity theory that will make it easier to understand Foucault's approach to history are *self-organization* and *emergence*. The idea of self-organization entails that apart from drawing on energy and information, systems are not organized or regulated by anything external to themselves, in the sense of a foundation or essential principle that is *ahistorical*.[24] It also explains how systems generate new patterns of activity through dynamic interactions over time. In relation to the concept of *emergence*, within any system both the macro-structure and micro-structure of parts interact, mutually affecting each other, and permitting indefinite recombination, thus ensuring new entities and structures, resulting in novelty and change (see Capra, 1996: ch. 2).

Of relevance to both self-organization and emergence, complexity theorists also typically represent the world as stratified, characterized by levels or sub-systems interconnected by interactions. Within complex systems, reciprocal interactions of various sorts will define relations at various levels. Within each level, different rules apply. Collective entities (e.g., brains) manifest properties (thinking) that the individual components (neurons and synapses) do not. Different entities are constituted by different elements that form a whole. Elements are related within the whole through organization, which, as Morin says, comprises 'a structure of relations between components to produce a whole with qualities unknown to these components outside the structure. Hence, organization connects parts to each other and parts to the whole' (1999: 115). Morin cites Dilthey to emphasize that 'a whole cannot be understood except by understanding its constituent parts, which cannot be understood except by understanding the whole' (1999: 115). Within complex systems, also, the interconnectedness of part and whole means that interactions of various sorts will take place. Interactions characterize relations, both at the microscopic (organisms, cellular life) and macroscopic levels. Such interactions can be of qualitatively different types, both linear and non-linear, and 'multi-referential' in Morin's sense (Morin, 1992: 47). Types of interactions that typify complex systems may be complementary or competitive, physical, biological, psycho-social, anthropological, economic, political, and so on.

For Morin:

> Interactions (1) suppose elements, beings or material objects capable of encountering each other; (2) suppose conditions of encounter, that is to say agitation, turbulence, contrary fluxes, etc.; (3) obey determinations/constraints inherent to the nature of elements, objects or beings in encounter; (4) become in certain conditions interrelations (associations, linkages, combinations communications, etc.) that is to say give birth to phenomena of organization ... (1992: 47)

New properties arise through the interactions of parts in the process of *emergence*. Emergents are defined as 'the simple effects of combined actions' (Morin, 2008: 100). Such processes operate within open systems where parts and wholes are linked in a dynamic, precarious, and unstable tension. Systems comprise 'polyrelational circuits' of 'whole/parts', made up of 'elements', 'interrelations', 'organization', and 'whole' (Morin, 2008: 102). 'In this circuit, organization plays a nuclearizing role', says Morin (2008: 102). As such, the system is 'a totality of polycentric dispersion', where small perturbations can derail and effect the whole (2008: 104). Society can be viewed in such a model as a complex dynamical system. In such a conception, the process of emergence is 'at the very heart of the theory of the system' (2008: 105). Within systems, 'emergents blossom' (2008: 102). As Morin explains:

> all systems comprise an immersed, hidden, and obscure zone, teeming with stifled potentialities. The duality between the immersed and the emergent, the potential and the actual, the repressed and the expressed, is the source, in the great living and social polysystems, of scissions and dissociations between the sphere of the parts and that of the whole. (2008: 102)

Within any system, both the macro-structure and micro-structure of parts interact, mutually affecting each other, and permitting indefinite recombination, thus allowing new entities and structures to emerge. Language, the brain, consciousness, and life can be seen as emergent phenomena. In this systems paradigm, the dynamic and non-linear assert themselves alongside the static and linear, and non-equilibrium and equilibrium operate as both temporary and intermittent. Additive and linear models are now supplemented by non-additive, dynamic, and non-linear ones. The ontological idea of a closed universe, an idea that was still operative during the Middle Ages, and that still characterized Hegel's thought, was replaced, as Alexander Koyré (1965; 1968) notes, by the conception of an open universe characterized by infinite possibilities, uncertainty, and chance.

Badiou's ethics

Complexity formulations go well beyond anything Foucault explicitly articulated, yet it is my contention that such formulations are homologous with the guiding principles of his own historical ontology and his radically different way of conceptualizing the world. Such an approach, broadly conceived, enables us to formulate the rejection of foundationalism and essentialism and adequately capture the contingency and specificity of the historical event. In this sense, there is a parallel between a complexity formulation as developed in my own work and the adoption of mathematical set theory as adopted by Alain Badiou (2005) in his treatise of the ontology of the event. Badiou is significant for a study of Foucault's ethics in that, like Foucault, he takes up an anti-humanist position against the 'more or less respectful humanism [of] ... Rawls, Habermas, Benhabib, Ricoeur, Rorty, Irigaray, and much of what has been called "cultural studies" in North America' (Hallward, 2001: xv). Badiou employs the mathematics of Georg Cantor to equate the idea of a situation or event with that of a set (*ensemble*). The set expresses the specificity of every situation. Yet while Badiou's thesis is pathbreaking, I reject his dependence on set theory for the purposes of expressing a normativity for Foucault on several grounds.

First, set theory doesn't adequately take account of the 'arrow of time' in its formulation. Prigogine's supplementation of 'reversible time' with a conception of the 'irreversibility of time' results in turn in formulations of historical openness, the multiplicity of possibilities, indeterminism, uncertainty, and historical novelty. In *Order Out of Chaos*, Prigogine and Stengers acknowledge Alfred North Whitehead, the father of 'process-relational' philosophy, and Martin Heidegger as two seminal influences on their work, both thinkers seeing 'time' and 'history' as integral dimensions (Prigogine and Stengers, 1984: 93–6 [for Whitehead], 32–3, 42, 79 [for Heidegger]). Both approaches are compatible in important respects with Foucault's emphasis upon historicity.

A second criticism of Badiou's reliance on set theory refers to the way that the theory compromises or undermines the specificity of the event or situation in important respects. As Peter Hallward notes, a set for Cantor:

> is defined exclusively by what belongs to it (its elements or members) without reference to the constituent relations that might exist among

these elements (in set theory the very notion of 'constituent' relations is a contradiction in terms). The situation is made up simply of its elements, considered in their solitary ontological isolation (as x, y, z ...). (2001: xxxi–xxxii)

Although useful as a metaphor for understanding human institutions and situations as 'infinite multiplicities' in order 'to grasp the specificity of any particular situation' (Hallward, 2001: xxxii, xxxi), the set metaphor overly simplifies the specificity of the historical situation by underemphasizing its dynamic features and tendencies as well as by subordinating relations to elements, as it were, by definition.

A third weakness of Badiou's thesis, again identified by Hallward, has implications for moral and ethical relativism. It concerns Badiou's attempt to derive ethics from the situation as such as 'fully internal to its situation', that is, as topologically inscribed in the set. In Badiou's formulation:

> As a general rule, every generic procedure is in reality a process that can perfectly well be deliberative, as long as we understand that it invents its rule of deliberation at the same time as it invents itself. And it is no more constrained by a pre-established norm that follows from the rule of deliberation. You have only to look at how the rule of deliberation in different organizations, in different political sequences, and in different political modes, is entirely variable ... Every time a plurality of individuals, a plurality of human subjects, is engaged in a process of truth, the construction of this process induces the construction of a deliberative and collective figure of this production, which is itself variable. (Badiou, 2001: 117, cited in Hallward, 2001: xxxiv)

The set acknowledges nothing outside itself, and in some way, never to my mind satisfactorily explained by Badiou, must somehow 'coerce' or 'pressure' the ethical truth from tensions or conflicts *within* the situation as such. Truth, says Badiou, is immanent, meaning that 'truth proceeds in the situation, and nowhere else – there is no heaven of truths' (2001: 42–3). In this sense, there can be no ground or basis for ethical decisions except that emerging within the situation itself. Given such a view, Badiou's mantra 'Keep Going!', although superficially close to my own formulation, can only amount to a 'distraction' or something to 'take one's mind off' the confusions and opacity of the present conjuncture. It functions in this sense only as a psychological crutch. On such a view, set theory, as such, cannot account for what we ought to do. We might say that it lacks the capacity to generate normative traction. As such, it cannot prevent the onset of nihilism.

My own criticisms of set theory parallel and build on Poincaré's criticisms of Cantor, expressed long before Badiou wrote. Poincaré not only criticized Cantor, but other logicians such as Peano, Frege, Russell, Zermelo, and Hilbert. He was critical of Cantor's logical-set theoretic method partly because Cantor's set recognized infinity as actual. As Poincaré said, '[t]here is no actual infinity, the Cantorians have forgotten that, and they have fallen into contradiction' (1908: 212–13; 1913: 484). Poincaré was a relational historical ontologist and conventionalist. Although Bertrand Russell had also criticized Cantor's set theory for generating 'contradictions' or 'paradoxes', Poincaré considered that these criticisms merely reflected Russell's neo-Platonism about concepts (Poincaré, 1909: 482). For Poincaré, logic could not be seen as separate from psychology and history. In this, he condemned 'the logical point of view' (Poincaré, 1909: 482). According to Brian Clegg, Poincaré considered logic as a 'dead end detour' and 'an illness that was afflicting mathematics' (2003: 153).[25] There is a very real sense in which he serves as a precursor of Foucault in relation to his views of history and knowledge. For Poincaré, knowledge and science were both historical and conventional. By conventional, he did not mean 'arbitrary', but rather grounded in 'historical experience' and embedded in 'language' and 'discourse' (Poincaré, 1907: chs. X and XI). Although a pragmatist and anti-realist with regard to scientific theories, he did not see them in any purely relativistic sense, but as supporting varying degrees of *maturity* depending upon such things as the length of time the theory had survived, its predictive success, as well as the extractive force that it had in terms of real-world effects (i.e., whether it worked). In *The Value of Science*, Poincaré says that:

> what guarantees the objectivity of the world in which we live is that the world is common to us with other thinking beings ... Nothing,

therefore, will have objective value except what is transmissible by 'discourse', that is, intelligible ... it is relations alone which can be regarded as objective. (1907: 135, 137)[26]

Influenced by Poincaré, the development of post-quantum complexity theory based on Prigogine and the Brussels School, as well European philosophers such as Gilles Deleuze (Deleuze and Guattari, 1987; Deleuze, 1990; 1994a) and Foucault himself, reconceptualized history and ontology to represent the contingency and specificity of the historical situation. In this model, any situation or event must be represented as open to its external environments, and both its internal dynamics and the arrow of time must be represented as real. As this study proceeds, when complexity insights are relied upon, they will be explained again, as necessary. I will claim later, following leads from Bachelard's writings on the historicity of concepts, that general concepts can in certain situations coexist with historicity and not curtail or undermine it. Just as Foucault's concept of 'governmentality' can be rendered compatible with its historical variable forms, so it will be claimed that the appeal to a generality outside of a 'set' can be rendered compatible with the historicity and specificity of the historical situation.

Power and the event

Complexity theory is compatible with two emphases in Foucault in particular in addition to its general conformity to his historical ontology: the first is his theory of *power* and the second, his theory of the *event*. Foucault's theory of power as ubiquitous throughout the social domain, including the domains of science and knowledge, constitutes a radical, even revolutionary challenge to the Anglophone academic world, which will have downstream effects on ethics and philosophy. Ethics for Foucault, as we shall see, is at the same time contextual or situational, political, and strategic. Ethics does not amount to arriving at a 'truth of the situation', as Badiou says, but concerns skills of judgement, decision, engagement, action, and comportment within an always contingent order of events in situations structured by power, where it is unclear if not opaque as to what is at stake. Ethics in this sense concerns 'how to live' in contexts buffeted by chance events; it concerns the discourses that guide and regulate actions and conduct in specific situations.

Given his thesis heralding 'the death of man',[27] Foucault's anti-humanism, taken up from Althusser's critique of Hegel, spells the end of any essentialized conception of the subject based on nature, and dictates, as we shall see, that ethics must look instead to the future. Notwithstanding Badiou's employment of the concept of the set, I will argue that we are not locked within a closed space of solipsism even within the historical situation, as Foucault suggests that limits can be breached and transgression can lead to us to grasp the truth of the situation, if only fleetingly and with difficulty. To me, Foucault suggests that far from being trapped in the quagmire of relativism, action entails that there are general principles or concepts that can assist interpretation in specific contexts, and that can usefully give reasons to guide ethical conduct that are not simply relative or arbitrary. For Foucault, action is contextualized in terms of the 'limits' and points of 'transgression' in specific situations. As Foucault tells us in the essay he dedicated to Georges Bataille:

> Transgression is an action that involves the limit, that narrow zone of a line where it displays the flash of its passage, but perhaps also its entire trajectory ... The limit and transgression depend on each other for whatever density of being they possess: *a limit could not exist if it were absolutely uncrossable and, reciprocally, transgression would be pointless if it merely crossed a limit composed of illusions and shadows.* (1998e: 73, emphasis added)

Being ethical involves action in relation to limits and points of transgression, constrained by the situation as well as the age or epoch within which they acquire their content and force; they cry out to grasp something real, something beyond the transgressed limit, 'where being achieves its limit and where the limit defines being' (Foucault, 1998e: 75).

Power structures the field that history crosses and writes its script, a fact that makes ethics difficult. For Foucault, power is neither unitary nor repressive. Relations of power traverse the social structure and operate in all contexts and situations. Rather than seeing power as repressive, flowing from a centralized source, from top to bottom, Foucault represents power as 'exercised' rather than 'possessed', as 'productive' rather than merely 'repressive', and as circulating at all levels and in every sphere of society.

The concept of the event also plays a central role in Foucault's writings on history, especially as regards his genealogical method. In his 1971 essay, 'Nietzsche, Genealogy, History', Foucault (1977d) elaborates a complex historiography without foundations or origins. Genealogy is concerned with tracing the historical processes of descent (*Herkunft*) and emergence (*Entstehung*) by which historical processes and events come into being and are subsequently transformed. Genealogical analysis aims to explain the existence and transformation of elements by situating them within power relations and by tracing their descent and emergence in the context of history. The event is thus a contingent and situationally specific historical apparatus (*dispositif*) constituted in the open terrain of history. For Foucault, Nietzsche's genealogy opposes itself to the search for origins (*Ursprung*). To search for origins is to attempt to capture the exact essence of things, which Foucault sees as reinstating Platonic essentialism.

Foucault's approach to history, in eschewing foundations and essentialism, expresses a compatibility with complexity science. His utilization of structural linguistics is important in this regard. Structural linguistics is concerned with the relations among elements, which enables Foucault to study social reality as a logical structure or a set of logical relations. The methods of structural linguistics also enable Foucault to analyse change. For just as linguistics undertakes synchronic analysis in seeking to trace the necessary conditions for an element within a structure of language to undergo change, a similar synchronic analysis applied to social life asks the question, in order for a change to occur, what other changes must take place in the overall texture of the social configuration (Foucault, 1994b: 827)? Hence, Foucault seeks to identify logical relations where none had previously been thought to exist or where previously one had searched for causal relations. While traditionally, analysis in the shadow of classical mechanics has referenced a linear conception of causality, in structural linguistics the concern is not with causality in a linear sense, but with revealing multiple relations of different sorts. In a 1969 paper, 'Linguistique et sciences sociales', Foucault calls these 'logical relations' (1994b: 824). It is, he says, the discovery of the 'presence of a logic that is not the logic of causal determinism that is currently at the heart of philosophical and theoretical debates' (1994b: 824). It is in terms of such an approach that one can understand Foucault's rejection of Marx and Hegel and his turn to Nietzsche and Heidegger. For Foucault, the totality always eluded analysis in terms of necessity or the ability to predict the outcome of future events, and rather must be characterized by incompleteness, indeterminacy, complexity, and chance. As Foucault says in his inaugural lecture at the Collège de France, 'we must accept the introduction of chance [*aléa*] as a category in the production of events' (1981a: 69). Such processes have also been enumerated by Ian Hacking (1975; 1990), who builds on Foucault's work to explain the emergence of probability and chance in present-day conceptions of science. As Hacking puts it, '[d]eterminism was eroded during the 19th century and a space was cleared for autonomous laws of chance' (1990: vii).

Further insights into Foucault's methods are revealed in his lecture notes at the Collège de France, as published initially in the four volumes of *Dits et écrits* (1994a). In these volumes Foucault reveals the importance of analytic methods and of the philosophy of language in relation to the analysis of discourse and history. In one essay, 'La philosophie analytique de la politique' (1994c), initially presented in 1978 in Japan, Foucault spells out the superiority of analytic methods as used in Anglo-American philosophy compared to dialectical methodology, as used by Hegel and Marx. Although Foucault (2016b: 22) admitted in the first of his lectures at Dartmouth College in 1980 that he was not an analytic philosopher (adding the phrase 'nobody is perfect'), as Frédéric Gros notes in his 'Course Context' for Foucault's 1982–83 lectures at the Collège de France, *The Government of the Self and Others*, 'the dialogue with the analytic tradition had already begun in the *Archaeology of Knowledge*' (Gros, 2010: 379).[28] What characterizes analytic methods is a concern not with the deep structures of language, or the 'being' of language, but with the 'everyday use' made of language in different types of discourse. By extension,

Foucault argues that philosophy can similarly analyse what occurs in 'everyday relations of power' as well as all the other relations that 'traverse the social body' (1994c: 541). Just as language can be seen to underlie thought, so there is a similar grammar underlying social relations and relations of power. Hence, Foucault argues for what he calls an 'analytico-political philosophy' (1994c: 541). Similarly, rather than seeing language as revealing some eternal buried truth that 'deceives and reveals', the metaphorical method for understanding that Foucault utilizes is that of a *game*: 'Language, it is played.' It is thus a 'strategic' metaphor, as well as a linguistic metaphor, that Foucault utilizes to develop a critical approach to society: 'Relations of power, also, they are played; it is these games of power (*jeux de pouvoir*) that one must study in terms of tactics and strategy, in terms of order and chance, in terms of stakes and objectives' (Foucault, 1994c: 541–2).

It is in such a context of disorder and contingency that ethics must take root. Such is likely to produce a radically different approach, freed from the reigning models of Aristotle, Kant, Hegel, Bentham, or Levinas. Like Foucault, in constructing a normativity that will necessarily go beyond him, I too will canvass both Anglo-American as well as Continental philosophical traditions of scholarship. This, indeed, will constitute a major aspect of this study. While in many respects both traditions have remained hermetically sealed off and distanced from one another, Foucault's own overtures towards Anglo-American philosophy set an example that – hopefully – can only be productive.

Outline of the book

In the chapters that follow I set out my scheme to develop a normative ethics that would both befit and honour Foucault. In the next chapter, 'Foucault and normativity', I seek to establish the central arguments of the book while also summarizing and critically interrogating a prominent recent literature on normativity in relation to Foucault's writing. The major author to be considered here is Mark Kelly, who claims that Foucault is anti-normative, and that he should not be normative. While in part Kelly's claims are agreed with, in part they are disputed. Three recent authors are then introduced who claim that normativity pervades life in general, and that intentionality itself is intrinsically normative. Different senses in which the normative influences or affects Foucault are also considered. While it is claimed that there are latent normative values expressed in his work, it is conceded that an adequate normative architecture and concept still need to be established. In this sense, Foucault's project is found wanting for a failure to attend to the normative, and Pierre Hadot's criticisms of Foucault's conception of the subject add further light on the different ways that such a lack of normativity manifests itself.

In Chapter 2, 'Life and error: Foucault, Canguilhem, Jacob', I explore the possible implications of Foucault's late interest in life philosophy and his work on Georges Canguilhem and François Jacob in order to further develop a conception of normativity that could serve to ground an ethics. A distinction is drawn between Foucault's persistent opposition to advocating prescriptions as to how people should live or what they should do, and the necessity of a normative architecture to guide his approach, which it has often been noted is lacking or undeveloped. It is argued that notwithstanding an apparently absent normativity to ground his ethical and political claims, the basis of an adequate normative architecture can be found within his project. Although for much of his career, spanning the entire period of his major books, such a normativity remained largely implicit and undeveloped, waiting to be unearthed and rendered visible, in his later years, from 1980 until his death, a more explicit dimension of normativity can be seen, as suggested through his engagement with the writings of Canguilhem on life philosophy and error. Foucault's attention to Canguilhem and Jacob is retraced in order to reveal how such an approach can normatively ground his own distinctive theoretical orientation, thus serving as a springboard to further Foucauldian studies on ethics, morality, economics, welfare, education, and normative political theory.

Chapter 3, 'Nietzsche's life philosophy: naturalism, will to power, normativity', examines Nietzsche's writings on normativity, will to power, and life. Building on the work of Maudemarie Clark and David Dudrick, I argue for an objectivist rather than subjectivist reading of Nietzsche as a moral philosopher. It is claimed that adding Nietzschean insights concerning normativity to those present on life philosophy in Foucault's reading of Canguilhem enables the development of a theory of normativity that can serve Foucault. The chapter starts by considering the issue of realism/anti-realism over ethical values, as well as the senses in which Nietzsche's conceptions of ethics and morality can be considered as normatively objective or subjective. It argues that while Nietzsche is a metaphysical anti-realist in that he rejects any notion of a transcendent metaphysical world, or any conception of ahistorical foundations, there is an important sense of normative objectivity over ethical values. This relates to Nietzsche's ontologizing of the future as constituting an uncertain and precarious terrain to be negotiated and crossed. The chapter goes on to consider Nietzsche's concept of the 'will to power' as representing an immanent normativity over ethical value creation. It argues that the function of Nietzsche's concept of the will to power in accenting the dynamic, creative, form-giving functions of life plays an important role in his theory of the ethics of becoming. The chapter concludes by examining the importance for value creation and ethics of Nietzsche's views on 'life philosophy'.

Chapter 4, 'Continuance ethics, objectivity, Kant', considers Kantian ethics, but before doing so it seeks to restate continuance ethics in relation to some of the major approaches to ethics in anglophone moral philosophy. The issues of objectivism and subjectivism in ethics are revisited here, this time in relation to anglophone philosophers, especially Derek Parfit, who is used as an interlocutor for the purposes of comparison to the life continuance approach. The chapter moves on to provide a critique of Kant's ethical system in terms of what I consider to broadly represent a Foucauldian position. There is not a great deal of reference to Foucault's own writings on Kant in the chapter: rather it seeks to formulate a critique of Kant's ethics based on how Foucault might reasonably be expected to respond. I *imagine* myself as Foucault and seek to consider Kant as a Foucauldian might reasonably be expected to do, while respecting Foucault's core philosophical views. Overall, the chapter identifies four senses in which Kantian ethics must be rejected, or surpassed, and seeks to justify the superiority of a Nietzschean-inspired 'continuance' perspective to Kantian ethics in these terms for the twenty-first century.

Chapter 5, 'Foucault, Hegel, Marx', examines Foucault's relationship to Hegel and Marx. As Foucault's position can be reassembled easily through his own writings, this chapter, unlike Chapter 4, seeks to present Foucault's own approach, tracing the influence on his thinking on Hegel of his teachers, Jean Hyppolite and Louis Althusser. The latter sections of the chapter then consider two contemporary variants of Hegelian scholarship in political philosophy and ethics. The first of these is the 'politics of recognition', initiated by Hegel and given contemporary significance by Charles Taylor. The engagement in this section is through a book by Patchen Markell, *Bound by Recognition* (2003), which serves as an interlocutor for issues thrown up in a consideration of recognition ethics. The second Hegelian-inspired domain of scholarship to be considered is the ethic of 'self-realization' developed by the British Hegelian T. H. Green, as encapsulating an ethic for the contemporary era. Both the 'politics of recognition' and the ethic of 'self-realization' are compared to the ethic of life continuance. Finally, the chapter turns to examine Foucault's comments on Marx and Marxism in order to highlight the enigma that he considered Marxism to be.

Chapter 6, 'Hobbes, God, and modern social contract theory', positions Foucault among a variety of anglophone and French thinkers, including Michael Ignatieff on rights, Albert Camus on the meaning of life, and Thomas Hobbes on his conceptions of nature and the state of nature, opting for a 'post-human' conception 'beyond nature' in order to adequately represent the global epoch. In seeking to justify continuance as objective in relation to the equality of all, the chapter asks whether religion is necessary to provide an adequate justification of the equal worth of all. After doing this, it turns its attention to an appraisal of the modern social contract tradition, specifically represented by John Rawls, in comparison to continuance ethics.

Chapter 7, 'A politics of pluralism', examines Foucault's commitment to pluralism, which it is argued constitutes the basis of his democratic approach to politics. The chapter starts by considering Foucault's conception of power in comparison to Baron de Montesquieu's conception of the separation of powers as represented through the lens of the jurist Charles Eisenmann, as well as Louis Althusser's writings on Montesquieu. It is argued that Montesquieu's conception, if correctly interpreted, is in important senses homologous to Foucault's and can permit an understanding of the normative workings of power and the function it plays in safeguarding democracy. The chapter reinforces the homology between Foucault and Montesquieu by considering Foucault's views on Adam Ferguson in his final lecture in *The Birth of Biopolitics* (2008). The remaining sections of the chapter utilize Foucault's interviews to further focus on how power relates to supporting democracy, ethics, morality, rights, democratic participation, and public engagement. The chapter concludes by relating pluralism to the topics of fundamentalism and the issue as to whether limits are required for pluralism in political life.

Chapter 8, 'Democracy, education, global ethics', continues the theme of ethical engagement and the senses in which Foucault's work can be said to support a democratic ethic. It starts by examining the critical commentary of Foucault by the American political theorist Ella Myers, in order to position Foucault in relation to her conception of democratic politics. The second part of the chapter turns its attention to a current of political philosophy in North America, notably Stephen K. White's 'weak ontology' thesis, and the ethic of 'presumptive generosity' that White, as well as influential philosophers such as William Connolly and Charles Taylor, have supported. After doing this, Foucault's relevance for education is explored, and the chapter concludes by seeking to relate continuance ethics to virtue ethics and asking what a Foucauldian ethic for a global world might look like.

Chapter 9, 'Ethical comportment', concludes this study by examining the issues of ethics and the subject. Drawing on writing on normative moral philosophy in relation to Foucault, the chapter introduces and critically examines the themes of personal responsibility, integrity, authenticity, and ethical comportment, drawing especially on the work of Judith Butler. It seeks to ascertain how the individual acts morally and engages ethically in a complex world and what ethical engagement, ethical motivation, and ethical commitment looks like from a Foucauldian point of view.

Notes

1 For a detailed list of Foucault's works on ethics, see Appendix 1.
2 To give an example, to the extent that Nietzsche adopts justificatory attitudes to 'suffering' and 'pain', I disagree with his views. Although some scholars have sought to defend Nietzsche, claiming that one must comprehend the nuances of the sophistication of his thesis in order to fully understand his specific comments, because I am not philosophically interested in his views on suffering, my approach is to adopt an approach frequently recommended by Nietzsche, and 'walk on by'.
3 Butler's 2005 book *Giving an Account of Oneself* takes a phrase used by Foucault in his last lecture course at the Collège de France as its title; she says it is the first she has written on moral philosophy.
4 See his last two 'Course Context' articles for Foucault's 1983 and 1984 lectures at the Collège de France (Gros, 2010; 2011), where it seems to me that Gros displays an interest in the issue of normativity in relation to Foucault.
5 In Greek and Roman antiquity, at least, Foucault stresses the importance of the other. See Foucault (1986a: 51–5, 1989b: 296; 1991a; 1997c: 287; 2005: 45, 60, 117, 202; 2011a: 90).
6 Judith Butler seems to agree with this point, but to lament it, when she writes: 'it seems right to fault Foucault for not making more room explicitly for the other in his consideration of ethics' (2005: 23).
7 It is true that Foucault rarely mentions Newton, yet he did dispute Newtonian themes with respect to determinism and free will, causation, and so on.
8 The phrase 'quiet revolution' is drawn from a description by Stuart Kauffman (2008: Preface).
9 For a general introduction to complexity approaches, see Rescher (1998), Mitchell (2009), Morin (2008), Érdi (2008).
10 For an account of downward causation, see Érdi (2008: 32).
11 See my articles 'Michel Foucault's Historical Materialism' (Olssen, 1996), and 'Foucault and Marx: Re-writing the Theory of Historical Materialism' (Olssen, 2005).
12 Materialism designates an approach in which all of life is considered to arise from the physical stuff of the universe in the context of evolution. Materialism is historical to the extent that events, objects, and properties are constituted and accounted for within a 'distributed' system characterized by contingency and evolution.

13 Planck's constant was formulated as part of his work to produce a mathematical expression that accurately predicted the observed spectral distribution of thermal radiation from a closed furnace (black-body radiation). This mathematical formulation is now known as Planck's law.

14 The scientific journal *Annalen der Physik* published four of Einstein's papers in 1905, which established a new foundation for modern physics, radically changing established views of space, time, mass, and energy.

15 Poincaré's contributions lay in recurrence theory, topography and dynamical systems analysis, and also importantly, in his specific work on the 'three-body problem'. See Poincaré (1890; 1891), and note 20 below.

16 If a film can represent motion running backwards in the same way as running forwards, then in physics it is said that time is reversible. The rotation of the hands of a clock is reversible, whereas tearing a piece of paper is irreversible. Prigogine does not deny that time reversibility has relevance, but wishes to add that in many areas, including life itself, time is irreversible.

17 Ergodic theory is a branch of mathematics that studies statistical properties of deterministic dynamical systems. Ergodic theory is concerned with the behaviour of dynamical systems when allowed to run for a long time. The ergodic hypothesis arose with James Clerk Maxwell's (1831–79) and Ludwig Boltzmann's (1844–1906) endeavours to give a precise specification to the kinetic theory of gases and statistical mechanics (Zund, 2002: 139). David Birkhoff had proved Poincaré's geometric theorem in 1913 through his research on celestial mechanics, and through his further researches on dynamical systems was led ultimately to his ergodic theorem. See Birkhoff (1913; 1931), von Neumann (1932), Petersen (1990), Zund (2002), Lasota and Mackey (1998), Walters (1982).

18 Restated by Henri Poincaré, the theorem expresses the cyclic time of the Stoics to formulate recurrence in an isolated system. It has reinforced among physicists the idea of irreversible time as merely subjective.

19 The amount of time taken for repeatability is known as 'Poincare cycle time'. In physics, the Poincaré recurrence theorem maintains that, after a long or very long duration, certain systems (continuous state systems) will return to a state arbitrarily near to, or (discrete state systems) exactly the same as, their initial state. The Poincaré recurrence time is the length of time elapsed until the recurrence. The theorem is commonly discussed in the context of ergodic theory, dynamical systems theory, and statistical mechanics.

20 Centrally important to the establishment of chaos theory was Poincaré's exploration and arguments concerning the 'three-body problem'. Briefly stated, prior to Poincaré, the paradigm of 'celestial mechanics' represented the solar system as predictable according to invariant laws of the cosmos. Poincaré showed that as soon as there were more than two bodies in the system, unpredictability became the norm. What he discovered was *chaos* (see Poincaré, 1890; 1891).

21 Although quantum theory had introduced notions of indeterminacy, through the interaction with measurement, for Prigogine such indeterminism is more centrally associated with 'strong mixing' in initial system interactions.

22 By defining order as a product of the system as a whole, as in a complex dynamical system, order or pattern associated with the macroscopic property of the entire system is not a property of the constituent elements of the system, yet can affect them through a variety of linear and non-linear processes involving 'feedback loops' or 'endogeneity', 'strong mixing', and 'downward causation'.

23 While I wish to note that writers such as Deleuze developed approaches broadly compatible with complexity science as formulated by Prigogine, I am not intending to develop the theme further in this context. For an introduction, however, see Protevi (2006).

24 Although laws apply, they operate as a consequence of the location of elements within a system, that is, relationally, and are contingent and evolutionary.

25 In support of these claims, Clegg references Aczel (2000: passim).

26 John Worrall (1989) sees Poincaré as a 'structural realist', although he concedes that Poincaré is typically represented as a 'pragmatic anti-realist' about scientific theories. Worrall's suggestion of 'realism' is related to the fact that Poincaré is not a sceptic when it comes to the validity of science. Regarding structuralism in mathematics, Poincaré opposes *ante rem* structuralism, where the system or structure exists prior to and independently of the parts (or 'places'), but sees the structure as emerging with the parts, thus manifesting an *in re* structuralism. Poincaré can be seen as a precursor of poststructuralism.

27 Foucault expresses the 'death of man' thesis in slightly different ways at the end of *The Order of Things* (1970: 322, 344, 386).

28 See Foucault (1972: 82–4 and passim). Gros notes also references to Austin and Searle in the 12 January lecture of the 1982–83 lectures at the Collège de France (see Foucault, 2010: 12 January, second hour).

1

Foucault and normativity

Foucault as anti-normative

> Listen, listen ... How difficult it is! I am not a prophet; I am not an organiser; I don't want to tell people what they should do. I am not going to tell them, 'This is good for you, this is bad for you!'
> (Foucault, 2016c: 137)
>
> The role of an intellectual is not to tell others what they must do. By what right would he do so? ... The work of the intellectual is ... to re-examine evidence and assumptions, to shake up habitual ways of thinking, to dissipate conventional familiarities, to re-evaluate rules and institutions ... to participate in the formation of a political will.
> (Foucault, 1989b: 462)

In claiming to establish a normative Foucault, what becomes manifestly evident to the informed reader is that such a project runs in opposition to much of the current literature on Foucault and normativity. In his book *For Foucault*, Mark Kelly (2018) argues that Foucault's approach is non-normative, non-political, and non-theoretical. This non-normative approach is also an anti-normative approach. Whereas Marx is a normative thinker who proselytizes on the political, Foucault rejects normativity. Just as Foucault is against 'advice-giving', as Kelly notes, he can also be found proselytizing against doing politics. As Foucault says in *Sécurité, territoire, population*, for instance: 'I only propose therefore this single imperative, but this will be categorical and unconditional: Never do politics' (Foucault, 2004: 6, cited in Kelly, 2018: 10). Kelly comments: 'I read this comment [by Foucault] as a condemnation specifically of normative politics' (2018: 10). He himself welcomes this tendency and speaks of his own academic career as 'presenting papers at conferences and seminars proposing that political philosophy be conducted in a "non-normative" way' (2018: 2). Noting that many audiences questioned the plausibility of his view, Kelly seeks immediately to restrict the definition of 'normative' 'as merely a by-word for prescription, which is to say for "oughts"' (2018: 2), and he cites Christine Korsgaard (2009) to lend authority to this claim.

This approach, says Kelly, challenges the 'ethical turn' in political philosophy of the 1970s, characterized by writers such as John Rawls in his *Theory of Justice* (1971), a book that sought to breathe 'new life into normative approaches to politics, and re-founding political philosophy as a distinctive normative enterprise linked to – but no longer entirely subordinated to – normative ethics' (Kelly, 2018: 2). Others who characterized such an approach include Jürgen Habermas, as well as a large number of writers who represent Marxist political thought. Against this trend of the 'ethicization of political thought … Foucault pushes in the opposite direction, for a political thought that stands against normativity' (Kelly, 2018: 3). Kelly further amplifies this thesis by referring to Foucault's 1978 paper, 'La philosophie analytique de la politique' (Foucault, 1994c: 534–51), in which he advocates an analytic method similar to that utilized in anglophone analytical philosophy. This, Kelly suggests, stands opposed to normative philosophy: 'I think it is in the end thoroughgoing methodological non-normativity that Foucault is proposing when he talks of a political philosophy that is purely "analytical"' (Kelly, 2018: 5). Foucault's supposed rejection of normative thinking, then, might seem validated by the image of a detached, neutral, almost positivistic style that pervades the 'grey' parchment of his genealogies. This whole approach implies that a normative method would have various negative consequences, for it would be overtly political and therefore prescriptive. Being prescriptive of the axioms and assumptions of normative thinking would in turn be dangerous, for it would, as Kelly says, 'restrict the possible audience for political thought to those who share [such views]' (2018: 7). This, says Kelly, would have various 'unintended consequences', for it would suppress the 'radically unforeseeable … complexity of the social world' (2018: 8, 9). He argues that 'normativity, politics, and theory need to be stamped out, primarily on the basis of their failure to account for social complexity' (2018: 15). Kelly builds his thesis on the work of Australian philosopher Paul Patton, who, Kelly says, has also interpreted Foucault as non-normative.[1] I will argue in this book, contra Kelly, that a viable normative theory is *required*, especially *given* the complexity of the world, if only in order to ground an ethics to guide political action.

Kelly notes in advocating his thesis that Foucault nowhere uses the term 'normativity' itself, but he considers this 'unsurprising given the term had limited currency in French at the time' (2018: 5). Kelly also observes how Foucault 'does not pointedly reject normativity as such', but he explains this as a consequence of the fact that 'this is in large part because his core political writings … were composed before the ethical turn in French thought began … Rather he was working in a context where non-normativity was already quite firmly established as the standard mode for political thought' (2018: 3). These observations are important from my point of view, as while I agree with Kelly that Foucault shows no interest in being prescriptive in the sense of proselytizing for a particular political position or 'giving advice', there are two points on which I disagree. First, Foucault was being normative in the more nuanced sense of normativity that I will define further below, in that his theoretical and methodological choices involved selections and exclusions of a normative sort. Secondly, whereas Kelly celebrates being non-normative, I think it is a liability and a disadvantage, especially as regards being able to support ethical, moral, and political claims. Kelly says that '[t]he burden should be on the normativist to explain why normativity is necessary or useful in political thought' (2018: 9). This is a challenge I intend to take up. For reasons that I will expand on further below and throughout this book, I think that a normative Foucault would have enormous benefits.

In order to expand on these points, I want to propose two theses: first, that it is hard, even impossible, to be non-normative in any total sense. Kelly himself is alert to the charge that to seek to avoid normativity is to render oneself 'incoherent' (2018: 10). Yet he cannot understand why:

contemporary political philosophers are in the grip of a largely unstated normative metaprinciple that they should be normative. By dint of this unconscious principle, the idea of a non-normative political philosophy simply does not occur to most specialists today, and when they see it, it looks to them like nonsense. When confronted with Foucault's work, most commentators either describe him as incoherent for his opposition to normativity or attempt to ascribe a deep normativity to him. (2018: 10)

I quote this passage because it demonstrates the limitations in the understanding of normativity that Kelly possesses, in my view. While one can seek to proceed, as Foucault did in his major genealogical researches, to eschew a concern with normative disciplines such as politics, law, ethics, or morality, and avoid commitment to a narrow political agenda, this does not mean that his methodological and onto-epistemological choices are not in and of themselves in an important sense normative. In his writing on Wittgenstein, Saul Kripke (1984) argued that all meaning is normative as well as descriptive because there exist criteria for the correct use of linguistic expressions. Such normative criteria relate to the selection of words, as well as methodological and epistemic choices.[2] Further, being normative must not be confused with being biased, and yet it seems to me that Kelly is equating the two. What Kelly fails to understand is that decisions and selections are normative not just in relation to taking a particular stand in relation to politics, or in 'telling people what to do', but in relation to any number of choices concerning what is practical or impractical, true or false, worthy or unworthy, healthy or unhealthy, productive or unproductive, and so on. Yet Kelly maintains that Foucault actively sought to expunge all reference to normativity from his methodology and that 'non-normativity is thus a methodological percept for Foucault' (2018: 9). Kelly doesn't accept 'that Foucault believed ... that it is strictly necessary ... to adopt even a single normative principle' (2018: 10). In my view, while Kelly captures something in Foucault's approach, he goes far too far.

Kelly goes too far because he advocates for being non-normative without differentiating the different senses of 'normative' that are entailed. Being normative can mean providing criteria that can support normative judgements, thereby escaping moral relativism.

This is a sense that Kelly does not consider. As stated above, Kelly thinks that it is a 'methodological non-normativity that Foucault is proposing when he talks of a political philosophy that is purely "analytical"' (2018: 5). I think Kelly is mistaken here. In my reading of Foucault on analytic philosophy, he is not referring to analytic philosophy as excluding the normative, but rather in relation to proposing a methodology for talking about power with reference to the precision of ordinary language philosophy. As Foucault would have been aware, analytic philosophy supports a strong tradition of normative and moral philosophy. Putting this point to rest, Kelly's admission that Foucault does not use the term 'normativity' as such, together with his argument that Foucault is 'against normativity', are too general and include too many different senses of what being normative can possibly mean to be useful.

It is my contention that Foucault's theoretical orientation must be seen as more nuanced and more complex than Kelly has allowed for. Rather than saying that Foucault actively avoided being normative, or that he was anti-normative *in toto*, I would rather say that Foucault clearly did not want his own theoretical methodology to be infected by any partisan, hidden, or camouflaged political ideology or theory. But I think a stronger and more nuanced statement is warranted here, for in my view, Foucault didn't simply reject all values of a normative sort, which would have been impossible, but stood very emphatically against certain metaphysical and theoretical traditions, notably Marxism and Hegelianism, as well as Platonism, and modernist conceptions of the subject, and so forth. While he showed little interest in normative theorizing in the 'prescriptive' or 'utopian' senses associated with these positions, this was because he didn't want his own historical genealogies to be contaminated by a specific ideological, political, or narrowly theoretical stance of an inappropriate sort that might contradict the Nietzschean onto-epistemology that largely guided his work. On my reading, it was not that Foucault was not committed to *any* normative values, but rather that he did not want to have the *wrong* values infect his own normative approach. It was not so much an agnosticism over or antipathy to normative assumptions, but a question of identifying with the values he wanted his project overall to be identified with. In this sense, it is not a question of being against normativity as such, but only against certain narrow senses of being normative (moralizing, advice giving, etc). What I would maintain also is that while Foucault did not articulate any normative principle that could ground his project overall, the development of a normative architecture that could support an ethics, and give concepts such as *critique, resistance, states of domination, practices of the self,* and *parrhēsia* some normative grounding against arbitrary power and relativistic incoherence, would be useful.

The pervasiveness of the normative

The basis of the discussion so far is that I believe it is impossible not to be normative in certain senses. Further, I maintain that to develop a normative architecture that could ground ethics is quite different to what Foucault opposed, which was essentially 'moralizing', 'sermonizing', 'advice-giving', or 'preaching'. My own view is that Kelly has not differentiated these different senses adequately. I want now to summarize three views on the pervasiveness of normativity in our lives, and discuss these with reference to Foucault. Before doing so, let me define normative in the way Kelly has done, and consistently with G. H. von Wright in *Norm and Action*, as referring to prescriptive statements about what ought (or ought not) to be the case. As von Wright says, '[a] normative statement ... is a statement to the effect that something or other ought to, or may, or must not be done (by some agent or agents, on some occasion or generally, unconditionally or provided certain conditions are satisfied)' (1963: 105). In this sense, normative discourse is used to refer not just to terms such as 'ought' ('ought not'), but also to terms such as 'may' ('may not'), 'prohibited' ('allowable'), 'advisable' ('discouraged'), etc. Normative is the adjective from norm, which governs actions, and includes such things as 'laws', 'rules', 'prescriptions', 'customs', 'moral norms', 'directives', and 'ideals', says von Wright (1963: ch. 1). Synonyms for norms are words such as 'pattern', 'standard', 'type', 'regulation', 'rule', 'law'. 'Directives' and 'prescriptions' are said to be normative. It is said that customs exert normative pressure, that is, pressure as to what citizens ought to do (von Wright, 1963: chs 1, 5).

In his paper 'The Deontic Furniture of the World', Jaap Hage presents a complementary analysis and codification of the basic concepts that embody normativity. Although normativity pertains to what ought to be, ought must not be taken in a narrow sense, pertaining solely to the moral, but can relate to moral, ethical, prudential, instrumental, aesthetic, political, or religious values. It can be *ex ante*, related to the guidance of behaviour, or *ex post*, related to the evaluation of behaviour. Although the conception developed in relation to Foucault will be constructivist, it will, as it does for Hage, recognize deontic facts ('Judge Judy has the duty to apply the law') and deontic rules ('Judges have the duty to apply the law') (Hage, 2013: 87).

Ralph Wedgwood

According to Ralph Wedgwood, normativity pervades our lives, including the concept of intentionality. Consistent with von Wright and Hage, Wedgwood defines normativity as what ought to be (2007: 1). Any time we intentionally act, we are in part being normative. Any selection as to what determines actions as right or wrong, good or bad, appropriate or inappropriate, in different contexts, presupposes a normative orientation. In this sense, the normative inhabits the realm of the discursive and provides rules for arbitration over standards of evidence, appropriate methods, as well as any intentionality expressed in and through discourse. Normative properties are irreducible and causally efficacious. Because normative discourse is irreducible, any narrow naturalism that is reductive must be rejected.[3] For Wedgwood, 'the intentional itself is normative' (2007: 8). Intentionality is the 'subject of the mental ... all mental states – are *about* something; they are "concerned with" or "directed towards" something' (2007: 159). This constitutes, he says, a 'metaphysical claim' (2007: 159). As he states:

> I propose that we should interpret the claim that the intentional is normative as the claim that in giving an account of the nature or essence of intentional states, we must mention normative properties or relations ... In that sense, intentional facts are partially constituted by normative facts. (2007: 159)

The key point here is that any adequate account of the subject's functioning *must* require normative terms. An intentional state requires at least two elements: '(i) a content, which is composed out of *concepts,* and (ii) a *mental relation* or *attitude* such as belief, desire, hope, fear, and so on, towards that content' (Wedgwood, 2007: 161). Hence, on this model, even conceptualization and reasoning are normative, or involve normative activities, in that they entail selection, prioritizing, classification, and so on.

Normative discourse is about what ought to be, but ought applies here in context-specific ways across all of the multiple domains of life. According to Wedgwood, concepts such as 'good', 'right', and 'ought' are 'profoundly context-sensitive, so that they express different concepts in different contexts' (2007: 23). Normativity thus conforms to an 'internalism', says Wedgwood, in that there is 'an essential internal connection between normative judgements and practical reasoning or motivation for action' (2007: 23). Normative judgement is thus broader than moral or even ethical judgement in that it concerns all 'oughts' against a background habitus of survival, not simply those of justice, fairness, equality, and rights. Wedgwood states that '[t]here is extensive linguistic evidence that there are in fact several different kinds of "ought": the term "ought" expresses different concepts in different contexts of use' (2007: 117). Not only is 'the term ought ... systematically context-sensitive', so is the term 'best' (2007: 119, 129). As for intentions, motivations and judgement are context-sensitive and intrinsically normative too. Any account of the subject's action must mention the normative dimension to action. There is even, says Wedgwood, a normative element in being rational, or thinking clearly. To think clearly means that certain social conditions that defeat 'rational', 'clear' thinking must be absent (2007: 160). For Wedgwood, moreover, normativity is real, yet constructed, rather than 'psychological' or 'expressivist' in the tradition of writers such as A. J. Ayer or Simon Blackburn or Alan Gibbard, who see normative statements as having meaning only in psychological terms (Wedgwood, 2007: ch. 2; Ayer, 1946; Gibbard, 1990; 2003; Blackburn, 1993; 1998). Wedgwood maintains 'that there cannot be any *reduction* of the normative to the mental' (2007: 175). This conception of the irreducibility and non-psychological nature of the normative will be essential to the theory I wish to construct for Foucault.

What I also take from Wedgwood is that subjects are intrinsically normative, and mental choices and intentions are related to dispositions or actions that by definition constitute selections between an indefinite range of possible options. This entails that there are 'better' ways to arrange the environment of the subject, and demonstrates the normativity of the subject as a *necessary* 'chooser' and 'problem-solver' in a complex terrain of multiple possibilities as they go about their lives. To select A and not B involves reasons for A being 'better/worse', 'more satisfying/less satisfying', 'more efficient/less efficient', 'more appropriate/less appropriate', 'more effective/less effective', 'healthier/less healthy'. Any or all of these constitute a form of normativity, just as the multiple bifurcations of life require choice, decision, judgement, and selection, which presupposes normative criteria according to which such plans are assessed and executed.

The content of normative commitments is determined for Wedgwood not simply by mental states and emotions, but by actions and practices, and are both individual and collective. Normativity is implicated in any judgements concerning courses of action as to relevant futures. Ethics constitutes a sub-branch of the normative in that it constitutes a set of actions that guides individuals and collectivities, involving a consistent set of beliefs and plans, what Wedgwood calls, following Allan Gibbard (1990), 'a *hyperplan* – roughly, a complete and consistent plan about what to do and what to think for every conceivable circumstance' (Wedgwood, 2007: 45). As mental states are normatively governed and constructed, normativity is thus public and operates across all of life, and yet it is individually appropriated, mediated, and interpreted in context-sensitive ways. In that norms are socially constructed, and involve actions for the future, they necessarily entail a myriad of conflicting rules over what we ought to do for any particular course of action. Wedgwood cites Crispin Wright (1992: 74), who characterizes normative discourse as 'a thoroughly disciplined discourse' involving 'certain standards of justification and warrantedness' in terms of 'rules' (Wedgwood, 2007: 47). Rules become the way that normativity is institutionalized and enacted.

Hannah Ginsborg

Another recent thinker who maintains that normativity pervades our lives is Hannah Ginsborg in her book, *The Normativity of Nature: Essays on Kant's Critique of Judgment* (2015). Ginsborg offers a revision of Kant's *Critique* as representing a central contribution to the understanding of normativity and of human cognition more generally by drawing out the philosophical significance of normativity for the notion of judgement (as written about by Kant in his third *Critique*) and showing its importance to possibilities of reinterpretation of Kant's philosophy as well as for the contemporary view of human action and ethics. Ginsborg's reinterpretation of Kant:

> rejects the traditional dichotomy between the natural and the normative, taking nature itself – both human nature and nature outside us – to be comprehensible only in normative terms ... To possess the capacity of judgment ... is to respond to the world in a way which involves the recognition of one's response as normatively appropriate to the objects which cause them. (2015: dust jacket)

The priority of the normative is thus central to Ginsborg's revision of Kant. As she states: 'to recognise normativity in the natural psychological processes responsible for perception and empirical judgment ... [w]e must be able to regard the sensory and imaginative responses which those objects elicit not only as natural psychological ends but also as governed by normative rules' (2015: 327). Overturning Kant's priority of teleology over mechanism, Ginsborg reincorporates the concepts of 'end' and 'purposiveness' back into a reformulated conception of judgement *as normative*:

> judgment amounts, in effect, to the principle that the relation between nature and our cognitive faculties is a normative one ... The idea of nature's purposiveness for judgment is the idea of a normative fit between nature outside of us and the natural psychological processes through which we perceive and conceptualize it. (2015: 329)

If organisms have a natural normativity, then, this leads, says Ginsborg, 'to a conception of organisms as natural ends'

(2015: 328). As such, Ginsborg's thesis constitutes a reformulation of the traditional dichotomy of both Kant and Kantians between the natural and the normative. Although credit where it is given is only to Wittgenstein, and although the term poststructuralism is not mentioned, Ginsborg's thesis represents very decidedly a poststructuralist revision of Kant's *Critique of Judgement* in important senses.[4] What is important here, however, is not her detailed analysis and rewriting of Kant's third *Critique*, but her own reformulations with respect to normativity. Kant's theory, says Ginsborg, 'rests on our entitlement to ascribe normativity to nature in ourselves' (2015: 6). She sees the faculty of judgement as the basis of such an immanent normativity. Here, importantly, however, she claims that Kant only *implicitly* saw judgement as normative in this sense ('while not articulated explicitly by Kant ... is implicit in his treatment of the topics with which the *Critique of Judgment* is directly concerned' [2015: 5]).[5] In responding to the world outside us, and exercising perceptual, imaginative, and judgmental activity, we steer a course between what is appropriate and inappropriate guided by an immanent quest for survival constitutive of the immanent normativity of life itself. This at least is the thesis that I would like to take from Ginsborg's analysis of Kant.

Thomas Scanlon

Finally, a third contemporary account of the normative is provided by Thomas Scanlon, an Anglo-American social contract theorist. Scanlon offers a defence of the irreducibility of normative truths concerning reasons for action in his book, *Being Realistic about Reasons* (2014). Such truths, he says, exist in a 'domain' which, although he doesn't use the word, is clearly a discursive domain quite compatible with the sense of discourse in Foucault. Central to this 'domain-centred view', says Scanlon:

> I believe that the way of thinking about these matters that makes most sense is a view that does not privilege science but takes as basic a range of domains, including mathematics, science, and moral and practical reasoning. It holds that statements within all of these

> domains are capable of truth and falsity, and that the truth values of statements about one domain, insofar as they do not conflict with statements of some other domain, are properly settled by the standards of the domain that they are about. (2014: 19)

In that each domain has its own standards for considering questions, although reason is internal to each domain, it can also answer questions across domains and deal with 'mixed statements' (2014: 20). Scanlon considers possible criticisms as to whether or in what sense domains could be said to 'exist', and concludes that, like Carnap's concept of 'framework' (or it may be inserted, Foucault's concept of 'discourse'), 'the question about domains is not whether they exist, but whether they provide a helpful way of discussing certain matters' (2014: 23). Adapting Gilbert Harman's famous 'explanatory requirement', originally applied to justifying the use of certain concepts in the natural sciences, Scanlon employs the concept as justifying our 'reason to be committed to the existence of things ... if they play a role in explaining what happens' (2014: 26).[6]

Scanlon argues that in the normative domain, 'reasons for actions have determinate answers' that are 'independent of us' (2014: 30). Scanlon provides an objectivist account of the normative realm, with its own truth criteria as well as standards of assessment. In the normative domain, what is distinctive, says Scanlon, is not individual reasons, but 'normative relations such as being a reason for something, or being a sufficient or conclusive reason' (2014: 30). Hence, 'what is special about normative claims ... is the relation of simply counting in favour of some action or attitude' (2014: 30). Whether something is a reason depends upon 'circumstance' (2014: 30). Through the concept of the normative as a relation, Scanlon builds in contingency or specificity to action, representing something being a *reason for something* as involving what he calls 'a four-place relation ... holding between a fact p, an agent x, a set of conditions c, and an action or attitude a' (2014: 31). It is no accident that the representation of an irreducible normative domain parallels the ascendance of vital materialism in the Continental tradition of philosophy, and indirectly legitimates notions such as *discourse* and *dispositif*, as used by Foucault.

Normativity in Foucault

Although each of these perspectives on normativity, developing as they have within the Anglo-American theatre of philosophy, must be adjudged unsatisfactory from Foucault's point of view – especially as regards the relations between individual and collective, as well as the importance of power and democracy – with regard to how the normative can guide policy, all three views expressed above constitute important statements of the revival of a normative 'turn' in philosophy, that is, as a field of understanding and exploration that cannot be sidestepped.

Extending on from this, in the broader, more general sense in which I have (with Wedgwood's, Ginsborg's, and Scanlon's assistance) developed the concept here, there appears to be a very obvious sense in which the concept of discourse as developed by Foucault is itself capable of incorporating a dimension of normativity. In *The Archaeology of Knowledge*, where Foucault theorizes the concept of discourse, he is clearly interested in the '*rules* of formation of discourse' – the '*group of rules* that are immanent in a practice, and define it in its specificity' (1972: 46, emphasis added). For Foucault, discourse constitutes an irreducible domain. He points out that the unity of discourse lies not in the objects it classifies and refers to, but in the '*rules of formation*. The rules of formation are conditions of existence (but also of coexistence, maintenance, modification, and disappearance) in a given discursive division' (1972: 38). While not using the term 'normative' (or 'normativity'), the unity on which such discourses form include 'the identity and persistence of themes' (1972: 35). Such a thematic unity manifests 'its own internal force, and its own capacity for survival' (1972: 35). The rules of formation of discourse, he says, form a 'group of rules' (1972: 34). This group of rules 'simultaneously, or in turn, make possible purely perceptual descriptions' (1972: 34).

Although Foucault does not use the term, the rules of formation of discourse are at least in part normative, as indeed rules *necessarily are*, as consistent with the view I have argued above. The rule governing the formation of discourse 'lays down what must be related, in a particular discursive practice, for such and such an enunciation to be made, for such and such a concept to be used, for such and such a strategy to be organized' (1972: 74). And although Foucault does not use the term 'norms' in this context either, it would seem that the rules of formation of discourse include such things as 'interests', 'facts', 'desires', 'relevant themes', 'norms', and 'practices' pertinent to survival within a particular historical milieu, as dictated 'by the *function* that the discourse under study must carry out *in a field of non-discursive practices*' (1972: 68). What is evident here is that the system for the formation of discourse contains a normative dimension, although it is worth noting that this judgement constitutes a re-reading of Foucault's *Archaeology of Knowledge* after the 'normative turn', rather than Foucault's own nomenclature. It is my conjecture here that Foucault would agree that the construction of discourse combines both normative and non-normative elements.

If, in Foucault's genealogies, epistemic rules govern the production of his text in myriad ways, more generally rules constitute patterns of behaviour in the sense of suggesting, enforcing, or proscribing actions in social life. Given the priority of historical nominalism in the theorization of rules in *The Archaeology of Knowledge*, certain parallels are also possible between Foucault and Wittgenstein. For Foucault, as for Wittgenstein, rules are not mental states, nor platonic objects, but historical and communal (Wittgenstein, 1967: 342). Both writers also utilize the metaphor of the game, and see a multiplicity of ways in which a rule can be obeyed.[7] In this sense, for both writers, rule following is a social practice that presupposes common agreement, and a normative principle or principles that guide action.[8] Rules thus maintain a high degree of systematicity and normative unity in the sense that rule following doesn't simply apply to language but to all domains. This is also to say that practices of social behaviour are insufficient in themselves to guide behaviour. While one cannot always codify what one ought to do or why, the normative rules, even if not always transparent, are implicit in any situation. While independent of persons, rules thus are behaviour-guiding and important psychologically in motivating how people act.

Analysing Foucault's works, or drawing parallels with Wittgenstein, is quite different to accepting that Foucault's works contain normative presuppositions, yet this is another dimension or aspect of normativity that tacitly affects his work, and that warrants scrutiny. This constitutes a further aspect of the challenge I started out with above, that it is difficult not to reveal one's normative presumptions, and this is to claim that such presuppositions can readily be found in Foucault's writings, both in his more formal studies as well as in his interviews and commentaries. This is important for, as already noted, Kelly does 'not believe ... that it is strictly necessary for us to adopt even a single normative principle' (2018: 10). In the light of my references to Wedgwood, Ginsborg, and Scanlon above, as well as of the embedded assumptions in Foucault's own work, it would appear that this claim is hard to defend. Kelly is undoubtedly correct that Foucault was not interested in expounding any explicit normative position in relation to his canonical genealogies, but that is not the same as proving that there are no embedded normative assumptions in his work. Denying Marxism and Hegelianism, in preference for a conception of pluralism, is itself a normative position, as is adhering to a Nietzschean-inspired conception of genealogy. That the various different elements of Foucault's *oeuvre* spanning more than thirty years reveal a particular normative moral-philosophical orientation is something that would seem undoubtedly to be the case.

In his 'unfashionable interpretation of Michel Foucault', James Johnson (1997) maintains that Foucault's commitment to normative concepts and principles, such as liberty, fairness, reciprocity, openness, and democratic justice, can be suggested by a normative analysis of power latent in his work. Johnson supports his case by tracing references in canonical works such as *Discipline and Punish* (1977) as well as in Foucault's interviews and articles. In *Discipline and Punish*, Foucault speaks of institutions such as prisons and schools as having the role of 'introducing insuperable asymmetries and excluding reciprocities' (1977a: 222). Here Foucault talks of the disciplines as being 'essentially nonegalitarian and asymmetrical' (1977a: 222). Johnson accepts a view, contra postmodern and other interpretations of Foucault, 'that disciplinary power is *normatively objectionable* [for Foucault] precisely *because* it imposes unequal, asymmetrical, nonreciprocal relations and because, in doing so, it obliterates the sorts of extant communicative relation that, potentially at least, could produce social relations characterized by equality, symmetry and reciprocity' (1997: 572). Hence, says Johnson, power relations for Foucault are 'objectionable because they subvert relations of communication, relations of the sort that – if more fully specified – might sustain the vision of political agency that is implicit in his commitment to resistance or dialogical ethics' (1997: 572). As against approaches such as Marxism and Hegelianism, the normative position of Foucault's work is that all power relations must be characterized by *openness*.

Such a view is supported in many interviews and articles. In the interview, 'The Ethic of Care for the Self as a Practice of Freedom' (1991a), for instance, Foucault discusses the concepts of 'non-domination' and the 'equalisation of power relations' as necessary to overcoming domination. In certain political situations, power relations, in terms of which liberty is realized, make its expression impossible. In this situation, says Foucault, there results a 'state of domination' (1991a: 12). In a state of domination, power relations become 'fixed in such a way that they are perpetually asymmetrical and the margin of liberty is extremely limited' (1991a: 12). Foucault illustrates this with reference to traditional conjugal relations of the eighteenth and nineteenth centuries:

> we cannot say that there was only male power; the woman herself could do a lot of things: be unfaithful to him, extract money from him, refuse him sexually. She was, however, subject to a state of domination, in the measure where all that was finally no more than a certain number of tricks which never brought about a reversal of the situation. (1991a: 12)

Such states of domination entailed relations of power that 'instead of being variable and allowing different partners a strategy which alters them, find themselves firmly set and congealed' (1991a: 3).

Similarly, in his criticism of Habermas, discussed in the same interview, Foucault proceeds to state a conception whereby power relations can be equalized in order 'to give oneself the rules of law, the techniques of management, and also the ethics, the *ethos*, the practices of self, which would allow these games of power to be played with a minimum of domination' (1991a: 18). In this situation, power relations presuppose 'free subjects'. As Foucault states:

One must observe also that there cannot be relations of power unless subjects are free. If one or the other were completely at the disposition of the other and became his thing, an object on which he can exercise an indefinite and unlimited violence, there would not be relations of power. (1991a: 12)

Paul Patton argues that the concept of the 'state of domination' in Foucault is non-normative, as Foucault envisages instances where domination is legitimate and non-punitive. As Patton puts it, 'domination allows more or less predictable control of the actions of others' (1998: 68). Pedagogical relations utilize a measure of domination based on asymmetrical power relations which, says Patton, 'are not in themselves evil' (1998: 68). This may well be true, but notwithstanding specific contextual structurations (or exceptions), reference to states of domination as arbitrary power enforcement *is* normative, and Foucault is very clear about the different ways in which he utilizes the concept and how it is to be interpreted in each context. Clearly suggested in his writing is that there are legitimate and illegitimate ways to structure power. Even in pedagogical or family relations, where asymmetrical relations of power might be deemed legitimate, there is still a normative reference that pertains to legitimacy, as there is also when asymmetrical relations are illegitimate. For Foucault, power relations are not something good or bad in themselves, but nevertheless, as he makes clear in his interviews, 'the only ethic one can have with regard to the exercise of power is the freedom of others' (Foucault, 2016b: 137).[9]

A systematic survey of embedded normative references in Foucault would yield a much larger result. To do so, however, would add little further weight to what can already be concluded: that it is in fact impossible to escape all reference to normativity. That Foucault did at times seem intent on excluding the presence of normative values from his work is a pertinent point that Kelly makes, and that can be accepted. This is largely because the studies Foucault was undertaking were not obviously prescriptive in the way that the theories he opposed were. In a purely theoretical sense, while normativity might pervade our lives, it was still clearly possible for Foucault to emulate the 'grey' neutrality of a positivist style of presentation. This does not mean that immanent normative values do not infuse his methodological and theoretical choices. Nor need it mean that a normative architecture that remains faithful to his approach cannot be erected and serve a positive function. This would not be advice-giving of the sort Foucault opposed. Rather it would constitute a meta-ethical conception that could be appealed to justify ethical, moral, and normative claims.

Criticisms of Foucault

Such a normative framework would offset criticisms of Foucault on the grounds of normative relativism that were prevalent in the late 1970s and 1980s. Foucault was aware of the criticisms of his project on the grounds of relativism that were levelled by Jürgen Habermas in *The Philosophical Discourses of Modernity* (1987: 276–9). Many others had made similar criticisms. As Nancy Fraser put it:

> Because Foucault has no basis for distinguishing ... forms of power that involve domination from those that do not, he appears to endorse a one-sided, wholesale rejection of modernity as such ... Clearly, what Foucault needs, and needs desperately, are normative criteria for distinguishing acceptable from unacceptable forms of power. (1989: 32–3)

Pierre Hadot's criticisms of Foucault raise the issue of normativity not directly in relation to power, but in relation to the constitution of the subject. Because Foucault did not wish to recognize or posit any transcendent metaphysics of exteriority in order to ground ethics, Hadot claims that he effectively reduces the Stoics' conception of the self and way of life to a thinly based set of aesthetic exercises without any spiritual dimension or telos that rightfully belongs to it. This makes it difficult, Hadot suggests, for Foucault to consider any criteria that could determine which of any ways of life were better or worse in moral or ethical terms.

The criticism of Foucault that Hadot levelled is that while he articulates the historically varied forms of the practices of self, he also understates and shows little interest in the extent to which such practices are concerned with the ethical or moral dimensions of life, or the extent to which they manifest common features underpinning their varied forms. In his studies and writings on ancient ethics, Foucault draws on Hadot's article 'Exercices spirituels' (1976) in order to describe ancient philosophy as an 'art, style, or way of life' (Hadot, 1995: 206). Whereas Hadot terms these practices 'spiritual exercises', however, Foucault labels them 'arts of existence' or 'techniques of the self' (Hadot, 1995: 206–7). Hadot finds a problem here, for as he sees it, Foucault's description 'is precisely focused far too much on the "self", or at least on a specific conception of self' (1995: 207). Hadot's point essentially is that the portrait is too narcissistic. Hence, distinctions made by Seneca in his twenty-third *Letter* between 'pleasure' and 'joy' (*voluptas* and *gaudium*) are obscured by Foucault. As Hadot maintains, 'Foucault presents Greco-Roman ethics as an ethics of the pleasure one takes in oneself' (1995: 207). Hadot's point, then, concerns the very absence of the ethical and moral sense of self in Foucault's account:

> If the Stoics insist on the word *gaudium*/'joy', it is precisely because they refuse to introduce the principle of pleasure into moral life. For them, happiness does not consist in pleasure, but in virtue itself, which is its own reward. Long before Kant, the Stoics strove jealously to preserve the purity of intention of the moral consciousness. (1995: 207).

As a consequence of this, says Hadot, Foucault's account of the Stoics fails to adequately acknowledge the moral dimension of the self, the higher aspect of the self, in which joy is located. Foucault never explores what this moral dimension that the Stoics insisted upon comprises or how it operates. While it could be accessed through joy, it certainly could not be accessed through pleasure. Hadot cites Seneca, who says that joy is to be found 'in the best portion of the self', in 'the true good' (1995: 207).[10] For Seneca, joy is to be found in 'perfect reason' (1995: 207).[11] Joy is located 'in the conscience turned towards the good; in intentions which have no other object than virtue; in just actions' (1995: 207).[12]

It is this normative dimension of the self that Foucault neglects. The Stoics aim to 'go beyond the self and think and act in unison with universal reason' (Hadot, 1995: 207). Hadot surmises that Foucault overlooks these aspects for a particular extra-theoretical purpose which drives his studies: 'His description of the practices of the self ... is not merely an historical study, but rather a tacit attempt to offer contemporary mankind a model of life, which Foucault calls "an aesthetics of existence"' (1995: 208). Hadot seems to be accusing Foucault of being normative here, but in a way that he does not approve of, and in a way that neglects the possibilities of morality. The overarching criticism seems to be that Foucault offers us an overly 'hollowed-out' self, a self that is devoid of ethical, moral, or normative compass. There is no feeling, Hadot claims, in Foucault's self of belonging to a greater whole, the 'human community', the 'cosmic whole', or, in one of Seneca's phrases, 'the totality of the world' (Hadot, 1995: 208). There are, in short, no normative criteria in terms of which the moral dimension of selfhood can be understood.

Clearly Hadot's objection suggests that he is at least somewhat out of sympathy with what Foucault is trying to do, as well as suggesting that Foucault sacrifices important aspects of the self in the Greco-Roman world for the purposes of an ulterior theoretical motive. Yet some writers have rallied to Foucault's defence. As Orazio Irrera notes: 'Hadot's strained attempt to include the concept of transcendence in order to conceive unitarily of performativity, of the therapeutic value of the entire philosophical discourse of antiquity, introduces in reality *a theory of universality as normative exteriority* in regard to consciousness' (2010: 1008).[13] Irrera's point is that to take Hadot's criticisms on board is likely to derail Foucault's entire genealogical project concerning Greek and Roman antiquity. In my view, however, Foucault's project would be more potent in terms of its theoretical effects if the normativity of the subject *had* been taken on board.

What appears to concern Hadot, who was himself an inspiration for Foucault, is that Foucault's self appears to fall short of *our sense of self*; it appears somewhat bare, lacking a genuine inner normative sense, or (we might even say) *moral or ethical capability*. Hadot seems to be saying that Foucault's self lacks any ethical dimension, for to attribute ethicality to the subject, outside any reduced ethical conception of faithfully attending to oneself (which might appear somewhat narcissistic), would come dangerously close to incorporating an exterior metaphysics of morality. It would seem that if Hadot's criticism has a larger message, it is that central to any account of the practices or care of the self is that the self is not simply detachable from a normative reference, input, or telos.

Is Foucault's overly 'thin' and 'hollowed-out' conception of the self the 'price' that Derrida speaks of, which we have not yet finished paying in relation to the Heideggerian deconstruction of the metaphysics of the subject?[14] Although it was important to Foucault's own approach that he describe the ancient practices of the self without recourse to their transcendent beliefs if he is to avoid the impression of an overly empirical representation of the subject, it would seem that he needs a more effective way of theorizing this, not in terms of their relation to a transcendent world of metaphysics, but rather to their immanent normative capacity as living beings who are serious and have moral values. In other words, in order to ground ethics, for the purposes of doing ethics, Foucault needs a minimal metaphysics that is not a *metaphysics of exteriority*, to use Irrera's expression, but one that is *immanent to life*, from within the finitude of experience, from within thought as it functions in and through experience. Hence the *télos* of the care of the self, the *tekhnē tou biou*, is not just the *télos* of the *self*, but the *télos* of *life itself*, embodied in the value that life gives to life, that leads human selves to want to live well, to construct organizations and modify institutions in order to seek a more noble existence. This much at least is needed if the eclipse of any solid ethicality in Foucault's later writings, so succinctly expressed by Hadot, is to be restored.

The question posed by the title *Who Comes After the Subject?* (Nancy, 1991), which raises the prospect of an impoverishment of the subject as a consequence of postmodern deconstruction, can also be more satisfactorily answered – at least with respect to Foucault – with these amendments.[15] If life has an immanent normativity, then the problems of relativism are possible to overcome, with ethicality and morality restored. While Foucault clearly intends to present an account of the techniques and tests that constitute life, with the aim, as he puts it, 'precisely to form the self' (2005: 448), he also believes that such tests and practices of self act as aids to *life*, or have general relevance for *life*. It is how life is lived, how one tests one's life, what tests one undergoes, that will define one's *life* in relation to how one deals with the events of *life*, that will enable one to form the best possible relationship with oneself and with others.

There is a distinct sense here that such tests and ascetic practices serve both as therapy and as general aids to life. Foucault shared Hadot's view that in antiquity the care of the self exalted philosophy as a *way of life*. One can note the analytical philosopher Bernard Williams[16] telling Richard Sorabji that 'philosophical analysis cannot be therapeutic', to which Sorabji responded: '[w]hat is under discussion here is the role of philosophical analysis as relevant to life' (2000: 2249/7341).[17] One cannot be certain that Williams's position would be shared by analytic philosophers generally, but Sorabji's rejection of Williams's view, and defence of the ways in which philosophical analysis can and does contribute to life, reflects the division between what – using Foucault's bifurcation – we might well call the Delphic and Socratic routes in Western philosophy. Sorabji makes the case that the Stoic analysis of emotion is not simply 'far more rigorous than modern analyses' (2000: 2249/7341), but that their philosophical orientation to *life* as therapeutic can be defended on a number of grounds: it provides the necessary motivation to do philosophy; it focuses the arguments; it clarifies thought; and it determines action on issues of importance.[18] What Sorabji is in fact arguing is that there is an immanent normativity in life that is both ethically and epistemologically productive. It is productive because ultimately such a mode of life philosophy is linked to the survival of humanity, indeed to life itself. Furthermore, to make philosophy relevant to life, as a way of life, might also be seen as providing philosophy with an important 'test' of its own relevance. If Williams had put his view to Foucault, the issue would have had an added dimension, for Foucault would claim that Williams relies on a conception of self and of philosophy that was inaugurated by Descartes and consolidated by Kant. This is a view that Foucault disputes, and accepting the consequences of that dispute, he has no option but to view philosophy as a 'way of life' concerned with the constitution of the self and the rectification of ills. In this sense, the techniques that serve as aids to the constitution of the self also define the self, and assist the self to live. What is of interest here is whether we can in fact constitute a theory of normativity that can account for the embedded normative values that we can glean, and that can also characterize Foucault's poststructuralist project, without doing violence to his central principles. This is the task of this book. If such a poststructuralist normativity could be fashioned, we could possibly talk of a Foucauldian ethics, even a Foucauldian morality, and could in addition frame policy advice and action from a Foucauldian perspective. I have worked largely from a Foucauldian perspective in my own work on politics and education over some thirty years now, and have experienced first-hand the difficulties associated with what Kelly might celebrate as the 'non-normativity' of Foucault's thought. To have a broad, general, normative framework that could offset any charges of relativism, and guide politics and ethics in a global world, would to my mind be an advantage.

Notes

1 See Kelly (2018: ch. 8). Patton's characterization of Foucault as non-normative applies only to his earlier work. With regard to Foucault's later writings, Patton characterizes him as normative, although Kelly dissents from such a view (2018: 147). See also Patton (1989; 1998; 2004; 2005; 2010).
2 Brożek (2013) also maintains that meaning and semantic rules are prescriptive, and further, that when assembled, they have normative implications of a philosophical kind.
3 The word 'naturalism' is being used here as equivalent to scientific reductionism.
4 Postulating the irreducibility of the normative parallels in certain respects the articulation of concepts of discourse, vital materialisms, and the themes associated with life philosophies, which will be developed further in later chapters.
5 Later in her book, Ginsborg makes an even stronger concession that her views regarding normativity are not Kant's, but that her work represents very much a *revision* of Kant. As she says: 'As noted at the outset, while I take the view I have been developing to correspond to an insight

of Kant's, I have not tried to argue here that it does in fact represent Kant's view. More specifically, I have not tried to argue that it is what Kant himself has in mind when he argues to the legitimacy of aesthetic judgment by appeal to the conditions of empirical concept acquisition' (2015: 200). What she fails to acknowledge is that her *revision* of Kant could only have been made *after poststructuralism* and represents a major accommodation of Anglo-American philosophy belatedly to the major insights and themes developed by poststructuralism.
6 See Harman (1977: ch. 1). Scanlon also considers the issue and resolves it in relation to Quine's famous essay, 'On What There Is' (Quine, 1990). He claims that '[i]n Quine's case, exclusive emphasis on the physical world is build in from the start … [which] immediately excludes the normative, absent some naturalistic reduction' (Scanlon, 2014: 18).
7 See Wittgenstein, where he says: 'obeying a rule has many faces' (1953: §235), and utilizes the concept of 'language-games' (1953: §§2, 23, 65, 66, and passim). For Foucault on the game metaphor, see 1994c: 541–2.
8 See my article on Wittgenstein and Foucault (Olssen, 2017a).
9 The interviewer was Michael Bess, who conducted the interview in San Francisco on 3 November 1980.
10 Seneca, *Letter*, 23, 6.
11 Seneca, *Letter*, 124, 23.
12 Seneca, *Letter*, 23, 7.
13 Hadot's detailed criticisms, regarding 'joy' and 'pleasure', can be accepted. Apart from this, however, Irrera's rebuff seems accurate. The technical detail of Hadot's argument is more complex than I have presented and demonstrates the way his criticisms are related to each other. Referring to Foucault's writing about Seneca's letter to Lucilius (no. 13), Hadot seizes on the fact that the joy one finds in oneself is found 'in the best portion of the self'; this, says Hadot, is what foregrounds the opening to a transcendent level. For a more detailed treatment of the debate, see Irrera (2010) and Flynn (2005). Irrera points out that Hadot makes charges both in relation to 1) historical inaccuracy in Foucault's account, and 2) that the 'ethical model of existence appears as "too narrow and insufficient"' (Irrera, 2010: 996). The second criticism quotes Hadot from 'Le sage et le monde' (Hadot, 1987: 346).
14 Derrida says: 'A concept (that is to say also an experience) of responsibility comes at this price. We have not finished paying for it' (1991: 108).

15 The point of asking such a question is dictated by the inference that Foucault's postmodern reconstruction of subjectivity is overly 'hollowed-out' and needs further work.
16 Seminar in Oxford, 1 November 1996; see also Williams (1997).
17 Citing the Kindle edition of Sorabji's book.
18 This is my own summary of his points as I understand them.

2

Life and error: Foucault, Canguilhem, Jacob

This chapter argues that a philosophy of life can provide, in part, a normative meta-ethical conception that can ground ethics, that can also justify why reciprocal relations of power are normatively preferable to subjugating ones, and that can therefore provide a useful framework for the resolution of political and ethical disputes. I say 'in part' because the conception will not be complete until other elements have been added, and this will require reading later chapters, especially Chapter 3 on Nietzsche. The concepts of life and error are important to the overall conception, however, and it is these that will be considered here.

This chapter argues that towards the latter years of his life, Foucault became interested in two new concepts, those of *life* and *error*, and that these can be utilized to construct a normative basis for Foucault's work. What I will not claim is to represent Foucault's own agenda. While he was aware of the absence of any normative grounding for his approach, he also showed little interest in developing a meta-ethic that could resolve matters. His late interest in life philosophy is suggestive, however, and, augmented by the likes of Bachelard and Canguilhem, I believe that it offers the possibility for a normative grounding of sorts. Building on Spinoza, Hume, Nietzsche, Heidegger, Bachelard, Canguilhem, Jacob, and Deleuze, I outline what is central to life philosophy and how these thinkers can be represented as providing a new basis for normative political philosophy that conforms to the conception of 'weak' teleology that I will later suggest. The chapter explains how such an approach can be seen as supported by other philosophers, such as Nietzsche, Bachelard, Canguilhem, and Jacob, and how life philosophy can avoid functioning as a universal principle that can be 'applied', but still function to steer and set limits to evaluations that are genuinely cross-cultural, as well as link to democratic politics.

A brief history of *Lebensphilosophie*

Herbert Schnädelbach (1984) has identified three forms of life philosophy. The first is what he refers to as metaphysical life philosophy, which posits a conception of life as an exterior noumenal substance beyond (outside or underneath) the domains of human perception and consciousness. Schnädelbach gives the example of Henri Bergson's *élan vital* as an illustration. For Bergson, *élan vital* refers to an inanimate ahistorical principle or substance beyond the realm of human experience that could ultimately only be verified through 'intuition' or direct apprehension. In this conception, life represents a permanent universal substrate that lies behind and explains human and non-human experience. It constitutes a metaphysics of exteriority. It relies upon a fundamental dualism between conceptual experience and the supposition of something beyond the realm of experience that is ahistorical. Life philosophy in this sense is something that functions as a permanent animating principle or basic metaphysical force.

Schnädelbach's second form refers to life philosophy as a philosophy of history. This is represented by historians such as Oswald Spengler, who theorizes the rise and fall of historical cultures as forms of growth and decay, where historical cultures are treated as parallel to organisms, and where history involves a process of struggle equivalent to the struggle depicted by Darwin between species and life forms in history. Societies in this model are depicted metaphorically as life forms that are like species, or vegetation, that unfolds, decays, bursts forth, and develops. As Alastair Morgan notes, such a perspective 'collapses any distinction between culture and nature in a fateful identification of the processes of life with those of a politics that emphasizes growth, vigour and the healthy. The move from such a philosophy to the concepts of race and Social Darwinism intrinsic to National Socialist ideology is obvious' (2007: 9).[1]

Schnädelbach's third form is ethical life philosophy, which he identifies with Friedrich Nietzsche. This form distinguishes between what is living and what does not live and identifies a normativity immanent in life itself. I will maintain towards the end of this chapter that such a conception can be fully materialistic in the sense that it recognizes no vital spirit or entelechy. What enhances and sustains life in this sense grounds a conception of value and becomes the basis for establishing all value. As Morgan puts it, it 'becomes the grounding for all values and norms' (2007: 9). It is primarily this conception that is the focus of this chapter. Although I could garner support from a wide variety of thinkers, including Spinoza, Hume, Heidegger, Bataille, Nietzsche, and Deleuze, apart from Foucault, it is as these authors' views are expressed in the writings of Georges Canguilhem, and with recourse also to François Jacob (who was also influenced by Canguilhem), that I will chiefly proceed.[2] For Nietzsche, as reason and ideology coalesce, the only basis for evaluation is related to that which supports or does not support life. This is why he recognizes authentic existence as that which seeks to sustain and enhance; concerned, as Ansell-Pearson (1994: 18) says, with 'abundant health and strength'. This is why Nietzsche writes in *Beyond Good and Evil*: 'The falseness of a judgement is to us not necessarily an objection to the judgement ... The question is to what extent it is life-advancing, life-preserving, species preserving, perhaps even species breeding; and our fundamental tendency is to assert that the falsest judgements ... are the most indispensable to us' (Nietzsche, 1966: §4). If things are valued for the sake of life, Nietzsche defines life as 'a multiplicity of forces connected by a common mode of nutrition', in which 'the different contenders grow unequally' (1968a: §641, §642). As Lester Hunt puts it, '[l]ife is a hierarchically integrated system the members of which have a common means of support. Perfection is the state in which this integration is fully achieved (*volkommen*). To "enhance life," then, is to increase the extent to which this state has been achieved' (1991: 126). Whether historic associations with perfectionism, teleology, or even possible remaining residues of vitalism are satisfactorily dispensed with by all three of Schnädelbach's classification of types remains to be seen.

Life and error

Foucault wrote the introduction to the first English translation of Georges Canguilhem's *Le normal et le pathologique*, published by Reidel in 1978.[3] This then appeared in *Ideology and Consciousness* as 'George Canguilhem: Philosopher of Error' (Foucault, 1980b), was reprinted in the *Revue de métaphysique et de morale* in 1985 (Foucault, 1985b), and finally reproduced, in slightly modified form, as 'Life: Experience and Science', in James Faubion's edition of Foucault's *Essential Works* (Foucault, 1998b).[4] Although Foucault's entrée to life philosophy came too late to warrant attributing to him a self-consciously worked-out normative dimension, if we are mindful of the parallel life philosophies of Nietzsche and Heidegger, as well as the deep influence of Canguilhem over Foucault's first books,[5] we can seek to extend such a normative conception to Foucault's approach, thus assisting with combating moral relativism, and creating a normative architecture to anchor ethical, moral, and political choices.

In 'Life: Experience and Science', Foucault traces a perspective on life in the writings of Canguilhem, which he describes as being concerned with the avoidance or elimination of *error*.[6] Error, he says, is at the centre of the problem of life in Canguilhem's work.[7] Life is described as a process of coding and decoding and conceptualizing, which confronts contingency, as Foucault puts it, where 'the processes of coding and decoding give way to a chance occurrence that ... is something like a disturbance in the informative system, something like a "mistake." In this sense, life – and this is its radical feature – is that which is capable of error' (1998b: 476). Foucault speculates that it is this 'contingency' or 'datum' that accounts for the fact that 'the question of anomaly permeates the whole of biology' (1998b: 476). Likewise, it is error that accounts for 'mutations and evolutive processes to which they lead' (1998b: 476). 'With man', says Foucault, 'life has led to a living being that is never completely in the right place, that is destined to "err" and to be "wrong"' (1998b: 476). And if error, Foucault continues:

is the reply that life itself has given to that chance process, one must agree that error is the root of what produces human thought and its history ... The historian of rationalities ... is a philosopher of error – I mean that error provides him with the basis for posing philosophical problems; or, let us say more exactly, the problem of truth and life. (1998b: 476–7)

Foucault speculates that in the history of humankind, the 'power effects that different societies and different institutions link to that division – all this may be nothing but the most belated response to that possibility of error inherent in life' (1998b: 476). Moreover:

if the history of the sciences ... can be analyzed only as a series of 'corrections' ... the reason, again, is that 'error' constitutes not a neglect or a delay of the promised fulfilment but the dimension peculiar to the life of human beings and indispensable to the duration [*temps*] of the species. (1998b: 476)

In his interpretation of Canguilhem, Foucault is saying that error is at one level a response to complexity in the context of life as it is lived. To err is to make a mistake or at least a wrong turn; related to the body it constitutes anomaly, disease, monstrosity, pathology, and death; related to the social, it introduces the realms of ethics, morality, and politics; in the domain of everyday life it results in unexpected developments, crises, or catastrophes. It presupposes at the most immediate level the type of genealogy that Foucault develops from Nietzsche's and Canguilhem's reading of the tasks of the life science process. Error allows for a break with the idea that life and knowledge of life move in ways that are linear, cumulative, and logical, and, rather, affirms the power of events, contingencies, unexpected mutations, wrong turnings, and so on. Additionally, in that it presupposes all this, it also presupposes, albeit in relation to an open future of endless possibilities, that there is some sense in which the various strategies, actions, decisions, and paths for life are seen as objectively better or worse from the point of view of negotiating life's obstacles.

My argument here, presupposed in the conceptions of life and error, is that there are objectively better and worse ways to live, despite, or in addition to, the necessity of its unpredictability, the inevitability of 'chance occurrences' and 'accidents', together with the necessary uncertainties, partialities, distortions, and limitations as a consequence of the necessity and frequent opacity of the conceptual mediation of the real.[8] These mean, given the complex environment in which life operates, that error cannot be – in any complete sense – eliminated; yet traversing or negotiating error will depend to variable extents on skill, expertise, and luck. Life constitutes a force that endures in time by modulating or adapting itself contingently in different times and places through a multiplicity of strategies and/or perspectives.

Colin Gordon summarizes the core of Canguilhem's life philosophy in three distinct propositions. The first is that 'life is an irreducible concept and one which is necessary to science'; the second is that 'its content is given through our experience as living beings as well as our observation of living beings'; and the third is that 'our conceptual activity in general is a continuation and extension of our existence as living beings' (Gordon, 1998: 185). Gordon stresses (both for Canguilhem and Foucault) the importance of life incorporating and articulating a principle of normativity. He notes that Canguilhem's work on the history of the normal both anticipated, and was acknowledged by, Foucault, for *The Normal and the Pathological* deals not only 'with the concepts of the normal, the norm and the normative, but with the history of practices of normalisation' (Gordon, 1998: 186). He cites Canguilhem who, he says, undertakes something of a genealogy:

> from the grammatical norms, by way of industrial and hygienic norms, to the morphological norms of men and horses established for purposes of national defence ... Between 1759, the date of the appearance of the word '*normal*', and 1834, the date of the appearance of the word '*normalise*', normative class conquered the power to identify – through a fine example of ideological illusion – the function of social norms with the use it made of those norms whose content it itself determined. (Canguilhem, 1975: 182–4, cited in Gordon, 1998: 186).

By understanding this constructivist mechanism, Gordon also recounts how the normativity of life is expressed in relation to conceptualization and knowledge. Citing Foucault from his article on Canguilhem:

[t]hat man lives in a conceptually architectured environment does not prove that he has turned away from life by some forgetfulness ... *To form concepts is a way of living and not a way of killing life*; it is a way of living in complete mobility and not of immobilising life. (Foucault, 1980b: 60, cited in Gordon, 1998: 184)

As Canguilhem comments in the introduction to *Knowledge of Life*, 'thought and knowledge are inscribed within life so as to regulate it ... Thus, the universal relation of human knowledge to living organisation reveals itself through the relation of knowledge to human life' (2008: xviii–xix).

Conceptualization is important to life, says Foucault, 'insofar as it is one of the modes of that information which every living being takes from its environment and by which conversely it structures its environment' (Foucault, 1998b: 475). At one level, this is because we interact with an environment where the context for interaction is already established. Yet Foucault is also maintaining that forming concepts matters to life and how successfully it is lived. Conceptualization in this sense is normative. As Foucault says, '[conceptualization] is a very special type of information' (1998b: 475). This is the sense in which conceptualization is itself endlessly creative and plural. The impetus is always on living, on surviving, on developing, on creating. In this it receives assistance from the sciences. Canguilhem cites the German neurologist and psychiatrist Kurt Goldstein, who says: '[b]iology has to do with individuals that exist and tend to exist, that is to say, seek to realize their capacities as best they can in a given environment' (Canguilhem, 2008: xix).[9]

The rejection of the metaphysics of certainty and order

While lived experience is thus always conceptually mediated, conceptual mediation confines human beings to the world 'for-us'. Contra phenomenology and empiricism, Foucault argues that lived experience cannot constitute 'under any circumstances an independent empire in nature' (Foucault, 1998b: 474), in the sense that, 'since Kant, philosophical discourse has been the discourse of finitude rather than of the absolute' (Canguilhem and

Foucault, 2013: 5).[10] Concepts are not monological expressions of any singularity of lived experience. Rather, subject only, based on Canguilhem, to the norms that permit life to continue at all, lived experience is an infinitely original response to the contingently mobile conditions of existence. It is in this sense that life is by its very nature normative, which means that living entails acceptance and rejection of norms. As Canguilhem puts it, 'living means preference and exclusion' (1991: 136).

If this is metaphysical, it constitutes an immanent metaphysics that foregoes certitude of the world beyond experience, but can still attempt scientific knowledge from the vantage of experience as it is lived.[11] It is in this sense that a philosophy of life itself borrows 'from "information theory" – codes, messages, messengers, and so on' (Foucault, 1998b: 475–6) and makes bridgeheads with the normative, which can inform morality, politics, ethics, and policy sciences (1998b: 476). For it is life that enables Canguilhem to distinguish the 'normal' from the 'pathological'. Error here introduces the possibility of creativity and originality.

Error, for Canguilhem, thus constitutes an evolutionary and pragmatic path to knowledge. For Foucault, the upshot of such a view is that knowledge, 'rather than opening onto the truth of the world, is deeply rooted in the "errors" of life' (1998b: 477).[12] In a complex world, the recurrence of error becomes a fundamental ontological postulate. Such a theory entails that 'the whole theory of the subject be reformulated' (Foucault, 1998b: 477) as both historically contextualized, yet creative and experimental, and as ushering forward a conception of 'limit-experiences' bounded yet open, and certainly in uncharted seas, in terms of the viable possibilities for life for the future. In such a context, Nietzsche's emphasis on 'experimentation' becomes a core educational and epistemic method.

Ways of living are also affected by the norms and ideas of each age. 'For Canguilhem', says Foucault, 'error is the permanent contingency [aléa] around which the history of life and the development of human beings are coiled' (1998b: 477). Foucault then posits an important link between error, life, and normativity when he notes that for Canguilhem, '[i]t is the notion of error that enables him ... to bring out the relationship between life and knowledge [*connaissance*] and to follow, like a red thread, the presence of value and the norm within it' (1998b: 477). What Foucault acknowledges in interpreting Canguilhem is that values are intrinsic to norms of life. Life seeks to live. The norm of life continuance is immanent to life itself and irreducible. As Gordon notes, 'Canguilhem asserts the biological primacy of the normative over the normal' (1998: 183). The biological institutes a range of possible modes of existence, variable and plural to particular times and places. Normativity is immanent to life in this sense, yet at the same time is compatible with unending creativity and originality. Gordon cites Canguilhem from the original French edition of *Le normale et le pathologique*, where he says that:

> The term 'normative' is applied in philosophy to any judgement which assesses or qualifies a fact in relation to a norm, but at bottom this mode of judgement is subordinate to the person who institutes the norms. In its fullest sense, normative means that which institutes normal. And it is in this sense that we propose to speak of a biological normativity. (Canguilhem, 1975: 77, cited in Gordon, 1998: 183)

Gordon also cites Canguilhem on health and illness in relation to normativity: 'The ill person is ill by incapacity to tolerate more than a single norm ... abnormal not because of the absence of the norm, but because of the incapacity to be normative' (Canguilhem, 1975: 122, cited in Gordon, 1998: 183). Gordon says that 'cure, then, is the recovery of normativity' (1998: 183). There is a 'priority of normativity over the norm' (1998: 188).

Canguilhem reiterates these same points in his later work when he says that 'life is a polarity and thereby even an unconscious position of value; in short, life is in fact a normative activity' (1994: 339). He continues: 'Any normality open to possible future correction is authentic normativity, or health' (1994: 352). Hence, 'health is more than normality; in simple terms, it is normativity' (1994: 351). By normative here, Canguilhem means not simply a judgement 'which evaluates or qualifies a fact in relation to a norm', but 'in the fullest sense of the word ... that which establishes norms' (1994: 339). The fundamental notion here, as Paola Marrati and Todd Meyers summarize Canguilhem's understanding of normative, is 'that living beings are not, and cannot be, indifferent to the conditions of their life, both to the internal conditions of the organism ... and to the external conditions provided by the natural and social milieu in which they interact' (2008: ix). For Canguilhem, then, 'wherever there is *life* there are norms. Life is a polarized activity, a dynamic polarity, and that in itself is enough to establish norms' (1994: 351). Norms are thus immanent to life. Life itself constitutes a set of vital potentials that offers an open set of possibilities to which individuals manifest 'preferred behaviors' (1994: 351).[13] The normal constitutes, therefore, 'a universal category of life' (1994: 351) that is irreducible. The normal is not a single uniform path but a large framework of endless variety within limits accepted by life itself.

Importantly, for Canguilhem, it is only through a relationship to the environment that normality is approximated. The organism by itself is not normal, and neither is an environment, in and of itself. In his essay 'Normality and Normativity', Canguilhem says, 'normality is determined by the interactions between structures and behaviors, on the one hand, and environmental conditions, on the other ...' (1994: 352). Further: 'It is the relation between the environment and the living thing that determines what is normal in both' (1994: 354). Hence, '[t]aken separately, the living being and his environment are not normal: it is their relationship that makes them such' (1991: 143). Canguilhem argues further that 'an environment is normal when it allows a species to multiply and diversify in it in such a way as to tolerate, if necessary, changes in the environment' (1994: 354). A healthy person 'is a person capable of confronting risks. Health is creative – call it normative – in that it is capable of surviving catastrophe and establishing a new order' (1994: 355). The individual 'lives in a world of possible accidents ... where there are leaks, holes, escapes and unexpected resistances' (1994: 356); or, '[h]ealth is a regulatory flywheel of the possibilities of reaction. Life often falls short of its possibilities, but when necessary can surpass expectations' (1994: 357). In such a model, '[t]o be sick is to be unable to tolerate change' (1994: 354). Such a perspective is repeated consistently throughout Canguilhem's writings. In *The Normal and the Pathological*, his medical thesis first published in 1943, he says that 'health is a margin of tolerance for inconsistencies of the environment' (1991: 197). Here, Canguilhem represents health as normative, by which he means 'capable of following new norms of life' (1991: 200). To be cured does not mean a return to some previous state but involves 'physiological innovation' (1991: 196). 'To be cured is to be given new norms of life, sometimes superior to the old ones. There is an irreversibility of biological normativity' (1991: 228). Hence, what Canguilhem does is to redefine illness and health in terms of normativity, and away from binary dualisms of 'normal/abnormal'. Health, illness, and cure reveal the openness and irreversibility of life as normative. In that this suggests vitalism, we shall assess to what extent this is objectionable below. Canguilhem held that such a thesis was necessary to augment and correct Darwin's theory of natural selection, which represented development and survival as shaped purely by external circumstances. As Canguilhem put it in 'Le vivant et son milieu', written in 1947, 'a living thing cannot be reduced to a sum [*carrefour*] of influences' (1952: 154).

Responding to the new biology: the writings of François Jacob

One aspect of Canguilhem's work that caught Foucault's interest was the way his writings on medicine, biology, and the philosophy of science drew support from and extended the new researches on molecular biology, genetics, and heredity associated with Crick and Watson, Monod, and Lwoff in the late 1950s. This operated in several senses. The consistent theme of error in Canguilhem's work, from his 1943 thesis onwards, asserting the error proneness of living beings in their conduct if not in themselves, was directly affirmed by the new biology.[14] Modern molecular genetics provides an interpretation of biological individuality as a 'communication of information', presupposing an identification of life with concept, information, or *logos*. As Canguilhem says in 'The Concept of Life', 'there is a logos inscribed, preserved and transmitted in living beings', hence 'life is concept' (1994: 317, 318).[15] Although initially drawing from his self-acknowledged master, Kurt Goldstein's *Der Aufbau des Organismus* (1934),[16] Canguilhem also noted how the revolution in molecular genetics supported such a perspective. It was for this reason, as Jean Gayon notes, that Foucault saw 'The Concept of Life' as Canguilhem's 'most inventive text' (Gayon, 1998: 320; see Foucault, 1998b). Molecular biology had introduced a new conception of life as information or *logos* by admitting that there is a *logos* or concept inscribed in all living things. Foucault interpreted this to have profound implications for the theory of the subject, and for identity. Molecular biology had called into question the idea of the individual as the basis of life. In Foucault's view, this meant that the living thing is not fundamentally tied to an individual subject; rather life is 'a pure repetition anterior to the singularity of the individual in the course of evolution. The living thing was a reduplication machine well before it was an individual organism' (1994e: 969). Reproduction can exist, therefore, without clearly defined individuals. In this sense, the new biological research suggested a re-understanding of life, radically transforming the domains of both knowledge and thinking. Foucault's point is that the basic mechanisms of all living things, as illuminated by Crick and Watson, Monod, and Lwoff, do not warrant positing any mysterious source of life, substance, or essence (*ousia*). Rather, the cell functions according to a programme, as a 'living system' (*système vivant*) (Foucault, 1994e: 970–1).[17]

It was on the same ground that Foucault spoke enthusiastically with regard to François Jacob's book, *Logic of the Living: A History of Heredity*. In his review of Jacob's book, entitled 'Grow and Multiply', published in *Le Monde* in 1970,[18] Foucault (1994e) notes that both Canguilhem and Jacob reconfirm the central theses of molecular biology in relation to the errancy and errors of living agents in relation to norms and normativity. As Talcott summarizes it: 'all living happens according to norms that are posited by living individuals for themselves as they attempt to realize positive values and avoid negative ones' (2014: 258). Jacob's history of genetics had especially demonstrated how molecular biology called into question what was previously known, meaning that knowledge itself was no longer secure or assured, that everything known now became questionable. Jacob's history had disassembled the very idea of an orderly 'chain of being' which posited life as it was meant to be in its nature or essence. The cell as system was itself complex, permitting diverse permutations and possibilities (Jacob, 1973: 11).

In this, Foucault reaffirms theses outlined initially in *The Order of Things* (1970) and *The History of Sexuality, Volume I* (1980c). Jacob, like Canguilhem, had confirmed the central complexity insights with relation to science. The revolution in biology had confirmed the 'shocks' (*secousses*) and 'wounds' (*blessures*) that the new science had inflicted on 'the oldest knowledge [*savoir*] in the West', and the demands it made upon us to relearn how to think (Foucault, 1994e, cited in Talcott, 2014: 267). The new biologists had, for Foucault, identified the arbitrary code that resided at the base of what linked nucleic acids and proteins. They had confirmed the importance of chance and discontinuity in all of life. Both the history of biology and the new genetics 'teaches us that the dice govern us [*les dés nous gouvernent*] in our very biology' (Foucault, 1994e: 968). This makes not only chance central, but creativity as well. Molecular biology reaffirms the central importance of discontinuity, chance, and irregularity in both epistemology and ontology. In this sense, Jacob and Canguilhem inspired Foucault to harness a 'historical epistemology attuned to errancy, error, and experimentation' (Talcott, 2014: 254).

Molecular biology also militates against reduction, since the mechanism by which living things function and maintain themselves cannot explain all of life's phenomena. Relations between elements within living systems generate novel interactions with diverse possibilities and outcomes. Hence, Foucault says of Jacob that 'describing a living system, is to refer to both the logic of its organization and the logic of its evolution' (1994e: 971; Jacob, 1973: 300). Foucault further cites Jacob, who says that 'the arbitrary traverses the fundamental structures of the living cell, and this is an absolutely universal mode' (Foucault, 1994e: 970–1). There is no predetermined meaning to any of the mistakes or errors that occur in translating code into proteins. Evolution, according to such a picture, occurs according to error and errancy. What is pivotal here, as Talcott notes, is that 'man does not become man by the single, continuous modification of an original cellular ancestor' (2014: 270). Rather, changes occur in a system where 'each mosaic of change ... has evolved in its own way and at its own pace' (Jacob, 1973: 319). Although within everyday life things maintain their regularity, in a theoretical sense prediction becomes impossible: 'each organism ... is a mosaic produced by millions of years of aimless evolutionary experimentation, [which] makes it really impossible to predict how one form emerged out of another' (Talcott, 2014: 270). The biological revolution in the post-war period thus depicts as deeply flawed the reigning metaphysically infused conception of individuals as basic and primary with a natural impetus to develop. It is for these reasons that Foucault considers Jacob as having produced 'the most remarkable history of biology that has ever been written' (1994e: 972).

Opposing vitalism

It is commonplace for commentators to refer to Canguilhem's vitalism, but it is frequently not made clear what this means, or whether it should be considered objectionable. As Gayon (1998) points out, a sense of vitalism is invoked by Canguilhem when he claims in 'Le vivant et son milieu' that the living being is always 'an absolute and irreducible system of reference' (Canguilhem, 1952: 154).[19] While various senses of individuality in Canguilhem are documented by Gayon, he notes that individuality is defined in 'La théorie cellular', initially written in 1945,[20] not as a being, but as a relation. Canguilhem defines the individual specifically as 'that which cannot be divided without losing its characteristics. It is a minimum of being ... The individual implies its own relation to a wider being' (Canguilhem, 1952: 71). In that molecular biology acknowledges a *logos* inscribed in all living things, Canguilhem thought that the biological and genetic revolution reinstated a form of Aristotelianism in that a knowledge of life must draw the idea of the living thing from life itself. As Canguilhem says in 'The Concept of Life', '[f]or Aristotle, soul was not only the nature but form of the living thing. Soul was at once life's reality [*ousia*] and definition [*logos*]' (Canguilhem, 1994: 303). This squares with the idea that living things cannot be accounted for solely with reference to external forces, as Darwin held, and as noted above. Aristotle's concept of soul was ambiguous, as Gayon (1998: 324) notes, in that soul was both a formal and eternal principle, as well as an active mechanism, functioning contingently in a generative sense in particular situations.

Notwithstanding Canguilhem's appeal to Aristotle, in my view he avoids associating life with classical representations of vitalism that recognized a hidden interior, entelechy, or vital force that characterizes life as spontaneity in opposition to mechanism or science. This is to say that vitalism is not appealed to as an already preformed biological doctrine, but rather as a fertile domain of exploration. It seems to me that Canguilhem is groping for a sense of the subject that is entailed by his researches and the biological revolution. While life can be represented as emergent, such emergence is constituted as a composition purely from material elements. Classical representations of 'spirit', 'vital principle', or 'vital force' in the tradition of Barthez, Bichat, Driesch, or van Helmont (see Canguilhem, 2008: ch. 3) or links to 'animism', in the tradition of George Ernst Stahl (see Canguilhem, 2008: 71), are not invoked or endorsed. A return to life philosophy is not a return to mysticism or to being chimerical (Canguilhem, 2008: 65). Neither does it invoke a particular representation of cell theory.[21] While it does attest to the limits of mechanism, mechanism is supplemented by complex systems of causation, processes of emergence, and non-linearity, as necessary to being adequate to representations and processes of the world as we experience it. Although Paul Rabinow (1994) describes Canguilhem as a 'vital rationalist', the reinstatement of life is not vitalist in the important senses in which the doctrine was objectionable, that is, as Canguilhem describes it, as *'the philosophically inexcusable fault [of the] classical vitalist [that] accepts the insertion of the living organism into a physical milieu to whose laws it constitutes an exception*' (2008: 70, emphasis added). Rather, in Canguilhem's words again, '[o]nce one recognises the originality of life, one must "comprehend" matter within life, and the science of matter – which is science itself – within the activity of the living' (2008: 70). Such a doctrine can be described as Canguilhem denotes Diderot, or as Deleuze can also be characterized, as a 'vital materialism', just so long as one is clear as to definitions and the new meaning of life that emerges from the complexity motif, as fully a product of material processes.

Nor does such an entrée to life philosophy reinstate Hegel or the Romanticism associated with the likes of Novalis, who sees the state as a supra-moral institution, 'willed by God', as Canguilhem

(2008: 42) puts it, to which the individual therefore owes both deference and submission. In this sense, unlike the vitalist biology that influenced the Romantics, life philosophy is no supporter of totalitarian movements or structures. The life philosophy being described, therefore, draws neither on 'the political philosophy of the *Aufklärung*, [nor] the community conceived by Romantic political philosophy' (Canguilhem, 2008: 41). Rather, the forms of complexity developed by Foucault, and before him Canguilhem, offer a new and different understanding of science, which retains notions of life, indeterminacy, systems effects, novelty, uncertainty, and unpredictability, without reducing analysis to individualism, or celebrating collectivism in its non-democratic forms.

For his part, Foucault was most emphatically keen to escape any hint of vitalism, as such would conflict with his conception of the subject as historically and socially constructed. In this sense, Foucault's elaboration of the concept of biopower in *The History of Sexuality, Volume I*, says Talcott, 'can and should be read as an attempt, at least in part, to take up the challenge of molecular biology and rethink the human being while also developing an alternative to Canguilhem's account, and its emphasis on the living individual as the touchstone of experience and value' (2014: 272). As Talcott points out, Foucault sought the DNA of social life in biopower rather than risk being confused with a form of vitalism. Biopower, in this sense, becomes a way of understanding human subjectivities and identities, and permits Foucault to rethink politics as historical construction.[22] In this sense, Foucault can be seen as extending both Canguilhem and Jacob to reinterpret politics in response, as Talcott puts it, to 'contemporary events in the life sciences ... Biopower was Foucault's way to rethink the old question of man as a political animal in terms of a power, or a politics' (2014: 255, 256). The new researches in molecular biology and heredity required a new 'grid of analysis' for both the life sciences and politics, and, by extension, I will claim, ethics. Although, like Talcott, I see Foucault as remaining faithful to Canguilhem, rather than representing him as a vitalist, Foucault represents him as a philosopher of error, in a mosaic of life as a collective system of trial and error, as well as luck, skill, and chance. In like fashion, he interprets both Canguilhem and Jacob as supporting his thesis against the centrality of the subject in Western philosophy (see Foucault, 1978a: 442; 1985b: 1595).

It is possible to defend Nietzsche on the charge of vitalism as well, especially given Foucault's debt to Nietzsche. Heidegger's massive four-volume study (1962) was an attempt to rescue Nietzsche from any such charges of vitalism or biologism. In his book *Of Spirit*, Jacques Derrida says that Nietzsche rejects the philosophy of life as vital spirit without 'conferring the meanings "vital" or "biological" on the totality of entities' (1989: 73). Indeed, Derrida quotes Heidegger, who says that Nietzsche does the opposite:

> It would be necessary to do the opposite, which is also something quite different: to reinterpret the vital on the basis of the will to power. This has nothing 'vital' or 'spiritual' about it; to the contrary, the 'vital' (the living) and the spiritual are, as belonging to entities determined by Being in the sense of the Will to Power. (Heidegger, 1991: II, 300)

Life, says Derrida, 'is not a stable semantic determination' (1989: 73), yet it struggles to survive. It does not do this in any particular way and does not express a constant 'template' (1989: 73) of nature; rather it is characterized by 'death' (or the attempt to avoid it) and 'vulnerability'; and yet it responds to the horizon into which it is 'thrown' (to use Heidegger's term). Although Foucault was influenced by both Heidegger and Nietzsche, it is notable that he avoids appropriating Heidegger's early use of the concept of *Dasein* as too anthropocentric.[23] With Nietzsche, too, Foucault rejects, as did Heidegger, any suggestion of a 'biologistic, zoologistic or vitalistic reappropriation' (Derrida, 1989: 73). In that there is any way to interpret Nietzsche as advancing a metaphysics of subjectivity, Foucault rejects it, as he did with Hegel, whose *Geist* emanated from Descartes' *cogito*. Any echo of unconditioned subjectivity is rejected, and spirit is no longer *Geist* or the unconditioned subjectivity of the will to power. As Derrida argues, subjectivity, as either rationality of spirit (*Geist*) or animality of body, is rejected by Nietzsche (1989: 73). This was also the basis on which both Nietzsche and Foucault claimed to reject idealism and vitalism and subscribed to materialism in their analyses.

Foucault's appropriation of life philosophy

In his essay, 'Life: Experience and Science' (1998b), Foucault brings forward a crucial insight, displaying the real value of his and Canguilhem's perspective. Here he asks whether, though the Enlightenment of Descartes, Kant, and Hegel oriented philosophy towards concerns with the concepts of truth and subjectivity, relating them to a nature that functioned as a ground, we should not now reorient philosophy towards questions of life. More exactly, should we not, with Canguilhem, propose a 'philosophy of error, or the concept of the living, as a different way of approaching the notion of life' (Foucault, 1998b: 477)? Is not the question of what advances and maintains life the pertinent question for us to ask in the current horizon? There is a historicity then to our chosen normative concepts, yet in the milieu in which they operate they still effectively guide us. It is not a question of abandoning them, but rather of adjusting their position in a hierarchy of prominence. In this sense, it can be observed that the concept of *life* and its continuation, like Foucault's concept of *governmentality*, can operate at a level of generality that renders it consistent with a principle of historicity. Just as governmentality focuses on different governmental forms in different eras, so life continuance relates to different agendas for traversing the future. In such a context, the existence of new, emergent pressures on the biosphere may warrant a departure from the reactive naturalism of Hobbes, Locke, and Kant. The original Enlightenment, Foucault suggests, inappropriately normatized technical and scientific rationality; it promoted a form of rationalism 'of which we are entitled to ask what part it may have played in the effects of despotism where that hope lost itself' (1998b: 469); and the enthusiasm for science promoted conceptions of 'rationality' and 'universal validity' 'as a mirage tied to a domination and a political hegemony' (1998b: 469).

Canguilhem's philosophy of life, Foucault suggests, assumes a possible normative role at this juncture of re-asking the question of *Aufklärung*, 'for the West to become aware of its present possibilities and of the freedoms it may have access to, but also as a way to question oneself about its limits and the powers it has utilized' (1998b: 470). What is at stake here is altering the norms that regulate the '*concept* in *life*' in the context of an 'historical-epistemological perspective' (1998b: 475, 473). For 'the processes of elimination and selection of statements, theories, objects ... take place at each instant as a function of a certain norm' (1998b: 473). This norm then generates the mode of information by which each element of life appropriates and structures its environment. What Foucault suggests is a shift in conceptual modality contingent upon changing materialities, from a history exclusively concerned with or focused around the true and the false as it was at the onset of modernism, to one focused around critical control over error and its elimination in order to implicate a 'new way of "truth telling"' (1998b: 471). It applies to individual subjects and to institutions, and is especially relevant given an horizon characterized by new dangers, such as those associated with climate change and viral pandemics. It becomes a central way of orienting to the world. Foucault seems to be suggesting that it is a new way of truth telling that is crucially pivotal in the present conjuncture.

The affinity between Foucault and the tradition of philosophical pragmatism can be noted here, in the sense that the warrant of theories and conjectures test themselves in an effort to eradicate errors historically. The success of a scientific approach, and the maturity of a scientific armature, depends on its predictive and explanatory success, and on its ability to recognize and correct errors. The principle of disputability operates in relation to theoretical argumentation. Signs of stress or intolerance are another such test which might operate in the political or social domain. Just as error enables certain 'corrections' to ideology, in that 'vital' life norms also circulate together with their ideological shadows, they still constitute the basis of what guides us. In this sense, as Catherine Mills says, there is a distinction between vital life norms, which are immanent to life itself, and social norms, which are not. As she puts it, '[i]n other words, vital and social norms may be empirically inseparable, but they are nevertheless analytically distinct' (2005: 94). She notes further Foucault's caveat in *The History of Sexuality, Volume I* (1980c: 143) that 'life constantly escapes or exceeds the techniques that govern or administer it' (Mills, 2005: 97).

One can see that Foucault's interest in the normative aspect of the concept of life was evident in his earlier studies. In the *History of Sexuality, Volume I*, Foucault outlines his argument concerning the transformation that occurred in the eighteenth century from a regime of sovereignty to a regime of biopower. Whereas sovereignty focused on disciplining individual bodies, biopower, made possible by the rise of nation-states and new developments in the sciences and statistics, became concerned not so much with discipline but rather with the management and control of populations. As Foucault puts it, '[one] consequence of the development of biopower was the growing importance assumed by the action of the norm' (1980c: 144). For Foucault, 'a normalizing society is the historical outcome of a technology of power centred on life' (1980c: 144). Apparatuses such as the normal curve made deep assumptions of unity by which individuals could be compared on the same conceptual space to the entire population.[24] Hence, notions of normalcy become important. Such a technology effectively constituted a new way of reconciling the relations between the one and the many where exceptions and anomalies could be more uniformly identified and treated. Biopower constituted a new arm of power from the eighteenth century that focused on managing errors in aggregate as well as individual terms via disciplinary power. It instantiated a new regimen of social and political regulation concerned with normalization.

In his last lecture course, *The Courage of Truth*, given at the Collège de France from January to March 1984, the theme of life in a normative sense also interested Foucault in relation to Plato's texts and the theme of the care of the self. Foucault claims to detect a shift in Plato from *Alcibiades* to *Laches*, which differ, he says, in a crucial respect: *Alcibiades* is concerned with soul (*psukhē*), whereas *Laches* is concerned with life (*bios*). This shift from *psukhē* (soul) to *bios* (life) is what Plato introduces in *Laches*. This constitutes a bifurcation point in the development of Western ethics, for Foucault. As he puts it, 'it is at precisely this point, that I would like to [highlight], starting with the *Laches*, a text in which *bios*, much more than soul, appears very clearly as the object of care' (2011a: 128). Foucault says that *Alcibiades* and *Laches* mark 'two great lines of development of Socratic veridiction in Western philosophy' (2011a: 161). So here we have 'the *Laches* as starting point for this question of the care of the self, as "test of life" and not as "knowledge of the soul"' (2011a: 128). In *Laches*, 'we are led to *bios*, to life, to existence and the way in which one conducts one's existence' (2011a: 160). In this new-found compact based on life, survival and well-being must be seen as *willed* from the present in order that contingencies can be accounted and adjusted for, rather than as evolving through a naturalistic teleology with the implication of being set for all time. Such a conception must be framed constructively, not naturalistically.[25] The compact for moving forward is between motley beings, rather than rational actors in a hypothetical contract situation. Such a switch from naturalist to constructivist is also effected by Deleuze in his essay *Pure Immanence: Essays on Life* (1994b). This work constitutes an 'affirmative biopolitics', in Roberto Esposito's sense (2008: 191, 194). It celebrates life as an indefinite series of relations, where norms are internal to the movement of life, or in Esposito's words, where the norm is made 'the immanent impulse of life' (2008: 194). Such a postulate is formulated by Canguilhem when he says, 'it is life itself and not medical judgement that makes the biological norm a concept of value and not a statistical reality' (1994: 343). *Bios* thus expresses a biopolitical spectrum that articulates life as a unified process across multiple forms of difference. Esposito notes how Nietzsche imparts an 'underlying biopolitical relevance' in that '[t]o assume the will to power as the fundamental vital impulse means affirming at the same time that life has a constitutively political dimension and that politics has no other object than the maintenance and expansion of life' (2008: 9). This is to say that 'politics is nothing other than the possibility or the instrument for keeping life alive {*in vita la vita*}' (2008: 46). The immanent normativity of life continuance is thus the source of our ordinary understandings of ethics and morality. Consistent with this, Esposito (2008: 191–4) recounts how Deleuze, in *Pure Immanence*, conceptualizes a 'singular life' where all forms of life are interconnected and where harming one potentially harms all. The incorporation of a harm principle as an element of the continuance calculus is itself justified by the interconnectivity of all forms of life.

What life may provide here in terms of what Foucault (1998g) terms 'the limit' of the 'outside' is a conception of a normative baseline located in the present, registering in the development of growing levels of intolerance once conditions of life themselves are experienced as 'intolerable'. Intolerance is a test of the 'limit of the "outside"'. Just as falsification is a test of the limit in the epistemic domain, intolerance is one criterion that operates in the domain of the political.[26] This was the test utilized by the Prisons Information Group (GIP) in its founding statement made by Foucault at a press conference on 8 February 1971. As the statement reads:

> Let what is intolerable – imposed, as it is, by force and by silence – cease to be accepted. We do not make our inquiry in order to accumulate knowledge, but to heighten our intolerance and make it an active intolerance. Let us become people intolerant of prisons, the legal system, the hospital system, psychiatric practice, military service, etc. (Foucault, 1994d, 1044)

Life is important in both the sciences and the political domain, where it constitutes the direct basis of normativity linked to urgent social tasks in the horizon of the present. In the sciences, says Foucault, the concern with life constitutes 'the search for the normativity internal to the different scientific activities, as they have actually been carried out' (1998b: 473). For Canguilhem, it is solely this conception of life as a normative value that enables the distinction between the 'normal' and the 'pathological' in the sciences of medicine. Life thus constitutes a norm which lives *in* science, as it lives elsewhere, and as a norm it simultaneously implicates a theory of value, a basis for critique, and a normative agenda.[27]

Central to any idea of instituting the normative in Foucault, then, is the requirement to confront the infinite permutations of power. In this, universal rights are necessary to offset or counter the perilous and infinitely unpredictable disorganizing propensities of power as it operates in the world and impacts differentially on different individuals and groups. Conceived of in this way, although life points to a broad direction of travel, and a general end compatible with a plurality of different ways of life, in the context of a complex world constitutive of unintended consequences, actions from a distance, and structural inhibitions and constraints, working out what will, as opposed to what will not, enhance or continue life best will be forever a matter of uncertainty, conflict, argument, speculation, and debate.

Furthermore, although knowledge can, through the elimination of error, challenge ideology, for Foucault it can never succeed in eliminating it once and for all. As he expresses the point in *The Archaeology of Knowledge*, for instance: 'Ideology is not exclusive of scientificity ... By correcting itself, by rectifying its errors, by clarifying its formulations, discourse does not necessarily undo its relations with ideology. The role of ideology does not diminish as rigour increases and error is dissipated' (Foucault, 1972: 186). In addition to this, life permits no easy guide to resolving conflicts or pointing the way. Many of the 'big questions', such as those concerned with bioethics – euthanasia, assisted suicide, abortion rights, etc. – will not be easily resolved by knowing that we must do the best for life itself. Yet, no matter what the difficulty, such a conception of life frames action as itself normative, in that to act is to act under a description relative to an end or a purpose.[28] This end or purpose entails commitments and pledges, and is amenable to reason through argument and evidence. Theoretically, the concept of life exonerates postmodernism from the charge of relativism. If this means that an essential message of teleology is reinstated, this time it is without appeal to 'final causes' or 'essential purposes', 'nature', or frameworks of 'design'. Life, then, is the background presence that answers Habermas's question: 'Why fight at all?' The answer is, in short, so that we may keep living as best we can. And more, we act in such ways as to be consistent with the continuance of life for all.

A life philosophy of error also enables Foucault to answer the question concerning what guides the 'courage to truth' or *parrhēsia* (Foucault, 2010; 2011a). It provides a broad, general context, in terms of which 'speaking truth to power' is justified and circumscribed, as well as establishing grounds by which some truths rather than others can be stated. In this, it absolves Foucault from the charge of anarcho-libertarianism, whereby any old challenge, mobilized for any old reason, is justifiable as a political response or form of resistance. *Parrhēsia* is a particular type of ethical comportment or truth telling oriented to challenging those in power to provide justifications for their conduct as well as demonstrate their legitimacy.

Institutionalization becomes the condition upon which interdependent and connected individuals coordinate to resolve conflicts and confront power. Institutions, says Giorgio Agamben, constitute sets of practices and networks 'that aim to manage, govern, control and orient – in a way that purports to be useful – the behaviours, gestures, and thoughts of human beings' (2009: 12). Institutions constitute 'the *oikonomia* of apparatuses that seek to govern and guide them toward the good' (2009: 13). In seeking to elucidate Foucault's conception of apparatus (*dispositif*), Agamben states: 'I shall call an apparatus literally anything that has in some way the capacity to capture, orient, determine, intercept, model, control, or secure the gestures, behaviours, opinions, or discourses of living beings' (2009: 14).

Conclusion: applying 'Foucauldianism'

By specifying norms of life and its continuation, we come close to Nietzsche's view that all ethics and morality are but labels that we attach to whatever facilitates survival. Yet such a view has affinities in important respects with writers in Anglo-American philosophy such as Philippa Foot, whose book *Natural Goodness* (2001) describes ethics and morality within a framework of naturalism.[29] Foot tries to ground ethics in a concept of neo-Aristotelian teleology. Plants, she points out, seek to recover their strength; animals and humans seek strength, health, flourishing too (Foot, 2001: ch. 2, esp. p. 38). She describes these patterns of excellence, defect, and so on as 'patterns of natural normativity' which give rise to a 'structure of judgement' (2001: 38). As Foot continues, if 'this is possible, [it] is to imply that some at least of our judgments of goodness and badness in human beings are given truth or falsity by the conditions of human life' (2001: 38). Darwin also incorporated such an insight into his theory of natural selection. Nietzsche observed that, directly or indirectly, our moral language stems from such. Ethics in this sense is practical. Although in later chapters I will argue against Aristotelian and naturalist conceptions, to locate an immanent normativity within life establishes a single principle that can constitute the source of normative claims.

Life provides the immanent force that extrinsically constructs the normative. As such, life, for Foucault, constitutes a mosaic that escapes or exceeds any naturalist blueprint that predetermines outcomes. It is life that generates the normative as adjunct to the sphere of being. Rules develop historically and are imposed on the world and have real-world effects. If one plays the game, one adheres to the rules. It is life that provides a justification for morality as 'commands without a commander', as Soniewicka (2013) says, or, to cite Foucault's favourite poet, René Char, as *Le Marteau sans maitre*.[30] To merely advocate that we respect life is at one level hopelessly general. It will not exclude any number of groups or political organizations, but it will exclude those who advocate violence, murder, evil dictatorships, and non-democratic forms of government, since non-democracy, it can be cogently argued, will endanger and imperil the possibilities for commodious living and the future of life on earth for all or any. When evaluating either the fairness or appropriateness of the present organization of reality it is important to ask, says Canguilhem, 'whether the norms that it embodies are creative norms, norms with a forward thrust, or on the contrary, conservative norms, norms whose thrust is toward the past' (1994: 352).

Shaping norms leads to institutionalization, which results in the formulation of plans and specification of purposes, in terms of what counts as reasonable and what counts in favour of something. A common basis in life constitutes a ground for dialogue over a world with finite resources that must be shared in common. Any decision regarding norms, says Canguilhem, 'is understood only within the context of other norms' (1994: 372). A plan represents 'the unity of a unique thought ... The plan is the hidden dress of the idea of Providence' (1994: 373). The validity of a norm 'depends on its insertion in a coherent system, an order of hierarchized norms, drawing their binding power from their direct or indirect reference to a fundamental norm' (1994: 375). While there is thus a relativity of norms to social structures, 'the norm of norms remains convergence' (1994: 375). In this sense, Canguilhem sees a 'correlativity of social norms – technological, economic, juridical – [which] tends to make their virtual unity an organization' (1994: 375). In such a social organization, 'the rules for adjusting parts into a collective which is more or less clear as to its own final purpose ... are external to the adjusted multiple' (1994: 376).

Life and error: Foucault, Canguilhem, Jacob

Canguilhem's theory of life overcomes relativism, for although all entities and events are shaped by the genealogical structures of the past, as an effect of power, life incorporates immanent values of survival and continuance, which can be accessed with difficulty through the fog of culture and convention from the standpoint of the present. Given the immanent normativity of life, survival and well-being must be seen as *willed* from the present as a compact among motley beings; there is a *right to life*, based on the equality of each and all, justified on the basis of simply existing, that is, seeking to *stay alive*. Macro-social policy must frame agendas with a view to minimizing the likelihood of *ressentiment* among different groups and interests, enabling all to cohabit. This constitutes the best prospect for continued peace and security for each and all. In the next chapter, Nietzsche will be called upon to deepen this vision. Specifically, his own conception of normativity and his philosophy of the future will be recounted in order to support the concept of life so far discussed.

Notes

1 I am indebted to Morgan for originally drawing my attention to Schnädelbach's work.
2 As well as Canguilhem's own works, I also refer to secondary literature, notably Gordon, (1998), Lecourt (2008), Macherey (1998; 2009), Rabinow (1998), and Talcott (2014; 2019). Foucault's writing on Jacob is noted later in this chapter as extending his insights on Canguilhem.
3 This was originally published without Foucault's introduction in 1943, and again in 1966 by Presses Universitaires de France. A second edition of the 1966 volume included three new short essays written between 1963 and 1966.
4 This translation was by Robert Hurley.
5 See, for instance, Davidson (1994; 1997), Lecourt (1975). Although Foucault was deeply influenced by Canguilhem in his early works, the initial influence was in terms of Canguilhem's conception of epistemic formation and concepts. Only later did Foucault write about Canguilhem's concept of life in a specifically normative sense.
6 Dominique Lecourt questions placing Canguilhem as a 'philosopher of error' in this way (Lecourt, 2008: 5–6). According to Samuel Talcott,

this is most likely 'because he believes that it diminishes Canguilhem as a philosopher' (Talcott, 2019: ix). The point also serves to underscore that my reading of Canguilhem here is largely through Foucault's eyes.

7 Canguilhem taught a course entitled 'Science and Error' over the years 1955–56. But his notes from 1943–44 also show an early concern with 'error' and 'errancy', a concern that developed in both scope and rigour throughout his career (see Talcott, 2019: 258–9).

8 Hence, Foucault's characterization of error in terms such as 'mistake', 'being wrong', or 'to err' (1998b: 476). It was this chasm between finitude and the absolute that for Kierkegaard resulted in 'tragic crises'.

9 In 'Thought and the Living', the title of his introduction to *Knowledge of Life* (2008), Canguilhem cites Kurt Goldstein. Goldstein first developed the concept of the 'organism as a whole', in terms of which 'self-actualization' takes place. His work was to later influence Abraham Maslow's theories (see Goldstein, 1995).

10 The phrase was used by Foucault in the context of an homage at the memorial service to Jean Hyppolite at the École Normale Supérieure on 19 January 1969.

11 Kant defines immanence in the *Critique of Pure Reason* as pertaining to those principles 'whose application is confined entirely within the limits of possible experience' (1928: B 352/A 296).

12 Rabinow (2003: 48–9) introduces parallels between Foucault and John Dewey in relation to the form of pragmatism entailed here, noting similarities especially in relation to the utilization of the concept of 'problematization' by Foucault.

13 Canguilhem takes this concept of 'preferred behaviors' from Goldstein (Canguilhem, 2008: 354–5). See Goldstein (1995).

14 Canguilhem responded to the questions posited by molecular biology in the second edition of his famous essay, especially the chapter entitled 'A New Concept in Pathology: Error' (see Canguilhem, 1991: 276–8). The concern with error, although less emphasized in the 1943 essay, also received amplification and refinement in his course on 'Science and Error' of 1955–56 (see Talcott, 2014). François Dagognet (1977) argues that all of Canguilhem's work can be understood as a consistent 'deepening' of his 1943 thesis concerning the 'normativity of life'.

15 First published as 'Le concept et la vie' (1966). Reprinted in *Études d'histoire et de philosophie des sciences* (Paris: Vrin, 1968; 2nd edn, 1970; 3rd edn, 1975). English translation in Canguilhem, 1994: 303–20.

16 The book was published by Nijhoff (Haag) in German in 1934. Published in English under the title, *The Organism*. See Goldstein (1995).

17 Talcott (2014: 258) notes that 'living system' is the phrase that Foucault and Jacob prefer to 'life' (*la vie*), although sometimes, like Canguilhem, they refer to 'the living' (*le vivant*).
18 Published under the title 'Croître et multiplier', *Le Monde*, 15–16 November 1970, p. 13.
19 I am indebted to Jean Gayon (1998) for translations from this essay.
20 This article is reprinted in Canguilhem, 1952: 43–80. Partial English translation in Canguilhem, 1994: 161–77.
21 See Canguilhem's essays 'Cell Theory' and 'Aspects of Vitalism' (Canguilhem, 2008: esp. 55–7, 66–7).
22 Other writers who elaborate the concept of biopower, albeit for different purposes, include Michael Hardt and Antonio Negri (2005), Georgio Agamben (1998), Melinda Cooper (2008), Thomas Lemke (2011), Roberto Esposito (2008), and Nikolas Rose (2007).
23 It is well known that Heidegger also refrained from using the concept after the 1930s, which saw the 'turn' ('*die kehre*') from *Dasein* to language in his thought. *Dasein* was too human-centred, a criticism also made by Ryle (1970; 2009). After the 1930s, language is seen as ontologically prior to, and more basic than, the constitution of *Dasein*. Language was viewed by Heidegger as productive rather than simply as a transparent or neutral medium of communication (see Williams, 2016: 92).
24 See Olssen (1993) for an elaboration of this point.
25 This is a major difference between Foucault and Canguilhem, as well as writers such as Aristotle and Hobbes, who also place value on life. Both these latter thinkers develop a naturalistic conception of life, seeing nature as a ground for life's value. The linking of survival and well-being can be observed in Aristotle, where he links *zoē* and *bios* by identifying 'some noble element' as 'possibly' existing in 'mere life' (Aristotle, 1905: 1278b), as well as in Hobbes's *Leviathan*, where he says: 'But by Safety here, is not meant a bare Preservation, but also all other Contentments of life, which every man by lawfull Industry, without danger, or hurt to the Common-wealth, shall acquire to himselfe' (Hobbes, 1968: 242).
26 'Falsification' is the concept used by Karl Popper (1959) as part of his solution to the problem of induction in the philosophy of science.
27 Many of these themes can be traced back to Gaston Bachelard, who influenced both Canguilhem and Foucault. In his 'historical epistemology', Bachelard iterates the ideas that extra-epistemological norms, developed in life or lived experience, permeate science and *savoir*; that this means that ideology circulates alongside epistemological norms

internal to the sciences; that to avoid transcendental idealism means that knowledge is seen in some important sense as being a 'reflection' of social structure; that what assures the epistemological status of science is its concern with rectification or the elimination of 'error'; and that such an approach represents objectification as itself internal to the historical process, and avoids traditional forms of 'realism' which posit the object of knowledge as outside the knowledge process, thus effectively denying mediation. Bachelard also theorizes the constructive and inventive role of discursive production, including the production of *concepts*, as central to scientific activity (*savoir*) and life itself. His theorization of 'error' occurs in many of his books and essays (see Bachelard, 1928: 245, 249; 1934: 22; 1938: ch. 1; 1940: 8; 1949: 58). He says, for instance, 'I have found no possible solution to the problem of truth, other than dispelling finer and finer errors' (1928: 244). Bachelard saw 'error' as accounting for movement in science, the process proceeding via 'ruptures', 'oscillations', 'breaks', 'corrections', and so on, that is, being 'non-continuist'. In his study of Bachelard, Dominique Lecourt says that the process of science takes place through 'progressive objectification by successive rectifications which reveal, by way of recurrence, the raw material on which thought works' (1975: 60).
28 This poststructuralist proposition seems to me to be homologous with G. E. M. Anscombe's (1979) conception of discourse.
29 See also Kraut (2007), Thompson (2008), and Brewer (2009) for similar analyses.
30 This is the title of René Char's book, published by Éditions Surréalistes in 1934.

3

Nietzsche's life philosophy: naturalism, will to power, normativity

Naturalism in Nietzsche

Anglo-American philosophy on Nietzsche has not generally interacted with those writing in the Continental philosophical tradition.[1] Although Nietzsche was a major influence on Foucault, and although Foucault's friend, Gilles Deleuze, wrote a book on Nietzsche (entitled *Nietzsche and Philosophy*, 1983), very few in the Anglo-American world have engaged with such work. At a conference at the University of Southampton some years ago, Brian Leiter told me he had never read Deleuze's book, although he added that he had heard it was very good. In my view, Deleuze's book is a minor classic, and I encouraged Professor Leiter to read it. There is a difference, however, in how the Continental philosophers read Nietzsche. They interpret him as an anti-foundational thinker, and this has major implications for how they view the issue of naturalism. Writers such as Foucault and Deleuze do not see Nietzsche as being a naturalist in the sense that he posits a ground or foundation in human nature, or nature generally, in terms of which political, moral, or ethical beliefs could be explained. The issue is complicated by the fact that not all of the Anglo-American philosophers who write on Nietzsche today view him as a foundationalist, as Leiter does. Indeed, in my view, related to Nietzsche studies especially, there has been a major convergence between the two philosophical traditions over the last three decades, with the Anglo-Americans' views tending to converge with the views of the Continentals.[2] What was significant about writers such as Foucault and Deleuze is that they saw Nietzsche as being in an important sense 'beyond nature'; that is, rejecting nature as a ground.

Brian Leiter (2002) identifies Nietzsche as a naturalist in two senses. He considers Nietzsche a naturalist on the grounds that he rejects supernaturalism, teleology, metaphysics, and God. This kind of naturalism Leiter terms *s-naturalism*. Leiter also sees Nietzsche as a naturalist in a narrower sense whereby philosophy should take its path from methods of science. He terms this form of naturalism *m-naturalism*. As Leiter explains, 'the speculative theories of m-naturalists are "modelled" on the sciences most importantly in that they take over from science the ideas that natural phenomena have deterministic causes' (2002: 5).

I agree that Nietzsche was a naturalist in the sense that he rejected supernaturalism, spiritualism, and metaphysics, but he was definitely not a naturalist in the sense of seeing nature as a ground, or template, or as establishing a historical constant. As this view seems to be embedded in Leiter's m-naturalism thesis, I would dispute that Nietzsche was a naturalist in this 'narrower' sense that philosophy should follow the methods of the sciences. It is not that this is wholly untrue, but rather that it requires a far more nuanced understanding. As Christine Swanton maintains, Nietzsche's naturalism is of a very general sort, rejecting supernatural or non-empirical explanations in preference for a form of explanation that is 'empirical, in the broad sense of an approach based upon experience as opposed to theological dogma or doctrine' (Swanton, 2015: 11). Within this broad approach, scientific models and terms can indeed be criticized and rejected. This approach she terms 'spare naturalism', which rejects 'bald naturalism, and both scientistic and scientific naturalism' (2015: 11).

Christopher Janaway (2007: 350) notes that while Nietzsche seeks explanations that cite causes in ways that do not conflict with science as a general discourse, he also wants to change the model of science. In this respect, Janaway argues that Nietzsche is a not a naturalist *precisely* in the way that Leiter identifies. In Janaway's view, Leiter sees Nietzsche's:

> explanation of moral beliefs in terms of a fixed set of psycho-physical characteristics of the individual, which Leiter refers to as 'type-facts.'

Leiter suggests the following is a 'typical Nietzschean form of argument': 'a person's theoretical beliefs are best explained in terms of his moral beliefs and best explained in terms of natural facts about the person he is'. (Janaway, 2007: 346, citing Leiter, 2002: 9)

Leiter's characterization of Nietzsche represents him as subscribing to a biological or instinctual foundationalism by which cultural values are seen as expressions of deeper instinctual processes in the individual. Janaway posits as a 'corrective' to Leiter's view the fact that 'explanatory facts about me, even if somehow located in my psycho-physiology, are essentially shaped by *culture*' (2007: 346). In this sense, Janaway sees Leiter's account as too foundationalist with respect to instinctual processes being 'hard-wired' into the nature of the individual. Leiter is not willing to give up his foundationalism, however, for he argues that anti-foundationalist views of Nietzsche are 'significant misreadings' (2002: 112). That Leiter subscribes to such a foundational reading is a puzzle, for such readings of Nietzsche have long since been discredited, and no Foucauldian would ever accept them.[3]

Although Nietzsche says in *Beyond Good and Evil* (1966: §230) that he is 'translating man back into nature', his phrase is aimed at his rejection of the metaphysics of those who seek to trace ultimate foundations pertaining to metaphysics or the divine. Janaway goes on to characterize what I would rather refer to as a consistent historical materialism, with respect to Nietzsche's theory of human drives. According to Janaway, Nietzsche's theory of drives conveys the following claims:

> (a) that we have such complexes of affects 'for' and 'against'; (b) that our having such affects is explanatory with respect to our moral judgments and our rational justification of them; (c) that it is to a variegated past of social and conceptual arrangements that our present feelings and meta feelings owe their origins; (d) that those past cultural arrangements themselves are explained by their function as discharging, preserving, repressing, or transforming pre-existing affects or those who participated in them. (2007: 346)

Nietzsche is only, then, a naturalist in Leiter's s-naturalism sense in that he rejects the idea of the supernatural, and rejects as well metaphysical beliefs that can be known beyond the realm of experience.

His announcement that 'God is dead' (1974: §§108, 125, 343), as well as claims to 'de-deify' nature (1974: §109), provide testimony to this. In this sense, Nietzsche is a defender of the Enlightenment while rejecting the idea that such an Enlightenment is based solely on rationalism, a correspondence between mind and world, or of knowledge based on or secured in foundations, whether God, Forms, *cogito*, biology, or *conatus*. He advances what some contemporary philosophers might term a kind of 'fallibilism' that recognizes no ultimate critical standards, foundations, or Archimedean points.[4]

Given the various uses and meanings associated with naturalism in Western philosophy, one needs to be particularly cautious in using the term. Moreover, one wonders whether there are not more accurate ways to characterize and label Nietzsche's views of the world.[5] Foucault shared Nietzsche's rejection of metaphysical and supernatural entities, and yet refrained from describing either Nietzsche's or his own position as 'naturalistic'. Foucault saw naturalism as characterizing the representation of nature as a ground, the depiction of historical constants (the nature of man, the state of nature), or 'historical laws' (the self-regulating market). Foucault would argue that when philosophers invoke 'nature' as the basis for claims, they merely reinforce their own prejudices derived from a particular historical regime of truth.

From the seventeenth to the nineteenth centuries, naturalism in relation to morality held that moral truths followed upon the natural laws governing human beings. Hobbes saw morality as deriving from the natural laws of desire and self-preservation that governed human beings and forms of life more generally. Others, such as Galton and Darwin, saw hereditary instincts as constituting a basis to explain human variations. If we go back to the Greeks, we find distinctions in Epicurus as to those things that exist by nature, and those that exist by convention. One could see Plato, and later Spinoza, as naturalists in the sense that both saw qualities such as good and evil as being part of the immovable order of the world. It is in the sense that naturalism refers to foundations that determine or shape experience that Nietzsche and Foucault are definitely not naturalists. In this sense, both refrain from describing or relying upon the fixed world of the in-itself, a world outside of experience.

This for Nietzsche would be a metaphysical world, and anathema to his devoutly anti-metaphysical approach. When Marxists such as Gramsci talk of 'naturalization', they are referring to the natural as an invariant law that is resistant to historical modification and yet often serves ideological purposes. Hence, Gramsci was convinced that certain historical phenomena, such as intelligence, could be presented as constituting natural variations among classes, thus concealing the extent to which the differences were themselves socially and historically produced and therefore transformable (Gramsci, 1971). In the sense that certain regularities were naturalized, history was presented as having an essential and immovable character expressing invariant laws of development and resistant to change through human agency. Nature in this sense functions to confirm an ahistorical foundation that limits or regulates the extent to which change can take place. Naturalism in such a view constitutes an unbridled essentialism. Foucault's concept of *eventalization* serves to expose and dislodge such historical constants where they occur (see Foucault, 1987: 104–5; 1997f: 31).

In discussing prevailing models of eighteenth-century science and philosophy – organicist and mechanist – in *The Gay Science*, Nietzsche's views against both foundationalism and the juridification of nature come to the fore:

> Let us beware of saying that there are laws in nature. There are only necessities: there is nobody who commands, nobody who obeys, nobody who trespasses ... There are no eternally enduring substances; matter is as much of an error as the God of Eleatics ... When will we complete our de-deification of nature? When may we begin to '*naturalize*' humanity in terms of a pure, newly discovered, newly redeemed nature? (1974 §109)

He approaches things empirically, and is a naturalist in the sense that he recognizes certain material necessities and rejects the world beyond experience, the metaphysical world. These are the limited senses in which calling Nietzsche a naturalist is warranted. In this, Nietzsche follows Kant in rejecting any possibility of direct knowledge of the noumenal. Partly, these claims to knowledge of the noumenal world outside of experience manifest themselves as the arrogance of those who claim to know the truth. While

Nietzsche followed Kant on this, he also took the view that Kant was unfaithful to the rule he had posited, and found ways to reintroduce metaphysical categories (such as God) back into his analysis. Beyond his rejection of a world beyond experience, however, Nietzsche's criticisms of Descartes and Kant meant that the sense in which he was a naturalist in supporting science was always tinged with suspicion, and needs to be qualified. As Christa Davis Acampora expresses the point:

> Nietzsche is clearly a naturalist in seeking a focus on natural, observable phenomena for garnering our understanding of the world and our place within it … The problem of science for Nietzsche is that it quite often sneaks in principles or articles of faith that smack of the very metaphysical and theological conceptions that it seeks to overcome. (2006: 316–17)

Normative objectivity and anti-realism

Nietzsche can also be labelled a constructivist in the sense that Kai Nielsen uses the term, that there is no structure to be 'unearthed … but something to be forged – constructed – by a timely and resolute use of the method of reflective equilibrium' (1996: 17). Nielsen describes 'reflective equilibrium' as a 'coherentist methodology' of explanation and justification used in ethics, philosophy, and epistemology, articulated in recent Western political philosophy by the likes of John Rawls, Nelson Goodman, and Stuart Hampshire (Nielsen, 1996: 17). It is a method that starts with one's considered judgements and convictions and revises them incrementally, forging them into a considered and provisionally consistent whole. With Nietzsche, the method would start with a suspicious experimental orientation to the problems of one's experience and seek to take different perspectives seriously in order to arrive at a more comprehensive valuation based upon considered principles. I will dub this Nietzsche's *method of perspectivism*.

Something similar is described by Maudemarie Clark and David Dudrick in arguing the case for Nietzsche as a moral objectivist. According to Clark and Dudrick, objectivity is increased as one grasps multiple perspectives in depth. Such a view starts from Nietzsche's thesis concerning the *'perspectival* character of valuing', which is always 'based on a partial view of things' (Clark and Dudrick, 2007: 219) but seeks greater comprehensiveness through exposure, and they document various sources in Nietzsche, such as the preface to *Human, All Too Human*, as well as *On the Genealogy of Morals* (III, §12), to make an impressive case that this 'method of perspectivism' was actually what Nietzsche himself was driving at.

Leiter (2002: 137) argues that Nietzsche's naturalism implies a non-realist view concerning moral and ethical values. He sees Nietzsche's meta-ethics as subjectivist in the Humean expressivist sense. As Clark and Dudrick point out, also part of Leiter's view is 'that such anti-realism entails or is equivalent to a denial of moral objectivity' (2007: 192). This represents a position that has been the mainstay of anglophone philosophy on Nietzsche, yet Clark and Dudrick argue for a view of him that 'does and can consistently claim that his evaluative position is objective and that this is a central component of his understanding of himself as a philosopher' (2007: 192). Although in his early writings, such as *Human, All Too Human* (1878), Nietzsche's position was cognitivist, denying 'that moral claims have normative objectivity, that they deserve acceptance by others' (Clark and Dudrick, 2007: 193), by the time of *The Gay Science* (1882), and even more obviously by the time of *On the Genealogy of Morals* (1887), 'Nietzsche offers a conception of objectivity according to which such claims can be objective, and ... Nietzsche's new conception of objectivity is connected to a new understanding of the nature of philosophy, and therefore his own task' (2007: 193).

This conception of moral and ethical objectivity in Nietzsche is a conception that I wish to affirm, if not for Foucault, then certainly as a Foucauldian.[6] While I accept Leiter's and Clark and Dudrick's position that Nietzsche is metaphysically anti-realist, I will maintain that he developed an immanent conception of life that could ground a certain conception of ethical and moral objectivity. This is to say that Nietzsche sought to identify a *norm of life continuance* in terms of his philosophy of the future as immanent to social and historical existence. Nietzsche came increasingly to develop the view that philosophy constituted a weapon for the advance and protection of civilization, and that in this process, ethical and moral values held a certain objective sway. This thesis was central to his philosophy of the future. That is, certain values either did or did not contribute constructively to the critical interrogation of the present, the clearing away of myths, thus enabling navigation to the future to proceed in a viable way. While Nietzsche agreed in *Human, All Too Human* that there was no metaphysically realist foundation to values, either in Plato's Forms or Kant's 'thing-in-itself', the whole point of his substantial discussion of values, ethics, and morality is not to subjectify them or render them without authority, but to validate them precisely as the title to his book confirms – as '*human-all-too-human*'.

This reading differs in some minor respects from that of Clark and Dudrick, and also more seriously from Leiter.[7] I am going to use these writers to frame my own view concerning realism and objectivity with regard to ethics and value, as the view I argue for has implications for the poststructuralist ethic I wish to construct. According to Leiter, in *Human, All Too Human* Nietzsche is an anti-realist not just about metaphysics, but about values, which means that he sees value merely as a reflection or expression of his own 'idiosyncratic' personal perspective. If he were a realist about ethical values, he would be able to claim that his values *deserved to be considered seriously by others*. The realist, says Leiter, maintains 'that there are *objective* facts about value' (2002: 137). Leiter sees Nietzsche as a realist about 'prudential value', but an anti-realist about ethical and moral values. He also maintains that for Nietzsche, anti-realism entails a denial of moral objectivity. Clark and Dudrick accept Leiter's position as it applies to *Human, All Too Human*. This book, they point out, is 'widely acknowledged as marking a turning point in Nietzsche's career, the point at which he turns his back on the metaphysical or quasi-metaphysical commitments of his early works and embraces science as that which provides access to the "disclosed" or "real nature of the world"' (Clark and Dudrick, 2007: 195).[8]

Clark and Dudrick claim that Leiter's evidence for Nietzsche as anti-realist stems from his perspective on naturalism, specifically in this instance from 'the psycho-physiological roots of our value judgments' (cited in Clark and Dudrick, 2007: 195). If goodness and badness stem from the instinctual roots of our characters, then the evaluations can be represented as merely personal and not objectively valid. Leiter advances Nietzsche as a subjectivist, and it is this view that I will dispute. While Nietzsche advances complex arguments against the possibility of a metaphysical world 'beyond experience', my interest here is solely concerned with what we mean by the terms 'anti-realism/realism', and the related issue of the objectivity of values. Will it be possible to say, as I have suggested above, that Nietzsche subscribes to an 'immanent', 'human-all-too-human' sense of realism and also of value objectivity? Can he do this by focusing on the difficult and fraught passage to the future? Can Nietzsche claim that through 'reflective equilibrium' or the 'method of perspectivism', a norm of continuance can be identified that can be differentiated from mere convention or from the happenstance of history? That can save human beings from their own degeneration? These questions form the hypotheses that I will entertain.

Clark and Dudrick on normative objectivity in Nietzsche

Clark and Dudrick initially agree with Leiter's characterization of Nietzsche as anti-realist and also with his denial of the 'normative question of moral objectivity ... whether his own values are deserving of acceptance by others' (2007: 198). The issue of 'moral objectivity' concerns, they say, 'whether moral statements are objective and therefore worthy of our acceptance' (2007: 198). Clark and Dudrick conclude on this point by saying that:

> Leiter therefore appears to be correct in thinking that Nietzsche denies moral objectivity at the same time that he embraces anti-realism about moral properties. Such moral claims are all erroneous, how could anyone's be worthy of acceptance by others? In fact, Nietzsche goes further. He denies that one's moral claims are worthy of acceptance by oneself. (2007: 200)

The agreement between Clark and Dudrick and Leiter is short-lived, however. Clark and Dudrick maintain that Nietzsche changes his position after *Human, All Too Human*, retaining 'anti-realism about moral properties' but establishing a commitment to moral objectivity by giving up his 'cognitivist assumptions concerning moral discourse' (2007: 200). They proceed in the later sections of their essay to establish how Nietzsche effected this change in *The Gay Science*. Here they claim that there is a change in Nietzsche's view 'on the possibility of normative objectivity for value claims' (2007: 201). They point out that Nietzsche still appears committed to 'value anti-realism', yet his abandonment of a 'cognitive reading' that sees values as expressing a cognitive belief, for a non-cognitive reading where they express 'a non-cognitive state, such as emotion' (2007: 202), offers the possibility that values can be seen as objective. In order to establish that moral claims can be objective, they start by noting Nietzsche's more explicitly constructivist approach in *The Gay Science* as opposed to what they term the 'error theory' of *Human, All Too Human*. The constructivist approach emphasizes human beings as *creators* of values rather than seeing values as representing some sort of false mystification (or error) that reflects their psychic state. Nietzsche also affirms that 'nature itself lacks normative properties, but [insists] that through the act of valuing, human beings bestow normative properties (goodness, rightness, etc.) on things, persons, or states of affairs hitherto lacking them' (Clark and Dudrick, 2007: 205). While this has led many writers on Nietzsche to confirm 'normative subjectivism', Clark and Dudrick argue for 'normative objectivism', the view that 'the source of the normative authority of values is to be found outside "the particular inclinations that make up an individual's will"' (2007: 205).[9] The nub of their position is that 'the non-cognitivism Nietzsche endorses in GS has the resources to overcome normative subjectivism and to endorse normative objectivism: the view that things are objectively valuable, that their value does not depend on our attitudes towards them' (2007: 207).

The crux of their argument emphasizes that value creation is not merely a cognitive activity, but sees objectivity as increasing with education and widening perspective. Clark and Dudrick focus on Nietzsche's reference to 'ethical teachers' in *The Gay Science*, who are 'the teachers of the purpose of existence' (1974: §301). For Nietzsche, they say, it is 'higher human beings, not humans in general, who create values for the world that can be said to contain normative properties' (Clark and Dudrick, 2007: 207). This creation of ethical values is a process of increasing comprehensiveness through ever-widening perspectives. As Clark and Dudrick say:

> by instituting practices of non-prudential reason-giving, the 'teachers of the purpose of existence' bring into existence the space of reasons, and that it is only this space that makes it possible for anything to be a bearer of normative properties, e.g., to be good or bad, right or wrong. (2007: 213)

The baseline assumptions subtending such a view are that to value something presupposes reasons and not just desires, and that 'reasons exist ... only for beings who can appreciate reasons' (2007: 213). Further, they claim that this is a conception of objectivity that shows 'how philosophers can be justified in creating values' (2007: 213) and that Nietzsche demonstrates in his later works the fruits of perspectivism as a method in increasing both comprehensiveness and objectivity in both knowledge and ethics, that is, in knowing what one ought to do.[10] Nietzsche comments in *Human, All Too Human* that 'the importance of knowledge for life *ought* to appear as great as possible' (I, §6). Clark and Dudrick cite Nietzsche from *Beyond Good and Evil* in support of their claim:

> *True [eigentlichen] philosophers ... are commanders and law-givers*: they say 'thus it *shall* be', it is they who determine the Wherefore and Whither of mankind ... they reach for the future with creative hand, and everything that is or has been becomes for them a means, an instrument, a hammer. (1966: §211, cited in Clark and Dudrick, 2007: 216)

This conception of objectivity appears only in Nietzsche's later works, after *Human, All Too Human*, they say (2007: 217). Furthermore, Nietzsche 'endorses the possibility of objectivity in others precisely because he thinks value claims can express commitments taken up *justly*' (2007: 217). Hence, Clark and Dudrick's central argument is that Nietzsche sees a 'training in objectivity' as possible (2007: 220). There are, they say:

> preconditions for creating values ... whereby the philosopher actually inhabits quite opposed perspectives, e.g., those of the dogmatist, the skeptic, and the critical philosopher, because precisely this is necessary to 'run through the range of human values and value feelings'

and 'consciences' that have stood the test of serious philosophical examination. (2007: 221)[11]

They compare Nietzsche's method here to the 'objective standpoint' of Thomas Nagel (1989: 147, cited in Clark and Dudrick, 2007: 221–2). This is the conception of objectivity that one arrives at as one detaches oneself progressively from one's own personal perspective and adopts a more impersonal one. Such a conception of the 'objective standpoint' seems close, say Clark and Dudrick, to the conception of objectivity found in *On the Genealogy of Morals* (2007: 221). Their final adjudication as to Nietzsche's objectivism bears something of such a viewpoint: 'On this view, objectivity is a matter of degree: a person's value judgments are more or less objective to the extent that they reflect a process in which she has taken up and inhabited evaluative perspectives other than her own' (2007: 223). Although this represents an important statement of objectivity in Nietzsche through his method of perspectivism, Clark and Dudrick point out that such a method does not necessarily guarantee convergence or consensus, which may well be difficult to achieve.

Building on the objectivist reading

While Clark and Dudrick's argument constitutes a case for ethical objectivism in the context of metaphysical anti-realism in Nietzsche, in my view there is a further element to the argument that strengthens even further the case for considering Nietzsche as an objectivist on the question of values. What must be focused on more specifically is the forces that Nietzsche identifies that serve to explain a convergence in perspectives. Clark and Dudrick make very little of these, specifically Nietzsche's concern with the future as a precarious and uncertain terrain that must be traversed if life itself is to continue. The object of creating values on the part of higher human beings is to forge a pathway to the future, which represents for Nietzsche the 'danger of dangers' (1996: Preface). While we can accept that Nietzsche is a metaphysical anti-realist, at the same time he is a social and historical realist in a certain sense, and it is in this sense that he is an objectivist about knowledge and ethical values. This is the sense that, while crises are produced in history, they are not determined by the individual subject, and are, in fact, external to each subject. Inasmuch as we might disagree regarding the best way to proceed to the future, we are constrained about what we agree and disagree on. On some matters the future constitutes itself as a demand for agreement over definite acts and for abstention from other acts, and it is in relation to these demands that pressures for convergence arise.

Navigating the future requires mutual accommodations that must be achieved as best as possible, not simply through the method of perspectivism, as Clark and Dudrick suggest, but by averting the 'danger of dangers' – death, annihilation, failure. Importantly here, Nietzsche's concern *for the future* in terms of value creation can be represented as being both a *collective* and *individual* concern, in that he is concerned with the *continuation of life as a whole*. Averting the 'danger of dangers', as well as forging 'agreement' or 'convergence' through the method of perspectivism, presupposes not simply perspectival convergence, but historically real and objective challenges. Such concerns indeed constitute non-metaphysical, 'human-all-too-human' challenges for the continuation of life. Such a process can anchor ethics and morality and underpin the concept of normative objectivity. For avoiding death, like vulnerability and pain, are normative in 'upshot' if not in 'content', to utilize the distinction made by Robert Audi (2013: 18). Hence, navigating the future requires mutual accommodations that must be achieved as best as possible through the method of perspectivism, leading optimally not just to agreement, but to *action* as well.

To claim objectivity for such values without positing a metaphysical beyond can be justified further. In his book *On Nietzsche*, Georges Bataille takes the view that, for Nietzsche, navigating the future represents the struggle for survival and security that constitutes a non-moral yearning once 'God is dead', a goal that stretches out before one 'independently of moral goals or of serving God', and yet imposes an object that 'surpasses all others in value' and translates 'as a demand for definite acts' (2004: xviii, xvii). Traversing to the future forces either convergence or conflict over values and actions, by virtue of the fact that normative beings who seek above all to survive confront, in Hannah Arendt's words, a 'common world [that] gathers us together and yet prevents our falling over each other' (2000: 201). Such a shared world arises, as Kant puts it, 'by virtue of the right of common possession of the surface of the earth' (Kant, 2006: AK 8, 358), constitutive of a world with *finite and limited resources that are shared together*. It is the indisputable materiality of this shared common concern that grounds the argument for the objectivity of value. To put it bluntly, arguing over limited resources and space constitutes pressure for an accord between humans over values associated with survival. While such an accord generates values that are conventional, they adhere to a norm for survival that is analytically distinct from mere convention or social dissensus. The future paradoxically itself becomes interpreted as a moral obligation; the future *generates* such obligations. The future represents our greatest fears, our greatest hopes, the things we take most seriously, what we are prepared to fight over, and kill for. Concerned ultimately with the avoidance of death, the 'narrow gauge' of the future is the source of normativity in all its forms.

Nietzsche understands the seriousness of the future only too well. The future constitutes a major trope in his philosophy. In *Human, All Too Human*, Nietzsche refers to 'The world's increasing gravity. The higher the culture of a man rises, the greater the number of topics are removed from joking or mockery' (§240). In *The Gay Science*, the theme of the future of humanity and of the world abound. Here Nietzsche speaks of 'venturing out to face dangers' in an 'open horizon' (§343). Such a future horizon is 'infinite' (§124). Further, 'we have burned our bridges behind us' (§124), 'what is needed is a new justice! And a new watchword. And new philosophers' (§289). In *Thus Spoke Zarathustra* the language becomes even more metaphorical, but much of it can be interpreted as endorsing Nietzsche's ontologizing of the future: 'I teach you the overman. Man is something that shall be overcome' (*Prologue*, §3).[12] The themes of danger and difficulty abound: 'Man is a rope, tied between beast and overman – a rope over an abyss. A dangerous across, a dangerous on-the-way, a dangerous looking-back, and dangerous shuddering and stopping' (*Prologue*, §4). The need to construct a way forward is a constant theme in Nietzsche: 'The time has come for man to set himself a goal. The time has come for man to plant the seed of his highest hope' (*Prologue*, §5). Finally, *Beyond Good and Evil* is subtitled 'Prelude to a Philosophy of the Future'. Those who will be necessary to lead, says Nietzsche, must be the '*new philosophers* ... spirits strong enough to make a start on antithetical evaluations and to revalue and reverse "eternal values"' (§203). They must have 'a rare eye for the collective danger that "man" himself *may degenerate*' (§203).[13]

It seems as if, for Nietzsche, traversing the future will be difficult proportionate to the difficulties on the horizon, and this historical task itself will constitute the force that results in a particular reconciliation of the one and the many, and constitute also its own force for shared objective values without any need to posit a metaphysical beyond. It is also apparent that the future represents a *collective idiom* in Nietzsche, which questions the possibilities of continuance as a fundamental ontological question for humanity. Paul Patton says that '[i]n some passages in *The Will to Power*, this takes the form of a cosmological theory' (1993: 151). While knowledge necessary to traverse successfully to the future can only be gleaned through the 'method of perspectivism', with no guarantees of convergence or agreement, or the prevention of war, estimations and difficulties concerned with traversing the future nevertheless constitute a yardstick that anchors normative objectivity for Nietzsche.

While the conception of justice that I read in Nietzsche seeks continuance for each and all on equal and fair terms, as well as for spaceship earth, in my opinion this was also his own view.[14] Nietzsche clearly thought that 'the higher human beings ... [who] see and hear immeasurably more, and see and hear thoughtfully' (1974: §301) would play a more decisive role in 'steering the ship'.[15] Normative objectivity has a yardstick that ranges from near universal agreement (that murder, or wanton violence, is wrong), to highly disputed, to actively fought over. The future looked perilous enough to Nietzsche, with certain tropes of Nazism already on the cultural horizon, yet he was unaware of climate change, viral pandemics, global population growth towards ten billion, or the possibility of nuclear annihilation. However, he was aware of continuance into the future as anchoring a normative conception of objectivity, and further, he accepted the sociological and historical realism entailed in such a proposition as placing a check on conventionalism or subjectivism. As a consequence, this constitutes a conception of objectivity which, although not possessing the metaphysical status of Kant's 'thing-in-itself', is nevertheless determined by a process (navigation of the future) that is independent of particular individual human beings.

Will to power as immanent normativity

One means by which Nietzsche attempts to articulate his philosophy of life is through the concept of the will to power. Nietzsche's will to power expresses the quest for freedom constitutive of the immanent value of life, a normativity, if you like, at the base of life. The first error to clear away is that the will to power is a minimal or limited concept solely concerned with self-preservation. Nietzsche's focus on life is much broader than this. The will to power is central to what Nietzsche calls becoming. As Gilles Deleuze tells us, 'the will to power is not wanting, coveting or seeking power, but only "giving" or "creating"' (1983: xii). Its potency as a concept is brought to bear most poignantly in *On the Genealogy of Morals*, where Nietzsche discusses evolution and natural selection. Will to power for Nietzsche offers a more powerful analysis of evolution and surpasses the concept of adaptation used by Darwin. Although Darwin provided for a detailed theory of natural selection to understand how life develops by natural processes, unaided by conscious design, what he never emphasized was the normativity of life itself in its quest to survive. In *The Will to Power* Nietzsche notes how Darwin overemphasized the role of the 'external environment' on development. As Nietzsche puts it: 'The influence of "external circumstances" is overestimated by Darwin to a ridiculous extent: the essential thing in the life process is precisely the tremendous shaping, form-creating, force-working from within which utilizes and *exploits* "external circumstances"' (1968a: §647).

In *On the Genealogy of Morals*, Nietzsche critically assesses the concept of *adaptation*, here in reference to Herbert Spencer rather than Darwin, and by directly invoking the notion of the will to power.[16] Again, the focus is on adaptation as a mere passive response to external circumstances. Adaptation, says Nietzsche, is 'a second-order activity, a mere reactivity' (1996: II, §12). In terms of this concept, he says:

> even life itself has been defined as an ever-more expedient inner adaptation to external circumstances (Herbert Spencer). But this represents a failure to recognize the essence of life, its *will to power*, this overlooks the priority of the spontaneous, attacking, overcoming, reinterpreting, restructuring and shaping forces, whose action proceeds 'adaptation'. (1996: II, §12)

The will to power constitutes for Nietzsche an immanent normative principle of life defined as 'an essential activity' (1996: II, §12), emphasizing what he calls the 'form-shaping forces' (*gestaltenden Kräfte*) 'in which the vital will manifests itself actively, and in its form-giving capacity' (1996: II, §12). This constitutes 'the theory of a *will to power* manifesting itself in all things and events' (1996: II, §12). In his book *Viroid Life*, Keith Ansell-Pearson, in commenting upon this theme, notes that:

> Nietzsche's critique of English Darwinism lies at the heart of [his] postulation of the notion of a 'will to power' to account for the primacy of spontaneous and form-giving 'activity' (*Aktivität*) in the becoming of complex life ... In contrast to an emphasis on the influence of 'external circumstances' (*ausseren Umstände*), he stresses that the essential phenomenon in the life process is precisely the 'tremendous shaping, form-creating force'. (1997: 92)

It is this immanent normativity at the heart of life, which seeks not self-preservation, or egoistic advancement, or pleasure, or happiness, but the creative values and actions necessary for the continuance of life, that Nietzsche seeks to express through the concept of the will to power. According to Ansell-Pearson, the will to power was 'inspired by the work Nietzsche read in the early 1880s in experimental embryology (notably Wilhelm Roux) and orthogenesis (notably Carl von Nageli)' (1997: 93). Nageli's theory of evolution had emphasized the 'double process and resultant play between the interior and the exterior which amount to the complex reality of variation' (1997: 93). Nietzsche derived from this, says Ansell-Pearson, the insight regarding the theory of evolution or becoming 'that the "use" of an organ in no way serves to explain its evolution' (1997: 93). It is not simply through 'adaptation' that evolution takes place. Rather Nageli saw both external and internal forces as operative 'under the influence of molecular forces' (1997: 93). Hence, for Nietzsche, says Ansell-Pearson, 'the will to power is active in a complex evolution' (1997: 94). It represents an active factor in organic matter that later helped inspire the vital materialism of Gilles Deleuze (see Deleuze and Guattari, 1987), and that was also present in Foucault's approach to history. Nietzsche's development of the will to power expands 'the different types of components' through which one understands 'a complex adaptive system' (Ansell-Pearson, 1997: 94). It is linked to Nietzsche's attack on mechanism, says Ansell-Pearson (1997: 94), and it stands in contrast to Darwinism:

> The extent ... to which Nietzsche formulated his conception of life as will-to-power in terms of an alternative to the depiction of life offered by English Darwinism has been overlooked. For Nietzsche the life process evolves in terms of the shaping, form-creating forces working from within, utilizing and exploiting external circumstances as the arena to test out its own extravagant experimentations. (1997: 97)

The link between the will to power and activity is realized through the concept of force. As Nietzsche says, '[t]he *victorious* concept of "force", by means of which our physicists have created God and the world, still needs to be *completed*: an inner will must be ascribed to it, which I designate as "will to power"' (1968a: §619). The will to power is thus the form-giving force of life. As Deleuze says, '[f]orce is what can, will to power is what wills ... The will to power is thus added to force' (1983: 50–1). It is thus 'both the genetic element of force and the principle of synthesis of forces' (1983: 51). It constitutes the force in life that seeks survival, that seeks life. This is also Foucault's appropriation of Nietzsche.

Nietzsche's concern here, as revealed by his use of terms such as 'enhancement', 'higher', 'lower', and so on, relates to a thesis concerning evolution and humanity as well as applying to individual actions. In this sense, the concept of the will to power functions in both a collective as well as an individual sense, and an objective as well as a subjective sense. In a subjective sense, will to power functions as a 'feeling of power' that results from an objective sense as an 'enhancement', 'advance', or 'heightening' of power in individuals, groups, and culture. Nietzsche says in *The Anti-Christ*, for instance: 'What is good? – All that heightens the feeling of power, the will to power, power itself in man. What is bad? – All that proceeds from weakness. What is happiness? – The feeling that power *increases* – that resistance is overcome ...' (§2). Or, again from *Daybreak*: 'the *feeling of power* has evolved to such a degree of *subtlety* that ... it has become his strongest propensity: the means discovered for creating this feeling almost constitute the history of culture' (§23). The will to power is thus an *active force* in human beings that functions in a psychological, sociocultural and historical sense. It portrays the development of the human being and represents a theory of human agency. It represents the human subject as a subject of power who acts in terms of forces and capacities. Nietzsche's theory at this level is a theory of human action.

At the same time, Foucault's other inspiration, Heidegger, notes how Nietzsche also links the will to power to his philosophy of the future for life as a whole. Heidegger's point here is that the will to power represents a *collective* dimension of Nietzsche's thinking as well as an individual dimension. Nietzsche indicates this dimension repeatedly, in references to 'the world', the 'future', 'the death of God', and with his general concern with the 'future of humanity' and 'life itself'. This is why Nietzsche can write '*the world is the will to power – and nothing besides!*' (1968a: §1067). The will to power thus expresses, says Heidegger, 'the fundamental character of beings as a whole'. It is for this reason that '*Life* is will to power' (Heidegger, 1991: 18).

In this sense, for Heidegger, the will to power is 'the principle of a new valuation' (1991: 15). This is the sense in which the principle of the will to power alters and supplements Darwin and provides a new ontology of vital materialism. For Heidegger's reading of Nietzsche, 'a new valuation means to set different perspectival conditions for life' (1991: 17). The word *value*, says Heidegger, is 'essential for Nietzsche' and 'came into circulation partly through Nietzsche' (1991: 15). 'Value for Nietzsche means a condition of life, a condition of life's being "alive". In Nietzsche's thinking *life* is usually the term for what is and for beings as a whole insofar as they are' (1991: 15). As with Ansell-Pearson and Deleuze, Heidegger dissociates Nietzsche's will to power from advocating a Darwinian thesis as the 'struggle for existence', but sees it as supporting 'self-transcending enhancement' (1991: 15). Heidegger continues: 'As a condition of life, value must therefore be thought as that which supports, furthers, and awakens the enhancement of life. Only what enhances life, and beings as a whole, has value – more precisely, *is* a value' (1991: 15–16). Heidegger says that for Nietzsche, 'the essence of life is life-enhancement' (1991: 16). Enhancement here means '*over-beyond-itself*' (1991: 16). 'This means that in enhancement life projects higher possibilities of itself before itself and directs itself forward into something not yet attained, something first to be achieved' (1991: 16).

Modifying Nietzsche's concepts

In that the concept of the 'will to power' demonstrates a latent concern with hierarchy, with progression, with quantitative and qualitative increase, Heidegger's interpretation incorporates the multiple senses in which Nietzsche employs the concept and articulates most accurately the work that the concept does in his writing as a whole. Yet, from a Foucauldian viewpoint, some of Nietzsche's concepts require critical revision. The concept of 'enhancement' seems deficient in that it represents the thesis of the will to power at the level of agency or actions by individuals or groups in a way that could be seen to resist historicity in important senses; senses that are also integral to Nietzsche's own philosophy. By resisting historicity, I mean to say that if one takes historicity and context into account, then what constitutes enhancement will likely mean different things in different times and places, as well as registering differently in the developmental histories of different living beings. In some of these meanings, the word enhancement may not itself be appropriate. In some contexts, enhancement may mean *self-aggrandizement*; for others *dominion* and *control*; yet for others, simply a sense of *sustainability*, or even *gratitude*. Patton says that Nietzsche recognizes enhancement as relating to an increase in a 'feeling of power' as one of the 'elements of a complex theory of human agency' (Patton,

1998: 74). Patton quotes *Beyond Good and Evil* to the effect that it is through the combined effects of willing and action that Nietzsche says that an individual 'enjoys the increase of power that accompanies all success' (Nietzsche, 1966: §19, cited in Patton, 1998: 74).

The ambiguities associated with some of Nietzsche's concepts, and the possibility of different interpretations in different contexts, have contributed to his poor image, and to misunderstandings over what he meant. Enhancement is one concept that seems to resist historicity in that it cannot be easily translated into different contexts. For the most part, it would appear that Nietzsche recognizes an ultimate contingency in terms of the way causation propels outcomes at the level of psychology. Examples abound in Nietzsche's texts. One such example of behaviour in a marketplace is provided in *Daybreak*, and serves as an illustration of the fact that there can be no basis in human nature or world for reliably predicting human drives as consistently the same in all times and places:

> Suppose we are in a market place one day and we noticed someone laughing at us as we went by: this event will signify this or that to us according to whether this or that drive happens at that moment to be at its height in us – and it will be a quite different event according to the kind of person we are. One person will absorb it like a drop of rain, another will shake it from him like an insect, another will try to pick a quarrel, another will examine his clothing to see if there is anything about it that might give rise to laughter, another will be led to reflect on the nature of laughter as such, another will be glad to have involuntarily augmented the amount of cheerfulness and sunshine in the world – (Nietzsche, 1998: §119)

In another example, also in *Daybreak*, Nietzsche describes the existence of dreams as subject to a multiplicity of arbitrary interpretations produced by a multiplicity of overdetermined causes which exert their variable effects in contingent sequences, unique in that their number and relative contributions will never exactly be repeated. Hence, a dream may be a consequence 'of the motions of the blood and intestines, of the pressure of the arm and the bedclothes, of the sounds made by church bells, weather-cocks, night-revellers and other things of the kind' (1998: §119). Not only all this, but the dream is itself an interpretation that 'is commented upon in such varying ways, that the inventive reasoning faculty imagines today a cause for the nervous stimuli so very different from the cause it imagined yesterday, though the stimuli are the same' (1998: §119). Hence, Nietzsche concludes 'that all [of] our so-called consciousness is a more or less fantastic commentary on an unknown, perhaps unknowable, but felt text' (1998: §119). There can be no universal basis for explaining what happens, and therefore there can be no science of reliable prediction based on the likelihood of repetitions of behaviour. Drives, thus, are *overdetermined* by a contingent array of variables or features of the context, and contexts infinitely return but are also infinitely different. A finite list of elements – maybe. But differently related and organized – certainly!

Yet, if such contingency operates in the determination of responses in a marketplace or in dreams, what do we make of the concept of 'enhancement'? There will be a sense in which it will mean very different things in different contexts. My concern is that the concept is too narrow, or too inflexible, to accommodate such multiplicities of use. While what living beings seek might sometimes be represented as a 'quantitative increase', or a 'heightening', or 'enhancement', such a process might not manifest itself as the same phenomenon, either objectively in terms of *actual effects*, or subjectively in terms of *feelings of power*. As a consequence, I believe the term *life continuance* avoids imputations of a univocal sense of hierarchy and quantitative elevation both at the individual subjective levels, as well as the cultural and historical levels, in relation to Nietzsche's philosophy of the future. The term life continuance can also retain the important collective sense in which Nietzsche's philosophy moves with reference to the idea of a *different* future, a future as yet to be decided, or even ascertained; a future that establishes new conditions for life, 'better' only in the sense that it surpasses a past that is increasingly unworkable. In this sense, the term continuance can incorporate the senses in which Nietzsche's philosophy of the future also reflects the will to power in terms of 'self-overcoming' or 'self-transformation', in terms of which 'all great things bring about their own destruction through an act of self-overcoming' (Nietzsche, 1996: §161). In that the term does not necessarily imply or assume a particular 'heightening', or 'increase', or 'elevation', continuance is more compatible with a Foucauldian principle of historicity in that it does not posit a substantive universal developmental trait or direction that is supposed to operate in all times and places, which terms such as 'enhancement' or 'self-overcoming' or 'elevation' are potentially in danger of doing.

In addition, continuance is also normatively regulating in that what contributes to the orderly transition to the future can be deemed of positive value, and what impedes, of negative value. This, in my view, accurately encapsulates Nietzsche's own views as to how *true* normativity operates. This is also the view of Richard Schacht, who says that Nietzsche's 'attempted "overcoming of morality" ... is more its *Aufhebung* than its abolition' (2001: 152).[17] *Aufhebung*, as Schacht footnotes, is an 'excellent Hegelian term with frequent aptness in Nietzsche; it conveys the threefold idea of elimination, preservation, and supersession, with the last sense prevailing' (2001: 179, n. 4). Schacht also says that '[o]n a Nietzschean view of the matter, there *are* moralities that are *more appropriate* than others' (2001: 155–6). It is my conjecture that the term continuance can serve these purposes, notwithstanding that it constitutes an 'extra-moral' source for normativity.[18] The term continuance also avoids possible imputations of elitism that might be claimed to exist with terms such as enhancement, advance, heightening, or other terms Nietzsche used, especially if linked to the organic intellectuals ('new philosophers', 'Superman', etc.) that Nietzsche saw as the orchestrators of such a transition. Continuance can therefore incorporate and normatively regulate enhancement; hence the two terms are not mutually exclusive. Enhancement, where it occurs, in its potentially very different forms, can in this sense be conceptualized *in terms of* moving towards the future, and can be acceptable in that versions of enhancement conform with the orderly continuance *to* the future. Continuance, in short, captures Nietzsche's theme of proceeding to the future as an unknown, uncertain, and dangerous journey. Continuance to the future can thus serve as the principle of a *new valuation* for a new and different future that constitutes the essence of Nietzsche's will to power, and ultimately will be able to normatively ground ethics, morality, and practical wisdom. It constitutes a new standard for Nietzsche's '*attempters*', that is, his 'new philosophers' (1968a: §§42–4). Ultimately, this puts a prioritization on knowledge and skill (*tekhnē*) as essential to the future, as Heidegger discusses in chapter 4 of the third volume of his four-volume study of Nietzsche (1991).[19]

The immanent value of life

As David Farrell Krell (1991: xxii) reminds us, when Nietzsche invokes the concept of 'life', he does so ontologically and not biologically. This is to say that life contains an *immanent* normativity,[20] which also makes naturalism an unattractive designator of Nietzsche's approach, for the normativity of conceptual judgements poses problems for naturalism, at least as traditionally understood.[21]

An immanent normativity guided only by life and the quest to continue, in an uncertain and dangerous world, is a hallmark of Nietzsche's concepts of life and will to power. It is the normativity immanent in life that grounds Nietzsche's use of words such as 'embark', 'bloom', 'blossom', 'ripen' – what Kaufmann refers to as the 'garden imagery' (Nietzsche, 1974: 232, n. 15) that underpins '[t]he theme of fashioning evil into good' (1974: 232, n. 15). It also makes sense of Nietzsche's concepts such as 'flourishing', 'development', 'preservation', 'growth', and 'advancement'.

Nietzsche frequently regards existing moralities as expressions of sectional interests and as having regressive and conservative effects. Nietzsche's critique of moralities doesn't mean that he sees no valid basis for normative values, however. The source of legitimate normativity in Nietzsche is *life*. This point has also been made by Schacht, who says: 'morals ... are not merely all-too-human, or pathological phenomena, but are constructively and crucially operative in what he calls "the service of life" and its "enhancement" ... that for him, is the trump consideration in all matters of meaning and value' (2001: 158). This is why, says Schacht, for Nietzsche, 'all normativity is ultimately of extra-moral origin' (2001: 158). Life expresses itself through the immanent normativity of the will to power. It is the concept of the will to power that is the 'ultimate origin – the *Ur*-source of normativity', says Schacht (2001: 158). This normativity is to survive and prosper, which establishes 'forms of life' (to use Wittgenstein's term), or communities of practice governed by norms. Although Schacht acknowledges that value is relative to a form of life, he fails to fully see, in my view, that the 'forms of life' themselves express the immanent normativity of life that also propels the philosophy of the future and vision of a new life, and that also grounds a conception of objectivity that goes beyond any single form of life, yet is nevertheless 'this-worldly', non-trivial, and non-metaphysical. Nietzsche's critiques and genealogies, which so inspired Foucault, seek to clear the way for his more positive philosophy of the future of humankind. Opposing both metaphysical views of a world beyond, as well as teleological views of historical destiny towards a set end or goal, Nietzsche saw the issue of how life and the future will be constructed as of crucial significance.

What, apart from Nietzsche, it can be asked, is the evidence for this claim that life has immanent value and seeks to continue? Nietzsche's main philosophical influence, Spinoza, sets out in Part III of his *Ethics* how human beings 'follow the way of nature' directed by their *conatus*, or striving.[22] When animals or humans are born, they seek to preserve themselves. The Stoic *oikeiosis* refers to 'selfhood ... as the foundation of any animal's life' (Long, 2001: 253). 'By its reflexive formulation, "self-belonging" characterises the disposition of care and ownership that an animal has in relation to itself' (2001: 253). 'From the moment of birth', animals and humans act in 'self-preserving ways' (2001: 253). Nietzsche's innovation was to represent this in relation to the future as imposing definite tasks.

If will to power is the '*Ur*-source of normativity', what type of ontology is being presupposed here? It is at this level of generality that it is tempting to say that living beings have a nature, yet one must be cautious. It is important not to turn an immanent normativity of life into a psychophysical theory of instincts, for such a normativity expresses itself differently in different environmental contexts. There can be no biological determinism here, for the biological, cultural, and historical interact and express the context for how living beings seek to survive and prosper. It is living within a context that establishes the case for the expression of normativity in relation to life. As Schacht expresses it:

For Nietzsche, as for Hegel, I suggest, and on my own view of the matter as well, the primary locus is the indisputably real historically engendered, culturally configured and socially encoded macro- and micro-*forms of human life* or broader or narrower *Lebenssphären* ('spheres of life') ... in which our human reality expresses and develops itself. (2001: 159)[23]

Schacht does not believe, as do Hegel and Kant, that any higher kind of normative validation is available, other than these 'forms of life' he refers to. At the same time, he points out that such a relativism does not render the 'historically varying and contingent sociocultural formations, institutions, and practices ... [as] subjective and capricious, any more than are the rules of chess or the norms of conduct associated with the practice of medicine or the conduct of scientific enquiry' (2001: 165). Yet the rules of the game, in that they express the immanent normativity of life to survive and prosper, go beyond *specific* forms of life to form *bridgeheads* between and across them. At the same time, it is admittedly a lesser form of objectivity than would be granted by a metaphysical conception of the likes of Plato's Forms or Kant's 'thing-in-itself'. Those kinds of objectivity are not possible, however. Beyond life continuance, there is no more robust sense of objectivity possible. Limited as it is, it is the basis for 'being appalled' at what goes on elsewhere – next door, in the village, in some far distant country. Hence it is the norm of *life continuance*, rather than the 'form of life' or of a 'community of practice', that enables the circumvention of relativism.

Schacht has made an important point in terms of how normativity and morals work in and through communities.[24] Although the immanent normativity of life expresses itself as an imperative of survival and well-being, it does so through constituting community structures and forms of life. Morals as norms have nothing to be keyed to apart from duties operative within forms of life, yet so long as such forms of life are oriented towards survival, there is *some* basis for cross-cultural objectivity in the constraints imposed by the materiality of the world on living beings as they endeavour to sustain life.

While Nietzsche expresses himself as a 'philosopher of the future', and sees 'the great task and question [as] how shall the earth be governed?' (1968a: §957), the presence of unpalatable or unacceptable attitudes in Nietzsche is an issue that many find disturbing.[25] It is here that Foucault becomes important to this study, as he accepted Nietzsche's core philosophical views, while those aspects and attitudes that affront our progressive political and moral sensibilities in the twentieth and twenty-first centuries are rejected. This is to say, also, that the attitudes in Nietzsche that most commonly offend are not centrally important to his work. What is central are his distinctive (non-)metaphysical views, which differ from all other political and metaphysical viewpoints in the Western intellectual tradition. Foucault acknowledged Nietzsche as his primary philosophical influence, with Heidegger playing an important secondary role. As he famously said in a much-quoted statement: 'For me Heidegger has always been the essential philosopher … I nevertheless recognise that Nietzsche outweighed him … these are the two fundamental experiences I have had' (1988e: 250).

With regard to ideas of the subject, power, history, and genealogy, Foucault seeks effectively to operationalize Nietzsche. As Paul Patton notes, Foucault's conception of the subject is like Nietzsche's in that Foucault sees the subject as 'a body composed of forces and capacities' (1998: 66). In accepting conceptions of the subject and power that are compatible with Nietzsche's views, it is possible to fit Foucault out with a normativity that has been identified in Nietzsche. This is in a way to link Foucault to his historical precursors, and to identify him as a part of the poststructuralist tradition that is correctly his home. For Foucault, the challenges of survival give life its own rules: it takes on the form of a game, with its own tactics and strategies, gambits and risks. Also important in this sense is that power and action become crucial for ethics. In that free actions when considered or reflected upon constitute ethical actions, ethics denotes the considered, conscious decisions that are made, rejected, or negotiated differently in a world where such decisions must be made repeatedly on an ongoing basis, and where individuals act in a context with others. In a complex, already given world of historically constituted and embedded constraints and structures, bifurcations or alternative multiple possible pathways confront the individual subject as repeated decision points. Such decision points implicate the normative. Zarathustra makes such choices in Nietzsche's great classic, *Thus Spoke Zarathustra*, when he selects one rather than another pathway at a fork in the road. Selecting one and not the other constitutes his subjectivity in one way rather than another way, with irreversible effects. The next chapter will look at Kantian ethics and related issues in order to better contextualize what we mean by life continuance.

Notes

1 See Appendix 2 regarding the Anglo-American and Continental traditions of philosophy with respect to Nietzsche studies.
2 This is simply a personal impression, based on the fact that many of the most published Anglo-American scholars on Nietzsche have appeared to criticize the traditional stereotypes concerning him, and accommodate positions close to or identical with Continental readings.
3 For accounts that see Nietzsche as a non-foundationalist, see Ansell-Pearson (1994; 1997) and Deleuze (1983).
4 See Peirce (1955: 59). Karl Popper, Friedrich Hayek, Kai Nielsen, and Nelson Goodman can also be considered as subscribing to fallibilism in this sense.
5 My own preference is to describe Nietzsche as materialist and generally in support of the ethos of science. A similar position is taken by Robert Audi, who says that 'naturalism in its most prominent forms is strongly associated with one or another kind of materialism' (2013: 27).
6 As Foucault never wrote on the issue, it is important to recall the title to this book, which suggests that I am 'constructing' Foucault's ethics.
7 Leiter opposes non-foundational readings of Nietzsche, and believes that his naturalism entails anti-realism, that is, that there are no objective facts about value. My own approach is non-foundationalist in the sense that I do not believe that Nietzsche recognizes any grounds in human nature to account for any *fixed characterological conception of the subject*. I would cite Deleuze (1983), Heidegger (1991), and Ansell-Pearson (1994) in support. All three cite ample textual support against foundationalist readings of Nietzsche. Apart from s-naturalism, which defines Nietzsche against supernaturalism, I also disagree with Leiter on objectivity and the other senses in which he claims that Nietzsche is a naturalist.
8 Clark and Dudrick are citing Nietzsche from *Human, All Too Human*, §§10, 29.

9 The last phrase cites Bernard Reginster (2006: 58), who maintains that Nietzsche is committed to 'normative subjectivism'.
10 Clark and Dudrick cite evidence from Nietzsche on increasing 'objectivity' of perspective from *On the Genealogy of Morals* (III, §12 and II, §11), and on the increasing comprehensiveness of perspective from *Human, All Too Human* (I, §6).
11 Clark and Dudrick are citing Nietzsche from *Beyond Good and Evil* (§211).
12 I accept Gilles Deleuze's depiction of the overman as representing 'the transhistoric element of man' (1983: xiii), constituting an affirmative ethical response ('the only affirmation of power'), rather than as a special class of person (Superman) here.
13 Further examples abound in Nietzsche. See his later works, for instance *Daybreak* (1881) and *Twilight of the Idols* (1889).
14 I appreciate that such a statement is contentious. It is unproductive here to become side-tracked by the specific values that Nietzsche sought to privilege, as such an issue is tangential to the argument for objective normativity that I am seeking to advance.
15 There are various ways in which such beings can be interpreted. It is perfectly conceivable that Nietzsche's 'higher human beings' had the benefits of an enriched early social environment and better education, and this is the key to the distinction between 'higher' and 'lower' that he makes.
16 Robin Small notes that it is generally recognized that Nietzsche was not well informed about Darwin's theories, and his approach to Darwinism is often through dialogue with Paul Rée and Herbert Spencer (see Small, 2007: 122).
17 Schacht cites Nietzsche from *Beyond Good and Evil* (§32).
18 In that continuance posits a non-moral source for normative, ethical, and moral claims, G. E. Moore might accuse me of committing 'the naturalistic fallacy'. For Moore, the naturalistic fallacy occurs when 'good' is defined in terms of anything other than 'good', such as a natural object such as 'pleasure' or 'evolution', or indeed a metaphysical object, such as 'the real' or 'eternal'. Moore criticizes Spencer's evolutionism because it holds 'that we need only to consider the tendency of "evolution" in order to discover the direction in which we *ought* to go ... that we ought to move in the direction of evolution simply *because* it is the direction of evolution' (1903: 54, 56). Moore's fallacy does not apply to continuance theory because continuance is a constructivist and not an evolutionary theory. In this sense, it is not 'defining' good in relation to a natural process or entity, but rather

specifying the generative conditions for the emergence of irreducible normative values. This is to say that continuance *is* a normative process that must be conjectured, calculated, decided upon, and enacted, either with or against the path of evolution. The constructivist nature of continuance means that it is not the same as evolution, and Moore's criticisms of Herbert Spencer's evolutionary theory do not therefore apply (see Moore, 1903: 54, 56). As Nietzsche said, 'we have created the world that concerns man' (1974: §301). The concepts of good and evil are for Nietzsche human inventions embedded in discourse and in need therefore of continual interpretation and judgement. At this point, it is also important to say that one must not be intimidated by Moore. While Moore highlights definitional problems as they apply to simple terms (such as 'good' or 'yellow'), his approach essentially amounts to a pluralism of simple, undefinable entities that he assumes must exist in some non-natural realm. The naturalistic fallacy is advanced as a logical fallacy, and Moore's own solution leads him towards, as Daly puts it, a 'non-naturalist solipsism' (1996: 30). In the Foucauldian world, everything is material, and Moore's dualism between the natural and non-natural must be replaced by what Stelmach (2013: 144) refers to as a nominalistic ontological monism. According to Stelmach, it is by positing a dualism that must be overcome, and at the same time determining that 'any attempts which try to overcome the naturalistic fallacy are doomed to failure' (2013: 140), that Moore constitutes his 'open question technique' as an impossible and illegitimate trap.

19 Chapter 4 is entitled 'Knowledge in Nietzsche's Fundamental Thought Concerning the Essence of Truth'.
20 Immanent in Kant's sense, as within the domain of the phenomenal or world-for-us. As developed by Deleuze, immanent refers to the forces, energies, intensities, that operate within the plane of existence.
21 Naturalism has traditionally sought to reduce normativity to self-interest. As John McDowell (1994: 73) argues: 'The structure of the space of reasons stubbornly resists being appropriated within a naturalism that conceives nature as the realm of law.' However, if normativity is not reduced to self-interest, but attaches generally to the objective conditions of life continuance, then there is no necessary conflict with an attenuated conception of naturalism as is being argued for in this chapter. For an argument as to the compatibility of naturalism with the normativity of conceptual judgement, albeit from a different philosophical perspective, see Papineau (1999).
22 See Spinoza 'On the Origins and Nature of Affects', *The Ethics*, Part III (Spinoza, 1993).

23 Schacht points out in a footnote that neither Nietzsche nor Hegel use the term *Lebenssphären*, which belongs, he says, to Wittgenstein. But, he says, both would find it satisfactory.

24 I acknowledge several debts to Schacht's excellent article 'Nietzsche and Normativity' (2001) here. Although I disagree with him on several points, I consider his article as pathbreaking in opening up a whole new domain of inquiry in Nietzsche studies.

25 Schacht notes various misrepresentations of Nietzsche: the most important he labels the '"blond beast" blunder ... [which] consists in taking Nietzsche to be advocating a return to or revival of the sort of thing he labels "master morality" in the first essay of GM' (2001: 153). Bertrand Russell, he notes, gave this criticism 'a classic expression' (2001: 153) in his *History of Western Philosophy*. While Schacht notes that Nietzsche does in fact 'evince a kind of appreciation and even admiration for that sort of morality' (2001: 153), he argues that Nietzsche's genealogical analysis is not intended as and should not be confused with his own normative vision of the future. This is an insightful point and makes it possible to reject Nietzsche's unacceptable attitudes while accepting his historical-ontological approach to overcoming metaphysics. In my view, Nietzsche is a misogynist, at times an elitist, and his views on suffering (e.g. 1968a: §957) appear cruel and excessive. We can say, further, that even if Nietzsche did 'inject' his normative vision of the future with the 'serum' of certain undesirable moral attitudes, there is no obstacle to detaching his philosophically novel ontology of the future from his own contingent and historically situated attitudes concerning politics, culture, gender, biology, slavery, and so on.

4

Continuance ethics, objectivity, Kant

Life continuance ground rules

Life continuance simply articulates or names the principle that constitutes the normativity of an ethic for life. For without consciously naming it, we act in terms of it. It implicitly regulates our conduct and orients our actions in relation to the future. This is to say that the norm of life continuance under conditions that are fair for all 1) is itself necessary for each of us to survive and prosper; 2) constitutes the yardstick at this juncture in history by which normative objectivity for values can be established; and 3) simply codifies common sense, or approximates our considered values and beliefs. This latter point was claimed by Immanuel Kant in the eighteenth century and by the American political philosopher John Rawls in the twentieth century for their own respective philosophical viewpoints. In the *Critique of Practical Reason*, Kant (2004: Preface, §14) claims that the universalization principle simply encapsulates the way that ordinary people actually go about making moral decisions on a daily basis. Rawls claims much the same thing in *A Theory of Justice* (1999a: xi, xviii). The neutrality over issues of fairness achieved behind the 'veil of ignorance' reflects the way that ordinary people make ethical decisions about what is fair and just.[1]

The fact that both conceptions stipulate a universal rule form of morality (see Ferrara, 1999: ch. 1) that is then applied to everyone uniformly has been one basis for criticism of both Kant and Rawls. Life continuance constitutes a principle that also claims to articulate what people actually do in relation to ethical and moral decisions. One aim of this chapter is to show that it is more successful than previous efforts to do this. The difference from universal rule type moralities is that it treats different situations differently according to circumstances. Such a rule of difference constitutes an important principle for Foucault. This entails that rather than comprising a universal rule to be imposed, it constitutes a framework or template that serves as an axis for reflection, deliberation, and judgement in particular situations. In this chapter, I will claim that continuance represents a conception of good, in the sense that the norms of continuance represent values that are external to the individual and that are instrumental in terms of how an individual defines their life and how they make decisions. In that continuance represents a 'preferred way forward', it applies not simply to individuals, but also to groups, societies, governments, and institutions. While there may be a plurality of possible actions, plans, or pathways that could be adopted in continuing one's life, there will be certain actions, plans, or pathways that are not optimal, as well as some that are terminal. The fact that some ways to act are better or worse in terms of how to live one's life is one way of denoting what is meant by saying that continuance ethics is objectivist rather than subjectivist. Certain actions are objectively better, independent of the person concerned.

The distinction between vital and social norms requires a judgement in each situation. It is this distinction that means that continuance norms are not merely conventional. There will be an optimal way forward premised upon a conception of what is fair and just for each and all. Judgement in turn presupposes knowledge, deliberation, and foresight. The conception entails a form of social realism. Sharing a world of finite resources commits humans to such rules of the game if they are to claim to participate in that game on a fair and reasonable basis. Given that the future is characterized by uncertainty and danger, although it constitutes a yardstick for ethics and morality, as well as practical policy making, these domains will equally be characterized by different viewpoints, adherence to different principles, and the possibility of innumerable conflicts and disagreements. Yet notwithstanding this, a war of all against all will contradict the good of continuance itself; hence the minimal requirement for social beings who wish to participate in the game of life is agreement to participate and to dialogue, which includes the democratic resolution of disagreements and disputes.

Because continuance of life constitutes a deeply shared commitment, it enables recognition that the best prospects for life either rest upon or imply a relation between the individual and the future of society as a system, based on the acceptance that what damages one damages the other, and what damages the structure, damages the part. That there are better ways to live one's life is put forward by all of the major religions, which each specify their own systems of rules and beliefs and justify these with reference to a metaphysical world beyond. This is one way of writing, or overwriting, the script of continuance, but it is not the only way, and not a necessary way. One cannot live without being committed to continuance norms, and while these won't prevent disagreements on moral issues, such norms do set limits, and in this sense the limits establish a zone of discretion, which is a zone of liberty. Our moral attitudes are always held in relation to the norm of continuance, even when we disagree with each other. Hence, while two individuals might disagree over abortion rights, both will invoke the norm of continuance with regard to the seriousness with which they consider the issues involved, the fact that in whatever decision they arrive at, basic concerns over respect for life, the rights of both the mother and the child, and so on, have been taken into account. We could say that even when they conflict, such beliefs and arguments operate in reference to a norm of continuance, which is always an important background consideration. In this sense, the norm of continuance sets limits outside of which actions and conduct become unacceptable. This applies to arbitrary violence, murder, cruelty, corruption, dishonesty, deceitfulness, and so on.

While this might sound like common sense, the main approaches to ethics for the last several hundred years have entailed a belief in a metaphysical world beyond the world of experience, either in Plato's world of Forms, Aristotle's teleological conception of the good, or a divine command view that posits God. Such metaphysical views are frequently supported by a theory known as intuitionism, which claims that such moral truths can be intuited by virtue of a special faculty and that therefore no argument or rational justification is needed. After intuitionism failed to convince that it was connecting with anything beyond experience, a doctrine known as subjectivism came to prominence, which claims that ethical actions and attitudes have no objective basis in anything outside the individual, but are simply expressions of subjective feelings or preferences. To complete the picture, the other standard approaches in the modernist era have been idealist, utilitarian, or Kantian. Idealism was a version of metaphysical ethics, as above, which frequently utilized intuitionism as a method for apprehending moral and ethical truths. Utilitarianism conceptualized right action in terms of the good of aggregate welfare, defining good in terms of maximizing pleasure, or in seeking to promote 'the greatest happiness of the greatest number' (in Bentham's phrase).[2] Kant's moral theory opposed utilitarianism on the grounds that individuals would be sacrificed on the altar of the good, and advanced a deontological rights-based ethics that located ethical and moral action in *a priori* categories in the nature of the subject, articulated in terms of the 'moral law'. Although Foucault has affinities with Kant on several issues, his opposition to Kant's conception of the subject as itself metaphysical means that Kantian theory needs revision. For Foucault, nature is also beyond experience, and a version of metaphysics. To claim to recognize an ahistorical subject with *a priori* categories of cognition is simply to access the metaphysical or noumenal world via a different route. The rest of this chapter and the following two will seek to consider several of these approaches, employing several analytic philosophers' views for the purpose of engaging them as interlocutors.

Objectivism and intuitionism in ethics

Ethics and morality stem from a relationship between individuals and the collective. When I refrain from throwing litter on the ground I play my part as regards a network of which I am a member. This might be partly because if everyone threw litter, not only would society be very untidy, but ultimately order might break down. Such an insight is Kantian, for to ask 'what if everyone did that' can be derived from the formulation of Kant's universalization rule.[3] I refrain from dropping litter because, in an ideal sense, I am interested in shaping my subjectivity as consistent with a world that I would like to inhabit. While the insight can be attributed to Kant, this way of thinking, and the capacity to think in this way, goes back well beyond Kant to the Stoics, and even beyond them, to the Greeks. Such a reflective way of thinking is encapsulated in the Golden Rule ('Do unto others as you would have them do unto you'), which derives from biblical times. Kant spends considerable effort in differentiating his principles of universalization from the Golden Rule, yet he only did so because there appears to be an obvious affinity. Derek Parfit analyses Kant's writing on this in detail, and because it is tangential to my concerns I am not going to get sidetracked.[4] All I want to say here is that both the Golden Rule and Kant's universalization principle constitute a form of reflective thinking that, without deflecting from Kant's contribution, have in different ways existed for millennia. The practices of the self must be compatible with a world that it is at least *possible* to live in. I am conscious also that only in such a world is my *safety* and that of those I love truly assured. It is also best for life itself, another value I hold dear.

When I take a stand against climate change, it is on similar grounds. While many people choose to understand such imperatives as deriving from otherworldly sources, such as God, it is on the requirement for life continuance that our ordinary understanding of such concepts is based, and from which it derives its necessity. While I maintain that we cannot pontificate about matters such as God, if she did exist, she would surely subscribe to such a view too.[5] However, as far as my argument is concerned, it is in terms of this-worldly purposes that the immediate rationale for such views must be understood. For, while certain events do in fact impede or facilitate life continuance in this sense, affecting both the individual and the whole, continuance maintains, to some degree at least, an objective basis located in the uncertain and contested estimations of how the future can best be traversed. The argument is that this norm is in fact implicit in our ways of acting and living, and is causally generative for our ethical and moral codes, indeed, of the normative itself. That is to say, certain events, ways of life, customs, and beliefs do in fact impede or facilitate the ability of life to continue, although not all actions necessarily affect it with the same force or in the same manner. Given this fact, there are good reasons for the ethical and moral rules we observe and act upon. Either directly or indirectly, life continuance in terms of how we traverse the future constitutes the measure by which normative objectivity in values is established.

Partly in order to clarify distinctions and the use of concepts, and partly because there exist within the Anglo-American philosophical world some exceptionally fine commentators on Kant, my own understandings and considerations have drawn from such notable figures as Christine Korsgaard, Allen Wood, Barbara Hermann, Derek Parfit, and Hannah Ginsborg. In this chapter, Parfit's theory of moral objectivism, as well as his critique and revision of Kant, will be focused upon. Parfit's three-volume *On What Matters* (2011a; 2011b; 2017) makes a noteworthy contribution as regards his defence of moral objectivism, which is his belief that there are objective moral truths and other normative values that subtend and should guide action and belief. It also contributes in terms of his critique of Kant. Parfit's work has been influential for my own analysis and revision of Kant. However, Parfit's analysis agrees with my own position, as developed from Nietzsche and Foucault, only in certain very limited respects.

Indeed, the agreement on most issues may be more apparent than real. We both claim to assert a view of moral and ethical values as objective. I agree that there are objective reasons for values, which is to say that some normative beliefs are objectively valid. Parfit does too, but he defines objectivism differently to me. He rejects the scepticism that goes back to Hume and beyond Hume to the beginnings of philosophy itself, as echoed in Plato's arguments against ethical scepticism and subjectivism. In this sense, he is a metaphysical objectivist who sees some external moral source for ethics and values. I am a metaphysical sceptic and anti-realist, but still claim to locate the objectivity of value as emergent in the will to survive. I am in this sense a sociological and historical realist, but see the objectivity of value not as merely conventional but tied to, validated by, and contingent upon the immanent quest of life to survive and prosper. I claim that the quest for survival coerces a certain standard of objectivity that is independent of mere convention. This may be a 'lesser sense' of objectivity than Parfit can claim, but I would argue that it still constitutes objectivity, especially when compared to subjectivism in ethics. Further, of course, I would also claim that Parfit's claimed objectivity is completely bogus. The important point of agreement between me and Parfit is that, like Parfit, I do not see ethics are merely a matter of subjective whims of individuals. As to the sources of objectivism, I claim that the very cadence of the quest to survive and prosper *dictates* objective values for both individuals and collectivities that are 'this-worldly' and 'non-metaphysical' and that form links ('bridgeheads') between (i.e., across) forms of life and communities. These facts about value have normative objectivity in that they deserve acceptance by others. It is for this reason, after all, that we can hold each other to account. On this point, and on what objectivism means precisely, philosophically, and in practice, there are, then, major differences between Parfit and me.[6]

One other difference concerns Parfit's allegiance to his philosophical paradigm of choice. Parfit claims adherence to intuitionism, by which he maintains that we have intuitive abilities to recognize objective normative (and moral) truths. For intuitionists, moral truths exist as naturally right or wrong and are '*independent* in the sense that they are not created or constructed by us' (Parfit, 2011a: 367). According to Parfit, '[w]e have *intuitive* abilities to respond to reasons and to recognize some normative truths' (2011b: 544). Although Parfit claims that this does not necessitate a belief in a non-sensory capacity, intuitionism has historically suffered from a congenital inadequacy of theorization as regards what is really going on, especially as it seems to suggest an immediacy of apprehension through some non-sensory, non-empirical, non-physical process. What is termed intuition can all too easily be suspected of being a process that synthesizes and integrates a multiplicity of previously incorporated sensory inputs, jumbling together a diverse array of elements such as direct observation, learning, secondary reports, religious beliefs, dominant ideology, social conditioning, sheer prejudice, and so on. The lack of any adequate account of how the mind works, as well as the lack of critical self-reflection among adherents to the doctrine regarding the possibility that our own consciousness is inhabited by ideological ghosts and cultural beliefs carried through the ages from generation to generation, seriously question the validity and reliability of intuition as a method.[7]

It is in relation to Parfit's justification of normativity with regard to the natural/non-natural distinction that another serious disagreement arises. Parfit maintains that normative truths, although objective, have no causal impact on the world (2011a: 306, 497, 503, 510, 517, 518, 532, 618). My objection here has also aroused the criticism of others, who basically agree with or are sympathetic to Parfit's other claims relating to objectivism in ethics, but find this claim strange. Larry S. Temkin finds Parfit's view 'puzzling' and at odds with any reasonable assessment of the situation. While there can be many causes of an action or event, 'it seems plain', he says, 'that one of the causes of action can be the reasons that led the agent to perform that action' (2017: 5). He gives the example of stopping at traffic lights, and notes that this is:

> recognizing and responding to the normative fact that I ought to stop – that is, to the reasons that there are for stopping in a country where the rules of the road require that drivers stop at red lights, and where the possible consequences of failing to stop can be dire – I put my foot on the brake, bringing my car to a halt. (2017: 15)

Rather than argue this case independently, let me just say, to adapt a well-known British political slogan, that 'I agree with Larry':[8] 'the normative reason that I had a good reason to stop, or that I ought to have stopped, had a causal impact on my stopping' (2017: 5). The normative fact that I ought to stop at red lights is derived from a collectively shared normative imperative, which human beings are fortunate enough to have sufficient rational capacities to implement. It is, therefore, a bad idea to ignore the lights and try to run them.

Temkin is also instructive on why Parfit might have claimed that normative facts do not have a causal impact on the world. Because for Parfit normative facts are not events and are not physical, they are not natural. Natural, for Parfit, as Temkin puts it, appears to be what the sciences study – matter, physical stuff, etc. Temkin suggests that Parfit possibly sees the issue as akin to that of substance dualism, which denies 'that immaterial substances can have a causal impact on material substances and vice versa' (2017: 7). So Parfit appears to take the view that normative facts are non-natural and that the non-natural cannot be the cause of the natural. As Temkin elaborates, Parfit no doubt labours under the view 'that causes of events in the natural world are the domain of science, but that non-natural normative facts are the domain of philosophy' (2017: 7).

Parfit also possibly shares the widely held view 'that causation is a relation that only obtains between *events*' (2017: 7). And as normative facts are not events, then they cannot have a causal impact. In addition, says Temkin, to posit non-natural normative facts as causing natural world events might well be seen as invoking 'supernatural', 'mystical', or 'occult' substances (2017: 7). That the issues raise difficulties is something of which Parfit is keenly aware, and this clearly lies behind his discussion of the concept of 'existence', where he distinguishes 'narrow' and 'wide' senses of something existing (2011a: 469–70) and claims that non-natural normative facts 'exist' in the 'wide sense'. This is something that Temkin (2017: 7) is also unhappy with, as am I. It not only raises insuperable problems as to the epistemological and ontological status of 'narrow' and 'wide', and whether the latter is somehow subordinate to or variously tangential or 'less real' than the former, but it reveals a commitment to an antiquated metaphysics and an inadequate theoretical understanding of the status of the discursive in philosophy. What will become clear is that any consideration from the perspective of Foucault will take a very different approach to Parfit on such issues.

These dualisms presupposed and invoked by Parfit are unfortunate, and nothing is lost, though much is gained, by giving them up. Normative facts and orderings arise when individual, group, and collective strategies are rendered concordant with norms for survival that are immanent to life itself and constitute a strategy of survival that all living things manifest. The dimension of natural/non-natural is unhelpful here.[9] So are the 'narrow' and 'wide' senses of what it means to exist. In the Foucauldian universe, the natural/non-natural would be seen as unhelpful in this context because it is poorly conceptualized, and confused frequently with the human/non-human, the discursive/non-discursive, or even the material/immaterial. Any talk of a non-natural realm would be rejected *tout court* as metaphysical. In most cases, talk of the non-natural simply refers to the discursive, and both the discursive and the pre- or extra-discursive are represented as constituting material realms. Normative orderings constitute a part of the discursive that constitutes, as Foucault put it in his review of Deleuze's book *The Logic of Sense*, an 'incorporeal materialism' (Foucault, 1998f).

They are as material as rocks, gravity, quarks, protons, grains of sand, or strategies of survival. As such, they constitute a network of signs and rules that regulate moral and ethical behaviour in terms of what we human beings ought to do if we are indeed concerned with the survival of life on earth. In this sense, normative facts both motivate and guide behaviour, are mind-independent, and in that they adhere to standards, are both constitutive and regulative.

Where I also disagree with Parfit is that while I support a certain sense of objectivism, I also argue that there is an irreducible deontic or subjective dimension to ethics, as an effect of the fact that individual identities are *emergent* within the whole and *develop* their own integrity in relation to it *through time*. A number of recent critics have questioned whether the objective/subjective divide in ethics is as deep or whether it operates as Parfit represents it. This is the sense in which the objective realm that guides ethics and morality is not represented in the life continuance perspective as some quasi-Platonic realm of immovable, unchanging Forms, beyond the world of experience, independent and unrelated to the subjective realms of motivation and life. Temkin himself advocates such a view when he makes the point that 'reasons are always reasons for creatures like us ... that is, normative facts only serve as practical reasons for beings whose cognitive capacities (faculty of reason) enable them to understand and appropriately respond to whatever reasons there are' (2017: 33). Julia Markovits (2017: 54–81) also claims that subjectivism and objectivism converge on the basis that the reasons that we adhere to fundamentally express our collective wants and desires. To render her claims in my language, continuance ethics asserts that it is wants and needs generated by life itself that are rendered objective. Such wants, says Markovits, are *collective*. It is because they are collective and express life itself that they also express the view of *homo sapiens* as a group. Such wants are the basis of life and constitute its objectivity. Markovits terms her approach as leading to an 'optimific subjectivism' which refers to the desires we have *in common*. No doubt by retaining the concept of subjectivism she avoids confusion with Parfit's metaphysical conception of objectivity, but not to recognize a 'softer' sense of objectivism that is clearly more than 'desires', and that maintains a sociological reality by virtue of being 'common', seems to me to be unnecessary on her part. I would rather term such an approach a non-metaphysical objectivism, on the grounds that it has intersubjective warrant, notwithstanding that there may be difficulties in distinguishing it from mere conventionalism. Her approach diverges in important respects from Parfit, who maintains a rigid separation between objective and subjective, external and internal, claiming that we have external reasons for acting that do not come from anyone's wants or desires. Given the historical ontology I subscribe to, Parfit's metaphysical view is simply not tenable. What Markovits identifies is a neglected system or social process by which individuals' wants are turned into collective norms, which in my view constitutes an objective basis for individual and group ethics.

Continuance thus is not some mysterious, occult quality, nor does it constitute some non-natural normative fact characteristic of what J. L. Mackie termed 'queerness' (1977: 38, 40).[10] To see structural or system characteristics or discourses that inhabit our world as 'queer' demonstrates the naivety with regard to social realism that I have already noted in general above.[11] Continuance characterizes life by codifying its norms, and thereby differentiates it from the inanimate. As Canguilhem pointed out, such norms are immanent in life itself. They concern the quest to survive and prosper. Just as we share physical properties, such as eyes and bones, so life possesses certain normative properties that are not particular to individuals, but that inhabit life itself, and hence *are* collective. Indeed, ontologically this immanent value is part of life rather than of individual humans per se, although it *inheres in* each individual. Because continuance constitutes the norm that all of life shares, it is a collective template that orients it to a future, as a defining feature of what life is. It is this imperative for survival and well-being inserted by life that constitutes the objectivity of ethics and morality. It makes the discernment of error in life theoretically possible, although in many instances practically difficult. The paradox of objectivity is that although there might be a best course for life to take, we humans are charged with working it out through experimentation, trial, and error. It is the indiscernibility of the open spaces of possibility in front of us, with the innumerable choices they require, that constitutes the matrix of ethics and the hope of 'justice to come', to use Derrida's phrase (Derrida, 1992).

Subjectivism in ethics

Like Nietzsche, Foucault, as I will construct his normative position, would not see ethical attitudes as merely expressive of desires. Continuance constitutes an objective basis for ethics and morality, with objectivity precariously defined in reference to the possibilities of life traversing to the future.[12] It is what will enable me to classify certain desires or values as irrational or immoral if they deny reasonable possibilities for continuance. Some readers may by this stage wonder why I am defending such a point, but the dominant trend in ethics and moral philosophy since the collapse of intuitionism in the first half of the twentieth century has been what is called subjectivism, expressed variously under a number of different labels, such as 'emotivism', 'prescriptivism', 'expressivism', or 'irrealism', and based on a sceptical or relativist view about ethics and moral beliefs reinforced by logical positivism in the nineteenth century.

Parfit spends an entire chapter (2011a: ch. 3) opposing subjectivism in ethics, and I also oppose it. A major culprit as regards subjectivism is David Hume. Hume held the view that reason could help us instrumentally to get from means to ends, but could not decide what we ought to do in the first place. This was simply a matter of what we desired or wanted, and desires and wants were merely subjective, with no possibility of objective justification. Since Hume there has been a long line of Anglo-American philosophers, from the logical positivists, notably A. J. Ayer, and including also such notables as C. L. Stevenson, R. M. Hare, J. L. Mackie, Simon Blackburn, Allan Gibbard, and Bernard Williams, who all hold to the idea that moral or ethical values are merely subjective utterances that cannot be objectively true or false.

That there is something very wrong about this subjectivist theory of ethics can be seen when one considers the implications of the theory and its deep incoherence in relation to what people, liberal philosophers included, actually do and believe. This is to say that they don't act in their own lives as if subjectivism were true. To the extent that ethical attitudes are subjective one would surely expect a range of views to be expressed on any particular issue, and even to be tolerated. Even Rawls believes that there are no external criteria for moral reasons, so that if a man believes that unrelieved suffering is what makes for the best life for a person, then that is the life that is worthwhile for that person. Similarly, if someone believes that a worthwhile life is to be achieved by counting grains of sand on the beach, then there is for the subjectivist no way to contradict the meaningfulness of such a life.

In the continuance perspective based on Nietzsche that I am advocating, desires and actions are in error if they frustrate optimal conditions for life continuance and fail to respect life itself. This is the constructivist value that life gives to life by the very fact that it exists. Such actions are morally objectionable and irrational on those grounds. If ethical and moral values were merely matters of taste, or subjective wants or desires, there would be no argument about them, for we do not argue about matters of taste. That you like onions with your burger rather than avocado is not regarded as a matter for argument but accepted as a subjective want, desire, or preference, which is therefore not a matter for debate. It is because ethical matters are *not* mere subjective preferences that we *do* argue over them. Both ethics and morality have an objective or external reference, and hence we argue over them all the time. While harming oneself has not been considered irrational for most subjectivists, it is for me. It is both irrational and wrong, for harming oneself frustrates the immanent norm of life. Burning fossil fuels is also wrong and ought to be addressed based upon norms of life continuance that are immanent in life itself as a matter of urgent national and global policy. There are distinct reasons in ethics and morality for acting one way rather than another.[13]

Kantian ethics

A Foucauldian ethics differs in important respects from Kant's ethics. There are also some major similarities. As Foucault says in *The Order of Things*, Kant's philosophy 'forms the immediate space of our reflection. We think in that area' (1970: 384). Kant places the importance in ethics on the process of reasoning conceptualized individualistically and through the articulation of maxims expressed as categorical imperatives. For this he distinguishes initially between hypothetical and categorical imperatives. Imperatives are formulas that enable the expression of practical principles of reason. Hypothetical imperatives suggest that *if* we act in a certain way, *then* we can expect a certain result to be produced under certain given conditions. Categorical imperatives, on the other hand, are unconditional commands or instructions. In Kant's view, it is these categorical imperatives that constitute ethics and express the moral law.

Although Kant's universalization rule implicates the whole and the consequences for the whole if individuals act a certain way, he sees such a logical process as an expression of the autonomy of each individual. The function of the whole in the universalization algorithm is only to ensure the consistency of each individual's behaviour. Kant holds that noumenal, undetermined, or uncaused freedom is a central feature of the human condition and as such constitutes the cornerstone of his philosophy. The grounding for the categorical imperatives that articulate the moral law resides in the rational nature of each individual as an end in itself, as expressed through the autonomy of the individual's will. These are the grounds of moral obligation.[14] Kant maintains that when we are able to universalize our actions in terms of maxims that can apply to all rational beings, the resulting generalizations constitute necessary laws of nature, and therefore laws of conduct. Contradiction – between the individual's maxim and the moral law – is the sole criterion of morality.

But what Kant also means is that ethical and moral actions are characterized by the purity of the motive propelling them. One does not claim, for instance, that one is being ethical if one's actions are motivated by an ulterior purpose, but only if one acts according to principle on the basis of duty and irrespective of the consequences. Similarly, one does not act morally in order to achieve pleasure or happiness. As Kant famously explains in the opening pages of the *Groundwork*, it is the motive of a good will alone that serves as the basis of ethics rather than the nature of the consequences produced by the action.[15] To act in pursuit of a particular end or good would be consequentialist, and this was a form of ethical reasoning that Kant opposed. True principles in ethics are established *a priori*, says Kant: they are metaphysical. *A priori* knowledge refers to maxims that are prior to experience, such as in maths or logic where there would be a contradiction in denying that they were true. Universalization establishes whether actions are contradictory for one's will. *A priori* knowledge, like mathematical knowledge, is not derived from empirical observation of the world but is based upon pure thought or reasoning. Kant thought that ethics in this sense was like mathematics.

Kant's general principle here is to 'act so that the maxim of your action were to become by your will law universal', or expressed negatively, 'it is wrong to act on maxims that one could not will to be universal laws' (Parfit, 2011a: 285).[16] As Parfit (2011a: 286) suggests, Kant intended to ask through this formula, 'What if everyone did that?', and 'What if everyone thought like you?' It is thus intended to constitute a formula to decide the rightness and wrongness of actions. According to the standard interpretation of Kant, universalization results in unconditional categorical imperatives that permit of no exceptions, a consequence that means it is never right to lie or break promises, or contradict categorical moral rules. This presents a multitude of problems for, as many commentators have argued, there are circumstances where it is held that lying or breaking a promise is the right thing to do, ethically or morally.

In real life, situations are often more complicated than Kant's rule seems to allow for. Parfit maintains that while some maxims are wholly bad or wholly good, what Kant failed to see was that many are 'morally mixed' (2011a: 293), including maxims such as 'never lie'. As Parfit puts it, 'Kant's formula assumes that acting on some maxim is either always wrong, or never wrong' (2011a: 293). Should one break a promise to do x if on the way to do x one encounters an accident where rendering assistance, and therefore breaking the promise, might save lives? Similarly, in what is a well-worn example used in this line of argument, and a matter that Kant wrote about in a notorious article, if a murderer asked the whereabouts of his intended victim, would one not reason that the appropriate ethical response is to lie, and endeavour to save the intended victim from an almost certain terminal fate? This as well as many other illustrations might suggest that Kant's universal law formula is not always helpful in deciding what is right and wrong, a fact that has led many leading commentators to criticize it as 'radically defective', that 'no one has been able to make work', or that 'gives either unacceptable guidance or none at all'.[17]

There are many other problems with Kant's ethical system that put it in need of drastic revision or change in the twenty-first century. Foucault highlights many criticisms of Kant in his own writings (see Foucault 1970; 1972: 203–4; 1984c; 1997f; 2008b). While I will argue for modifying Kant, my criticisms will be no less severe than those of others, such as Bernard Williams, who is unhappy that Kant saw morality as located in the individual but tied to a transcendental determination. According to Williams: 'Kant's work is in this respect a shattering failure, and the transcendental psychology to which it leads, where not unintelligible, certainly false. No human characteristic which is relevant to degrees of moral esteem can escape being an empirical characteristic' (1971: 23).

Through what mechanism or agency does the moral law work? Kant says it is from the will, but whence comes the will? For Kant it is transcendental, and metaphysical. This is a matter on which Kant has been harshly criticized. As Allen Wood puts it: 'Kant falsifies the finitude of the human condition when he attempts to place the good will beyond the reach of nature and fortune' (1990: 153). Hegel had already insinuated in *The Philosophy of Right* that Kant fails to rigorously define will in the sense that Hegel would like him to define it: naturalistically or historically. This is similar to the 'empirical' sense that Williams employs (in the quotation above). As McCumber puts it:

> [b]ecause he does not rigorously define 'will', Kant misses the fact that the definition can be formulated entirely in naturalistic terms – which means that philosophically considered, will is a modification of natural phenomena. Hegel is trying to *retain* Kant's account of will while giving it a naturalistic, rather than a transcendental basis. (2014: 152)[18]

Universalization also ignores context. It ignores the fact, as we saw above, that truth telling and theft and promise keeping are sometimes more important than at other times, and not always to be implemented in the same way in all times and places. Is it not true that moral truth operates more on a 'continuum' as regards the truth in certain situations? Do we not 'stretch the truth', tell 'white lies', or 'fibs,' when dealing with our children, friends, or partners? Can Kant's rigid distinction between moral and non-moral accommodate such flexibility? Kant's inflexibility results from the fact that he insists that categorical imperatives are unconditionally good and cannot be altered or qualified under any circumstances.

What, it may be asked, about other formulations of the categorical imperative? Are these not clearer guides to action? Kant gets much closer to expressing a viable definition of what morality is, or what its source is, which could answer the question 'Why be moral?', or 'What does it mean to be moral?' in one of the alternative formulations of the categorical imperative, the Formula of Humanity. This reads: 'Act in such a way that you always treat humanity, whether in your own person or in the person of any other, never merely as a means, but always at the same time as an end' (Kant, 1959: §429). This at least formulates an imperative with a moral message – to accord all human beings value, to treat them with dignity. This formula was not simply a consistency rule, as Hegel characterized the first formulation, for it 'presupposes that ... humans live' (McCumber, 2014: 164; see Hegel, 1942: §135).

What Kant clearly means by the Formula of Humanity relates to positing humans as worthy of equal respect and dignity as rational beings. Kant's principle is helpful only to the extent that it is not treated deontologically as a reformulation of the first and third principle (which Kant thought it was),[19] but as a general end that is justified within the finitude of the for-us on the grounds that all of humanity and indeed life are worthy of respect and dignity. This seminal idea underpins Kant's strong rejection of utilitarianism and its endorsement of pleasure or happiness as ethical goods that can motivate action. Yet, as important as they are, the principles of respect and dignity cannot help us in most instances decide which actions are right or wrong, or what to do in specific situations. We can also sense potential conflicts or contradictions where the principle of dignity, an end which we are to accord to all people, might conflict with the requirement, for example, to keep promises or not tell lies. In such situations, even if we were free to use the different formulations of the categorical imperative to check each other, it is not at all clear which should be regulative.

Revisions of Kant

Many authors insist that because Kant sees moral imperatives as unconditional, he allows no flexibility. Yet among his more recent commentators, one senses an attempt to revise this view of Kant. Allen W. Wood, for instance, presents a more nuanced if somewhat revisionist view. As he puts it:

> For Kant, a rational normative principle (or 'imperative') guiding our action is 'categorical' if its validity is not conditional on having set some end to which the action is to serve as a means. This does not entail, however, that the validity of rules which, *when they are valid*, are categorical imperatives, cannot be conditional upon particular circumstances, or that there cannot be grounds for making exceptions to a generally valid moral rule. (2005: 131)

Wood certainly has a point that if Kant's ethics permitted no flexibility to moral reasoning, it would be 'ridiculous'.[20] Yet many other commentators on Kant would appear not to notice where precisely Kant allows for such flexibility. According to Wood, in order to ascertain 'how often' such exceptions occur, we can also relate the universal imperative 'do not lie' to other formulations of the categorical imperative, viz. 'treat every rational being as an end in itself', in order to arrive at an assessment. Wood also notes how Kant treats '*exceptivae* (exceptions to moral rules) as one of the twelve fundamental categories of practical reason' (2005: 131; see Kant, 2004: 5, §66). In this respect, he observes that 'the twenty-odd "casuistical questions" that Kant raises about specific duties in the Doctrine of Virtue deal mainly with cases in which there may arguably be exceptions to rules that hold generally, though not universally' (2005: 131).

Wood's reappraisal of Kant certainly provides a richer picture than those who emphasize the first formulation at the expense of the later ones. And many of Hegel's criticisms have been dealt with in a rich literature, to which Wood (1990; 2005) himself, as well as Karl Ameriks (2000), Sally Sedgwick (2000a; 2000b; 2012), Barbara Herman (1993a; 1993b; 1993c; 2007a; 2007b), Christine Korsgaard (1996a; 1996b; 1996c; 1996d; 1996e), and

Hannah Ginsborg (2015) have all contributed. Korsgaard's *Sources of Normativity* (1996) revises Kant significantly to take on board many of the poststructuralist innovations and criticisms expressed over the last several decades, and Wittgenstein is appealed to substantially to rewrite matters with regard to language, the social nature of the self, and much else besides. Barbara Herman's account in *Moral Literacy* (2007) stimulated a considerable debate that did much to revise Kant away from a narrow concern with deontology to representing him as the theorist of practical rationality based upon norms. These readings of Kant 'after poststructuralism' have gone some way to correcting the matters that Hegel, Hamann, and others had raised over two centuries ago.[21] It is true, also, that Hegel's own criticisms, as McCumber (2014: 154) points out, were often inspired by Hegel's interest in building his own alternative system. It appears to me after reviewing criticisms of Kant, as well as the substantial work in Kant scholarship spoken of above, that the following criticisms, consistent with Foucault's general position, are still valid.

The metaphysically closed and didactic nature of universal moral obligations

Kant is highly critical of making exceptions to strict moral rules, and notwithstanding the attempts to revise him, this is how he is regularly, and understandably, interpreted. In terms of the traditional interpretation, Kant specifies universal categorical rules that apply in an invariant fashion in all times and places. This is because, for Kant, human nature is ahistorical and fixed for all time, and so is nature. While Wood's idea of 'triangulating' particular actions across the different formulations of the categorical imperative is appealing, Kant himself held that each formulation was meant to be a repetition of the same fundamental idea. If, however, when the SS guards appear at your door asking the whereabouts of the Jews you have hidden in your basement, you lie, thus breaking the imperative of the first formulation (which says in this instance, 'never lie') on the grounds of the second formulation (that to tell the truth would not be to treat the Jewish family as 'ends in themselves'), then this would certainly solve a problem in relation to seeing Kant as imposing inflexible unconditional rules. But this would introduce a whole assortment of new issues, for instance as to the status of the different formulations of the categorical imperative, which ones were to be 'regulative', and on what grounds they were to be regulative. Foucault certainly would not support the application of a 'univocal rule ... [as] all uniform, rational models arrive very quickly at paradoxes' (2000h: 378). Kant's system is no exception. It constitutes a universal rule type of morality which Foucault steadfastly opposed.

Kant neglects consequences and real-world structures and effects

In arguing for 'duty for duty's sake' against the prevailing utilitarian emphasis on happiness or pleasure as the ultimate principle guiding morality, Kant refuses to consider treating any ethical decision or action with reference to its consequences. The reason for obeying such commands is simply because it is the right thing to do, independent of the consequences. By doing so one abides by and respects the moral law that Kant held to be within the individual. One's actions must be motivated purely by their good intention, rather than serving our self-interest or desires. This inflexibly prioritizes the deontic dimension of ethics and presents no way of reconciling situations where principles of duty conflict.

It is of further related concern that structural and political features of the world do not come in for critical scrutiny in Kant's ethics. The concern is purely related to how individuals exercise their moral duties or obligations. The focus is *always and only* on *contradiction* (between individual maxim and universal law). There is also a presumption that the present arrangements of the world are just. This is a criticism made by Hegel (1942: §135). If a bank lends you money on the understanding that you will pay it back by a certain time, the Kantian moral is that such obligations must be honoured. What it does not question is whether the system of banking is just in the first place. Kant's concern is solely with the obligations of individuals. Universalization is Kant's method for establishing the content of the moral law *for individuals*. This effectively excludes matters to do with issues such as banking, or matters concerned with the structural and political organization of society in general. It accepts the world outside as a given and, in this sense, it does not consider whether contextual issues could alter individual obligations. There is no answer to the question in Kant regarding whether there are situations where it could be considered morally legitimate for individuals to steal. The issue of theft in fact reveals that Kant's moral theory presupposes not just an ideal world ('if everyone did that') but also a representation of *the present world idealized*. Hence, while prescribing that it is always wrong to steal (or lie, or break promises), it simultaneously implies the justness of existing property arrangements, rules of banking, usury, interest, and so on.[22]

Kant's conception of will is metaphysical and non-empirical

Kant fails adequately to define will. As John McCumber states, Kant's conception of the will appears as a 'mysteriously non-natural fact hanging in the transcendental air' (2014: 154). 'The various definitions he gives are loose, context relative, and even sloppy' (2014: 150). McCumber shows that in the attempt to define will, Kant shifts first to reason,[23] and then to principles, generating a case of '*obscurum per pariter obscurum*' (2014: 150). Hegel could charge Kant with 'bad idealism', says McCumber, for denying 'that experience, even of the "facts" of our own consciousness, is always infected with at least possible contingency' (2014: 151). Kant must deny that such contingency operates on humans on the ground that:

> this principle of morality ... on account of the universality of the law ... makes it the formal supreme determining ground of the will regardless of all subjective differences, [and] is declared by reason to be at the same time a law for all rational beings insofar as they have a will. (Kant, 1902: 5, §32, cited in McCumber, 2014: 151)

It further follows from this that Kant's theory of the individual subject's development and their action in the world is compromised by the metaphysical colonization of the subjectivity of the subject with respect to will. In such a conception, there could be no scope for a theory of development or maturity, as the individual is duty-bound to exercise reason in order to follow the moral law. The metaphysical basis of the will thus also means a metaphysically ahistorical and pre-social subject whose capacity for 'clear and distinct ideas' has been incorporated from Descartes without evidence or argument. Kant's account of the will is therefore universalistic and non-empirical. In focusing upon will it also short-circuits matters such as 'convictions', 'anxieties', or a broader conception of 'desires'.[24] It also places priority on the will as the determinant of ethics and morality, rather than on the particular object to be willed in terms of its significance for survival and well-being. Poststructuralist and Continental philosophers have long made a great deal of these criticisms of Kant's theory of the subject and will, largely because a social and historical conception of will would be eminently possible.

Kant's concern to 'transcendentalize' will is something that Foucault also questions. In his first lecture course at the Collège de France, *On the Will to Know*, presented between January and March 1971, Foucault introduces Nietzsche's criticisms of Kant as regards the will. Foucault asks: 'is it really reasonable to pick out the notion of will as central for an analysis of kinds of knowledge ... Is this not another way of once again reintroducing something like a sovereign subject?' (2013: 3). Foucault's view was that Kant builds in a metaphysical conception of the subject that has exaggerated powers for both reason and autonomy. In addition, Foucault would hold that Kant's insistence on the centrality of the will as the ontological grounding of reason encapsulates his overly formal and subjective approach to ethics and morality. Will encapsulates Kant's subjective and metaphysical view of morality as a purely self-imposed and individualistic imperative of duty.

Kant's moral theory is too formalistic and impositional, leaving a diminished sense of effective agency for the subject

Kant's moral laws may be premised on free will, but they constitute a code-type morality that is practically empty of content. As experience for the subject is universally legislated for by an all-determining moral law, there is little room for effective agency, notwithstanding the metaphysical freedom that Kant gives to the subject. This is to say that the concept of experience is not adequately theorized. For Kant, freedom is only freedom to comply or not comply with the moral law. Universalization tells us how to identify when to act on a maxim, but does not establish how and why we should so act upon it in the first place or in relation to variable situations. Why should I tell the truth to a murderer in any circumstances? What makes telling the truth at all times and places ethical? At best it constitutes a general sociological indication of what the consequences would be if everyone told lies or broke promises. So, in general, we can say that not telling lies is a good thing.

To pose questions like this is to debate the issue on Kant's own terms. It is also apparent that universalization is a passive, defensive, reactive, and overly individualistic approach to ethics. This is to say, while it provides an algorithm for the individual to screen proposed actions as moral or immoral, it doesn't prioritize an ordered list of social and political tasks or pay particular regard to the social, ecological, and political contexts in which people live. In this sense, Kant's moral system is too imperatival and overlooks what Nicolai Hartmann calls 'the fullness of life' (2007: 36). By this, Hartmann means that Kant overlooks emotional, sexual, aesthetic, spiritual, cultural, and political issues concerned with what sort of life one should live. As such, the categorical imperative is too limited to provide a satisfactory explanation of why or how one should act. How can Kant's rules determine which tasks I should work on first? Or work on at all? How can Kant's moral law assist in deciding 'what needs to be done?' Or in hierarchically ranking tasks or obligations in order of their importance at a particular time? In Kant's theory, also, the metaphysical weight on moral choices is distributed equally. Are the rules of engagement experienced by individuals in all times and places universal and constant? Is telling a lie of equal significance in all contexts and times? There is no recognition of variably weighted contexts where, say, not telling a lie might range from being 1) of the utmost importance and seriousness, to 2) being moderately important, to 3) being not important at all, to 4) being practically useful, to 5) being morally justified. What about a situation of multiple conflicting options or duties all of variable importance or significance? If for instance you are anguishing over whether you should stay and look after your ailing, elderly mother, or go and join the French resistance to fight the Germans, how will Kant's categorical imperatives help you decide? The political or social context is not figural in Kant's theory to establishing obligations. His categorical imperative thus has only limited practical relevance.

It was in relation to the issue of inflexibility that Nietzsche criticized Kant's system of categorical imperatives. For Nietzsche, Kant was constrained by a linear view of causation and the corresponding uniformity that he sought to impose on the world. As he said in *The Gay Science*: 'What! You admire the categorical imperative within you? This "firmness" of your so-called moral judgment? This "unconditioned" feeling that "here everyone must judge as I do"? Rather admire your selfishness at this point' (1974: §335). Nietzsche's more nominalist view was that no two situations or contexts were alike and that the very prospect of codifying maxims according to universal rules was doomed to failure. In Nietzsche's view, 'there neither are nor can be actions that are the same; that every action that has ever been done was done in an altogether unique way, and that this will be equally true of every future action'. Nietzsche concludes this aphorism by saying that while actions 'may lead to some semblance of sameness ... in any particular case the law of their mechanism is indemonstrable' (1974: §335).

Nietzsche took the view that as far as the individual was concerned, Kant had placed them in a metaphysical 'headlock', compounded by the fact that he had reintroduced ideas of 'God', 'immortality', 'soul', and 'freedom' in the *Critique of Practical Reason* which he had argued were indemonstrable in the *Critique of Pure Reason*.[25] Responding again to the term, 'categorical imperative', Nietzsche says:

> The term tickles my ear and makes me laugh ... It makes me think of old Kant who had obtained the 'thing in itself' by stealth – another very ridiculous thing! – and was punished for this when the 'categorical imperative' crept stealthily into his heart and led him astray – back to 'God', 'soul', 'freedom', and 'immortality', like a fox who loses his way and goes straight back into his cage. (1974: §335)

Life continuance restated

In *The Imperative of Responsibility* (1984), Hans Jonas claims that the altered character of human action in reference to a new relation between the local and the global, as well as the consequences of action at a distance, where what a person does in one place has consequences elsewhere, constitutes an imperative to reshape ethics beyond the Kantian system based upon subjective rules of universalization. Many of his formulations encapsulate the continuance perspective and are therefore useful for me to restate here. Ethical responsibility, he says, is only possible relative to an agent's knowledge and power with regard to their actions, that is, relative to their capacity to affect the outcome. Whereas Kantian ethics is individualistic and universalistic, continuance enables ethics to be applied both individually and collectively, as a normativity immanent in life oriented to the future. In this sense, contingency and institutionalization become important dimensions of ethics in a Foucauldian world. Normative reasons can be true or false in relation to these dimensions. While the future is always in an important sense ungraspable, conjectured, estimated, worried about, a subject of study, it is nevertheless the traversing of this always present yet somewhat opaque standard that anchors objectivity in relation to ethics, politics, morality, law, and the prescriptive sciences. While Jonas's view of ethics as needing to be reshaped to respond to new technologies has merit, it is also a question of challenging established ways of thinking, and established traditions in terms of which thinking takes place. The biosphere in general must now become our duty to protect, he says – humans, animals, vegetation, and the environment. Policing new technologies has become another core duty for human beings as part of this larger goal. There is a sense, too, in which we are all responsible for climate change now, whether we caused it or not.

Where Jonas is most insightful is in critiquing and reformulating Kant's categorical imperative. Kant had formulated it, says Jonas, so that 'action must be such that it can without self-contradiction be imagined as a general practice of that community' (1984: 11). He notes further with regard to Kant's categorical imperatives that 'the basic reflection on morals ... is not itself a moral but a logical one: The "I can will" or "I cannot will" expresses logical compatibility or incompatibility, not moral approbation or revulsion' (1984: 11). Instead of saying, 'Act so that you can will that maxim of your action that can be willed as a universal law', the new imperative must today become:

> 'Act so that the effects of your action are compatible with the permanence of genuine human life.' Or, expressed negatively: 'Act so that the effects of your action are not destructive of the future possibility of such life'; or simply: 'Do not compromise the conditions for an indefinite continuation of humanity on earth'. (1984: 11)

Jonas explains that 'the new imperative says precisely that we may risk our own life – but not that of humanity', for 'we do not have the right to choose, or even risk, nonexistence for future generations on account for a better life for the present one' (1984: 11). Also, Jonas's ethic stipulates that we have an obligation to the future, to what does not yet exist, and even to that which might never exist. By acting in accordance with the permanence of life, one acts in terms of the permanent continuation of life. His reformulated imperatives can also incorporate the possibility of a concordance principle: that when one acts one does not harm others, the world, or oneself. The imperative of responsibility addresses itself to public policy as well as individual conduct, whereas Kant's formulas were addressed solely to individuals. Indeed, as Jonas says, Kant's ethic was concerned with subjective intention (*Gesinnungsethik*) (1984: 12). In this sense, Kant's categorical imperative is simply a consistency rule. As Jonas puts it:

> Kant's categorical imperative was addressed to the individual, and its criterion was instantaneous. It enjoined each of us to consider what would happen *if* the *maxim* of my present action were made, or at this moment already were, the principle of a universal legislation; the self-consistency or consistency of such a *hypothetical* universalization is made the test for my *private choice* ... The new imperative invokes a different consistency: not that of the act with itself, but that of its eventual effects with the continuance of human agency in times to come. (1984: 12)

Jonas's point is that *real* consequences are not considered at all by Kant, which is to say that Kant's principle is one only of the subjective quality of my will, but not of objective responsibility or action in the world. In that Jonas's ethical theory is about keeping the welfare of all in mind whenever one acts, there is a major affinity with continuance ethics. Continuance as the basis for judgement takes account of context, situation, and contingency. This implies at the micro-level that each time I act in the world, I consult myself on how and in what sense my actions are consistent with the future of life on earth, and what effects they will have. In this, Kant's universalization rule can serve as a practical technique to aid judgement. So long as one accepts the limited role it can play, it can be incorporated within a broader approach to life continuance, as an informal, subservient, supplementary technique for gauging concordance in relation to particular actions.

Continuance is thus more practical than Kant's theory in that it can be regulative between deontic and consequentialist concerns in ethical decision making, adjudicating the relative importance of each in different situations. In this sense, continuance plays an impartial role as umpire between deontology and consequences. It must judge on a future that is always at best both uncertain and dangerous. Continuance to the future ontologizes the future as the new standard to render ethics normatively objective. Continuance in this sense provokes a reflective and deliberative process of assessment between the imperatives of survival and well-being for all, the present conjuncture of forces, and contemplated actions of individuals and collectivities, as well as the suitability and fairness of existing institutional arrangements. While actions that are held to contradict continuance are deemed unethical, the options and possibilities within continuance are multiple and varied. Unlike Kant's system, continuance ethics will enable both individuals and groups, non-governmental organizations and multinational corporations, governments and public institutions, to set 'continuance agendas' as well as prioritize issues of current concern. In this sense, despite the fact that continuance refers to a process without end rather than a fixed goal or purpose, it also constitutes a theory of good.

Continuance and the good

For Foucault, Kant founded the two great critical traditions between which modern philosophy has been divided. As James Miller notes, Foucault situates his own work within the critical tradition of Kant. The Kantian tradition, says Foucault, entails 'an analysis of the conditions under which certain relations of subject and object are formed and modified', and a demonstration of how such conditions 'are constitutive of a possible knowledge' (Foucault, 1970: 384, cited in Miller, 1994: 138). Continuance reinstates a conception of good where the good is understood in a constructivist sense as something practised and invented through collective work in history. It represents a shared interest and incorporates a weak sense of teleology as constituting a process without end. This is the sort of conception that Foucault advances in his interview with Michael Bess in 1980:

> What is good is something that comes through innovation. The Good does not exist ... in an a-temporal sky, with people who would be like Astrologers of the Good, whose job it is to determine what is the favorable nature of the stars. The good is defined by us, it is practiced, it is invented. And this is a collective work. (Foucault, 1988d: 13; 2016c: 138)

In this sense traditional conceptions of the right and the good can be redefined and the concepts repositioned to represent the poles of a system and parts, collective and individual, as conceptualized with the complexity perspective, and from a constructivist rather than a naturalist perspective. The dual theorization of macro and micro levels, or system and part(s), as well as the principle of non-reductionism, necessitates an understanding of shared supports to individual development. For the intertwined character of life dictates that the conditions for the development of *each* presupposes the maintenance of adequate conditions for the development of *all*. In this sense, the concepts of the right and the good can be utilized to denote these two poles in relation to the normative domain.[26] Regarding the relation between the right and the good, there is a strong argument to suggest that the good is necessary to the right if one is not to fall into contradiction. In an ontological sense, this is required if meanings and values are social and historical, as well as if there is a shared or collective dimension to personhood. It was in order to resolve conundrums that arise within deontological ethics that J. C. Ewing thought that 'Kant's deontological rule requires supplementation [by a conception of good]' (1953: 63).[27] This is because right and wrong presuppose a theory of good that defines what is right and what is wrong in order to establish their content. Importantly, as Ewing says, it will enable us to know how to resolve ethical conflicts when principles of duty conflict.

An earlier attempt at reconciling teleological and deontological ethics was made by the intuitionist moral philosopher David Ross, in *The Right and the Good*, initially published in 1930. Ross sought to find a compromise between deontological and teleological ethics by stressing the importance of consequences as determining the rightness of an action, while rejecting an exclusive emphasis on them. Further, he defended moral duties but rejected the absolute character of them as holding in all times and places. To this end, he introduced the idea of *'prima facie duty'* to 'signify an obligation that only holds subject to not being overridden by a superior obligation' (Ewing, 1953: 78). *Prima facie* duties covered situations where there might be a conflict of duties, or where the context or situation rendered what might normally be regarded as a duty perverse. An example might be telling a lie in order to protect the whereabouts of Jews being hunted by the Nazis. By acknowledging this, and 'relativizing' the notion of a duty in this way, Ross is, contra Kant, acknowledging the ultimate link between the right and the good or, in other words, the ultimate mutual dependence of the right and the good.

Right action in this model is not deprived of its deontic, rightful entitlement as a consequence of emergent individuation within the whole. Rightful action and conduct is characterized by time/space specificity, and the need for judgement in specific situations from a specific vantage point. As each person is emergent in the process of development, the constitution of identity (a precondition for right action) is also irreducible. In these senses, right action is also *not* defined as G. E. Moore defined right, as that which is 'productive of the greatest possible good' (1903: 147), nor is it defined as what maximizes aggregate welfare or happiness. The good of continuance is a norm that sets limits and boundaries. It is not being *aimed at or filled out*, but rather *conformed with*. It is the norm that expresses the conditions in terms of which life reproduces itself. Although in many instances, different actions will be classifiable in terms of their contribution to continuance, the nature of the continuance good, as a process without an end, does not detract from the emergent value of rightful conduct. The advantage of such a conception is significant in that, as noted by Ewing above, where duties, actions, or values conflict, it permits of reflective considered judgements in the interests of resolution. While this explanation may not overcome, as Cahal Daly has put it, the 'fear that belief in fixed moral standards will lead to fanaticism' (1996: 75), a fear that fuelled the rise of subjectivism in ethics, it does, from a Foucauldian point of view, more adequately and more accurately represent the changed nature of science and the world in the twenty-first century. It also puts paid to the clear sense in which the subjectivist view in ethics is not credible.

If the good must be retained to stop ethics from falling into contradiction, such a good is not to be understood in utilitarian terms, as privileging a value that prioritizes aggregate pleasure or happiness as the condition in terms of which the right of individual conduct is evaluated. Life continuance is not to be thought of as a quantitative value to be maximized but rather comprises a shared right to existence, as well as an end that varies contingently at different times and places, and that specifies no single ultimate value, such as pleasure or *eudaimonia*, to be maximized. This is the sense in which one does not get more of continuance; one conforms in terms of it; it functions, in other words, as a *regulative* norm. If we act on the provision that rights operate as important protections for individuals against the collective, and that duties or obligations cannot simply or easily be traded for the sake of supposed better consequences in the future, or some conception of the greater good, then we must reject theoretically the emphasis that utilitarianism has traditionally placed upon maximization. Neither maximization or 'the majority principle' are adequate to ground normative theory. Majority preferences are not relevant to defending minority religious rights, for instance. Rules of right are themselves sacrosanct for all because they ensure orderly conduct and fair play, that is, justice, without which the goods of stability and security, plus much else, would all collapse. They cannot be traded in any easy sense. Where there is conflict between the right and the good, resolution must proceed publicly, subject to due process in terms of law and democracy.

Compared to Bentham's 'felicific calculus', set out in his *Introduction to the Principles of Morals and Legislation* [1789], the means of calculating the value of an action is not the oversimplified method of his model of utility. Partly, the value of an action will be contingently related to time and place. In times of urgency, such as the present time of a global viral pandemic, when life continuance itself is threatened, the collective dimensions of selfhood will assume greater importance, and individual freedom will be constrained. In that the continuance calculus avoids the maximizing strategy, it also avoids the 'averaging' character of utilitarianism. Proof-bearing propositions and strategies, following complexity science, are those that are most likely to achieve success. This is to say, a society where people are treated justly is most likely to succeed. Agendas that respect the mutual dependence of each and all are more likely to succeed, at least in public policy terms. As regards the calculus of continuance, no actions or rules are prohibited unless they impede or are detrimental to continuance itself. Actions and rules that harm others, or harm oneself, or harm social structures, are prohibited or discouraged. To the extent that continuance operates as a form of political ethics and public morality, it will give a greater weight to outcomes and consequences than would be the case in respect of purely private moral matters. Having said this, as I will try to maintain in the later chapters of this study, it has general relevance in relation to ethics and morality as well. Its locus is both institutional and individual. Continuance is in this sense cognizant of consequences but not utilitarian. It values welfare, security, liberty and individuality, non-domination, as well as reasonable equality as constituting the conditions most likely to succeed for moving forward at this time in history. Except in times of crisis or urgency, rather than being concerned to promote the *best* policy, it seeks to establish limits and boundaries. Unlike utilitarianism, as Nagel says, '[where] the method of combination is basically majoritarian', and policy is enacted 'from a general point of view that combines those of *all* individuals', for the ethic of continuance, 'something is acceptable from a schematic point of view that represents in essentials the standpoint of each individual' (Nagel, 1978: 86). Thus, the specific standpoint of each individual or group from the contingency of their present situation constitutes a major departure from the universalizing tendencies of both utilitarianism and Kantianism.

While conflicts exist between the good and the right, they cannot be resolved as Kantians have tried to do by abolishing the idea of the good. A large number of liberal objections to the good are simply a method for establishing the exclusive legitimacy of a deontological moral framework. If the right presupposes the good, tensions and conflicts between them can only be resolvable through legal, political, and institutional processes, including norms of public scrutiny, transparency, and accountability. In political terms, conflicts between the right and the good, like the dangers of collective power, are resolvable when we recall that relations between the right and the good are political relations. This is to say that individual rights are ultimately protected through *legal machinery* and through *democratic mechanisms*. The central importance of democracy for Foucault dictates that this is the sort of resolution he would seek. Conflicts must be resolvable at the political level in terms of dispute-resolution mechanisms. Where there are conflicts between individual rights and collective ends, or between duties and consequences, these must be adjudicated through a publicly mandated institutional procedure in terms of public norms of transparency and accountability. In cases of personal morality, where one – say – breaks a promise to achieve a 'greater' good, this may be resolved by 'giving an account of oneself', to use Foucault's phrase (2011a: 161). In a complex society, structured by contingently varying conflicting situations, the possible types of conflict between rights and duties or rights and consequences will be infinite, not just in terms of content but also in terms of the application of principles. In this context, the good and the right must be justified in each situation. This requires institutionalization, including available legal aid.[28] In cases of conflict, depending upon the situation, one should be able to 'give an account of oneself', demonstrate veracity and sincerity, apologize, file a grievance, or take legal action. This is why a democratic culture is so important in a Foucauldian view of ethics, because democracy ensures that both individual and collective rights and entitlements can coexist, that one is not sacrificed on the altar of the other.

Importantly, in this sense, practical policy formulation proceeds according to the good, but nevertheless we can agree that individual actions must accord with those duties and obligations defined as right. This is because the right represents the rules of engagement that codify the way in which a good life is represented and operationalized for a multiplicity of projects that partake of it at a particular time. There is then a relation between the good and the right, but it is not helpful to attribute any categorical normative priority to one over the other. Rules of right represent the way the good life is operationalized and rendered available for all. In this sense, they regulate *process*, which establishes rules of engagement and action. It is in the public spheres of politics, law, and morality that the good and the right are accommodated, one to the other. Where individuals decide that the 'law is an ass' or 'morality is an ass', as might well happen in a complicated world, should they choose to disregard the right, they should be prepared to publicly demonstrate the legitimacy of their decision (i.e., they should keep the receipts!) It is collective publicly accountable authority, via democratic processes, law, and the institutions of personal integrity, that regulates the relation of right to the good, and ultimately saves us from the dangers that some see in 'aggregative', 'collective', or 'consequential' theorizing.

Conclusion

As it is assumed that all people will be in favour of the project of humanity being continued, that is, that life is worthwhile, this postulation of an immanent normativity meets the conditions of the unanimity rule. It may be the only postulation that can be unanimously agreed upon by all, but it is enough, as all other matters can in theory be resolved via a political process.[29] As it would be quickly decided that democracy offers the best chance of success at continuance, being the only method that would prevent 'a war of all against all', all others matters would be resolved via democratic processes. This would include the shape and character of the democratic process itself.

Such a good can also be justified as self-evident by philosophical analysis through reasoned argument, however. As von Wright tells us in *Norm and Action*, '[o]ne sense in which a norm can be said to be valid is that it *exists*' (1963: 195). The norm of life continuance can be validated empirically through reflection for humans and for all living beings. From tying one's shoelaces, to 'grasping' and 'sucking' reflexes that new infants manifest, beyond saying that it constitutes the background habitus to our lives far more than we ordinarily acknowledge or are possibly aware of, it is also so obviously true on serious reflection as to warrant further argument for such a thesis.[30]

From a Foucauldian standpoint, Kant seriously overstates the clear-headedness and moral autonomy of individual subjects, reminiscent more than anything of both the individualism and the arrogance of the early Enlightenment, a movement in which Kant was a major advocate and champion. If we adjust for metaphysics, Foucault would seem to give the subject more 'effective' freedom than does Kant. It is here that it is necessary to modify and reformulate Kant in certain important ways if he is to be resurrected for value today as we face a new and different horizon. First, the value to life is a value given by life to itself; as such, it applies to all living beings, not to all 'rational beings', and not just to humanity. We can charge Kant here with anthropocentrism, which doesn't merely entail that he confines his observations to human beings and ignores animals,[31] but, more importantly, that he locks this value that he recognizes into each and every individual human being rather than seeing it as a characteristic of *life itself*. Hence, the charge of anthropocentrism results in a further charge: that of individualism.[32] Kant's ethical obligations apply only to individuals. Furthermore, it is not the fact that human beings are rational, or that they are autonomous, that is significant; it is the value of life, that is, *the immanent value that life accords to itself*. The problem for ethics is that by encasing these qualities of autonomy and reason as synonyms for worth in each individual, rather than taking the issue of *value* as the challenge for life itself in both an individual and collective species sense, Kant is guilty of failing to see the distinction between *the value of life and human beings' own limitations.*[33]

Realizing all of this effectively reorients ethics and social inquiry in the direction of Nietzsche. Autonomy, which is locked in metaphysically by Kant, instantiated because rational beings are exempt from natural causal chains in the physical world, is largely a product of the model of causation that Kant applies to nature as a consequence of living in a Newtonian world. Human beings may be able to freely intervene in the material or physical or social worlds, but just because they are free in this way doesn't mean they should be defined as 'non-natural' or 'autonomous'. Humans are material beings who have freedom by virtue of the fact that they are living beings. To call this freedom 'autonomy' based on the existence of 'rationality' (the fact that human beings can think),[34] and lock it in metaphysically, is not simply confusing and misleading but means that no viable empirical theory of human beings' limitations, development, and action can develop. It is to ignore the fact that while human beings are problem-solving animals, their consciousness is also inhabited by the ghosts and phantoms of ages past, which has made the exercise of reason far more difficult than Kant foresaw.

It is the institutions in our already-made world that induct us into continuance norms. Practical guidance for action is decided according to reasons and considered convictions or judgements via the process of reflective equilibrium constituted as a democratic process of investigating pathways to the future and revising appropriate norms to guide action.[35] Judgements must be revisable, subject to challenge and appeal, and protective of *parrhēsia*, in a process that continues indefinitely. Normative claims are true or false because some things can be determined as being objectively better for life than others. While discovering the truth and falsity of normative claims is in some senses obvious, in many cases it will require ongoing research and deliberation to amass knowledge that may be at best uncertain. As Thomas Scanlon has suggested, 'we can discover normative truths ... simply by thinking ... in the right way' (2014: 70). Scanlon also advocates the method of reflective equilibrium as providing the best answer to establishing normative truths (2014: 71). In his view, the answers arrived at constitute 'considered judgments' (2014: 78). The issue is not only one of establishing the truths, but also of how we characterize normative processes in order to clarify which principles and modes of reasoning are valid and which are not. Such thinking reflectively and deliberatively generates both norms that regulate collectively, and reasons that frame action for individuals and groups in day-to-day life. Both guide policies and structure the field of the normative according to standards of correctness that are democratically mandated.

Scanlon is a social contract theorist, a tradition of political thought that in the twentieth century reformulated the social contract tradition of Hobbes, Locke, Rousseau, and Kant in order to reformulate moral and political philosophy.[36] Its most famous exponent was John Rawls, whose book *A Theory of Justice* was published in 1971. It became ascendant in the twentieth century in order to combat the influence of utilitarianism and intuitionism in moral and political philosophy. I will consider contract theory in Chapter 6, where it will emerge that a Foucauldian approach rejects contract theory, replacing it with a norms-based historical approach. Whereas contract theory presupposes the possibility of rational agreement by parties coming together and reasoning in an attempt to recreate the naturalism of their classical mentors, a norms-based approach is bottom up, in which principles of social and political organization are the evolutionary outcome of interaction and contestation in history. The norm becomes an emergent property of such interaction.

Foucault, on this view, would be a political realist despite his rejection of metaphysical truths. Norms emerge in history. The path of continuance is the one that reason dictates is the best for each and all, the path that would be followed if we were fully rational, if we could see the future clearly, and if we had the power to act in concert. The best chance of emulating such a model is via democratic deliberation and contestation, through which the advantages of collective over individual decision making can best be ensured. Through politics, the norm of continuance can with difficulty be detected, which can arbitrate good sense from folklore and ideology, and which can establish agreed moral and political objectives against the pressures of social consensus and the possibilities of error.

Notes

1. Kant says that 'the sort of knowledge here in question has somewhat of an everyday character' (2004: §114, 10). Rawls says, 'it is this conception, I believe, which best approximates our considered judgments of justice and constitutes the most appropriate moral basis for a democratic society' (1999: xviii).
2. The early history of the slogan is usually traced to Adam Smith's mentor, Francis Hutcheson, who first wrestled with its meaning. However, Bentham incorporated it within his own system, and it has become associated with his writings on utilitarianism.
3. See Parfit (2011a: 334, 286). Kant's categorical imperatives, as stated in the *Groundwork of the Metaphysics of Morals* are: FIRST FORMULA: The Formula of the Universal Law [FUL]: 'Act only on that maxim through which you can at the same time will that it should become a universal law' (1959: §421); The Formula of the Law of Nature [FLN]: 'Act as if the maxim of your action were to become by your will a universal law of nature' (1959: §421); SECOND FORMULA: The Formula of Humanity as End in Itself [FH]: 'Act in such a way that you always treat humanity, whether in your own person or in the person of any other, never merely as a means, but always at the same time as an end' (1959: §429); THIRD FORMULA: Formula of Autonomy [FA]: 'the idea of the will of every rational being as a will which makes universal law' (1959: §431) or 'Choose only in such a way that the maxims of your choice are also included as universal law in the same volition' (1959: §439). Formula of the Realm of Ends [FRE]: 'Act in accordance with the maxims of a universally legislative member of a merely possible realm of ends' (1959: §439).
4. Kant himself considered that such a rule lacked the sophistication of the formula of universalization. See Parfit (2011a: ch. 14) for a summary and discussion of Kant's view on the Golden Rule.
5. The view is that agnosticism is the only rational view, for if we cannot prove God's existence, we surely also cannot disprove it. Agnosticism also entails that we do not know what the concept of God could entail or be.
6. Another way to put this argument is that in the very wide chasm between intuitionism's metaphysical objectivism and subjectivism's hopeless retreat to desires and preferences, there is room (surely) for a 'this-worldly' conception of objectivity.

7 My view in this respect is no different to that of many in the history of philosophy (see Mill, 1998: esp. 133, 586). Mill thought that intuitionism functioned as a conduit for authoritarianism and prejudice and was used to justify the status quo. Among other early intuitionists were the Cambridge Platonists, such as Ralph Cudsworth (1617–88), Samuel Clarke (1675–1729), Francis Hutcheson (1694–1746), and later in the eighteenth and nineteenth centuries, Thomas Reid (1710–96), William Whewell (1794–1866), and William Hamilton (1788–1856). Mill directed his criticisms at Whewell especially.

8 In Britain, the phrase was 'I agree with Nick', referring to Nick Clegg, leader of the Liberal Democrats, who on becoming the audience 'favourite' in the 2010 election television debate attracted the surprising support of his political opponents, David Cameron and Gordon Brown. In order to share in the reflected audience approval, Cameron repeatedly used this phrase.

9 In saying this I am not saying that the issue could not or should not be more fully discussed than I am proposing to do here. To give the matter its due would require a serious digression from what this study is concerned with, and thus I am simply stipulating my position in full confidence that it could be argued successfully.

10 As life continuance premised upon survival does not constitute a metaphysics 'beyond experience', it avoids the possibilities of being considered as 'queer' in Mackie's sense. It is somewhat worrying that Mackie seems to define 'metaphysical' not as 'that which is beyond experience', but as everything that is not classifiable by natural science in terms of what is deemed to exist in the physical world. It is this that betrays the deeply ideological character of his analysis, with the implications that social realist concepts (discourse, ideology, etc.) are represented by Mackie as 'queer'.

11 Thomas Scanlon also rejects Mackie's argument that positing normative truths results in 'queer' metaphysical entities that are incompatible with science. Mackie's view was that objective values were 'metaphysically odd', 'utterly different from anything else in the universe' (Mackie, 1977: 38). Scanlon claims that 'Mackie's objection seems to be based on the view that all of our ontological commitments must be understood as claims about what exists in the physical world of space and time' (2014: 17). Scanlon's view is that 'this is an idea we should not accept ... accepting a scientific view of the natural world does not mean accepting the view that the only determinate truth values are statements about the natural world' (2014: 17, 18). Hage takes a similar view to Scanlon, claiming that Mackie's view that facts cannot depend

on standards or norms results from a 'misunderstanding [which] is essentially that of applying an ontologically realist stance to domains in which such is less suitable' (Hage, 2013: 81).
12 Although it might be argued that this form of non-metaphysical objectivism should not be classified as objectivism, the point to be made is that it is not obviously similar in form to prevailing models of subjectivism either. If someone were to argue that non-metaphysical views of value should all be classified as subjective, then it becomes an issue of inappropriate labelling.
13 Given that I subscribe to these attitudes, I would of course oppose John Stuart Mill, who argues in *On Liberty* that harming oneself should not be a matter for regulation. Hence Mill seeks to justify drug taking and other behaviours of a libertarian type (see Mill, 1956).
14 See Wood (2005: 139). For Kant's discussions of 'rational nature', see *Groundwork* (1959: 4, §§427–8).
15 Kant's actual words were: 'It is impossible to think of anything at all in the world, or indeed even beyond it, that could be considered good without limitation except a good will ... A good will is not good because of what it effects or accomplishes, because of its fitness to attain some proposed end, but only because of its volition, that is, it is good in itself' (Kant, 1902: 4, §§393, 394).
16 See also note 3 above.
17 See Parfit (2011a: 293) for a summary of views, including notable Kantian commentators such as Wood, Herman, and O'Neill (responsible for the phrases in quotation marks in the order quoted).
18 See Hegel (1942: §5) for his own historical account of will.
19 This point is made by the Cambridge philosopher A. C. Ewing (1953: 62).
20 Wood's actual words in referring to such views is that they are 'ridiculously fallacious' (2005: 131).
21 Only some way, alas. For all of these Kantian writers, it is true to say that 'autonomy' is still 'ring-fenced' and not seriously questioned in the Kantian system; morality is still conceptualized narrowly as deriving from *contradiction* (between maxims and universal laws), and context is still not adequately taken into account as a variable factor in differentially weighting ethical duties. In this sense, it can be argued that the inclusion of Wittgenstein, and shifts in language from 'duties' to 'norms', etc., are, in many senses, cosmetic, and oriented to making Kantianism *seem* more 'contemporary'.
22 I have summarized and presented my conclusions here from a lengthy literature. As McCumber (2014, 164–5) says, the point developed by

Hegel in *The Philosophy of Right* (§135) is the reason he criticizes Kant's first formula as 'empty', not because the first formula when universalized does nothing, but because it presupposes the given nature of the world, in this case the given system of deposits in banking. I have examined Wood (1990: 157), Korsgaard (1996e: 86–7, 95), and O'Hagan (1987) on this, in addition to McCumber (2014: 164–5), and my view is that Timothy O'Hagan has stated the issue in the clearest way when he says that 'The standard of non-contradiction [Kant's sole standard for morality] can be applied only when a given institution or practice (in this case private property) is presupposed ... The content for [Kant] is imported more or less accidently from a given social order' (1987: 140).

23 At the start of the *Groundwork*, Kant says that the will is nothing but practical reason. See Kant (1902: 4, §412, cited in McCumber, 2014: 149–50).

24 Convictions is a concept that might suggest a more empirical concept of reason, that is, in that ideas are *considered* within the contingency of the present; anxieties might suggest *fears related to others, or the future*; and desires might be given an empirical definition that *subverts reason*. None of these issues are adequately considered by Kant.

25 This is a point made by Kaufmann in his notes on this section, where he also agrees with Nietzsche that the 'doctrine of the categorical imperative, the core of Kant's ethics, is untenable' (Nietzsche, 1974: 264, n. 60).

26 This is made easier because the intuitionists, such as Ross, Ewing, and Prichard, didn't define the concept of the good at all – *on principle*; leaving it as a sort of empty 'place-filler', enabling me to overwrite content for it from an entirely different philosophical perspective.

27 Bhikhu Parekh also undermines the ability of Kant's universalization rule to stand on its own when he notes that 'it is possible to universalize and consistently will the principle that one should always tell the truth irrespective of its consequences. It is equally possible to will consistently that one should tell the truth unless it causes harm to others. Since the Kantian test is met by both, it does not tell us which one to opt for' (Parekh, 2005: 22).

28 The erosion of legal aid under policies of austerity in the UK over the past decade has significantly limited the capacity of citizens to redress rights grievances.

29 I claim here that with regard to life continuance, unanimity, or very near unanimity, would be possible to infer even if articulated in different ways.

30 This is not to say that it doesn't constitute or could not generate interesting research questions; indeed, the studies of the concept of *habitus* (Aristotle, Bourdieu) constitute a particular way of addressing such issues, as do studies of genetics, and the recent revival of epigenetic and neo-Lamarckian approaches (see Jablonka and Lamb, 2014).
31 For Kant, duties to animals are indirect in that they derive from the duty to respect the ends of humanity, comprising rational animals, i.e., humans.
32 Robert Pippin (2008: 124) says that Hegel identifies a concern with 'liberal individualism' as being central in his critique of Kant.
33 It is my view that in seeing 'reason' and 'autonomy' as the grounds for normativity, Kant is committing the 'naturalistic fallacy' in one sense that Moore (1903) defines it. This is in the sense that reasoning from initial premises by logical deduction will not arrive at normative conclusions unless normative propositions are embodied in the premises. As reasoning is a procedural or methodological process, reasoning alone will not arrive at normative conclusions.
34 Many animal species can 'think' in the sense they can 'problem-solve', some utilizing what appear to be sophisticated strategies. The fact that humans are clearly superior to other species in this regard gives us no indication of the extent to which our reason is limited. This would appear to be a consequence of our finitude. It is not falsifiable in theory.
35 Rawls's method is a coherence theory that starts by identifying initial inputs about a subject and then accounting for them in an ongoing process of revision to form 'considered judgments' with the aim of achieving convergence. As Hage defines it, it entails 'some uncritical input which is then rationally reconstructed into a coherent whole' (2013: 101). Linked to democracy, such a process may be extended to incorporate checks and balances, including independent research, triangulation, knowledge, peer review, and so on.
36 Not all of the modern social contract theorists are uniformly influenced by Kant, Locke, and Rousseau in the same way. John Harsanyi (1953; 1976), usually considered a social contract theorist, remained utilitarian in important respects. Others in the tradition included Brian Barry (1965; 1989), James Buchanan and Gordon Tullock (1962), David Gauthier (1963; 1969), and Russell Grice (1967; 1977) (see Weale, 2020). Scanlon (1978; 1982; 1998; 2014) and Rawls (1971; 1980; 1999a; 1999b) were much more Kantian.

5

Foucault, Hegel, Marx

Foucault's critique of Marx and Hegel

Foucault stood steadfastly opposed to Marxist or Hegelian conceptions of politics. While he manifested strong ideals of justice and equality, his strong antipathy to Hegel meant that Marx's Hegelian view of history and method could not be countenanced. I have outlined Foucault's orientations to Marxism in other writings, so let me here only add some more recent material and thoughts, in as much as they are relevant for the issue of ethics and normativity. The first thing to say is that Foucault's opposition to Hegel and Marx can be seen to reflect his opposition to their teleological and monistic approach to history.

Just a word about Foucault's reading of Hegel, and my own reading of Hegel, to start. Foucault's reading of Hegel would not concur with the 'social reading' presented by commentators such as Charles Taylor (1977; 1979), which, as Yirmiyahu Yovel states, 'separates Hegel's more fruitful political theory from his less fruitful ontology' (2005: 2).[1] One has become accustomed to reading accounts of Hegel in the last several decades that seek to de-emphasize or overlook the unacceptable metaphysics and essentially rewrite Hegel in a form palatable for contemporary audiences. Charles Taylor has done this, offering an approach not dissimilar to and building upon Foucault's own social-historical conception of the subject, which Taylor had already studied (Taylor, 1984). These approaches that seek to resurrect Hegel, recruiting him as an unacknowledged ally to religious crusades, no matter how appealingly stated, should not be permitted to succeed. Foucault would claim that Hegel's politics cannot be separated from his metaphysics. For Foucault, Hegel is the philosopher of absolute knowledge, of closure, of the finitude of reason, of totality, and with a Cartesian theory of the subject. Foucault would situate Hegel as a post-Kantian, in the sense that Hegel sought to correct and go beyond Kant, to overcome Kant's limitations to the subject's consciousness with his conception of absolute idealism, but Hegel would not be credited with having succeeded.[2]

In Hegel, the whole dominates the parts, because, as Canguilhem observes, 'it is the whole which creates the relation among its parts, so that without the whole there are no parts' (1994: 301). In this conception, as Canguilhem acknowledges, the whole maintained ontological precedence to the parts; the whole is dominant. As Hegel famously asserts in the Preface to *The Phenomenology of Spirit*, 'the truth is the whole' (1977: 11).[3] In contrast to Hegel, Foucault's approach to history was both nominalistic and empirical, a basis on which he rejected Hegel's type of holistic approach whereby the meaning of specific events, or of the present, was interpreted within an all-encompassing whole, including past, present, and future.

There is a sense in which Foucault's critique of Marx and Hegel has similarities to those offered in Anglo-American philosophy by Popper and others (Popper, 1945; 1961; 1992). To compare Foucault's conception of Marx with regard to his manner of researching history with the view presented by Arthur C. Danto is informative. Danto maintains that Marx's way of doing history is 'theological', or 'that it has structural features in common with theological readings of history, which is seen *in toto*, as bearing out some divine plan' (1965: 9). As Danto continues: 'It is ... instructive to recognise that Marx and Engels, although they were materialists and explicit atheists, were nevertheless inclined to regard history through essentially theological spectacles, as though they could perceive a divine plan, but not a divine being whose plan it was' (1965: 9). Foucault's thesis on the subject of Marxism and totalitarianism was more directly focused on what was precisely at stake here: Hegel's conception of totality, truth, and the subject. Foucault's analysis in the *Archaeology of Knowledge* is clearly aimed at Marx and Hegel as philosophers who totalize history and who represent the state as a legitimate organ of domination and truth. For Hegel, it was dialectics that led to this totalization through the reconciliation of opposites by which all contradictions were overcome. Hegel had rejected the intuitionism of Fichte, Schelling, and Hölderlin, developing his thesis of the acquisition of knowledge through dialectical progression in history.[4] But the hidden and unacknowledged ghosts behind the scene were undoubtedly Newton, or perhaps all those who contributed to the deterministic, linear view of history as a closed mechanical system, which propelled evolutionism as the fashionable grid for analysis; and Kant and Descartes, for tying the subject to a founding conception. Hegel sought to account for mind as the outcome of a dialectical synthesis culminating in the Absolute. For Marx, it was the history of class struggles that achieved the same dialectical synthesis resulting in the communist utopia. These thinkers believed in 'final solutions', 'revolutionary goals and strategies', 'the march of history', 'dialectical progression', and identified power as emanating from a central agency in the state. Foucault agreed with Glucksmann's assessment that, influenced by thinkers such as Marx and Hegel, '[t]he Europe of states seeks to exclude the marginal' (Glucksmann, 1977: 119).

The notion of totality is important here if one is to understand Foucault's relation to Hegel. As I have already presented this in previous work (Olssen, 1999; 2006), I will be brief. Foucault's scepticism towards the idea of totality is developed forcefully in the introduction to *The Archaeology of Knowledge*, where he distinguishes between 'total history', which he opposes, and 'general history', which characterizes his own pluralist methodological approach; an approach that, he says, 'speaks of series, divisions, limits, differences of level, shifts, chronological specificities, particular forms of rehandling, possible types of relation' (1972: 10). The idea of society as an organic totality or whole had been an animating spiritual principle from ancient Greece through to the middle ages. The whole pertained to both the spiritual and physical order. Leibniz (1646–1716) had characterized society as a 'pre-established harmony' in his *Monadology*, based on the concept of the continuum; that the differences between things were differences of degree and were interconnected to the extent that 'each simple substance has relations and expresses all the others, and consequently ... is a perpetual living mirror of the universe' (Leibniz, 2008: §78). At the start of the nineteenth century Hegel witnessed modernity as ravaged by crisis, division (*Entzweiung*), diremption (*Trennung*), and social atomism, effected by the rising bourgeois order, and the question he sought to answer was: how is it possible to salvage the idea of unity given such a situation? The question was important for Hegel as he appreciated that human beings are in most respects products of their environment, and a fragmented society (*Bildung*) would mean a fragmented subject, pertaining both to the individual and to community.

Hegel's answer, which is also important for understanding Marx, was to historicize the notion. He sought to preserve the idea of a closed totality against the fragmenting forces of modernism by historicizing it and injecting it with an overarching spiritual significance in relation to progressive development. Influenced by the experience of the French Revolution, as well as the philosophies of Jean-Jacques Rousseau[5] and Sir James Steuart,[6] Hegel claimed to detect a suprahistorical process of reason whereby such disintegrations were reconciled, preserving the unity of totality overall. Foucault comments in *The Hermeneutics of the Subject* that Hegel was characteristic of much of nineteenth-century thought (Schelling, Schopenhauer, Nietzsche, Husserl, and Heidegger) in linking knowledge to spirituality (Foucault, 2005: 28). John Grumley makes the point that this spiritual principle in important senses supersedes Kant, and provides the major mechanism for preserving unity.[7] As Grumley puts it, 'Hegel's surprising shift from Kant to Jesus in "The Spirit of Christianity" represents a final rejection of Kantian moral asceticism' (1989: 18). Society could maintain itself and prosper notwithstanding fragmentary forces of division and diremption through processes of reconciliation and regeneration built into life itself. To use Grumley's metaphor, just as the body repairs itself from the conditions of disease and injury, achieving integration back to health over time, so too can the economy and society. Hegel's instances of violence and division are represented as but 'moments' in a larger dialectical process of reconciliation and adjustment whereby the totality reintegrates itself at a higher spiritual level of development. For Hegel, such a process was both sociological, historical, and metaphysical, and applied to the individual, the community, and society. The ravages of the rising bourgeois world were transcendable, preserving unity as a progressive, developmental, spiritual process, culminating in the Absolute, perfect knowledge, or God. It is fundamentally this spiritual/teleological principle that Foucault finds objectionable and that is central to his own anti-totalizing perspective. Closely linked to this is his rejection of dialectical method as a suprahistorical conception in terms of which historical change is schematically interpreted. As Foucault told Alessandro Fontana and Pasquale Pasquino, dialectic constitutes 'a way of evading the always open and hazardous reality of conflict by reducing it to a Hegelian skeleton' (Foucault, 1980e: 114–15).

Foucault's position on Marxism receives clear expression in his review of Glucksmann's *Les Maîtres Penseurs* in *Le Nouvel Observateur* in 1977, where he endorses Glucksmann's 'new philosophy' (Foucault, 1977b: 84–6),[8] offering a reciprocation of Glucksmann's positive endorsement of Foucault's thesis, and his earlier suggestion that political theory should take a 'Foucauldian turn' (Glucksmann, 1975: 17). Foucault's endorsement of Glucksmann's book signalled a number of important political and philosophical dimensions, even if only developed in embryonic form: first, a consistent anti-totalitarianism as an essential feature of his own philosophical pluralism; second, a disillusionment with 1968 and post-1968 revolutionary politics as potentially totalitarian; and third, a chance to crystallize his rejection of Marxism, Marxism-Leninism, Stalinism, and Maoism as political movements. Glucksmann had in *Les Maîtres Penseurs* analysed Alexander Solzhenitsyn's *Gulag Archipelago* as representing the culmination of Marxist historical dialectical development, ending up in the residues of totalitarian politics as expressed in the camps of Siberia, genocide and, by extension, Nazism. As Foucault wrote in his review of *Les Maîtres Penseurs*:

> Stalinism was the truth, 'rather' naked, admittedly, of an entire political discourse which was that of Marx and of other thinkers before him. With the Gulag, one sees not the consequences of an unfortunate error but the effect of the most 'true' theories in the order of politics. Those who hoped to save themselves by opposing Marx's real beard to Stalin's false nose are wasting their time. (1977b: 84)

Jean Hyppolite's Hegel

Foucault, for his part, found sustenance in the anti-statist and pluralist discourses that characterized his own early works, focusing instead on the 'micro powers' and 'disciplines' that underpinned the state and were prior to it. The relation to Hegel and Marx is central to understanding Foucault's methodology as well as his project as a whole. In a way, Foucault's entire approach reflects a conversation with Hegel. In his book, *Thinking the Impossible: French Philosophy Since 1960* (2011), Gary Gutting points out the central role of Hegel as the figure to whom French philosophy for much of the twentieth century has responded. Gutting makes the point that 'Foucault first came to full philosophical life when he encountered Jean Hyppolite'. Hyppolite taught a course on Hegel's *Phenomenology of Spirit* at the Lycée Henri IV, where Foucault underwent his preparation for his entrance to the École Normale Supérieure (Gutting, 2011: 13). Hyppolite was sympathetic to certain aspects of Hegel's philosophy, but at the same time highly critical of what he regarded as Hegel's 'system'. As he says in his book, *Studies in Marx and Hegel* of 1955, 'in that system the individual thinker and the historical individual disappeared. They were vanishing moments in a monumental history which represented the progressive realization of the Absolute' (Hyppolite, 1968: v).

In emphasizing the historical character of Hegel's philosophy, Hyppolite presented a quite different analysis to that of another interpreter of Hegel in France, Alexander Kojève. Kojève placed emphasis on the master–slave dialectic, focusing attention on the role of 'man' in the historical process. He was influential in the development of Jean-Paul Sartre's version of existential Marxism (see Poster, 1975: ch. 1). Hyppolite's more historical focus led him to find an important place for Nietzsche as interlocutor and critical voice by which the difficulties in Hegel's philosophy could be opened for examination. There is an important sense in which he sides with Nietzsche in opposing Hegel, or at least modifies Hegel in a Nietzschean direction, in order to move away from existentialist readings of Hegel's work. As Arkady Plotnitsky notes, '[Nietzsche's] idea of the

Dionysian is pivotal for the *Phenomenology*, which makes the book Nietzschean or makes some of Nietzsche's ideas Hegelian ... The contours of an artistic – Dionysian and Nietzschean – philosophy of the future emerge here – a more Nietzschean Hegel, a more Hegelian Nietzsche' (1996: xiii). Plotnitsky quotes Hyppolite in the English translation to his *Introduction to Hegel's Philosophy of History* to say that 'the notion of the [historical] spirit of the people and the tragic vision of the world ... [are] in the center of Hegelian thought' (cited in Plotnitsky, 1996: xiv). The aspects of Hegel that Hyppolite questions are the senses in which Hegel seeks to integrate all phenomenological experience, that experience of the 'unhappy' and 'partial consciousness', as but moments in a progressive realization of spirit's development through the historical process of dialectical synthesis, ultimately to a full unity in God (see Hegel, 1977; see also Hegel, 1953; 1956; 1975).

With respect to his understanding of Hegel, Foucault acknowledges in 'The Discourse on Language' that '[a] large part of [my] indebtedness ... is to Jean Hyppolite' (1972: 235). Unlike Hyppolite, however, Foucault felt little obligation to resurrect Hegel's system. His own predilection was more in accord with Georges Bataille's adage that 'knowledge is access to the unknown' (Bataille, 1980: 101). Although opposed to Hegel in this sense, influenced by Hyppolite's reading of Hegel, Foucault came to appreciate elements in Hegel's philosophy that could not easily be discarded. These include Hegel's focus on history and time, as well as his focus on historicity, language, and interpretation, rather than on mind. Especially important here was Hyppolite's later book on Hegel, *Logic and Existence* (1953), which, as Gutting tells us, 'moves more decisively away from the existentialists' anthropological reading and gives central place to language rather than human consciousness' (2011: 28). Existentialists such as Sartre and Marcel, atheist and religious in turn, both emphasized the unity of man, who was the foundation and starting point for analysis. Foucault shared both Hyppolite's and Althusser's concern to move away from the anthropological reading of the existentialists who emphasized human consciousness, moving instead towards a position where all experience is necessarily mediated by conceptual structures or discourses. If consciousness and mind are socially and historically constituted, then consciousness and lived experience themselves become subordinate to language and discourse. Hyppolite showed the path, says Foucault, 'by which one can get away from Hegel' (1972: 235). As Foucault states: '[f]or him the relation to Hegel was the site of an experiment, a confrontation from which he was never sure that philosophy would emerge victorious. He did not use the Hegelian system as a reassuring universe; he saw in it the extreme risk taken by philosophy' (1972: 235). According to Plotnitsky, 'the scene' of this 'great experiment' was 'a philosophy of the future, a philosophy for new stages of life and spirit' (1996: x). Foucault clearly credits Hyppolite, in the same way as Plotnitsky does in his foreword to Hyppolite's *Introduction to Hegel's Philosophy of History*, as presenting a Nietzschean reading of Hegel (Plotnitsky, 1996: xii). Hyppolite concludes his thesis with the observation that '[t]here exists in [Hegel's] thought an ambiguity. That ambiguity is that the reconciliation of subjective spirit and objective spirit, the supreme synthesis of this system, is perhaps not completely realizable' (1996: 72).

Hyppolite's reading of Hegel is represented by Foucault as being deeply sceptical and sets Foucault on a trajectory that takes him outside of the Hegelian system altogether, while retaining some aspects of it. Foucault certainly sees Hyppolite, if not as modifying Hegel in the direction of Nietzsche, then certainly as allowing Foucault to do so. As he says, '[i]nstead of conceiving philosophy as the totality at least capable of thinking itself and grasping itself in the movement of the concept, Jean Hyppolite made it into a task without end set against an infinite horizon' (1972: 236). It is, continues Foucault:

> [a] task without end and consequently a task forever recommenced ... the inaccessible thought of the totality was for Jean Hyppolite the most repeatable thing in the extreme irregularity of experience ... He transformed the Hegelian theme of closure on to the consciousness of self into a theme of repetitive interrogation. (1972: 236)

Notwithstanding this, certain aspects of Hegel – the interest in historicity, mediation, language, culture, and history – are retained while being adapted. Foucault was no doubt also aware of a certain non-foundationalism suggested by Hegel, especially concerning notions such as truth, knowledge, ethics, culture, and community, which could be retained while avoiding Hegel's overarching metaphysical system.[9]

Influenced by Louis Althusser, Foucault saw Hegel's concept of consciousness as contributing to an overly humanistic conception of the subject. Like Foucault, Althusser's writing is very much an effort to escape the influence of Hegel. Most noteworthy for his attack on humanism, Althusser drew parallels between his own anti-humanism and his criticisms of Hegel, in that Hegel, like the early Marx, had an essentialized conception of human beings ('consciousness', 'human freedom') at the base of his philosophy. In his book, *For Marx*, Althusser (1969: 227) attacks anthropological readings of Hegel. Central to his argument was that prior to 1845, Marx had contributed to humanism because he had followed Hegel. The year 1845 is seen as marking an 'epistemological break', after which the figure of man is displaced in preference of an anti-humanist emphasis on scientific practice. Both Foucault and Althusser maintained a view that the subject is not pre-given but constituted through practices. Having studied philosophy with Althusser at the École Normale Supérieure and having struck up a friendship with him in the late 1940s (see Macey, 1993: 25), Foucault accepted Althusser's lesson against the philosophy of consciousness and for a philosophy of the concept. He also rejected the central implication from structuralism that language or thought constituted a transparent representation of an objective reality. Rather, Foucault accepted the constructive role of language and concepts in shaping the world, a role that will become important for developing an ethics. The categories of thinking are not self-evident on the basis of reason, as Kant had posited with his conception of the transcendental subject, and as had been at the heart of Western philosophy since Descartes. Like Althusser, too, Foucault accepted that the freedom or interiority of the subject is not totally penetrated or eclipsed by dominant ideology. Rather, it was a question of how the subject could effectively deploy power through tactics and strategies to forge a path beyond the present.

Beyond this, Foucault was circumspect as to what he did and did not accept from Althusser, especially concerning the subject of Marxism. In an interview conducted by Alessandro Fontana and

Pasquale Pasquino in June 1976, Foucault reveals an uneasiness about the French Communist Party (PCF) and the restrictions it imposed:

> I wonder nevertheless whether among the intellectuals in or close to the PCF there wasn't a refusal to pose the problem of internment, of the political use of psychiatry and, in a more general sense, of the disciplinary grid of society. No doubt little was then known in 1955–60 of the real extent of the gulag ... it was a danger zone marked by warning signs. (1980e: 110–11)

Foucault's vision of the future was that there was no utopian ideal such as a communist society to be realized, but only a future that relied upon forces already present and active in the existing conjuncture of social and political relations. David Macey cites a comment made by Althusser on Foucault that 'even the meanings he gives to formulations he has borrowed from me are transformed into another, quite different meaning than my own' (cited in Macey, 1993: 196–7). Having studied separately with both Hyppolite and Althusser, it can be accepted that Foucault was very aware of how and in what senses his own philosophy departs from Hegel's.

Teleology

Central to what Foucault opposed in both Hegel and Marx was a conception of history which was teleological, which saw history as having inherent natural ends and purposes, and moving via the dialectic through successive stages towards those ends. Such a conception of teleology was rejected at the Enlightenment when science sought to explain nature mechanically (in terms of basic postulates such as size, matter, shape, and motion) without appeal to inherent ends or purposes. This notion in Marx and Hegel gave them an affinity with Aristotle's conception of teleology as a theory of final causes based on essentialist naturalism. It also implied a 'closed' Newtonian universe. This was the universe of both Hegel and Marx. As Alexander Koyré notes, while the doctrine of teleology described a universe that was finite and hierarchically ordered, the change in conception from a closed universe to one that is *open*, *indefinite*, and *infinite* alters the equation concerning how teleology ought to be configured. With the Enlightenment, this shift implied a rejection from science of all elements based on:

> value, perfection, harmony, meaning, and aim, because these concepts, from now on *merely subjective*, cannot have a place in the new ontology ... Or to put it in different words: all formal and final causes as modes of explanation disappear from – or are rejected by – the new science and are replaced by efficient and even material ones. Only the latter have the right of way and are admitted to existence in the new universe of hypostatized geometry. (Koyré 1965: 7–8)

While major figures such as Bacon (1561–1626), Descartes (1596–1650), and Spinoza (1632–77) embraced the rejection of final causes, as Monte Ransome Johnson points out, they did not reject this 'without qualification' (2005: 25).[10] In addition, says Johnson, 'later prominent scientific revolutionaries, such as Gassendi (1592–1655), Boyle (1627–91), Newton (1642–1727), and Leibniz (1646–1716) actively countenanced final causes, even in the context of natural science' (2005: 25). Many of these figures felt that the early modernists had been too radical and that it was not possible to reject final causes, or at least conform in all respects to mechanical method with respect to intentional agency, even if it was possible to conform to mechanism where nature and non-intentional agency was involved. Complexity science has moderated the importance of mechanism, supplementing it with emergent holistic types of analysis characteristic of non-equilibrium physics, implying a shift, as Ilya Prigogine puts it, 'from "being" to "becoming"' as a consequence of the effects of time irreversibility on 'the dynamics of large systems, thermodynamic systems and fields' (2003: 39). For Prigogine, '[t]he inclusion of "irreversibility" changes our views of nature. The future is no longer given. Our world is a world of continuous "construction", ruled by probabilistic laws and no longer a kind of automation' (2003: 39). It is to this conception, of a universe that is radically open, that is characterized by becoming, that thinkers such as Nietzsche, Foucault, and Deleuze subscribe.

While such a position rejects strong teleology, it is by no means clear that it dispenses with all aspects of teleological thinking. In her book *The Virtue Ethics of Hume and Nietzsche*, Christine Swanton claims that Nietzsche avoided commitment to what she calls 'strong teleology' of the Aristotelian sort (2015: 196), but still posits 'ends' and 'goals' in a different form. For Nietzsche, she claims, there is 'no telos proper to human beings qua human – rather we create ourselves in an ongoing process' (2015: 196). Swanton cites Simon May who says, 'for Nietzsche, unlike Aristotle, the perfect and final actualization of a clear and fixed potential is neither possible nor knowable nor should be sought' (1999: 109, cited in Swanton 2015: 197). She also cites Alexander Nehemas who asserts much the same thesis, saying that 'becoming does not aim at a final state' (2001: 261, cited in Swanton 2015: 197). This 'weaker' sense of teleology eschews conceptions of 'natural purposes', 'natural essences', 'inner forces', 'ideals of perfection', and allows for a conception of ends as an open-ended process that applies only to living beings and that is wholly compatible with science. The point of discussing teleology in this way here is that if Foucault is to be fitted out with a normative architecture of life continuance, a weaker sense of teleology that recognizes ends, goals, and purposes must also avoid positing occult or religious categories, entelechies or vital spirits, appeals to intelligent design, innate purposes, perfection, or incompatibility with science. If the concept of life continuance is open to criticism as marking a retreat to an unacceptable conception of already discredited teleological thinking, a form of thinking that Foucault himself opposed, then, by extension, any attempt to rehabilitate a normative conception of life continuance on this basis will also founder. As continuance posits only ends and goals that are those of life itself and that can realize themselves variously in an open field of possibilities, the notion of teleology adopted concerns action oriented towards ends.[11] Such goals and ends are constructed rather than natural. As such, there is no conflict with the guiding postulates of complexity science.

Accepting a weak form of teleology as positing a constructed end in an open and endless process also underpins at an ontological level the reinstatement of the good, which we saw in the last chapter was important to ethics and normativity, in that it recognizes the social and historical souces of value or normativity, and resolves the contradiction that deontology results in if it seeks to account for ethics alone. It is the *re-*inclusion of a form of teleological thinking that makes the reinstatement of the concept of good possible. This has been suggested by the German philosopher Otfried Höffe, who maintains that 'teleological and deontological ethics don't have to exclude each other' (2010: 270), with the important consequence that the good can be reinstated alongside the right. As Höffe continues:

> [A] primarily deontological ethics allows only for action-internal reflection, whereas a far-reaching teleological ethic also allows for action-external reflection over consequences ... ethics is more meaningfully, even necessarily, deontological in its foundation; and in contrast, ethics is teleological with respect to the 'application' of principles to certain regions of life and concrete situations. (2010: 270)

As argued in Chapter 4, the good of continuance can be regulative between rights and consequences, as well as with regard to conflicting duties, requiring judgements in specific situations. Such a good need not be seen, as in the classical era, as emanating from a teleology of nature, but rather as shared or collective ends as they expand or contract in different historical times. Joseph Schumpeter advanced this sort of view in *Capitalism, Socialism, and Democracy* (1943). According to Schumpeter, while we must reject the classical conception of good of old, in that it builds natural purposes into nature, there is nothing to 'debar us from trying to build up another and more realistic one' (1976: 252–3). Despite his antagonism towards the classical doctrine of good, Schumpeter sees nothing amiss with representing aggregate human interests in history as common collective interests, by which he means 'not a genuine, but a manufactured will. And often this artifact is all that in reality corresponds to the *volonté géneralé* of the classical doctrine' (1976: 263). Schumpeter continues: '[s]o far as this is so, the will of the people is the product and not the motive power of the political process' (1976: 263). As a conception of shared interests, the good of life continuance becomes realizable on this basis.

Based upon a complexity model, Foucault's vision of history enables a resolution of a core criticism of idealist philosophy by classical liberals. This concerns the overemphasis on unity, as expressed in the 'doctrine of harmony' between the state and the citizen. This was a consequence of the fact that, in Hegelian philosophy, the whole determined the character of the parts, resulting in uniformity. Liberals criticized the idealists for positing the person as a citizen who existed only as a public being in the shadow of the state (government + civil society = state) and was 'imprisoned by its own creation' (Seth, 1897: 291). Both German and Oxford Idealism posited as essential the unity between the individual and society. As James Seth explains it:

> So perfect was the harmony between the individual and the State, that any dissociation of the one from the other contradicted the individuals' conception of ethical completeness. It is to this sense of perfect harmony, this deep and satisfying conviction that the State is the true and sufficient ethical environment of the individual, that we owe the Greek conception of the ethical conception of the State. (1897: 282)

Foucault's model of the social system, through its emphasis on the reciprocal interaction of part(s) and whole, added to the postulates of openness and irreversibility, introduces a new nominalist conception of iteration where the future does not simply repeat the past but where repetition or reproduction of structures and identities over time both reproduces and also simultaneously individuates or differentiates their different elements in relation to the whole.[12] In this way, harmony or uniformity is theorized in terms whereby uniqueness and difference are simultaneously enacted. Repetition is characterized by difference and the future is marked by uncertainty and rupture. There is an irreducible dependence of the individual on the social and the general, yet also an infinite individuation and differentiation of each element within the whole. One consequence of this explains how the individual subject can be both historically and socially constituted, yet unique and separate. While each subject lacks an essence or substance (*ousia*) in Aristotle's sense, (de)ontological uniqueness is constituted in terms of differential effects of environment in relation to the different locations in space/time and through the differential effects on actions exacted as a consequence of time irreversibility. Every time an individual acts, they both reproduce the past and differentiate themselves in terms of it. Such a model of the self means that the issue of the separability of persons is assured.

The politics of recognition

In seeking to distance himself from Hegel, Foucault's conception also stood opposed to viewing ethical comportment in terms of Hegel's concept of recognition. Ethical comportment for Foucault was more related to actual inequalities and disturbances in power than to mere problems of recognition. This issue attests to Foucault's realism in the sense that ethics must be concerned with *practices* and *power* and 'not simply ... the proliferation of false or demeaning images of various people and groups' (Markell, 2003: 5). In his book *Bound by Recognition*, Patchen Markell points out that the concept of recognition was initially employed by Hegel in *The Phenomenology of Spirit* (1807), where he coined the phrase 'the struggle for recognition' (*Kampf um Anerkennung*) (Markell, 2003: 2). In more recent times, Hegel's concept has been popularized by Charles Taylor in his essay 'The Politics of Recognition' (Taylor, 1994). As Markell points out, while Taylor shares, and did much to proselytize, the critique of the liberal theory of the self and the world, as well as its unacceptable naturalism, his championing of the politics of recognition tends to share the Hegelian theme of a restoration of a perfect unity, via a purely educative process between the 'partial' consciousness and the Absolute, whereby discordant social views are reunited through mutual recognition. It is in this sense, says Markell, that 'the politics of recognition is characterized by certain important misrecognitions of its own ... [These] arise from the fact that the pursuit of recognition expresses an aspiration to *sovereignty*' (2003: 10). Markell defines sovereignty in terms of 'sovereign agency of the individual', which 'can be attributed as easily to persons as to institutions such as states'. In this broader sense, 'sovereignty refers to the condition of being an independent, self-determining agent, fully autonomous, characterized by what Hannah Arendt calls "uncompromising self-sufficiency and mastership"' (Markell, 2003: 11).[13]

Such a politics would not be embraced by Foucault, as Markell himself notes (2003: 28–9). Foucault's politics does not aim to restore the lost unity of the state, or of society, nor does it believe that such a lost unity could be achieved, but rather it aims to maintain equilibrium in an agonistic system of constantly shifting power alliances and identities that are always provisional, always being contested, re-won and re-made. Foucault's conception of selfhood and identity, in a way similar to Arendt's, is never 'sovereign' or 'fixed', and is never finally complete. Foucault sees identity on the terrain of the temporal as always being established, consolidated, and re-made, in the context of power within society. The self's identity is thus characterized by incompleteness, provisionality, frailty, and vulnerability. The individual's control and power are partial and relative; actions are characterized by risk and uncertainty; assessment is based upon partial and incomplete knowledge; and identity is characterized by degrees of fluidity and precariousness. Foucault does not conceive of a subject sufficient to itself, but represents identity as *always being-constituted*, as a shifting and fragile set of relations and temporary syntheses.

The fact that recognition politics seeks to restore unity, a fundamental theme associated with Hegel's conception of a closed totality, is mentioned by Markell as constituting the basis for his critique of both Hegel's original conception as well as Taylor's reformulation. The fact that Markell critiques both conceptions for their direct or implicit advocacy of a fully autonomous, sovereign subject indicates the influence of poststructuralism on the politics of recognition in the same way that many areas of philosophy and social science have been affected over the last several decades.[14] The Foucauldian critique of Hegel's theory of recognition would, however, not simply reject Hegel and Taylor, but also Markell's own reformulation, the 'politics of acknowledgment'. Hegel is rejected because recognition is ultimately constituted as a transition from 'partial' or 'unhappy' consciousness towards reconciliation with the Absolute in a process of convergence over time. Such a progressive teleology of history is simply unacceptable for Foucault. Hegel is certainly the most influential theorist of recognition, and undoubtedly the father of philosophical and political approaches to recognition in Western philosophy. His fundamental starting point concerned the 'struggle for recognition' as conceptualized in terms of the master–slave dialectic, which is set out in detail in *The Phenomenology of Spirit* (Hegel, 1977: 111–19). As Markell summarizes Hegel, he sought to explain the 'self-defeating tendency of asymmetrical structures of recognition, such as the master–slave dialectic' (Markell, 2003: 3). In this sense, he 'is the key source both of the norm of equal recognition, and of the vision of a just social order as one in which both individuals and groups are bound together by mutual recognition into a whole that does not suppress difference' (2003: 91).

Taylor is rejected in that while he claims to modify the Hegelian thesis, he restores sovereignty to the subject by following Herder, who sees the sovereignty of identity as achieved ultimately in the *Volk* (community). Although Taylor seeks to reformulate recognition politics within an acceptable pluralist political language, in order to speak to minority group rights in twentieth-century Canadian politics, the residual commitment to Hegelian theory, notwithstanding a more contemporary language of description, is ultimately grounded in the Hegelian goals of final reconciliation and unification. Taylor relates the philosophy of recognition to the philosophy of language and explains language as the background cultural context into which the individual is inducted. His critique of liberal individualist conceptions that posit the subject as pre-social and ahistorical, although now well known, still constitutes a powerful critique of liberal individualism. For Taylor, identity grows in 'dialogue', not 'monologue', and dialogue operates within a community; hence, Herder's significance in relation to the importance that is placed on community. Community interaction builds relations of equal respect and equal worth, which constitute the basis of mutual recognition. As Markell puts it: 'Taylor suggests that what we owe to each is a "presumption of equal worth", one which would draw us toward an engagement with others in which we ourselves might also be transformed, without pretending to know in advance what the outcome of that engagement will be' (2003: 57).

Taylor argues that recognition must be extended to all citizens. Yet, for a Foucauldian, the basis for this lies not in Hegel nor a politics of recognition, but must be traced directly to continuance as the limits imposed on us by the finitude of openness, uncertainty, and unpredictability in a pluralistic world characterized by unequal relations of power. For Foucault, the poststructuralist innovation to Hegel goes much further than Taylor's revisions: it releases recognition from the closed logic of a dialectical process by which the definitions projected by the more powerful become necessary and minority group claims are ignored. For Foucault, politics does not constitute a closed or rational process of reconciliation; rather, social existence is characterized by contingency, change, openness, plurality, and difference, within an ongoing process of contestation. Every ordering of society is characterized by pluralism and openness because identity implies difference, or rather, it generates difference and pluralism. Pluralism, in this sense, stands opposed to Hegelian unity and characterizes the open relations of power through which agents strategize to increase and consolidate their power and control. Action in the world for each individual or group is characterized by risk and uncertainty. Identities define themselves relationally, at least in part by who they are *not*, because of the specificity of their actions in time. This does not prevent the emergence over time of a unique self, as action is itself individuating, but identity is still at least partly defined by otherness, or who one is not, and is always precarious, vulnerable, changing, and partial. Similarly, Foucault's politics will not seek to liberate subjects simply by recognizing them, that is, by a process of mutual accommodation at the level of the cultural. Indeed, Foucault would reject recognition politics as too exclusively concerned with psychological or cognitive orientations, instead of institutional and political ones. The locus of change and the existence of equilibrium do not occur simply through recognition, but rather through political contestation structured within a democratic context. In this sense, recognition is too concerned, in Taylor's and Hegel's views, with the psychological, cognitive, and cultural dimensions of mutuality. For Foucault, the normative task is to equalize power relations, as the means to equalize recognition. Primarily, Foucault's politics are concerned with action in the world to redress injustices related to *both* redistribution *and* recognition as well as inequalities of power. That the politics of recognition prioritizes identity over action and therefore 'misunderstands the nature of identity and its relation to action' (Markell, 2003: 18) is indeed a primary objection that Markell has to traditional conceptions of recognition.

Having rejected the politics of recognition, Markell's favoured alternative is what he terms 'the politics of acknowledgment'

(2003: 32). Here he draws initially on James Tully, who endeavours to reframe recognition to represent it as a more open-ended, 'on-going process', as opposed to conceptualizing it as an 'end-state good' in preference to a good he calls 'acknowledgment', 'which consists simply in being treated as a co-participant in an ongoing political process' (2003: 33). After also discussing Stanley Cavell's conception of acknowledgement, Markell embraces the concept as more readily congruent with a conception of pluralist politics, claiming that acknowledgement is directed at the basic conditions of one's own existence and activity, including, crucially, the limits of identity as a ground of action, limits that arise out of our 'constitutive vulnerability to the unpredictable reactions and responses of others' (2003: 36). Markell claims to read this through an examination of Aristotle, as well as a correct reading of Hegel's *Phenomenology of Spirit*. Aristotle is reinterpreted by Markell as a complexity thinker, and he emphasizes themes in Aristotle that confirm such a view.[15]

Markell's reinterpretation of Aristotle as a complexity thinker is to prepare the ground for interpreting Hegel in the same way. Recognition is then reduced to acknowledgement, now within a reformulation of recognition theory subjected to a 'poststructuralized' and 'pluralistic' reworking. Although I doubt that he would consent to such a description of his work, Markell's thesis on recognition is a case of *reading Hegel after Foucault and Arendt*, and, also, of reading Hegel *after complexity theory and poststructuralism*. My difficulty with his concept of acknowledgement is that it functions within the same epistemological and ontological frame of reference as Hegel's traditional concept of recognition, and, on this basis, is not significantly different from it, despite Markell's insistence (see Markell, 2003: 32–8 and Conclusion). Acknowledgement would seem to me to have no warrant or effect separate from the mere fact of existence as such.[16] That human individuals and groups do acknowledge each other is both a legal and normative fact of existence, which is a shared norm of communities.[17] While such an indisputable materiality itself generates the normative and the intersubjective, for Foucault, to continue to be acknowledged must be seen as contested, fought over, won and re-won, in political battles over power, which represent the struggle for survival itself, contingently variable in terms of intensity and force at different times. To the extent that it is assured, it is assured through political stakes and objectives, and through victories regarding political rights and reforms. There is no need for a political psychology of acknowledgement or recognition in addition to this.

A further problem here is that, for Markell, this concept is still being articulated within a version of Hegelian theory. To offer a new poststructuralist interpretation of Hegel's *Phenomenology* at this late stage, after Foucault and Arendt, is like saying that Hegel was really a poststructuralist all along. But surely this is to contribute to a 'politics of confusion', given the way Hegel has traditionally been interpreted, and given also that if we are to start over again it would surely be better to do so through Foucault and Nietzsche, and/or Arendt, who were trying to achieve such an alternative complexity approach to politics all along.[18]

The British Hegelians and the ethic of self-realization

In that Foucault opposes Hegel, he also would stand opposed to ethical conceptions of self-realization, as developed by the British Idealists who adapted Hegel's philosophy to Britain and dominated British philosophy from 1850 until the 1930s, when Bertrand Russell, A. J. Ayer, and G. E. Moore knocked the Idealists from their pedestal. The concept of self-realization constituted an identificatory account of obligation whereby it was explained on the basis of the identity of the subject. Identity in turn was explained in relation to social roles, and conventionalism was avoided by anchoring these roles, in Green's writing, to the 'common good', and ultimately to God's will for humankind. Moral obligation for writers such as Green and Bradley depended upon the subject's identity, which was conceptualized as settled and developing over time. This development entailed increasing self-consciousness of one's moral duties towards full self-realization as a moral agent. While the source of this self-realization was God, in an intermediate sense it resided with the state which prescribed all social roles. While the British Idealists presupposed a fixed, essentially Cartesian theory of the subject, as Robert Stern notes, the more

Hegelian of them, such as Bradley, tended to see moral duties in terms of 'Hegel's social command theory', while Green, who was sometimes critical of Hegel, positioned himself also in terms of Aristotle and Kant, and tended to follow 'Kant's hybrid model' (Stern, 2013: 308). Both approaches relied on a conception of fixed identity, however, and both showed the influence of Hegel, albeit to varying degrees.[19] Green argues that moral goodness resides in the realization of one's capacities, which he argues in turn shape what a person will determine as pleasurable or desirable. Self-realization is the ultimate good and is itself regulative of all other desires and interests. As Green says in the *Prolegomena*, 'self-realization ... will express itself in their imposition on themselves of rules requiring something to be done irrespectively of any inclination to do it' (2003: §193). Many were not impressed by either the clarity or precision of the concept. Henry Sidgwick was of the view that it was both 'exceedingly obscure' and totally incapable of offering 'practical guidance' (1902: 73–4).

As Stern says, 'Green thus claims to have found here a version of a Kantian categorical imperative, but one which Kant himself wrongly overlooked' (2013: 312).[20] Green also claims that this new criterion of moral decision making is less formalistic than Kant's, yet is still based in the agent's own will, more specifically what Green calls 'self-satisfaction'. As Stern expresses the point:

> the agent can find in self-realization something that has value irrespective of what his desires or ends happen to be, where in identifying them reason has much more than an instrumental role, as here it determines the content of our desires themselves by establishing the proper object of our self-satisfaction. (2013: 312)

As a criterion of moral obligation, self-realization is intended by Green to permit a classification of development, in that it structures our desires in the light of this criterion as a fully rational good or end. While Stern is concerned that such a criterion does not maintain an 'imperatival force, or the kind of "necessitation" that Kant also took to be characteristic of morality for us' (2013: 312), Green would maintain that it dictates the content and progressive direction of morality over and above contingent or merely affective or instrumental concerns. It is in this sense that the influence of Hegel can be seen in relation to the concept of self-realization, even if not explicitly acknowledged. God is ultimately the source of 'self-satisfaction', and hence of all moral values.

The Foucauldian objections to Green are essentially the objections to Kant and Hegel: Green is positing a teleological conception of development which posits the good as unitary and naturalistic, rather than *multiple* and *constructed*. It is also highly individualistic and overlaid by a concept of religion, hence metaphysical. According to Muirhead, Green's concept of self-realization also presupposes 'eternal self-consciousness', defined by Muirhead as 'a will to betterment or to a fuller realisation of the self that is the source of the customs and institutions of society' (1924: 170).[21] Green typically defines 'eternal self-consciousness' in more Hegelian, and explicitly religious terms, however, as 'the law of nature or the will of God or its "idea"' (1986: sect. 17) or, 'freedom in the conscious union with God, or harmony with the true law of one's being' (1986: sect. 17). Important here in the idea of 'eternal self-consciousness' and its link with self-realization is the notion that the individual's will *unfolds* and, as it does so, God is progressively actualized in the individual and in the world (Green, 1986: sect. 17). It is clear, then, that the concept of self-realization presupposes a measure of both Kant and Hegel: it presupposes the central importance of *will*, which reproduces Kant's subjective insistence on the centrality of the individual as the ontological grounding of ethics and morality, as well as Hegel's teleological conception of dialectical progression towards a specific end of perfection in the Absolute.

Unlike Kant and Green, for whom the subject's development presupposes a primary focus on an autonomous will as both actual and normative (i.e., good), a Foucauldian does not see the free will of the individual as the core of ethics and morality in terms of determining conduct. For continuance ethics, the state of the world and the object to be willed must primarily be seen as important in determining the normative significance of action and conduct. Beyond this, there are major points of agreement between Foucault and Green. Both would see people as interdependent with others and reliant on the structures of social support. Foucault would agree with Green that insufficiency justifies a positive role for the state. Within poststructuralism, although continuance prescribes ends for development, these constitute an open set of possibilities, with their own risks, dangers, and opportunities. Although it constitutes a norm of development for each and all, the fact that it must be detected through the fog of conventional mores and ideologies is what generates the necessity for collective deliberation and democratic caution, at least at the macro-level.[22] This recognition of a collective dimension to personhood, and consequent collective functions for politics, is what classical liberals in the twentieth century shied away from, seeing any form of state power additional to a narrowly conceived negative role as potentially totalitarian.[23] Green was one of the few social democrats to oppose the main drift, and in this respect there is an affinity with the poststructuralist ethics of Foucault.

The difficulty for the classical liberals is that, as Foucault points out, collective politics and the positive state functions that result, although they are certainly dangerous, are also *necessary*. In this sense, priority is placed on political regulation as a positive state mechanism for the management and coordination of matters of urgency, economic failure, as well as for the provision of structures of services and opportunities for citizens. Although Green appealed to idealism on matters of mind and truth, and justified a positive role for the state on idealist grounds, writers such as Foucault theorized the rise of positive state power not, as classical liberals do, as an errant (or, for Green, deliberate) political choice, but unavoidably, as the result of materially instantiated changes in the structures and processes of the early modern period. For Foucault, positive state power, or *biopower*, represented a new material modality of power consequent upon the emergence of the state system and the necessity of state regulation. States pursued positive public purposes because *they couldn't do anything else*. Collective politics becomes more significant as societies change, manifesting increased shared concerns and interests.

A Foucauldian approach also enables a theorization of contingency in history concerning the domain of core values such as liberty, stability, and security. Nothing could be more evident in the first quarter of the twenty-first century with the emergence of new global issues around climate change, overpopulation, nuclear power, terrorism, and viral pandemics, than that the state's role is being altered. Contingent changes are altering the calculus of individual versus group interests in terms of which state actions and global agencies act. In this sense, climate change, or uncontrolled population growth, constitute potential 'tragedies of the commons', as Garrett Hardin claimed, indicating the interconnectedness between the collective and the individual. For Hardin, because of the rational pursuit of self-interest, both nations and individuals are led to overexploit and therefore abuse the commons, with the result that 'the freedom of the commons brings ruin to all' (1968: 1243). Yet this would entail that the greater the problems of security facing humanity, the greater the level of *shared* relative to *individual* interests, and the greater the shadow of the future over contemporary events. For, as danger in the outside world increases, the calculus of what constitutes self-interest (for an individual or group) and what constitutes a shared interest (of a group, nation, or humanity) also changes. What is being forged, indeed, is a new resolution of the one and the many, and the very dynamic that such an alteration implies.

Marxism's last rites

Just as Foucault is seriously critical of Hegel and Hegelian models of development, so too he is seriously critical of Marxism and Marx. Partly, this is because Foucault sees Marxism as parasitic on Hegel and on evolutionary approaches to history. In the 'Interview with Michel Foucault', conducted by Trombadori at the end of 1978,[24] Foucault celebrated the fact that a 'non-Marxist culture of the left was about to be born' (Foucault, 2000d: 263). In this interview, Foucault lays out the issues at stake in terms of 'how far can forms of reflection and analysis be constituted that are not irrationalist, that are not rightist, and yet are not tied to Marxist dogma?' (2000d: 265). In the same interview Foucault claims the credit for 'having been one of the first to say that ... Marx [was] among those most responsible for the gulags' (2000d: 268).

A similar thread on Marx and Marxism appears in Foucault's review of Jean Daniel's book, *Ere des ruptures* (*Age of Ruptures*), which appeared in *Le Nouvel Observateur* in late 1979, under the title 'An Ethic of Discomfort' (Foucault, 2000e). Here

Foucault approaches the issue in relation to the question, 'What is Enlightenment?',[25] which he translates for the purposes of his review as 'What are we now? What is this ever so fragile moment from which we cannot detach our identity, and which will carry that identity away with it?' (2000e: 443). This is a more stinging attack on the relevance of Marxism than his comment to Trombadori, above. It is an attack that is present in many of his other, larger works and interviews, but in this little review it is presented succinctly, in a direct and unambiguous form. Jean Daniel was the editor of *Le Nouvel Observateur*. Foucault starts off by noting that everything is changing and laments that the rapidity of change makes maintaining an identity difficult. This change of identity has engulfed the left, Marxism included. Daniel has spoken of his 'surprise' as the relevance of old, taken-for-granted categories of thought had fallen away, become irrelevant, lost their hold. The idea of the 'Left' as a 'moral identity', a 'home', had had its day. It had galvanized the identities of several generations. It was: '[c]redentialed by the Resistance, supported by the USSR and the "socialist camp", and wielding its doctrine, the Communist Party exerted a triple legitimacy, historical, political and theoretical. It laid down the law to everything that claimed to be of the Left' (2000e: 445).

Foucault's uneasiness with Marxism was linked to its utopianism and what that meant for ethics. He opposed a politics of utopia, because it sacrificed the means to the ends in pursuit of a violently realized, future communist state. Personal action in Marxism is given meaning within a future yet to be realized and in relation to a collective project of history that is both communal and utopian. People conduct their lives not for the present in the light of a future, but *for the sake of* an ideal posited in the future. In this respect it bears an affinity with the eschatological, messianic, religious approaches to ethics. This is an ethics of the future where human beings find their place in a world *yet to come*. The eschatology distinguishes between means and end, the present and the future, action and end, the imperfect present and a glorious future destiny. A strong sense of teleology is internal to the process of history: as in religious ethics, earthly life is sacrificed for future salvation. Rather than progress being unconditional, Foucault sees it as conditional. His ethics, by contrast to strong teleology, is an ethics of 'discomfort', oriented in terms of the present, but which considers the effects of one's actions for both the present and future in 'real-world' terms. Continuance includes the future in terms of the present as the locus of responsibility and as the basis for judgement. Obligations and duties do not issue from a specific goal, as yet unrealized in the future; neither do they sacrifice the present for a future ideal society or state of affairs. Foucault's ethic based on life continuance is, in this sense, non-utopian, non-messianic, and non-teleological.

One interesting question, given that Foucault is critical of Marxism, is how and why interviewers and many in the reading audience over the 1960s and 1970s thought that he was in some way aligned to Marxism. The answer to this question revolves around the fact that Foucault never quite knew or could articulate what exactly Marxism was. While at one level, he was careful not to be seen as criticizing Marxism too harshly, he also thought that Marx's own project was mistaken in important respects. It was because of this that he thought a new beginning grounded in Nietzsche and Heidegger might offer a better chance of realizing something like the hopes of Marxism which Marx had gone the wrong way about trying to achieve. Yet when he was able to confront precisely the different aspects of Marxism, in a theoretical sense, Foucault was always consistent. As he said to André Breton in an interview on 7 May 1981: 'Marxism ... made reference to an entire realm of historical analysis upon which, in a way, it was stuck' (2014a: 237). By its method of focus it left many issues unexamined. In any case, says Foucault, 'Marxism, or a concrete Marxist history was not, in France ... very well developed' (2014a: 237).

This criticism that Marxism dealt only with generalities was linked to the view that it was not very useful when dealing with, as Foucault wanted to, the 'interior' or lived experiences of groups like the 'mad', with 'sexuality', or with 'discipline and punishment'. He sought to ask about the cultural and social study of experiences such as madness in more specificity than Marxism, which offers, he says, 'a one size fits all approach to [such] developments' (2014a: 237). How could Marxism assist in connecting subjective experiences to the whole social field? Foucault asks: 'Is there or is there not an experience of madness that is characteristic of a given society or type of society such as ours?' (2014a: 237). Marxism couldn't assist in his interest. As he notes, the issue of madness had more to do with 'the question of limit-experiences' (2014a: 238) which in turn raises the issue of critique or the critical attitude and includes those 'border-line experiences that put into question the very things that were considered ordinarily acceptable. So, in one sense, to turn the history of madness into an interrogation of our own system of reason' (2014a: 238). For Foucault, it was the contemporaneity of philosophy since Kant that enabled the posing of a succession of important questions that enabled us to question our use of reason, our place in society, in history, in reference to the assumptions of modernity. Kant in this sense was more useful than Marx.

Such reflections led directly to his own conceptualization of power as *relations* and as *governmentality*. Foucault would in other words examine each of Marx's concepts in terms of its viability. This is what he told Michael Bess in San Francisco on 3 November 1980, when he spoke of resistance in relation to unequal power relations. When asked 'Was he a Marxist?', he disclaimed to know exactly what Marxism was:

> [W]hen someone speaks to me of Marxism, I would say: which one? The Marxism taught in the German Democratic Republic, *Marxismus-Leninismus*? Is it the vague, woolly, and hybrid concepts used by someone like Georges Marchais? Is it the body of doctrine that some English historians refer to? Well, for myself, I do not know what Marxism is. (2016c: 131)

Foucault was in the difficult position of having to respond to interviewers, of not wanting to be anti-Marxist, to the extent that Marxism was seen as progressive on many issues; yet for all that, in that Marx drew on Hegel's strong teleology of history, he was opposed at a deeper philosophical level. What is clear, however, is that the approach to history and the future that he develops, inspired by Nietzsche and Heidegger, resists the totalizing approaches of Hegel and Marx. Also, while different from liberalism in important respects, Foucault's approach signals its alignment with openness, democracy, rights, justice, and pluralism, as constituting the most important technologies needed for continuance to the future that are possible in the world today.

Notes

1 While this distinction is insightful, and while Yovel's translation and commentary are very accessible for the English-speaking reader, as Evangelia Sembou argues there are some disagreements with the reading of Hegel being proposed, regarding which I agree with her. Yovel fails to stress sufficiently, or prominently enough, immanent development as a central theme in Hegel's conception of mind, but more importantly, he likens the development in the final stage towards the Absolute (2005: 82–3) to 'where time's progressive direction becomes the eternal recurrence of the same' (2005: 82). This is Nietzsche's phrase, and to conflate the two thinkers by interchanging concepts in this way gives a misleading impression, as for Nietzsche, it is will that drives the process. Nietzsche's views of Hegel's philosophy were also, in the main, negative. In the same vein, Yovel makes several claims that spirit 'progresses in a semi-linear way modified by detours and regressions' (2005: 83; see also 9, 14). Sembou says: 'I cannot not see in the *Phenomenology of Spirit* itself, or indeed, in any other of Hegel's texts ... any regression' (Sembou, 2018: 3). This tendency of writers to read ascendant present-day cultural values into historical scholars' works, thereby reinterpreting them, is of course common. But because Yovel inadvertently or advertently gives Hegel something of a 'complexity spin', his commentary and translation has only a qualified approval.
2 See Pippin (1989; 2008), Hartmann (1972), and Pinkard (1988; 2002; 2012), who represent Hegel's philosophy as an extension of Kant's project.
3 Consciousness progressively converges with the Absolute in a dialectical process over time, ultimately achieving unity in God.
4 Fichte had developed an account of subjective idealism, while Schelling and Hölderlin subscribed to a version of intellectual intuition drawn from the Romantics.
5 Hegel was impressed initially both by Rousseau's ideas of democracy as well as his thesis concerning the disintegration of society under the force of economic and social developments.
6 See Plant (1973: 65–6). Plant argues that in *An Enquiry into the Principles of Political Economy* (1767), Steuart develops a progressive, evolutionist approach to political economy. The thesis is included in Hegel's early essay 'The Spirit of Christianity and its Fate' (1798–1800) (Hegel, 1948).

7 See Hegel (1948). I am indebted to John E. Grumley (1989) for his excellent discussion of the importance of religion in Hegel's early writings.
8 This article is translated as 'The Great Rage of Facts' (Foucault, 2016a).
9 The view that Hegel's philosophy can be interpreted to represent truth and knowledge in distinctively non-foundationalist and non-metaphysical terms has been suggested by many thinkers, for instance, in recent decades, Klaus Hartmann (1972), Merold Westphal (1979), Gillian Rose (1981), Stephen Houlgate (2009), William Maker (1994), John Sallis (1995), and Kimberley Hutchings (2003), to name but some.
10 These mainly concerned the applicability of teleology to intentional or living beings (see Johnson, 2005: ch. 1).
11 Such a notion of teleology is also adopted by Theodore R. Schatzki when he says, 'By "teleological" I mean orientated towards ends: the teleological character of activity consists in people performing actions for ends' (2010: xiii).
12 For a philosophical elaboration of this model, see Deleuze (1994a).
13 Markell cites Arendt (1957: 234).
14 I have already noted how contemporary Kantians such as Ginsborg (2015) and Korsgaard (1996a; 1996b; 2009) have revised their language, as well as conceptions of the subject, and other dimensions, with reference to poststructuralist themes, in their cases in reference to Wittgenstein. While it is true that Wittgenstein can serve as a repository for acknowledgement, it is also true that there was little understanding of much of the significance of Wittgenstein's theses until postructuralism popularized many of the conceptions now being incorporated into western philosophy and social science research. In many ways, it constitutes, if the metaphor can be excused, a 'great train robbery' by Western social science from poststructuralism, largely carried out by stealth and without acknowledgement.
15 For examples of 'complexifying' Aristotle, see Markell (2003: 79). Here Markell draws on Aristotle to highlight themes of 'non-linear causality', 'uncertainty', 'chance', 'recursivity', 'feedback loops', and 'doubling back', as well as 'vulnerability', 'plurality', 'contingency', 'unintended consequences', 'intersubjectivity', 'lack of control', etc.
16 One could compare it to Louis Althusser's (1971) concept of 'hailing'. In this case, however, in that one is 'hailed' as a social subject or citizen by official power, the concept is epistemologically useful, and expresses the sense of 'acknowledgement' as it operates in society, institutionalized in such ceremonies as baptism or birth registration.

17 Acknowledgement is in this sense derivative from birth, birth registration, birth ceremonies, and the like.
18 This is yet another instance of the poststructuralisation of Western political theory by stealth.
19 Peter Nicholson (1990; 1995) maintains that Green was influenced by Hegel, but adds 'it is by no means clear how Hegelian Green is: and this is not a question Green would have thought important' (1995: 61). See also Wempe (2004) for a supporting view.
20 Stern refers the reader to Green's 'Lectures on the Philosophy of Kant' (1885–88: §§119–24), Irwin (1984: 31–56; 2009: 581–624), and Brink (2003: 92–106).
21 This is an eminently reasonable view, as Green says in the *Prolegomena* that self-realization needs to be 'relative to something beyond itself' (2003: §185).
22 This implies that a micro-level also exists, whereby each time I act in the world, I consult myself on how and in what sense my actions are consistent with the future of life on earth.
23 The negative role of the state was defined by Adam Smith (1976b) as including only security, defence, and limited public works that nobody would want to do. The negative vs. positive distinction in relation to liberty and the role of the state is most clearly stated by Berlin (1958). Central to propagating this thesis against positive state power have been modern social contract theorists such as Rawls (1971; 1999) and Buchanan and Tullock (1962), as well as political philosophers such as Berlin (1958), Popper (1945; 1961; 1992), and Hayek (1944; 1949).
24 First published in the Italian journal *Il Contributo* in 1980.
25 This was the question a Berlin newspaper put out in 1784, to which Immanuel Kant responded, after Moses Mendelssohn.

6

Hobbes, God, and modern social contract theory

Hobbes, rights, and naturalism

In his book *Human Rights as Politics and Idolatry*, Michael Ignatieff articulates the value of life continuance when he says, 'our species is one, and each of the individuals who comprise it is entitled to equal moral consideration' (2005: 3–4). Ignatieff continues, 'human rights is the language which systematically embodies this intuition' (2005: 4). This sentiment is expressed as the initial justification for human rights, yet there are a number of points that I would want to make regarding it. First, it is not solely our species of humans that is deemed to count, but life in general. It is true that many distinctions need to be made here, and the issue of animals, and of animals and humans, is important, but it can be stated that although life in general has value, and all forms of life are interdependent, it is to humans that it falls to act as custodians of the earth as a whole. Only humans have the capacity and intelligence necessary to plan and act in ways that can reconcile macro and micro aims and goals for life as a whole. Although not assured of success, only humans can appreciate the complicated nature of the challenges before us and the difficulties that are involved. Secondly, our species is one, as Ignatieff says, but it is also diverse on innumerable dimensions. It could also be said that our species is one on the basis that we are *living beings*. Thirdly, human rights is one way to protect the intuition that we are entitled to equal moral consideration, and it is a major way. Only in the twentieth century have individual rights taken hold. The juridical revolution in human rights, says Ignatieff, has occurred since 1945, with the Universal Declaration of Human Rights, followed by the International Covenant on Civil and Political Rights, the Geneva Conventions of 1948, the revised Geneva Conventions of 1949, and the International Covenant on Asylums of 1951. For Foucault, human rights accords were important to protect human freedoms, and in this sense, they constitute a marker that assigns protection to each part in relation to the whole. He was aware, however, that the issue as to how far human rights proliferated was contentious, not least because of the problem 'of reconciling an infinite demand within a finite system' (2000h: 377). The 'decisional distance' (2000h: 373) between governors and governed requires ongoing deliberations. Human rights accords do, however, constitute a powerful technology as part of a comprehensive conception of the good built around continuance norms.

It is this preliminary insight, that 'our species is one', which signifies also that life has value, and that Ignatieff simply 'throws in' in order to get to speak about human rights that I also find interesting. For it is this very basic claim, which at one level is so obvious, that subtends all moral and ethical claims. It is this claim that provides a general form of unity necessary to undergird pluralism, thus saving it from incoherence, and it is this claim also that, as we shall see, offsets charges of relativism and ethical scepticism. Sometimes it is necessary to state the obvious in order to forestall objections that might be otherwise raised.

What is it, then, that this simple appeal to life establishes? In that it seeks to survive and prosper, it is seen as having value. Value by and for whom? It is life itself that sees life as being valuable, that is, as worthy of persevering and continuing. Although, as I will discuss below, there are many religious arguments over whence the value of life derives, as well as concerning matters such as the equality and dignity of human beings, it would seem to me that life itself has value and ought to be continued. How it ought to be continued is another question, a question that generates endless debate and conflict, sometimes resulting in wars and violence. Some might say that simply recognizing a value in life and its continuance leaves everything to be resolved, and that it doesn't do very much. To which I would respond that it generates the reason to keep going and in effect turns all other matters into (mere) technical or procedural issues. Hence, while it will not resolve definitively how wide a human rights regime should be, that is, which dimensions of existence should be included as rights, or how to resolve conflicts, it will determine what the function of a human rights order should be, and it will countenance some mechanism for resolving conflicts.

One thinker apart from Foucault who supports a right to life is Thomas Hobbes, and in this sense, Hobbes is the thinker who can most ably support Nietzsche, Foucault, and myself in fashioning a non-foundational ethic for the global age. There is a slight problem over Hobbes's naturalism, but if we can reconfigure that, he could be a most worthy ally. In *Leviathan* Hobbes presents survival as the core value motivating humans; it constitutes, he says, an 'Inference, made from the Passions' (1968: I, ch. XIII, 84). He continues:

> The Passions that encline man to Peace, are Feare of Death; Desire of such things as are necessary to commodious living; and a Hope by their Industry to obtain them. And Reason suggesteth convenient Articles of Peace, upon which men may be drawn to agreement. (1968: I, ch. XIII, 86)

Hobbes calls these Articles the 'Laws of Nature', which given the above discussion will be now understood in my view to represent an unfortunate way of expressing things. Hobbes defines the Law of Nature (*Lex Naturalis*) as 'a Precept, or General Rule, found out by Reason, by which man is forbidden to do that which is destructive of his life' (1968: I, ch. XIV, 87). I would rather say, however, that these proclivities to continue life are immanent to life itself. It is what we humans, and in fact animals too, seek to do. Once one has said they are immanent to life itself there is nothing further to be gained by saying they constitute laws of nature. As Schopenhauer (2010: ch. 7) points out, in relation to Kant, the language of laws is unnecessarily juridical. Furthermore, reference to laws suggests a foundation that is simply not there. Immanence characterizes life in the present horizon. While life necessitates and presupposes an environment, that environment is itself transient and changing. Hobbes presupposes a distinction between 'nature' and 'culture' where nature constitutes a fixed ground plan that human beings, through civil association, seek to channel and control. Like Locke and Rousseau, Hobbes reads far too much into nature. All three posit a fictional social contract, which Hobbes accepts as a metaphor to reflect the agreement between people, first, to live in civilized society, and secondly, to form a government. The social contract is the mechanism by which human beings come out of the state of nature and by which they then organize government. But given that Hobbes says that the 'Passions encline man' and that 'Reason suggesteth', it is not clear why the 'social contract' is also required to account for social and political life. The nature/culture distinction is not necessary to the thesis. Furthermore, there are all sorts of advantages to getting rid of it.

Why do we need to get rid of talk of nature? Although at one level nature retains its place, this will be indirectly, as mediated by the context of the present via an imperative for survival. References to the 'state of nature' or 'nature' as a ground will, however, be displaced. At one level, we all think we understand what is being talked about when references are made to man's nature. This represents, we come to believe, more or less the sort of beings that we are, independent of our life in society; it lists our non-social, unchangeable, basic drives, so to speak. But as the term manifests itself in Hobbes, Locke, and the whole social contract tradition, all the way to Kant and beyond, there is, additionally, a certain unwanted baggage introduced by use of the term. This is compounded in Hobbes, who talks of 'Laws of Nature', as well as the 'State of Nature'. First, it can be noted that reference to a 'nature' or 'laws of nature' sets matters up in a particular way. It establishes an ontology, or conception of being, which posits the most basic considerations concerning the human being as being outside of society. This makes each person solitary, at least in terms of this basic original location, thus minimizing the important, although historically variable, sense in which people are always social, that is, interdependent with each other and with the structures of social support. In this sense, it establishes nature, or the state of nature, as *pre-social*, thus diminishing any sense in which *context* is a primary determinant of people's lives. While in one sense it is meaningful to inquire as to the nature of human beings in their basic constitution, prior to or independent of society and socialization, it has proved an inordinately difficult question to answer. More importantly, however, it structures the issue in a way that defends the vested interests that naturalists hold, usually geared to upholding the existing structures or values of society. Hence, naturalism entails an individualist ontology that tends to 'freeze' existing experience as somehow given and unalterable and that prevents the possibility of change.

For Hobbes, naturalism functioned in exactly this way. His conception of human nature is essentialist and ahistorical. It constitutes a radical individualism expressed throughout both *De Cive* and *Leviathan* as a way of opposing the Aristotelian conception of humans as social beings. This was an ongoing debate in Hobbes's own day, and critics such as Ralph Cudworth sought to defend the Aristotelian view against Hobbes. Aiming his sights directly at Hobbes, Cudworth observed that 'a man cannot apprehend himself as a being standing by himself, cut off, separated, and disjointed from all other beings ... but looks upon himself as a member lovingly united to the whole system of all intellectual beings' (cited in Hampton, 1986: 10). In *De Cive*, Hobbes famously speaks of human beings as 'even now sprung out of the earth, and suddenly like mushrooms, come to full maturity, without any kind of engagement with each other' (1840: 109). It affects every aspect of his writing. When he talks of language, as he does in chapter IV of *Leviathan*, Hobbes essentially takes the view, incredible as it might seem to us today, that our ability to speak is in no way a consequence of our formative social interaction or learning. For Hobbes, the solitary, pre-social individual is the source of language. Language merely constitutes a public marker for what in reality are only private and individual thoughts. They are 'marks' or 'signes' to aid our memory, or communication, so that we can fulfil our desires (1968: I, ch. IV, 12–13, 31).[1]

Secondly, the idea of the 'State of Nature' functions as a historical fiction, for as Hobbes was well aware, it never actually existed. It must be considered that it functioned for Hobbes very much as a heuristic device to more effectively enable him to challenge the Aristotelian world view. While this doesn't necessarily invalidate it as a metaphor or method, its use in Hobbes's analysis introduces a conservative social and political bias that seriously skews the analysis and makes it difficult to claim its relevance for either the present or the future. Thirdly, it gives rise to disputable assessments, for instance, over the question of what the true nature of human beings or of the world is. Hobbes took a more negative view of human nature than Locke or Rousseau. We can argue until the cows come home as to who is correct on this. All three thinkers advance beyond the limits of finitude to the noumenal realm in order to make claims as to what nature determines. Their assessments go beyond a minimal sense of what experience dictates to chart contentious theses about both human individuals and society. That humans can be aggressive is certainly true; they can also be generous and altruistic – so it may be 'context' rather than 'nature' that accounts for human conduct. These thinkers also started putting too many things into nature, hardwired against possible incursions by the state. Locke, for instance, saw bourgeois property rights as 'natural', an assessment that has become a core value of liberal philosophy and has been inscribed in the constitutions of many countries, notably the USA. Nature for both Hobbes and Locke constitutes an outside that both writers seek to fill with claims that are, when all said and done – from a Foucauldian point of view, at least – nothing but interpretations.

By getting rid of nature, laws of nature, or state of nature, we get rid of a foundation that purports to be fixed and ahistorical, and instead are permitted to represent the natural immanent quest for continuance as itself historically transitory in important senses. What is required for survival and 'commodious living' (in Hobbes's words) can vary according to all sorts of changes, such as population density, the availability of resources, as well as forms of technology. Increase the world's population to ten billion and the very nature of existence, including the relations between individual and collective, the one and the many, will also change. Asking what is necessary to survival and commodious living, because we value life, is all that is required to justify the existence of liberty, a certain conception of property, a conception of deep democracy, and a conception of government.

Getting rid of nature is essential to a Foucauldian constructivist approach. Naturalism was central not only to Hobbes, but to Locke as well. Nietzsche is often represented as a naturalist but, as Paul Patton points out, for Nietzsche, nature is not a constraint or fixed ground that limits and defines human beings, as it is for Hobbes. For Nietzsche, human nature is:

Hobbes, God, and modern social contract theory

something achieved or produced by the operation of the will to power in the contingent historical circumstances in which human history is played out ... Ultimately, the basis of the human capacity for self-transformation lies in the very nature of will to power as Nietzsche understands it; that is as a law of life in terms of which 'all great things bring about their own destruction through an act of self-overcoming' ... This is the second element of the secret revealed to Zarathustra by Life itself: I am that *which must overcome itself again and again* ... (Patton, 1993: 154)[2]

The difference from Hobbes could not be starker. The contrast extends also to their views of power. As Patton notes, for Hobbes, '[t]he only mode of increase of power is quantitative ... by gaining power over the power of others ... the subject of Hobbes' contract of government is defined by its lack of security and by its need to ensure self-preservation' (1993: 153, 154). Nietzsche's conception of power is quite different, however: 'Nietzsche offers an active conception in which power is defined only with reference to the activity of which a given body is capable. The active body is one whose activity is not defined by what it lacks but what it is capable of doing' (1993: 153). Patton's point is that, for Nietzsche, human beings can transform themselves through history: 'Nietzsche's conception of human powers and their increase or enhancement through a dynamic of qualitative self-transformation allows him to envisage the possibility of a sovereign individual "conscious of his own power and freedom ... with the actual *right* to make promises"' (1993: 159).[3]

Hobbes, Hayles, and non-foundationalism

Hobbes's more 'one-dimensional' conception of power fixes the character of the subject through his foundationalism. The privileged position of nature as a *foundation* characterizes the social contract tradition in political theory, and more generally can be claimed to characterize not just Hobbes, but the approaches of Locke, Hume, and Kant as well.[4] The importance of nature can be seen among contemporary advocates of these positions. In Christine Korsgaard's neo-Kantian approach, notes Katherine Hayles, she builds on and incorporates the Platonic model of an 'originary presence [which] authorizes a stable, coherent self that could witness and testify to a stable, coherent reality' (Hayles, 1999: 285). She incorporates a 'metaphysics of presence' that 'front-loads' an individual rational subject standing outside history into her analysis. This, essentially, is what Hobbes, Locke, Hume, and Kant do as well.

Hayles extends her critique of naturalism in a useful way. Normativity for Hobbes, Locke, and Kant is rendered possible because nature serves as a stable foundation and signification is grounded securely in a world where humans are considered rational while other animals are not. Wittgenstein began and established the idea of a self as social and historical, a self that Korsgaard is keen to incorporate into her own analysis, at least with respect to her revisions of Kant.[5] The open nature of systems with the consequences and possibilities for uncertainty, unpredictability, and contingency are not considered. The possibility that nature represents merely a material outside that exerts no unidimensional control or force, that it is itself transient and unfixed, or that decision making and behaviour exhibit a randomness characteristic of the role of evolution in open, complex systems is not considered. Naturalists anticipate a settled and ordered world that yields ideas of autonomous will, social contract, and sources of normativity that are universal and transcendental. Hayles proselytizes for a 'post-human' analysis that in avoiding naturalism, also avoids anthropocentrism, yet does not deny the uniqueness of humans, or other species of animals, either. In this sense, the post-human need not be negatively construed, for it signifies the 'exhilarating prospect of getting out of some of the old boxes and opening up new ways of thinking about what being human means' (Hayles, 1999: 285). In this account:

> emergence replaces teleology; reflective epistemology replaces objectivism, distributed cognition replaces autonomous will, embodiment replaces a body seen as a support system for the mind; and a dynamic partnership between humans and intelligent machines replaces the liberal humanist subject's manifest destiny to dominate and control nature. (1999: 288)

In this sense:

> the posthuman does not really mean the end of humanity. It signals instead the end of a certain conception of the human, a conception that may have applied, at best, to the fraction of humanity who had the wealth, power and leisure to conceptualise themselves as autonomous beings exercising their will through individual agency and choice. (1999: 286)

But the post-human is neither 'anti-human' nor 'apocalyptic' (1999: 288). Although 'distributed cognition' can function as a counter-check to 'local knowledge' and 'restricted cognition', it does not recognize a sovereign role to human agency or will. Rather:

> In the post-human view, by contrast, conscious agency has never been 'in control.' In fact, the very illusion of control bespeaks a fundamental ignorance about the nature of emergent processes through which consciousness, the organism, and the environment are constituted. Mastery through the exercise of autonomous will is merely the story consciousness tells itself to explain the results that actually come about through chaotic dynamics and emergent structures. (1999: 288).

By focusing on survival, one looks to the future, starting from the present, and one assesses the possibilities in terms of the contingencies that constitute the horizon. Outcomes are far from certain in an agonistic world. It gives rise to radical questions concerning the conditions under which survival is possible, given the availability of resources, the current threats to existence, as well as the necessary constraints and options. It asks: what is the conception of the subject that it is necessary to construct, what threats must be circumvented or controlled, and what rules should prevail that will be acceptable to all? Failure to take account of this last point would potentially threaten the security of life itself. What is natural in this view is simply what is necessary to survive.

Having posed the question in this way, we could work through Hobbes's *Leviathan*, page by page, accepting many of his conclusions but abandoning any reference to nature. We could work through Locke as well. Liberty is beneficial to survival, as is government, democracy, a separation of powers, a form of constitution, a free press, morality and ethics, and much more. These might not be strictly necessary, it might be conjectured, but given the increasing density of the world's population, plus other problems, sophisticated structures that permit a reconciliation of the one and many, under conditions considered by all to be fair and just, could well be considered necessary lest security, order, and peace break down completely. All of these factors certainly aid survival and increase the likelihood of success. Survival is the attempt to sustain life in any environment. In this way continuance can be represented as a drop-dead argument: if you want to survive you will need to support political and civic structures that support the project of life on earth. You will need to respect others in order that your own life and goals can be respected and not thwarted. And if you do this, ethics and morality follow on in turn.

There is further value to be extracted from Hobbes for continuance ethics in relation to his conception of *reason*. The conception embedded in the quote from Hobbes above concerning 'Feare of Death and commodious living' can be represented as rational in the sense that Hobbes describes reason *normatively* as 'a man is forbidden to do that which is destructive of his life'. As all lives are interconnected to each other and the whole, reason dictates more generally that one is forbidden to do what is destructive of life per se. This normative sense of reason in Hobbes presupposes a value placed by human beings on life itself, and contrasts with what can be called the instrumental view of reason, which proceeds logically from inference or premise to conclusion in a purely deductive-methodological sense. This latter view is Hume's expressivist sense when he sees reason as the servant of the passions. Reason for Hume is simply a neutral method. In itself it won't support a pro-value on life unless such a pro-value is contained in the premise. If reason is a neutral method then starting to reason is like starting to count from one upwards: it won't resolve anything unless it is put to work for a specific purpose – and on this ground, it lacks intrinsic normative relevance or reference. It was Hobbes's great strength to see reason normatively as 'avoiding destruction', and promoting what is 'constructive for life' as being central to reason itself. For Hobbes, then, reason *is* normative, and *in this sense*, life continuance *is* rational.[6] However, this is not the sense of reason that I am happy with, because it is not the way the concept of reason is normally used. Normally, reason refers only to a neutral method, a hypothetical-deductive method of moving from premise to conclusion through logical inference. Reason is procedural. In this sense, it is confusing and somewhat vacuous to talk of continuance being a rational process. Reason is certainly necessary as an under labourer in the process of problematization through which goals are set and judgements made. But beyond this, reason must be conceptualized only as a method of arguing, and not identified with the ends itself.

There is abundant evidence that we humans actually do put a pro-value on life as a form of public morality, ranging from public vilification of people in the media to the trials at Nuremberg after the Second World War. At Nuremberg, not only the leaders who gave the orders but also the civil servants and junior officers of the military who executed them were tried and found guilty. Eichmann's defence that he was simply a civil servant obeying commands and acting within the laws of the land did not hold sway (see Arendt, 2006). The immanent value of life was a law over and above human society. It is what, for the most part, guides human societies. Violations in relation to Nazi Germany, or more recent instances of ethnic cleansing as in Rwanda or the Balkans, testify to the pervasiveness and pre-eminence of such a norm. It is the only value to be truly universal, and in this sense constitutes an invariant norm of human existence.

Life, equality, and God

But why should life continuance be for all? Why is everyone equal? Hobbes argues without recourse to religion that everyone is equal in all important respects. For Hobbes, man's belief in God stems from his desire for knowing causes as to the beginning of things. In a sort of grounding ontology, Hobbes notes in *Leviathan* that 'The unformed matter of the world, was a God, by the name of Chaos' (1968: I, ch. XII, 75). Hobbes says in the introduction that the passions 'are the same in all men, desire, feare, hope', and further, human beings are equal in their capacities, or roughly so:

> Nature hath made man so equall, in the faculties of body, and mind; as that though there bee found one man sometimes manifestly

stronger in body, or of quicker mind than another; yet when all is reckoned together, the difference between man and man, is not so considerable, as that one man can thereupon claim to himselfe any benefit, to which another may not pretend, as well as he. For as to the strength of the body, the weakest has strength enough to kill the strongest, either by secret machination, or by confederacy with others, that are in the same danger with himself. (1968: I, ch. XIII, 82)

As for the faculties of mind: 'I find yet a greater equality among men, than that of strength. For Prudence, is but Experience; which equall time, equally bestows on all men, in those things they equally apply themselves unto' (1968: I, ch. XIII, 82). While Hobbes concedes that there may well be differences between people, they are not consented to; instead one relates all evaluations to 'a vain conceit of one's owne wisdom which all men think they have in a greater degree, than the Vulgar; that is, than all men but themselves, and a few others, whom by Fame, or for concurring with themselves, they approve' (1968: I, ch. XIII, 82). Thus, he says, from 'equality of ability', there emerges an 'equality of hope in the attaining of our Ends' (1968: I, ch. XIII, 83) which leads to conflicts with others over desires for unattainable objects. Life thus becomes a 'Warre of Every One Against Every One' (1968: I, ch. XIII, 84). Conflict arises between equal beings in disputes over scarce ends.

One can think of humans acting so in a context of material scarcity, and one can even think that this represents part of what can be represented as the nature of the human being so long as one also represents such a nature as a species template that can vary, according to 'circumstance', to use a term borrowed from Hume (1978: 13). At any rate, trying to adduce equality from the state of nature is doubly problematic in that being equal, or unequal, carries a certain normative judgement. It is surely much better to say that history so far has not thrown up any confirmation that some castes or classes are superior or inferior to others, at least not in a way that warrants different consideration. History has shown in fact that all humans are equally arbitrary, which is to say, in more positive terms, that each of us has equal dignity and equal worth, concerning at least our basic status as human beings. Even if history had presented evidence for the superiority of some over others, this does not mean, in moral terms, that those with superior intelligence or capability should be saved or advantaged. Such a proposition would fail in its own terms, but would also quickly give rise to massive *ressentiment* which would potentially endanger the survival not only of the human race, but of life on earth itself.

Locke doesn't think that equality is justified simply by nature, for behind his conception of the state of nature is natural law theory, or God. In his book, *God, Locke and Equality*, Jeremy Waldron maintains that for Locke, humans are morally equal by virtue of possessing reason, which is divinely given. Noting that 'there is precious little in the modern literature on the background idea that we humans are fundamentally one another's equals' (2005a: 2), Waldron considers the issue in relation to Locke. He argues that Locke considered that nature in itself was not adequate for establishing the equality of all humans, but depended on a natural law argument that God created the world. By virtue of humans being God's creatures, and because God gave us reason, humans can reason that each is morally equal and deserves an equal right to exist and not be harmed. Waldron claims that many liberals overlook the central importance of God as foundational to the order of nature for Locke. To this end, he questions whether equality of all is justifiable outside a religious context in relation to Locke's philosophy. For Locke, reason, given by God, is what enables human beings to comprehend their moral obligations.

While sensitive to the fact that religious explanations, if true, would make the justification of ethical and moral claims a lot easier, given the fact that many people do not believe religious explanations, and also the violence, war, and general conflict caused by religion over millennia, it is a moot point as to whether the ease of justification is outweighed by the disadvantages. To opt for a religious justification is to embark upon a highly contentious metaphysical claim, which like the concept of the state of nature in Hobbes, goes well beyond experience to make claims about the noumenal realm, a realm that Kant himself said it was impossible to have knowledge of. As observed above, Locke even claims that private property rights are natural, a disgracefully unjustifiable assertion that has formed the cornerstone of liberal political and economic theory as a bulwark to the capitalist economy.

Continuance ethics justifies rights, morality, and ethics as necessary discourses to survival, independent of God or nature. Indeed, in a context of climate change and increasing population, they are vital if we humans are serious about surviving. That many people, leaders and nations included, seem to suffer from what Lovibond (2002) calls, following Plato, *akrasia* – weakness of will, moral and emotional disengagement, not being really committed, generally prone to 'free-riding' on serious issues, etc. – confounds the issues but doesn't make their seriousness go away.[7] There is no fixed ground or constant reference point; indeed, nature itself, under the burden of climate change, is in danger of imploding. Even without theistic justifications, there is a wide agreement regarding survival; it constitutes the rationale for most of what we humans do, the implicit habitus that defines life itself. There is also wide agreement on basic values concerning terrorism, torture, violence, and killing, as evidenced at Nuremberg and in other forums. Moreover, as Waldron says, drawing on Dworkin, there is 'an obvious and generally accepted truth that governments must treat their citizens as equals' (2005a: 3).[8] The quest to survive creates, in fact, an 'overlapping consensus' around basic values.[9] Rather than a foundation, what we have is an ethos that supports a value that guides actions.

Waldron argues that once we have crossed the threshold of being a rational person, there might be new hierarchies of value that justify treating people unequally. This is correct, of course. Merit, effort, desert, skill, job status, and difficulty all justify differences in treatment, including differences in remuneration. These are in many cases quite legitimate, but do not alter the case for moral equality and also do not justify huge inequalities. The case must be proportionate, for while certain inequalities might be justifiable, each must be addressed on its particular merits. As Amartya Sen argues, 'it is difficult to see how an ethical theory can have general social plausibility without extending equal consideration to all at *some* level' (1992: 3–4). Even groups that are opposed to equality of outcomes, or opposed to the state establishing policies to encourage equality, still argue for *certain* types of equality. For example, says Sen (1992: 3), even Robert Nozick's libertarian approach supports the equal existence of 'extensive basic liberties' and he believes that there is a basic 'moral equality' between all peoples. He simply opposes the state taking action to influence the outcomes that occur from the free interaction of these morally free individuals. There is, it would seem, a widespread consensus today that all humans are morally equal and deserving of respect and equal life chances on this basis. It constitutes a reflective equilibrium that has triumphed historically and is hopefully irreversible. This has not always been the case, of course, and indeed has not been long the case. Yet it would hopefully be difficult having achieved such a position to regress. One does not need to go back far in history to trace the widespread effects of ideologies of class and caste concerning the role of women, or of different races, justified in religious or biological/evolutionary terms.

Reasonable equality can be justified in terms of continuance, just as democracy can be, on the basis that reasonable equality and democracy are more likely to ensure continuance to the future as optimally stable and without conflict, violence, or war. But what about deeper values and beliefs, for example towards suicide, and issues to do with the ultimate meaning of life. Can it really be said that an immanent normativity that has its source in 'this-worldly' criteria, and that rejects all transcendental, metaphysical justifications, can provide normative criteria concerning such phenomena as these? It is essentially this type of argument that Albert Camus comes to in *The Myth of Sisyphus*, where he asks the question, in the absence of eternal values or God, what reason is there for refraining from suicide? 'Judging whether life is or is not worth living amounts to answering the fundamental question of philosophy', he says (1975: 3). But even without God, and 'within the limits of nihilism it is possible to find the means to proceed beyond nihilism' (1975: 1). The issue as to whether life has meaning is his key question; it is 'the most urgent of questions' (1975: 4). Camus's answer – 'to live and to create in the midst of the desert' (1975: 1) – is one source for my claim that once one has determined that life has value, and is interconnected both with other life and with the structures of its support, the questions as to how to live intelligently are purely technical. To put it bluntly, it involves working out a way to live and cohabit with others. Given that there are no transcendent or eternal sources of value, it is life which, recognizing its own quest to survive and prosper, bestows value upon itself, constructing its own discourses for the purpose of continuing.

It is here that I have to admit, however, that continuance ethics can be strengthened by appeal to a version of agnosticism as to the existence of God. Agnosticism doesn't posit the existence of God, but it avoids atheism, which, like theism, crosses into Kant's noumenal realm in order to posit *the existence of the non-existence* of God, going well beyond the confines of the finitude of actual human experience. Like Nietzsche, Foucault would be more faithful to Kant's rule than Kant was himself. Agnosticism only posits God as a *possibility*, a case that could be justified on the grounds that we humans are incapable of evidencing God as a reality through the use of reason. Reason searches for causes, and as Thomas Aquinas observed, to posit an 'uncaused first cause' is rationally incomprehensible. As he says in his essay 'God as the Beginning of Things', 'nothing can be inferred from nothing'. Yet, '*In the beginning God created heaven and earth*, says that *create* means make something from nothing. So, God can make something from nothing' (Aquinas, 1993: 252, 253). Many sophisticated theologians accept that this claim is incomprehensible on the grounds of reason, and claim, thus, to believe in God on *faith*. To posit the non-existence of God also goes beyond the finitude of the phenomenal world where Kant said one could not go, and on that basis, is irrational. Agnosticism is rational because it claims not to know and hence doesn't break Kant's rule.

While God in this model is a *possibility*, it would seem to me that one could only *hope* on faith. Agnosticism doesn't affirm the existence of God, yet it doesn't deny such existence either. For certain doubting minds, this possibility could be claimed to bolster the argument to treat all humans as equal, and also to respect all other life forms. Notwithstanding the ingenuity of Camus, for many it might be seen as strengthening the argument as to why one shouldn't routinely commit suicide. Agnosticism thus possibly assists in relation to justifying deeper questions to do with the meaning of life. Having said this, one must behave as if there is no God. Life justifies life, and also the decision to end life. The norms of continuance can justify why we should have liberty, democracy, a stable society, robust institutions, as well as certain ethical and moral beliefs, because they assume that we are committed to survival. Survival, then, is, in Kantian terms, a hypothetical imperative: *if* we are committed to continuing life, *then* certain things follow – regarding ethics, the organization of society, and so on. In this sense, irrespective of any commitment to agnosticism, the value of survival has overwhelming agreement, constitutes an overwhelming consensus, a 'reflective equilibrium' in Rawls's (1971) sense, bolstered by the fact, perhaps, that for people who disagree, the exit strategy of suicide diminishes any real opposition.

Modern social contract theory

The social contract theories of Hobbes, Locke, and Rousseau received new impetus with the publication in 1971 of John Rawls's book, *A Theory of Justice*. Rawls sought to reformulate the classical contract of the state of nature by positing a hypothetical contract situation comprising contractors reasoning to establish principles of justice that could form the basis of the modern state.[10] As with the classical theory, the central concern was to harmonize the separate interests of individuals in order to reconcile the good of each to the good of all. Rawls's contractors operated from within a hypothetical contract situation, which Rawls termed the 'original position', where they reasoned principles of justice that would be both fair and impartial. Rawls utilized the idea of the 'veil of ignorance' (Rawls, 1971: 137, n. 11; 1999a: 118, n. 11), which he took over from John Harsanyi,[11] a hypothetical device by which the contractors to the original position would be deprived of knowledge of their own social positions and identities so that they could not be biased. The method of reasoning was that of 'reflective equilibrium', where the contractors would form principles of justice based on established forms of reasoning.[12] The idea of reflective equilibrium applied to contract theory was that contractors would start with particulars, subsuming them under general principles in a back-and-forth process with the expectation of convergence or agreement.[13] The original position simulated the state of nature of the classical contract theorists in that it was intended to provide neutral, ahistorical, that is, rational grounds on which explanation could proceed.[14]

The initial theoretical impetus to modern social contract theory was as a response to intuitionism and utilitarianism. Intuitionism was seen as implausible as a method of ethics.[15] Social contract theorists such as Rawls argued that the claim of intuitionists to apprehend the objective status of moral truths by a special faculty without justification was unacceptable methodologically. H. A. Prichard had famously questioned why one should bother to undertake duties from a sense of obligation, and answered, as a good intuitionist would, that one immediately apprehended them without argument or justification.[16] Not happy with such an explanation, the contract theorists argued that obligations were grounded in practical rationality and arguments needed to be advanced in order to account for them. A Foucauldian normative theory would agree with contract theory in its critique of intuitionism.

A Foucauldian normative theory would also agree with social contract theory in relation to utilitarianism. Utilitarianism was viewed as not taking seriously the thesis concerning the separateness of persons. This problem was initially raised by H. L. A. Hart (1979). As Albert Weale puts it, '[it] subsumed individuals in an hypothesized common good' (2020: 51). For Rawls the separateness of persons meant that utilitarianism could not account for the claims of individual moral worth. In that utilitarianism was held to deny the separateness of persons, can the same charge be directed at poststructuralism? Whereas utilitarianism sought to harmonize the relations between the one and the many by constraining individual differences in terms of a conception of good defined in terms of aggregate happiness, poststructuralism views individuals as socially and historically constructed, experiencing individuation within history through successive differentiation within time/space. Although individual actions must be 'harmonized' in relation to the good of continuance, the political function is to establish the limits of the necessary within which a zone of discretion operates.

The key point here is that 'continuance' is different to 'pleasure', in that regulation proceeds according to what is necessary, not on the basis of maximizing good. Although continuance ethics operates as a theory of the good, importantly, influenced by complexity dynamics, right action is not defined solely as what is *productive of good*, as was pointed out in Chapter 4. Neither is the good the sum of individuals' goods or interests in any aggregate sense. In continuance ethics, although the *source* of ethical and moral claims is social, the fact that individual conduct and action operates in space/time from particular vantage points means that all right action has its own specificity in relation to judgement, location, timing, and motive. Action thus has both a teleological and a deontic dimension, neither reducible to the other. This situational specificity of right actions gives each action its own value and distinctiveness. This means that the individual can exercise claims against the good. Furthermore, the good of continuance cannot be maximized or averaged. One does not produce *more* continuance; one acts *in accordance with continuance*. The good of continuance is thus not the same as the good of aggregate happiness. Continuance points to the norm of life in societies and among living beings. Such a norm inheres collectively in shared interests and social structures, and individually, in each living part as well. As such, continuance sets limits to action but does not dispense with right conduct or individual integrity.

How, one might ask, does continuance rank one duty over another? Continuance helps explain how duties are more or less important dependent upon a contingent array of factors constitutive of the situation in terms of which judgements are called for. It arbitrates between rights and consequences in the same way. While consequences will be important, they may be overridden by other factors, for consequences are subordinate to the norm of continuance itself. While what is optimal for continuance might be difficult to gauge, judgements will still be required, and acts of judgement require issues to be democratically appraised and balanced, that is, they require proportionality.[17] It will be considered in one situation that certain principles or practices are more important; in other contexts, more than one social practice might appear to impact on life continuance more or less equally. While in some cases continuance will assist directly with prioritizing or ranking matters of ethical concern, on the 'hard issues' where consensus cannot easily be obtained, it validates the democratic process as the best method for harmonizing conflicting interests.

Constructivism is another similarity between a Foucauldian and a contract approach. Constructivism sees ethical values as the outcome of the decision process.[18] It includes a sense of normative discourse as constructed in history and operating under certain specified conditions, from which can be derived justifiable principles of practice. Scanlon argues that:

> a constructivist account of the normative domain is appealing because it seems to offer a way of explaining how normative judgments can have determinate truth values that are independent of us while also providing a basis for our epistemological access to these truths and an explanation of their practical significance for us. (2014: 91)

For Rawls, 'the principle of political justice (content) may be represented as the outcome of a certain procedure of construction' (2005: 89–90). Constructivism also establishes that the explanation for social practices and principles of justice is not metaphysical in the sense of referring to a reality beyond experience. Although a Foucauldian would deny that social contract theory complies with this latter rationalization, that they think they are arguing rationally rather than appealing to metaphysics is central to their own self-understanding of their endeavour. In Foucault's view, in that modern contract theory is a reformulation of the classical contract theory of Hobbes, Locke, and Kant, it appeals to a naturalistic metaphysics and a highly contentious metaphysical conception of the subject with conservative social and political implications.

A Foucauldian would also agree with the principle of *justice as fairness*. While Rawls would argue that our considered judgements tell us that slavery is wrong, Foucault would not object to the conclusion, but he would object to the process whereby the conclusion was arrived at. The problem is the method, and as a method of ethics, contract theory is unreliable. This relates to the decision procedure by which contract theorists claim to arrive at their conclusions concerning knowledge of natural dispositions through reason. What I propose to do here is list and comment upon the major reasons why a Foucauldian would reject social contract theory.

Foucauldian objections to contract theory

From a Foucauldian point of view, the artefact of the social contract would be rejected outright as a foundationalist approach that claims to ground reason in order to discover agent-neutral principles of justice that can be arrived at through reasoning alone. The attempt to establish universal principles of justice that were to apply in all times and places constitutes a rule type morality that was anathema to Foucault. Foucault would also dispute that a universalizing strategy of reason from a neutral starting point that prevented knowledge of the context or situation from being taken into account, and was based upon a highly contentious model of the subject as a self-interested maximizer, could be sufficient to determine justice, assist with the practical functions of the state, or constitute the basis of a normative theory.[19] It is difficult for critics of contract theory to see how a supposedly neutral method that is claimed to be purely procedural can arrive at normative conclusions, and how reason can be applied to matters of social justice without any understanding of specific contexts or ends. While reason can assist, normative conclusions require appropriate normative and political premises.

Foucault would also deny that social contract theory was coherent on its own terms. In fact, the paradigm has been fraught with endless attempts to justify the model of the contractual situation ever since Rawls published his book (see Weale, 2020). As Albert Weale points out, to inspire confidence, the decision procedure would have to be confirmable independently, and yet it is far from clear that it meets such a condition (Weale, 2020: 367ff.). Although the hypothetical contractual situation is meant to *determine* the principles of justice for society, Rawls spends considerable effort structuring it in certain ways *in advance*. Various principles, such as the principle of equal worth, become mandatory, not as the outcome of the reasoning process, but as a *presupposition*. According to Weale, Rawls also maintains that 'the account of rationality of the contracting parties should be consistent with the economic theory of rationality' (2020: 66). Rawls seemed to be proposing, says Weale, that a 'well-established theory of rationality and choice ... should be incorporated into contract theory' (2020: 66). On whose say so, one is entitled to ask, does this structuration take place? Instead of structuring the hypothetical contract situation in a purely procedural way, Rawls 'ends up with a theory that has strong moral commitments at its core' (Weale, 2020: 67).

Rawls builds into the hypothetical contractual situation the various axioms of justice that the contractors behind the 'veil of ignorance' are supposed to deliberate and decide upon. As to where Rawls gets these principles that structure the original position from, Weale says that it 'looks like a return to a form of intuitionism' (2020: 67). It is in this way that Rawls 'front-loads' the hypothetical contract situation to protect rights. The question of whether the contractors might reason to conclusions wildly discrepant from sentiments prevailing in society no doubt concerned him. What if the contractors wanted to install socialism, or reinstall a social practice such as slavery, perhaps in a gendered form, as sexual slavery? Other social contract theorists front-loaded rights against the possibilities of change in other ways. James Buchanan and Gordon Tullock introduced a requirement for unanimity into their hypothetical contractual situation. The unanimity rule proposed that a veto by a single individual could prevent change, and that 'only if a specific constitutional change can be shown to be in the interests of all parties shall we judge such a change to be an improvement' (1962: 14). A constitutional change is defined by them in broad terms to include social welfare, taxation, property rights, and general economic structuring. In advocating the unanimity rule, Buchanan and Tullock have given rise to an industry of analysis and criticism which I am not intending to survey in detail here.[20] Suffice it to note that the demand for unanimity as a decision-rule romanticizes the market as the bedrock for politics, falsely claims to emulate science, and relies on a model of laissez-faire and competitive economics that is not realistic.[21] To be fair, a voting rule must be normatively meaningful.[22] The unanimity rule proposed as the optimal decision-rule for politics constitutes, as many have observed, a conservative defence of the status quo.[23] Paradoxically, if adopted as a universal rule, it would deny that different decision-rules may be relevant at different times; it enables the minority to tyrannize the majority and prevent change; it ignores the costs associated with engineering unanimous consensus and the sheer inertia that would result from a government's inability to carry out change (including its electoral pledges); and it fails to explain why other decision-rules (e.g., majority rule, two-thirds majority) are not satisfactory. Indeed, in a frequently cited article, Douglas Rae (1975) put forward a contractarian

Hobbes, God, and modern social contract theory 209

defence of majority rule, arguing that consensual decision making as put forward by Buchanan and Tullock doesn't lead to greater efficiency, and that it is simple majority rule that in fact maximizes the convergence between public choice and individual preference.[24] A Foucauldian takes the view that unanimity, like Rawls's attempts to front-load the hypothetical contract situation, constitutes an anti-democratic attempt to structure the political process in order to prevent or limit the possibility of change.

In addition to these criticisms, contract theory offers an unsatisfactory explanation of obligations. It is especially unreliable as a theory of obligation as it cannot show convincingly why *self-interested subjects* have obligations to act in accord with the principles of justice based solely on *compliance*.[25] Continuance theory justifies obligations directly as an expression of the wish to survive and prosper. Altruism is explained as a consequence of being alive, and of being as capable of altruism as of competition. Survival is any attempt to sustain life in any environment that supports multiple character traits that are operative in different contexts. Because it rejects naturalism as a foundation, self-interest is seen as a historically contingent aspect of socialization reflecting the structuration of environments at a particular conjuncture in history. This is not to deny that self-interested behaviour is not always a possibility, but rather to say that it is not given foundational status as the central defining trait of all persons in all contexts at all times. 'Prichard's dilemma', to use Scanlon's phrase (Scanlon, 1998: 149–50),[26] which essentially asks the question 'Why be obligated at all?', is met head-on because continuance claims to tap into an immanent normativity. Continuance ethics can in this sense explain social relations beyond 'what we owe to each other' (to use Scanlon's phrase),[27] also explaining ethical obligations *beyond* interpersonal relations – to animals, the environment, and beyond the call of duty (supererogation).

In the broader sense, there is a difficulty in contract theory in its reliance on a theory of consent, or compliance, within its model of the hypothetical contract on the basis of actors motivated solely by self-interest and mutual advantage. As Weale notes, there is a problem in social contract theory relying on a theory of compliance at all. Weale cites Hart, who notes how punishment is required *because* we cannot rely on voluntary compliance. As Hart says: '[w]hat reason demands is voluntary behaviour within a coercive system' (cited in Weale, 2020: 383).[28] The importance of a punishment regimen, and the theoretical weakness of a presumption of a concept of consent as the basis of social relations, would both be corrected by the continuance model in its theorization of system and individual requirements for continuing into the future. This is especially so given that democracy exists as a recognition of the collective dimension of selfhood and the fact that individuals cannot possibly survive by acting alone. On this basis, the general good can in some cases outweigh the claims of particular individuals, such as occurs in relation to strengthening or maintaining system factors to sustain or increase security for individuals, to consolidate prudence over interest, or to deploy affirmative action campaigns to correct system anomalies. The punishment regimen of a society is also a case in point.

In Foucault's view, contract theory exaggerates the reasoning capacities of the subject. When Descartes said 'I think therefore I am', he inaugurated the Enlightenment, exalting human beings' capacity to formulate 'clear and distinct ideas' by separating reason from unreason. For Foucault, this also initiated the arrogance of the Enlightenment, the over-confidence on human beings' part of their own capacity for reason. If Descartes was wrong, and reason and ideology, folklore and good sense, circulate together; if the 'evil genius' (of the first *Meditation*) cannot be so easily excluded from the process through which knowledge is generated – then is it not possible that the liberal Enlightenment has exaggerated our rational capacities?[29] A Foucauldian believes that placing the full burden on the individual acting and reasoning alone fails to recognize that while reason is an invaluable tool, it is not something that individuals always use well. Individuals do not always think clearly. As Marschak says, '[l]iving men and women are apt to misplace their decimal points; they often confuse the part for the whole; and they are not above confusing a sufficient condition for a necessary one. That is, they do not behave rationally' (1950: 111, cited in Weale, 2020: 98). Derek Parfit's thesis in *Reasons and Persons* in many ways complements Marschak's thesis, in that Parfit argues that we as often as not act against our own best interests, frequently labour under a false view of what our best interests are, do not fully understand our own motives for action, and possess values and moral beliefs that are self-defeating. In *The Birth of Biopolitics*, Foucault (2008a: 216–89) opposed the rational choice theory of Gary Becker, opting for a more limited concept of rationality than that implied by the idea of *homo economicus* (see Becker, 1962; 1993).[30] Herbert Simons's (1982; 1983) concept of 'bounded rationality' is insightful in this context because it suggests limits to our capacity for reasoning in relation to thinking capacity, restrictions on time, and the limitations of information. The fact that people are not always rational does not mean, of course, that there are not better and worse ways to live, and that reason cannot assist in ascertaining what to do. If practical rationality is a way of thinking things through – from *a* to *z* – then it is a *process without a subject*. In this case, it is not necessary to envisage hypothetical contractors reasoning from behind a 'veil of ignorance' in order to render oneself unbiased and check one's prejudices. The rational thing to do can be calculated via an algorithm. As for controlling bias and ensuring an effective process of reasoning, making decisions in a public context, through a process of deliberation that is open and scrutinized, that is, democratic, will far more successfully control prejudice or bias.[31]

To the extent that this holds true, normative reasoning must be testable in the open courts of democratic contestation through conjectures and refutations, proposal and counter-proposal; *not* on the basis of any special faculty of reason on the part of contractors acting 'in camera' from behind a 'veil of ignorance'.[32] Democratic methods of reconciling the individual and collective are also more effective given the factors concerning the agonistic character of social relations, the ubiquity of power imbalances in social life, and the commingling of reason with unreason and ideology. While collective politics has potential dangers, as the existence of totalitarian governments and episodes of ethnic cleansing and genocide document, perhaps the surest method of extending democracy and reconciling such interests is to adapt the method of the Stoics, by building *ascending concentric circles* of checks and balances from the local to the global. Modern communications technologies offer some possibilities for amplifying instances of abuse or shortcomings in a way not available to previous generations.

A Foucauldian alternative

Contract theory is thus incompatible with an acceptable normative theory for politics. Our considered judgements must be arrived at in open forums subject to the 'to and fro' of political contestation that is both epistemologically and methodologically necessary to the process of concordance, given the agonistic character of social relations and the fact that they are structured by power. Although in the debates with Habermas, Foucault's position opposed Habermas's argument that the 'strategic' and 'communicative' uses of language can be separated, enabling rationality to succeed in carefully structured contexts such as law or government, a solution to Foucault's distrust in the possibilities of an epistemologically protected political process would be to increase the political safeguards, that is, the number of alternative, countervailing powers, processes of appeal, and checks and balances generally, based on the general adage that the solution to the problems of democracy is more and better democracy. Foucault says of politics what he says of philosophy, that it should be 'precisely the challenging of all phenomena of domination at whatever level or under whatever form they present themselves – political, economic, sexual, institutional, and so on' (1991a: 20; see Habermas, 1984; 1986; 1987; Foucault, 1980d; 1984c; 1988e). In such a context, Foucault stands for a normative context whereby power relations operate on fair and equal terms free of any states of domination, *to the greatest extent possible*. Democracy constitutes a series of arenas where all participants who meet the terms of continuance can participate; democracy also constitutes a principle whereby *optimally* all viewpoints can be considered under fairly structured and protected conditions.

Given that knowledge is partial, incomplete, and prone to error, one implication of Foucault's view concerning the subject is that collective reasoning is more effective than individual reasoning. Such a statement has important implications for political ethics. In this sense, the democratic forum constitutes a safer and more reliable apparatus for decision making than does Rawls's 'original position', which places sole reliance on the process of reasoning conducted purely on the basis of laws of logic independent of the agonistic nature of society, with the ever-present possibility that reason will be contaminated by ideology or prejudice. The point Foucault would make is that rational reflection and deliberation *require* contestation and open debate, on the basis of the need to be vigilant as to the ever-present possibility of subversion through the abuse of power. Based on the adage that there is safety in numbers, democratic contestation is more likely to result in better decision making. Unlike the hypothetical contract, democracy constitutes a forum that permits feedback, is accountable, allows for interrogation and appeal, builds in checks and safeguards, and is optimally transparent.

While the concept of democratic forum refers to the apparatus of government, for a Foucauldian it also refers to the general structuration of social relations, including family, employment, industry, and civil society. While many of these arenas are not democratic, or not sufficiently democratic, the commitment to principles such as accountability, transparency, rights, and entitlements, as well as duties and obligations, constitutes them as suitable arenas for the extension of democratic norms and practices further into the heartland of civil society. In this conception, it may be noted, Foucault's politics are free from obligation to any authority except that of democratic contestation and rational democratic process, embodied in the norms of continuance itself. Because it accents contestation as a counter-discourse against the myriad abuses that power can adopt within social and political settings, it provides a more effective method of challenging prejudice or habitual thinking, as well as cronyism, gerrymandering, nest feathering, or other forms of corruption, which Enlightenment I has failed to curtail, and which Enlightenment II must now take up.[33]

In this sense, by linking life continuance to democracy, continuance ethics represents itself as both meta-ethical and normative. It is meta-ethical in that it can specify the ontological status of its normative values; it is normative in that it can articulate the content and type of its normative values. In terms of a method of ethics, it replaces the contract with the democratic forum, as well as replacing the solitary reasoning of the original position with rational reflection and debate. It says what many see contract theory as trying to say, but does so more plausibly and more directly.[34] Although consequences can be taken into account, they are not determining. It can also rank conflicting demands according to the priorities of continuance at a particular time. The rules for democracy rest on a non-metaphysical theory of objective value concerned with 1) survival as a collective and individual project, and 2) well-being, where well-being is satisfied if i) basic needs are provided for, and ii) opportunities, benefits, and burdens are distributed justly. Normatively, it specifies an ethic of equal consideration for all where such an ethic can be justified both instrumentally and probabilistically as constituting the best (i.e., most likely) policy to ensure life continuance for all. To effect this, it adopts 'Bentham's dictum', as expressed by Mill, the maxim that 'everybody to count for one, nobody for more than one' (Mill, 1910: 58).[35] Policies, values, actions, principles, and ways of life deemed to be valuable for traversing the future are claimed to constitute an objective basis for establishing a conception of good. Unlike utilitarianism, the aim is not to make the majority better off, or to maximize aggregate welfare, but to ensure the survival and well-being of all as the best policy for assuring the survival and well-being of each.

If not the contract, on what basis are the founding principles just mentioned justified? As the principle of continuance represents an immanent norm for survival and well-being, it constitutes an objective *red thread* by which human institutions are judged.[36] The clause of 'equal consideration' is justified in a social constructionist world on the grounds that there can be no natural grounds to justify difference; in this sense, everyone is *equally* arbitrary and unjustifiable, *equally* a disposable 'piece of shit' in Žižek's (1999: 157) sense, *equally* a 'pale blue dot' in Carl Sagan's words, or having *equal* dignity, depending upon one's preferred point of view. Žižek's manner of expression is useful in the sense that, in alerting us to the ease with which life can be disposed of, it also alerts us to the *equal right not to be disposed of*, and the importance of institutional forms of security for life in a crowded world to be protected. However one wants to think such issues through, the justification links to the immanent quest to survive and prosper for each and all, with democracy being represented as the best method for assuring continuance, that is, the method least likely to engender *ressentiment*, to misuse Nietzsche's concept, or, in Hobbes's phrase, the most likely to prevent a 'war of all against all'. Democracy can most effectively harmonize the interests of the one and the many.

In order to save the integrity of the process *as constructivist*, and to avoid positing principles *prior to* democratic deliberation, for all aspects, including democracy itself, the process and content of the rules are themselves subject to democratic confirmation. While conventionally defined, the actual norm of continuance provides a standard independent of mere convention. This is because one can always argue that a certain practice or policy *is not really best for life continuance itself*. While given the uncertainty of the future, the art of establishing what precisely facilitates continuance will be inexact and experimental, the existence of such a norm nevertheless constitutes an objectivist criterion. Rawls's principles of justice are justified on the basis of continuance, too, in that if resources are distributed *fairly*, according to egalitarian principles, *ressentiment* will be minimized and social *concordance* will be more likely. As well as distributing goods more fairly, it is also important, as writers such as Sen and Nussbaum maintain, to ensure the even (and fair) development of capabilities (Nussbaum and Sen, 1993). Conceived in this way, establishing morality on the grounds of a contract is rendered unecessary.

Notes

1 While it is true that Hobbes saw himself as opposing the Aristotelian world view, Aristotle's view of language was similar to Hobbes's, notwithstanding his view of man as a *zoon politikon* (political animal). For Aristotle, in *On Interpretation*, language is represented, as for Hobbes, as a 'marker' of 'vocal sounds' to reveal what was in the 'soul'. Locke held a similar view, seeing language as a vehicle through which ideas were represented and communicated. Words are also but 'signs' for Locke. See Locke's *Essay Concerning Human Understanding* (1994: 176–80). See Taylor (1997: 80–2).
2 Patton is citing Nietzsche twice in this statement. The first quote is from *On the Genealogy of Morals*, §161; the second is from *Thus Spoke Zarathustra*, §138.
3 Citing Nietzsche from *On the Genealogy of Morals*.

4 Christine Korsgaard (1996a: 91) says, 'Kant, like Hume and Williams thinks that morality is grounded in human nature'.
5 I am thinking here of *The Sources of Normativity* (Korsgaard, 1996a).
6 I am not particularly happy with Hobbes's definition here, however, and prefer Hume's. So, I say, life continuance is normative. Reason assists in bringing it into being. It is the 'servant of life' (to modify Hume).
7 My source for this comment is Lovibond (2002: 88–100, 109, 124n). The source in Plato is *Meno* (78a6) and *Protagoras* (358b7).
8 Waldron refers to Dworkin's *Sovereign Virtue* (2000: 128).
9 In an overlapping consensus, citizens all endorse a core set of values or laws for different reasons (see Rawls, 1987).
10 Among other modern contract theorists are Brian Barry (1965; 1989), James Buchanan and Gordon Tullock (1962), David Gauthier (1963; 1969), Russell Grice (1967; 1977), John Harsanyi (1953; 1955; 1976), and Thomas Scanlon (1982; 1998; 2008; 2014).
11 Harsanyi is credited as making the first modern use of the veil of ignorance idea (see Harsanyi, 1953).
12 Rawls first proposed the method in 1951 in 'An Outline of a Decision-Procedure for Ethics' (1999b: 1–19), and later in *A Theory of Justice* (1999a: 18, n. 7, 18–19, 42–5, 507–8).
13 Rawls describes it as 'a process of mutual adjustment of principles and considered judgments' (1999a: 18, n. 7).
14 Interesting here is that while modern contract theory presupposes self-interested subjects, there was considerable variation between writers such as Hobbes, Locke, and Rousseau in their conceptions of the subject. There was a difference also in the aims of analysis: classical contract theory sought to explain political obligation, whereas modern contract theory is interested in principles of justice.
15 The Cambridge Platonists, including W. D. Ross, are among the earliest modern representatives of the tradition (see Ross, 2002).
16 See Prichard (1912: 29), where he says, 'we do not come to appreciate an obligation by an *argument*'. See also Weale (2020: 50, 378), for discussion of the issue.
17 It is in this sense that continuance ethics are not consequentialist, as while consequences may well win out in a particular situation, they are not in themselves *determining* of ethical decisions.
18 Anglo-American philosophy and poststructuralism utilize a similar conception of constructivism, due to their common ancestry in Kant. See also Weale (2020: ch. 3) and Bagnoli (2013).
19 It is in this sense that the contract theory of Rawls, like Kant's theory, appears to commit Moore's 'naturalistic fallacy', by claiming that pure

reason, expressed as logical chains of inference, such as in the practical syllogism, can reason to a normative conclusion (see Moore, 1903).

20 See Rae (1975), Coleman (1989), Barry (1965; 1990), Shapiro (1990: 79–125), Nelson (2010), and Weale (2020: ch. 6). All of these authors raise serious criticisms of the unanimity rule.

21 In *The Calculus of Consent*, Buchanan and Tullock note the likelihood that the unanimity rule may not actually apply for any real-world decisions, and also acknowledge that unanimity may be costly and difficult to achieve (1962: 69).

22 While it claims to be merely aggregational and non-normative, as Shapiro says, the model actually '"distorts" preferences' (1990: 94) and 'rests on a misleading theory of action' (1990: 92) in that it unjustifiably privileges actions that mimic what the market would produce.

23 Buchanan and Tullock justify it on the grounds that 1) it is the decision-rule that would be chosen by self-interested subjects acting rationally; 2) it is by definition acceptable to all; 3) such a rule ensures the inviolability of the person; and 4) it is fully inclusive of all individuals. It also 5) mimics consumer preferences in the market and is sensitive to property rights distribution.

24 Buchanan and Tullock can also be accused of being ambivalent; hence they say, 'were decision-making costless, rational voters would choose a unanimity rule. Because decision-making is not costless, simple majority is the second-best solution' (1962: 215). The issue concerning ambivalence is a fairly standard criticism of Buchanan and Tullock. William Nelson notes, for instance, that, in chapter 8 of *The Calculus of Consent*, they proceed to argue 'that something closer to majority rule might be preterable all things considered given the costs of reaching a consensus' (2010: 83). See also Coleman (1989: passim).

25 Rawls tends to assume in *Theory of Justice* that citizens act on the basis of comprehensive doctrines. The point is taken from Weale, who argues that '[t]he ambition to produce a theory of obligation which shows how the sense of justice is purely internal and dispositional fails' (2020: 383).

26 The question that Prichard put was: 'Is there really a reason why I should act in the ways in which hitherto I have thought I ought to act?' (1912: 21). I am indebted to Weale (2020: 9ff.) for alerting me to this literature.

27 Scanlon's book is titled *What We Owe to Each Other* (1998).

28 Carole Pateman (1988) also raises the exclusive focus on consent as problematic and as central to understanding contract theory as a theory of domination. Rawls's theory will do nothing in Pateman's view to

reform or change patriarchy, as only what is in the direct self-interest of the parties would be engaged with. Consent also doesn't view what is required for the future as central compared to the present, in that infrastructural developments, punishment regimes, and other structural reforms might not be undertaken, or prioritized, by self-interested subjects. In short, Pateman suggests, a society of self-interested subjects would lack appreciation of the norms required to make society work. It is this fact that accounts for the problems in making the contract model work, and why Rawls had to 'front-load' the hypothetical contract situation as he did.

29 In the first of his 1641 *Meditations on First Philosophy*, Descartes imagines that an evil demon, of 'utmost power and cunning has employed all his energies in order to deceive me'. Although, for Descartes, the evil genius intends to create the illusion of an external world, the banishment of the influence also becomes a condition for 'clear and distinct ideas' in general.

30 For a critique of Human Capital Theory, see Brown, Lauder, and Cheung (2020).

31 It will also mean that justice can be seen to be done; a requirement that contract theory also appears to fail to meet under the stringent tests of Foucault's sceptical suspicion.

32 The very idea of the 'veil', although intended to remove biases, also has the effect, it could be argued, of protecting the contractors from the gaze of those external to the process, thereby installing a norm of secrecy – hence the use of the phrase 'in camera'.

33 This distinction between Enlightenment I and Enlightenment II provides a shorthand way of representing Foucault's view that the Enlightenment project has not been a complete failure, but must now develop new strategies and be concerned with issues not satisfactorily resolved by the initial project. Issues of rights and democracy concerned with gender, sexuality, race and ethnicity, marriage, and employment constitute suitable areas for future consideration and action.

34 It is in this sense that the concept of continuance to the future, rather than that of a hypothetical contract, provides a more realistic rationale for what it is 'not reasonable to reject' in interpersonal relations (see Scanlon, 1998). On this basis, continuance theory is capable of explaining interpersonal ethical comportment and why social relations generate moral and ethical obligations. As a further point here, continuance also enables a substantive (as opposed to a purely formal) argument as to *why* it is not reasonable to reject a particular argument.

35 Although Foucault did not invoke Bentham or Mill to assert this principle, his writings in general, and on life and Canguilhem in particular, emphatically affirm it.
36 The term 'red thread' is that used by Foucault, already cited in Chapter 2, when he posits the important link between 'error', 'life', and 'normativity' in noting that for Canguilhem, '[i]t is the notion of error that enables him ... to bring out the relationship between life and knowledge [*connaissance*] and to follow, *like a red thread*, the presence of value and the norm within it' (1998b: 477, emphasis added).

7

A politics of pluralism

Political pluralism: Montesquieu's conception

William Connolly says that 'pluralism is not the same as "cultural relativism", "absolute tolerance", or "the abandonment of all standards"' (2005b: 41). He acknowledges that 'many critics ... treat these perspectives as if they were the same' (2005b: 41). Connolly defines cultural relativism as 'the view that you should support the culture that is dominant in a particular place' (2005b: 41). In my language, cultural relativism specifies no principle or standard that can justify or be appealed to on moral or normative grounds to regulate limits to pluralism. Unless a principle that specifies limits is stipulated, then pluralism must accept any group or viewpoint as legitimate, including those that do not support pluralism or democracy. In a previous book I criticized Isaiah Berlin for arguing for a conception of pluralism that was potentially relativistic, providing inadequate criteria for excluding any groups, whether Nazi or terrorist, from the circle of legitimate political contenders.[1] Critics of Foucault who judge him a relativist, such as Jürgen Habermas and Noam Chomsky, have levelled similar charges against him.[2] I will argue in this chapter that the principle of life continuance can undergird pluralism with criteria of inclusion and exclusion. As democracy is necessary to continuance as a mechanism for the reconciliation of disputes within groups and between individuals, failure to genuinely support democracy itself constitutes the outer limit of unity within which pluralism must operate. Difference within unity is the only coherent policy in this respect.

Foucault arrives at political pluralism through his analysis of power. He opposes Marx's repressive theory of power, replacing it with a thesis that power is both repressive and productive, and ubiquitous throughout life. In this chapter, I want to understand the importance of political pluralism to his ethics by relating his conception initially to that of another French thinker on power: Charles-Louis de Secondat, baron de La Brède et de Montesquieu. Montesquieu's thesis of the 'distribution of powers' and Foucault's thesis of the 'ubiquity of power' constitute a potential homology that I believe is normatively productive of some form of alliance between these two thinkers. Foucault saw resistance to power as a force prompted by life itself. Rather than resistance constituting a purely arbitrary reaction, it is constituted, rather, as a reaction to oppression and the denial of life. As Foucault says in *The History of Sexuality, Volume I*:

> against this power that was still new in the nineteenth century, the forces that resisted relied for support on the very thing it invested, that is, on life and man as a living being ... life, understood as the basic needs, man's concrete essence, the realisation of his potential, a plenitude of the possible ... life as a political object was in a sense taken at face value and turned back against the system that was bent on controlling it. It was life more than the law that became the issue of political struggles ... (1980c: 144, 145)

This focus on life constituted a technology around two poles, says Foucault; one centred on the disciplines of the body, the other on the regulation of populations. While Foucault describes in detail the techniques used to maintain order, focusing on both poles – *disciplinary* and *biopower* – life must also have constituted a normative reference point for policy makers in that outside the issue of the techniques of control and order effected by governments, it would also need to be considered what preferred policies might be best from the perspective of saving life itself.

Such a normativity is implicit in the concept of *biopower* as concerned with an evaluation of the future, of 'what we are in the process of becoming' (Deleuze, 1992: 164). Such a question needs to be considered by those in government, but it would also be considered by those outside government, by elites throughout society, and by citizens generally. Especially after the emergence of states, it is obvious to ask, as many did, how life could best be benefited overall; how best could security be maintained. This would lead to critical reflection concerning whether our present grids of historical reflection were either 'adequate' or 'fair' in terms of how they functioned relative to the various interests in the polis and the task of benefiting life overall.

That many did ask such questions gave rise to serious disagreements and conflicts as to how best life could be served. At the same time, there could be surprising consensus on some basic issues – as Kant noticed – such as the acceptability of lying or cheating, the use of force or violence, the sanctity of contracts, promise keeping, etc., which undergird the normative domains of ethics and morality within the domain of the social, coincident upon enduring reliability in the ongoing conduct of the economy and the concerns of security. If life seeks to continue, then it functions as a safety valve, as Montesquieu appreciated, if power is distributed in a plurality of centres across the social domain. This insight can today be extended to include the global order generally. This is also the basis of Foucault's pluralism and the key to his political activism in support of prison reform, on behalf of the Polish Solidarity Movement, for the rights of victims of oppression, and against the Shah of Iran, when Foucault agitated regularly to redress power imbalances and secure the rights of marginalized groups.

The possible homology with Montesquieu, on the issue of power at least, is striking. So long as we can take life as both a normative reference point, as well as justifying governmental technologies, it would seem that both thinkers could support the distribution of powers as strengthening the possibilities for life continuance via democracy. Montesquieu and Foucault are complementary on this issue. Montesquieu did provide a normative analysis of power; Foucault theorized power as omnipresent but shied away from normative analysis. Yet concepts such as 'resistance', 'intolerability', and 'limits' are pregnant with possibility. Intolerability defines the limit at the level of the political, just as falsification establishes the limit at the level of the empirical. Both thinkers theorized power as capable of controlling power. In the *Spirit of Laws*, Montesquieu says that 'it is necessary from the very nature of things that power should be a check to power' (2015: 205). If generalized to consider the functions of power in society at large, the idea of *corps intermédiaires* comprising associations of every sort, all intent on watching and controlling the government and each other, constitutes one basis for pluralism in the sense of a democratic safeguard that can be applied within the nation-state as well as the global order of states.

Although it has become a commonplace to interpret Book XI of Montesquieu's *Spirit of Laws* as theorizing the 'separation of powers' in relation to the executive, legislature, and judiciary, as the basis of liberty, security, and moderation, Montesquieu was in fact, according to the French jurist Charles Eisenmann, theorizing the separation of powers more generally as a thesis concerning the *balance* or *distribution* of powers (1933: 163–92). For Montesquieu, says Eisenmann, the 'separation of powers' referred to the ability of institutions to 'check' or 'balance' each other in their actions. What concerned Montesquieu was the plurality of power centres as a guarantee of fair play, which constituted a safeguard against monopoly or abuse. While the executive, legislature, and judiciary were the three pertinent powers relating to government, Montesquieu's thesis is more aptly represented as pertaining to the distribution of *corps intermédiaires* throughout the entirety of civil society as a hedge against the excessive unity of the state. Expressed in such a way, Montesquieu's thesis can be extended to the global sphere as well, where certain institutions and agencies begin to command over time a *reputation* or *authority* by virtue of their perceived ethical or moral integrity as well as their effectiveness in relation to national or international affairs. Power is not just ubiquitous throughout society; some powers acquire normative significance or authority, both formally and by reputation. After his visit to England in 1729–30, Montesquieu even concluded that the monarchy, in its newly reformulated status after 1688, posed no threat to his republican model of politics, and could contribute to a deeper conception of democracy by constituting an additional check on, or counterpoint to, the activities of government (see Cranston, 1986; Shackleton, 1961; Starobinski, 1953). Whereas the old English monarch cancelled freedom, post-1688 the limited monarchy could serve freedom's cause. Montesquieu's message was that 'a monarchy made constitutional could assure freedom, and reconcile it with law' (Cranston, 1986: 21).

It is my supposition that Montesquieu's theory of the balance of powers, while normative, is homologous with Foucault's thesis that power is omnipresent, extending throughout society. It thus contributes to the possibility of a normative, non-Hegelian conception of ethics and politics within a distinctly pluralist frame of reference. As Foucault's teacher, Louis Althusser, says:

> Montesquieu at last reached the sphere of the political as such, and demonstrated his genius in a theory of the balance of the powers, so well arranged that power is itself the limit of power, thus resolving once and for all the political problem, which is entirely a matter of the use and abuse of power; for others, the political problems of the future. (1982: 87).

In offering this interpretation, Althusser himself draws on Eisenmann's (1933; 1952) writings; specifically, Eisenmann's view that the thesis of the 'separation of powers' constitutes a *myth*. In Eisenmann's view, says Althusser, '[a] whole school of jurists arose, particularly at the end of the nineteenth and the beginning of the twentieth century, which took advantage of a number of isolated formulations of Montesquieu's in order to impose on him a *purely imaginary* theoretical model' (1982: 88). This was the model of the separation of powers. In all there were three powers: the executive, the legislature, and the judiciary, and each would 'correspond precisely to its own sphere, i.e. its own function, without any interference' (1982: 88). Eisenmann showed, says Althusser, 'that this famous theory *quite simply does not exist in Montesquieu*' (1982: 88). 'A careful reading', says Althusser, shows that the executive encroaches on the legislature, since the king has the power of veto; that the legislature can to a certain extent exercise a right of inspection over the executive, since it checks the application of the laws it has voted; and that the legislature encroaches seriously on the judiciary in all manner of ways, policing its magistrates throughout civil society. Rather than a separation, Eisenmann's thesis is that Montesquieu is concerned with '*the combination, fusion and liaison of these powers*' (Althusser, 1982: 90).

Moderate and stable government, then, is achieved by a 'balance' rather than a 'separation' of powers. Montesquieu's thesis 'from the

A politics of pluralism

separation of powers to the equilibrium of the *puissances* dividing up the power' (Althusser, 1982: 96) provides a normative theory of how the equalization of the distribution of power itself constitutes a check on power. It is on this basis that the political organization of power should proceed, through which powers should be provisionally certified or rendered provisionally authoritative. It was in this general observation concerning the plurality of powers as constitutive of the deepening of democracy, which was itself the vital mechanism for the ongoing reconciliation of the interests of the one and the many, that Montesquieu's novel thesis lay (see Packard, 2002; Masterman, 2011). The distribution of powers across civil and global politics will function for Foucault, then, as a precondition of ethics as well as an important normative support for democracy.

Foucault's thesis concerning the ubiquity of power, manifesting constant resistance, itself mobilized by life, is freed from the interests of defending any particular class trying to cling on to power. Although Althusser suggests that Montesquieu was concerned to restore a decaying class to its traditional glory, no one would accuse Foucault of trying to save the nobility.[3] In advocating that we should 'cut off the King's head',[4] Foucault sought to replace the traditional conception of power as repressive and held only by the sovereign with a more plural conception that saw power as productive as well as repressive, concerned with the routine strategies and tactics that pervade daily life (Foucault, 1980e: 120–2; 1980c: passim; 1980d: 100–3). Foucault's own political activism – I will argue – reinforces this model of using 'power to challenge power', not just as distributed within or across the government apparatus, but throughout civil and global society *in toto*. For both Montesquieu and Foucault, then, notwithstanding their significant differences on other issues, this conception of 'power checking power' is the nub of a form of political pluralism, and constitutes an important basis of its normativity.[5]

Adam Ferguson's model of power and civil society

Complementary to Montesquieu's concept of the distribution of powers, Foucault's writing on Adam Ferguson in *The Birth of*

Biopolitics reinforces his commitment to pluralism as a normative thesis. In his final lecture, Foucault selects the model of the Scottish Enlightenment as expounded by Ferguson (1723–1816) in *An Essay on the History of Civil Society* (1783). Foucault's argument is that Ferguson's approach recognized governmentality as opposed to the centralized state, differentiated government from society, was compatible concerning a pluralism of the micro-powers, and yet permitted the economy to operate in terms of its own laws. It is here that Foucault announces that in the history of economics, as far back as one cares to go, the economic was never seen as a single domain with its own laws, models, rationality, and method, standing alone, but as existing always within a political form of civil society.[6]

Ferguson is represented as endorsing Foucault's own preferred axioms concerning the social nature of the subject, the fallacy of the theory of the social contract, the necessary complementarity of the political with the economic, the dispersion of powers across civil society, and so on. In addition, alternative models of civil society developed by Locke, Hobbes, Rousseau, and Hegel are all briefly entertained and rejected by Foucault (2008a: 308–9). Ferguson's model might be being recounted genealogically, but it is also represented normatively as the *best* model of civil society on offer.[7] With certain modifications with respect to naturalism and essentialism, Ferguson reintroduces Aristotle's conception of human beings as 'by nature intended to live in a polis' (Aristotle, 1946: 1.7.9). Ferguson reinstates, for Foucault, the elevation of the political over the economic, which was displaced in the seventeenth century as economic self-interest became ascendant and human beings became seen as predominantly economic subjects. Such a displacement of the political continued throughout the eighteenth century under the dominance of economic liberalism. With Ferguson there is a rearticulation of the human subject as a fundamentally political being who must live first of all in a social and political community and manage the economic motives in the confines of that community. Ferguson reintroduces what in the middle ages was the control of the market in the interests of continued political stability. As Karl Polanyi (1944) argues in *The Great Transformation*, markets played little role in many pre-modern societies. Indeed, during the middle ages markets were regarded with suspicion and kept under firm political and community control so as to minimize their dysfunctional and disequalizing consequences.

In this last lecture of *The Birth of Biopolitics*, Foucault utilizes Ferguson as a counter-balance to Smith to conceptualize how the economic must always sit within civil society. But, importantly, we learn something else of great interest to Foucault: '[c]ivil society is ... a concept of governmental technology, or rather it is the correlate of a technology of government, the rational measure of which must be juridically paired to an economy understood as a process of production and exchange' (Foucault, 2008a: 296). The Scottish Enlightenment carefully balanced economy and governmentality in a way that reintroduced elements advocated by the Physiocrats. Governmental regulation would be according to the 'Economic Table', which generated for the Physiocrats knowledge of the whole, of distributions, and of probabilities, as they affected stability, growth, and security, in terms of the continual likelihood of growth for the future. It is through these dual conjunctions of the economic and the political that governmental reason regulates the economic and the political along different lines, but simultaneously. As Foucault says:

> Political economy is indeed a science, a type of knowledge (*savoir*), a mode of knowledge (*connaissance*) which those who govern must take into account. But economic science cannot be the science of government and economics cannot be the internal principle, law, rule of conduct, or rationality of government. Economics is a science lateral to the art of governing. One must govern with economics, one must govern alongside economists, one must govern by listening to the economists, but economics must not be and there is no question that it can be the governmental rationality itself. (2008a: 286)

Foucault utilizes Ferguson to expound the notion of a civil society that will bed down economy and governmentality in a single regulatory pact. As Alexander Broadie summarizes in *The Scottish Enlightenment*, Ferguson's central thesis is that '[i]t would be fatal to civil liberties if the citizens dedicated themselves to commercial activities to the exclusion of political activity' (2001: 90). Politics was central to Ferguson's thesis as a corrective to the 'psychopathology of the commercial society' (2001: 97). *Homo economicus* was only a partial and incomplete view, which failed to achieve the detachment of Smith's 'impartial spectator' (2001: 100–1). Commercial relations, also, can, if uncontrolled, impede or disrupt family and social accord, which is why during the middle ages the market was tightly controlled and subservient to the community. Freedom is itself ensured and underwritten by culture and government. The law is the vehicle '[that] ensures our liberty to live civilised, cultured lives' (2001: 86).

For Ferguson, too, says Foucault, government replaces the state (2008a: 310). In this sense, Ferguson, like Paine, does not confuse 'society' and 'government' (2008a: 310). Governmentality operates across civil society, in diverse sites, through a balance of powers, via a certain conception of institutional autonomy, as powers that are awarded, or have earned, privileged status can resist and check the centralizing powers of a unified state. Given that the distribution of powers provides for checks and balances in the society overall, governmentality provides an opening for social democracy and for the death of the state as a unitary force. In Ferguson's seminal arguments against corruption, he argued strenuously for a system of checks and balances across the body politic in order to prevent corruption posing a threat to the system. This argument was central to his arguments against passivity and in favour of the political participation of citizens, says Broadie (2001: 88–90). As Broadie concludes, 'Ferguson is ... arguing for a form of republicanism: citizens should see themselves as the guardians of civic virtues and civic liberties' (2001: 90). It is in this way that Ferguson complements both Montesquieu and Foucault.

Such an analysis of Ferguson causes us to query the extent to which there has been an over-hasty incorporation of Foucault to an insufficiently elaborated thesis of anti-statism. There is no 'phobia of the state' (*phobie d'état*), simply a re-theorization and de-transcendentalization of the state.[8] Given that, as Foucault famously said, 'what socialism lacks is not so much a theory of the state but of governmental reason' (2008a: 91), it may be that Foucault felt it was necessary to invent a new form of governmentality for a new type of socialism that is non-statist (*'il faut l'inventer'*) (see Gordon, 2016, summarized by Provenzano, 2016). If this is so, then possibly Ferguson's model was not just a response to the past, but to the future as well.

Ferguson first provides a model of how the economic and the political, interest and right, are related and managed in terms of a governmental rather than a state-centric theory. What Ferguson introduced was a new reference point for governmentality, one that superseded the economic. As Foucault says, 'the art of governing must be given a reference, a domain or field of reference, a new reality on which it will be exercised, and I think this new field of reference is civil society' (2008a: 295). Foucault then asks: 'What is civil society?' And the answer is that it is a governmental technology that involves 'how to govern, according to the rules of right, a space of sovereignty which for good or ill is inhabited by economic subjects ... Civil society is not a philosophical idea, therefore. Civil society is, I believe, a concept of governmental technology' (2008a: 295–6). Civil society is what enables government on the basis of 'a self-limitation which infringes neither economic laws nor the principles of right' (2008a: 296). As Foucault continues to develop inspiration from Ferguson:

> Civil society, therefore, is an element of transactional reality in the history of governmental technologies, a transactional technology which seems to me to be absolutely correlative to the form of governmental technology we call liberalism, that is to say, a technology of government whose objective is its own self-limitation insofar as it is pegged to the specificity of economic processes. (2008a: 297)

Here Foucault conceptualizes governmentality as extending across society in the context of checks and balances, as represented by Ferguson, whose model of civil society, first, *governmentalizes the state* and, second, *protects liberal and market freedoms within limits*. Such a model would be capable of incorporating supply-side technologies, on an *ad hoc* basis, as part of a broader programme of social democracy. These limits or checks, however, are exactly what neoliberalism in the twentieth century, as advanced by the likes of Gary Becker, did away with. The logic of the market for neoliberalism 'break[s] with the tradition of eighteenth and nineteenth century liberalism' (Foucault, 2008a: 119). Rather, the market now constitutes a 'general index ... for defining all governmental action ... [Hence] the relationship defined by eighteenth century liberalism is completely reversed' (2008a: 121). Neoliberalism offers, then, 'the analysis of non-economic behaviour through a grid of economic intelligibility' (2008a: 248). There is a 'generalization of the grid of *homo economicus* to domains that are not immediately and directly economic' (2008a: 268), resulting in 'the economization of the whole social field' (2008a: 242). This is precisely what Ferguson says should not be possible, although, alas, it can represent itself to be so from time to time.

Power: symmetry and rights

Power for Foucault represents an ontological given; power is omnipresent, everywhere. Power characterizes all relations and is also crucial for ethics. In one of his last interviews, conducted by Michael Bess, Foucault repeats his nominalistic view that 1) power comprises a ubiquitous series of relations which are always 'mobile [and] ... not an oppressive system bearing down on individuals from above'; and 2) power relations are 'mobile and reversible'. Relations of power are 'not always forms of repression', but are variously characterized by inequality/equality; further, power often becomes 'frozen and congealed'. As he states, 'what happens is that in societies, in most societies ... organizations are created to fix and maintain power relationships to the advantage of some, in a social, economic, political, institutional, etc. dissymmetry, which completely freezes the situation' (Foucault, 1988d: 11–12; 2016c: 130).

Opposing *asymmetries* of power is a normative principle for Foucault. In this context, Foucault believed that it was important to challenge such asymmetries where they occur:

> No reality must dictate to us an inhuman and definitive law. To that extent, we may consider what we have to rise up against is all forms of power, but not just in the narrow sense of power as a type of government, or of one social group over another – that is just one of a number of elements. I call 'power' everything that actually aims to immobilize and render sacrosanct what is given to us as real, true, and good. (1988d: 11; 2016c: 127)

Michael Bess asks Foucault: 'Can there be open power? Or is it intrinsically repressive?' Foucault responds that '[p]ower should not be understood as an oppressive system coming from above and bearing down on individuals, forbidding this or that. I think power is a set of relations' (1988d: 11; 2016c: 128). Therefore, power is not always repressive:

> power is a relationship ... by which one conducts the conduct of others. And there is no reason for this conduct ... not to have in the end effects that are positive, valuable, interesting, and so on ... the only ethic one can have with regard to the exercise of power is the freedom of others. (1988d: 12, 13; 2016c: 135, 137)

The organization of power in civil society occurs through institutionalization whereby power is mobilized as resistance, enforcement, or persuasion. Foucault himself contributed to fighting on behalf of various causes. Democratic contestation was his sole manner of political engagement. Strategic intervention through the mobilization of power was the tactic to be employed. Such a method eschewed violence or revolutionary action. In the West he considered that the revolution had been effectively already won. Rights, universal education, habeas corpus, universal welfare – the issue was not any longer one of winning 'the war' but of ensuring effective intervention, correction, and implementation, the exposure and elimination of corruption in relation to 'specific battles'. To understand power is to understand how power can be mobilized; how strategies of intervention can be effective, and how change can be achieved.

Foucault's strategy, no matter what the issue or group involved, was always one of public engagement and democratic contestation. Although this was his general position, and although he expressed some cynicism towards the Marxist idea of 'revolution', in his article 'Is It Useless to Revolt?' he seeks a possible justification outside of a theory of Marxism:

> No one has the right to say, 'Revolt for me; the final liberation of all men depends on it.' But I am not in agreement with anyone who would say, 'It is useless for you to revolt; it is always going to be the same thing.' One does not dictate to those who risk their lives facing a power. Is one right to revolt, or not? Let us leave the question open. (2000b: 452)

The issue, says Foucault:

> is inseparable from another principle: the power that one man exerts over another is always perilous. I am not saying that power, by nature, is evil; I am saying that power, with its mechanisms, is infinite ... The rules that exist to limit it can never be stringent enough; the universal principles for dispossessing it of all the occasions it seizes are never sufficiently rigorous. Against power one must always set inviolable laws and unrestricted rights. (2000b: 452–3)

Here, Foucault is speaking normatively in a way that makes him potentially homologous in important respects with Montesquieu and Ferguson. His advocacy of 'inviolable laws' and 'unrestricted rights' is repeated in several of his political statements addressed to specific issues. In a statement published in *Libération* in June 1984, on the occasion of the announcement in Geneva of the International Committee against Piracy, Foucault says:

> There exists an international citizenship that has its rights and its duties, and that obliges one to speak out against every abuse of power, whoever its author, whoever its victims. After all, we are all members of the community of the governed, and thereby obliged to show mutual solidarity ... It is the duty of this international citizenship to always bring the testimony of people's suffering to the eyes and ears of governments, sufferings for which it's untrue that they are not responsible. (2000c: 474–5)

In relation to pluralism, there is clearly here, in Foucault's approach, a general conception of *democratic justice*. As against totalizing approaches such as Marxism and Hegelianism, the normative emphasis of Foucault's conception is that all power relations must be characterized by *openness* and *reciprocity*. His openness on the question of revolution reflects his view that intolerability constitutes the limit-experience that triggers political action irrespective what political activists, philosophers, or politicians might think. In that justice concerns the question of 'Who is due what?', only reflection, deliberation, and judgement in relation to the norms of life continuance at a particular juncture can provide an appropriate answer.[9]

State power, governments, and prison reform

In many of his political statements and speeches, Foucault continues the pluralist theme by indicating that he sees the state as constituting an essential force for impartiality and security: '[t]he right that it exercises to defend the people itself burdens it with very heavy responsibilities' (2000f: 441). After the Iranian Revolution resulted in new, brutal forms of punishment, Foucault's open letter to Prime Minister Mehdi Bazargan makes clear that:

> It is also the duty for each government to show everyone ... under what conditions, in what way, on what principle, the authority can claim the right to punish in its name ... And I believe this duty to submit to judgment when one intends to pass judgment must be accepted by a government with respect to all men throughout the world. (2000f: 441)

The role of the state is important, however. Foucault makes it clear in 'The Risks of Security' that he is no supporter of those who denigrate the state:

> In fact, the idea of an opposition between civil society and the state was formulated in a given context in response to a precise intention: some liberal economists proposed it at the end of the eighteenth century to limit the sphere of action of the state, civil society being conceived of as the locus of an autonomous economic process. This was a quasi-polemical concept, opposed to administrative options of states of that era, so that a certain liberalism could flourish ... But something bothers me even more: the reference to this antagonistic pair is never exempt from a sort of Manicheism, afflicting the notion of state with a pejorative connotation at the same time as it idealizes society as something good, lively, and warm. (2000h: 372)

It is in relation to establishing pluralism as normative that Foucault comes closest to enunciating continuance norms for the state. The following passage further reinforces his credentials as both pluralist and democrat:

> When I speak of arbitration and normativity ... I picture, in a more global sense, something like a cloud of decisions arranging themselves around an axis that would roughly define the retained

norm. It remains to be seen how to ensure that this normative axis is as representative as possible of a certain state of consciousness of the people ... I believe that the results of arbitration should be a kind of ethical consensus, so that the individual can recognize himself in the decisions made and in the values behind those decisions. It is under this condition that the decisions will be acceptable, even if someone protests and rebels. (2000h: 378)

This idea that governments have moral obligations is a theme that Foucault repeats on numerous occasions. To rebuke governments or individuals for not acting in accord with the norms of continuance was central to his political activism. Continuance provides a normative context in terms of which such commitments make sense, and it limits and regulates the context in which *parrhēsia* is exercised. In his work on prison reform, Foucault specifies norms that should guide governments. On 8 February 1971, Foucault gave a speech announcing the formation of Le Groupe d'information sur les prisons (the Prisons Information Group, GIP). The GIP constituted an important, ongoing political activity for Foucault. The intended purpose of the group, say Perry Zurn and Andrew Dilts, was to advocate on behalf of prisoners and staff 'by letting "those who have an experience of prisons speak"'. As Zurn and Dilts say, '[i]t was the GIP's mission to honor and circulate subjugated knowledge about the prison' (2016: 1; drawing on Foucault, 1994d). In his 'Interview with *Actes*', Foucault says that 'the GIP was a "problematizing" venture, an effort to make problematic, to call into question, presumptions, practices, rules, institutions, and habits that had lain undisturbed for many decades. This effort targeted the prison itself, but through it, also penal justice, the law, and punishment in general' (2000g: 394). This motivation to advocate on behalf of subjugated, repressed, forgotten causes is central to Foucault's conception of democratic justice.

Empowering the disempowered and bringing their cause and their plight to the gaze of the public is a legitimate means of harnessing power within pluralist politics. Foucault saw 'detached' activism as more effective than seeking to lobby through official routes or via 'hob-nobbing' with the powerful. The role of intellectuals was not to seek to ingratiate themselves with those currently in power. More often than not, such attempts were simply aimed at advancing the career or public status of the intellectual through their being associated with those in power. Foucault's own experience with governments was that politicians and state functionaries would simply take what ideas they wanted: 'Intellectuals were there to supply their names and lend support at election time, and they were not asked for anything else; to be exact, they were asked not to say anything else' (2000g: 395).

The approach to politics and reform was dictated then by the agonistic character of power and by Foucault's distinctive ontological conception of the social. It gives us some ideas of how pluralism functions, and the risks it entails. As Foucault says in the same interview:

> Nothing is ever stable. Whenever an institution of power in a society is involved, everything is dangerous. Power is neither good nor bad in itself. It is something perilous. It is not evil one has to do with in exercising power but an extremely dangerous material, that is, something that can always be misused, with relatively serious negative consequences. (2000g: 400)

Through encouraging prisoners to speak, GIP shone a spotlight on punishment in general and the functions that punishment serves in a society. Foucault invokes Nietzsche's comment that 'our societies no longer know what it is to punish' to highlight the multifaceted functions of punishment, 'which seem to have been deposited in layers, meanings such as the law of retaliation, retribution, revenge, therapy, purification, and a few others that are actually present in the very practice of punishment' (2000g: 397–8). Foucault focuses on the techniques of punishment in part to prompt questions such as 'could confinement be replaced with much more intelligent forms?' (2000g: 398). In highlighting the 'historical relativity of the prison form', he seeks a 'radical re-examination [of] what it means to punish, what is being punished, why there is punishment, and finally how punishment should be carried out ... The Enlightenment is not evil incarnate, far from it; but it isn't the absolute good, either, and certainly not the definitive good' (2000g: 98–9).[10]

Ethical pluralism, fundamentalism, and cultural relativism

Foucault's political pluralism presupposes and depends upon both metaphysical and ontological pluralism, which clearly differentiates his project from Hegel and Marx. It can also be repeated, as stated at the start of this chapter, that a concordance of difference and unity is a requirement of Foucault's thought if it is not to suffer from self-contradiction. While Foucault supports a conception of the politics and philosophy of difference in the sense that he opposes the monistic tendencies inherent in Hegelianism and Marxism, it is important that he does not privilege difference to the exclusion of any form of unity. Foucault is both a metaphysical as well as political pluralist, but unity is required at the limit where life would start to break down and democracy itself might be undermined.

As well as challenging power, and constituting a support for democracy, Foucault's sense of pluralism also goes well beyond Montesquieu's pluralism, and indeed, beyond liberal pluralism in general, in the sense that critique must confront and extend into previously unexplored domains. In this sense, it must explore and challenge our taken-for-granted assumptions about what is normal behaviour and the extent to which our behaviour is shaped and constrained by outmoded conceptions of nature or reason. The challenge to unnecessary societal conventions that the Cynics inaugurated must once again cause us to question the achievements of modernism in order, not so much to take the existing categories of science and nature for granted, but to seek to know the extent to which it is possible to go beyond. Is it necessary that the majority of the world's population live in poverty and hunger while a few own most of the resources and wealth? In what areas does exclusion operate today? To what extent do our presumptions concerning race, class, sexuality, gender, marriage, and employability build in and depend upon attitudes that have been historically conditioned, and that are no longer optimal for moving towards the future? To what extent are property relations seen as part of the order of nature or subject to revision? To what extent has the triumph of reason, inaugurated by Kant at the onset of the *Aüfklarung*, turned a whole new set of social, psychiatric, and physical scientific concepts and models into 'holy cows', which are represented as beyond criticism and yet which merely replace the phantasms and superstitions of the dark ages with a whole new set of solidified notions beyond criticism or questioning? Critique, then, constitutes an important *tekhnē* in the armoury of ethics, politics, and education.[11]

Pluralism in this sense stands opposed to fundamentalisms of every sort. Foucault's support for the right to free speech (*parrhēsia*) entails ongoing critical reflection on the limits of others' actions and conduct and also of the strains of fundamentalism that exist not merely within our societies, but within ourselves. In his preface to *Anti-Oedipus* by Gilles Deleuze and Félix Guattari, Foucault writes: 'Paying modest tribute to Saint Francis de Sales, one might say that *Anti-Oedipus* is an *Introduction to the Non-Fascist Life*' (Foucault, 1983: xiii).[12] The non-fascist life identified currents of fundamentalist thinking that inhabit even those who presume that they are free of such vices, the strains that would close down thought and discussion, that enable even the most liberal among us to maintain exclusions. As William Connolly says, 'all of us have strains of fundamentalism flowing through us ... no component of cultural life automatically escapes colonization by fundamentalist impulses' (1995: 106). Many of these strains appear obvious, of course. Although writing in relation to the American context, Connolly presents a useful general definition that could apply anywhere:

> Fundamentalism, as conventionally understood ... is a general imperative to assert an absolute, singular ground of authority; to ground your own identity and allegiances in this institutional source; to define political issues in a vocabulary of God, morality, or nature that invokes such a certain, authoritative source; and to condemn tolerance, abortion, pluralism, radicalism, homosexuality, secular humanism, welfarism, and internationalism (among other things) by imputing moral weakness, relativism, selfishness, or corruption to them. (1995: 105)

Watching the media, it often seems that fundamentalists are everywhere today: in the rise of far right political parties championing aggressive forms of nationalism; in the support for free-market, laissez-faire economic policies; in the neoliberal restructuring of public services and universities, usually supported by the rich and by organized business; in religious fundamentalisms that hark back to scripture, or some version of divine right, or natural law, or some version of divine communion; and in the prevalent hostility towards gay rights and feminism. Frequently these latter are represented as forms of moral decline and the corruption of civilization.

Perhaps even more interesting, regarding fundamentalism, is the fact that '[i]t is also a quality that leads most of us to recognise fundamentalism only in the "other"' (Connolly, 1995: 105). There are a number of dimensions to this. First, we often fail to acknowledge the material root causes of fundamentalism, located in poverty, disadvantage, or lack of meaningful employment opportunities; secondly, we fail to acknowledge that globalization has not delivered advantages or wealth for many; thirdly, democracy clearly doesn't transmit a clear message of representation for many; rather it appears as remote and disconnected from the ordinary, everyday concerns of most people. In this sense, as regards fundamentalisms, or in response to power generally, Foucault's model of pluralism instantiates questioning and speaking truth (*parrhēsia*) as a new ethical obligation. There is an obligation on all to uphold the norms of continuance to the extent they are agreed upon and democratically established through ongoing, collective, participative, global deliberation. Codes of morality are themselves evaluated or justified according to their compliance with continuance norms. Dissent from such codes of morality is itself public. As well as operating politically, pluralism therefore also operates ethically on the self, and applies equally to questioning ourselves and others as regards standards and modes of conduct, false opinions, ideologies, and the utility of societal institutions and structures. The formulae and practices of both Socrates and the Cynics constitute and can be re-read as contributing to a pluralist procedure of ethical interrogation within an agonistic society. Such a practice would occur according to democratically mandated and constantly revisable set of rules. And yet, as in the times of the Greeks or the Romans, responsible, active citizenship is still anything but safe. The deficiencies of democracy as regards the practical inability of most people to seek effective redress or exercise their rights, the practical impossibility of acquiring costly legal aid for the vast majority of citizens, the debasement of democracy by covert and overt opinion manipulation, the marginalization of people of colour, as well as unfairness in the distribution of property, wealth, and employment, are all in urgent need of reconsideration.

In going beyond liberal pluralism, whether that of Montesquieu or, in the twentieth century, those such as Isaiah Berlin,[13] Foucault's pluralism reconfigures the relation of the one and the many, and recognizes the immanence and historicity of that relation. In this sense, Foucault's pluralism is significantly more radical than liberal pluralism and interrogates the very basis of bourgeois morality and normalization. David Halperin quotes Didier Eribon (1991: x), who notes that Foucault's 'entire oeuvre can be read as a revolt against the powers of "normalization"' (Halperin, 1995: 152). As Halperin puts it, 'resistance to "normalization" informed and organized the complex interplay among Foucault's personal, professional, sexual, social, academic, and political practices' (1995: 152). Within the bounds of continuance, we can note, normalization secretes forms of power that are both necessary and unnecessary, constantly amenable to critical interrogation and revision. Within this complex and open structure, there is a zone of freedom, of discretion, offering plenty of scope to 'develop your legitimate strangeness', to borrow a line that Foucault was fond of quoting from René Char (cited by Eribon, 1991: x).

Finally, Foucault's pluralism captures the complex horizon of the future as an uncharted and uncertain terrain. It is very much in this sense that Hardt and Negri,[14] who recognize Foucault as a major inspiration to their own work, speak in *Multitude* (2005) of the concept of the 'multitude' rather than adopting the traditional language of first principles (*Being, Truth, the Good, God, Unity*), as a immanent historical concept that articulates the convergence of metaphysical and political pluralism enabling a theorization of plurality and unity, the one and the many, in the context of a non-transcendental historical approach such as Foucault's. The multitude speaks to a fragmented network, which is aleatoric and maintains a mode of unity that is immanent on the basis of limits imposed by the material conditions of existence, that is, historically variable, provisional, synthetic, and imposed from the outside by living beings on behalf of life, to reflect the imperatives of each age. As Artemy Magun summarizes Hardt and Negri's core thesis:

'the multitude has a mode of *acting together*' (Magun, 2013a: xiv). Such an imposition must be democratic rather than authoritarian as the condition by which it is allowed to proceed without opposition, without resistance, without inscribing deep *ressentiments*. As democratic, it must proceed through '*joint action*' (Magun, 2013a: xiv) in relation to set goals emergent within the horizon and united by a common interest or aim inclusive of all; inclusive, indeed, of life itself. For Hardt and Negri, as for Aristotle, 'a joint action was ... a way to unite the multiple' (Magun, 2013a: xiv), while remaining internally comprised of different parts, that is, while remaining internally differentiated. Hence, differentiation and proliferation of identities and life goals within the whole is compatible with a common purpose. Importantly, it is 'implied by a set of relationships rather than a single essence or attribute' (Magun, 2013a: xiv). It is 'generic' in Badiou's sense, says Magun, in that it represents unity as 'a set that systematically avoids any substantive criterion of inclusion' (2013a: xii). It thus represents 'the most influential attempt to formulate [the] idea of a true immanent unity' (2013a: xii).[15] Magun cites Gerald Raunig (2013), who calls this pluralism/unity articulation a 'con-division' (Magun 2013a: xiv), which refers to 'a mode of collectivity which is no longer composed of units but only exists in a centrifuge of differentiation and singularization' (2013a: xiv). Magun calls this a 'shared solitude' (2013a: xiv). Whatever one calls it, what is important is that the good has no substantive basis for its unity apart from the *concordant* relations among groups, institutions, and individuals who comprise the polis at a particular conjuncture, united only by an interest in the process of continuing life for all. As such, it is no longer defined or propelled teleologically; it is defined rather by its shared purpose between interdependent beings that have overlapping interests, needs, and goals.

Notes

1 See Olssen (2010: ch. 4). Although Berlin does seek to avoid relativism, I claim that his argument is not successful.
2 See Habermas (1987: esp. 241, 276–81); Chomsky labelled Foucault an 'anarchist' (Foucault, 1980f).

3 See Althusser (1982: 93). In my view, Althusser's argument is not tenable, in that Montesquieu himself saw his writings as supportive of both the French and American Revolutions, in the interests of democracy.
4 In an interview in 1977, Foucault said, 'We need to cut off the king's head: in political theory that has still to be done' (Foucault, 1980e: 120).
5 While Montesquieu accepted the main positions of eighteenth-century liberalism, and in this sense held to many conceptions that are at odds with Foucault (concerning sovereignty, the social nature of the subject, etc.), much of his materialist approach to history, as well as his theorizations on power, complement Foucault in the sense that the fundamental ontological positions of both thinkers do not preclude minor adjustments to bring them into accord.
6 This is what Foucault intends when he says that Ferguson's concept of civil society constitutes a 'historical-natural constant' (2008a: 298). By this he means that for Ferguson 'the social bond has no prehistory … however far back we go in the history of humanity, we will find not only society, but nature', which is to say that '[civil society] is as old as the individual' (2008a: 299).
7 See my article in *Materiali Foucaultiani* (Olssen, 2019) for a more detailed elaboration of this thesis.
8 See Dean and Villadsen (2016), who seek to go beyond Foucault, though in my view they do not exhaust the possibilities for state theorization present in Foucault's work.
9 The conception of justice as 'giving each person what they are due' I take from Plato's *Republic*, in the intermediate view provided by Plato, with the assistance of Adeimantus, after rejecting the views of Cephalus, Glaucon, Polemarchus, and Thrasymachus, before he reaches a more developed view in Book IV: 419–34. It leaves open the question as to what is due to whom.
10 Foucault advocates for a more 'restorative' model of punishment as opposed to 'retributive' models.
11 *Tekhnē (technē)* was the Greek spirit (*daimona*) of art and technical skill.
12 Foucault is clearly aware of St Francis de Sales's work entitled *Introduction to the Devout Life*. Edward McGushin makes the point that 'Foucault's claim was more than a simple allusion to the title of Saint Francis de Sales' book; it was a gesture toward the whole tradition of spiritual direction and ascetic practice out of which the book emerged. What's more, Foucault was heralding the return of this tradition within

which the philosophy book served as a "manual or guide to everyday life", a set of instructions in the "art of living counter to all forms of fascism"' (McGushin, 2007: xi, citing Foucault as above). Although, as McGushin notes, Foucault wrote this preface in 1977, prior to his turn to ethics, its themes consistently anticipate his growing interest.

13 Isaiah Berlin believed that 'the ends of men are many ... [and] that the belief that some single formula can in principle be found whereby all the diverse ends of men can be harmoniously realized is demonstrably false' (1958: 71). My counter argument to Berlin is that pluralism, to be intelligible, must presuppose limits, so that unacceptable views can be excluded. See my critique of Berlin (Olssen, 2010: ch. 4).

14 Although Hardt and Negri appropriate Foucault to their neo-Marxist cause, to good effect, Foucault himself had severe problems with Marxism, as I have shown. My own analysis positions Foucault, more accurately, as a social democrat, who would see a vibrant yet regulated market order as enabling the expression of liberty, creativity, serendipity, and other important values.

15 For the articulation of set theory, see Badiou (1999; 2005; 2009).

8

Democracy, education, global ethics

This chapter starts by considering Ella Myers's critique of the relevance of Foucault for democracy and disagrees with her assessments, noting the senses in which Foucault can be considered pertinent for democracy today. The chapter moves to examine the implications of a Foucauldian ethic for education and global politics to seek to ascertain what might be considered the first steps of a Foucauldian agenda for a global politics and ethics. The chapter concludes by exploring the possibilities of a global ethics inspired by the work of Foucault and argues for the limited relevance of virtue ethics.

The care of the self, ethics, and democracy: considering Ella Myers's 'worldly ethics'

Ella Myers challenges whether Foucault's writings on the care of the self can constitute the basis for a renewed ethics. Myers argues, extending from her concern that Foucault's approach is relativistic, that it inadequately links individual character to social structure or politics. As she puts it, 'unless the self's reflexive relationship to itself is driven from the start by a concern for a worldly problem, there is no reason to believe that self-intervention will lead in an activist, democratic direction' (2013: 24). She claims further that:

> although Foucault implies that arts of the self can provide the basis for a contemporary ethics and even avers that such a reflexive ethics, focused on the self's relationship to self, can alter the broad field of

inter-subjective power relations, the connection between self-care and socio-political dynamics is only weakly and inconsistently articulated. (2013: 23)

She thus argues that 'the care of the self is a flawed basis for elaborating a democratic ethics' (2013: 24).

In this sense, the links between critique and democratic ethos may appear tenuous. This is especially significant today in that democratic institutions depend for their maintenance as well as their vitality and relevance on the cultural habits of their citizens. As Myers argues: '[r]evived interest in ethics among postfoundational thinkers reflects a desire to consider connections between character and democratic activity, while remaining cautious about the imposition of uniform ways of being' (2013: 23). Myers claims that to see Foucault's techniques of self-care as promoting 'privileged modes of resistance often neglects his analysis of disciplinary power and biopower, which if read carefully should alert one to the limits of the care of the self as a strategy for reshaping power relations' (2013: 159, n. 2; see also Myers, 2008). In relation to William Connolly's work, which has sought to defend a Foucauldian ethics based upon the care of the self, she argues, further, that 'conceptualizing ethics primarily in terms of self-intervention is dangerous in the context of an American cultural environment that can fairly be described as narcissistic' (2013: 47).[1] Myers continues along these lines, with Connolly in her sights (see Connolly, 1995; 1999; 2005b):

> There is no doubt that a Foucauldian-inspired arts of the self [that] Connolly advocates are meant to challenge reigning ways of being and to transform individuals in ways that enable them to engage more effectively in collective projects, including critical and oppositional endeavours that aim to alter status quo arrangements ... Even Connolly's version of therapeutic ethics, which he wants to demarcate from unappealing forms of self-indulgence, runs the risk of being captured by prevailing habits and beliefs that can render arts of the self nondemocratic, even antidemocratic. (2013: 47).

That Connolly's proposals for a Foucauldian-inspired micro-politics might be 'captured' by anti-democratic forces is perhaps tangential to the fundamentally important issue that Myers highlights, which is the absence of appropriate normative criteria that could distinguish moral from immoral action. Indeed, there is no way – independent of the power of some privileged judge – to distinguish *parrhēsia* from *athuroglottia* (rude babbling), a point with which many Greeks, including Plato, agreed. Myers's work highlights the difficulties Foucault gets into unless a normative architecture of the sort developed in this study is appended to his approach. Yet once that is appended, Myers's criticisms suddenly lack traction.

One further response to Myers here is that Foucault never claimed that his studies of the care of the self in Greek and Roman antiquity were intended as guides to ethics or democratic politics in contemporary Western societies. He was in fact very careful to avoid such an imputation. That Myers accuses Foucault of something he did not sign up to makes her own critique somewhat confused. Having said this, Foucault did see the development of the self, in relation to an appropriate *ēthos*, skills, and knowledge, as an important component for self-formation, and an important precondition for the development of an ethical self. Yet Foucault never believed that the care of the self would, in itself, *produce* a political ethic. As he says:

> I think we may have to suspect that we find it impossible today to constitute an ethic of the self, even though it may be an urgent, fundamental, and politically indispensable task, if it is true after all that there is no first or final point of resistance to political power other than the relationship one has to oneself. (2005: 251–2)

What is needed, it might be conjectured, is a macro-normative framework which Foucault never articulated, which could undergird his genealogies and give direction to his political activism and attitudes. In this context, it is my claim that a normative meta-ethic of life continuance can constitute an immanent normativity that furnishes a criterion for excluding that which is objectionable while allowing for a diversity of ways of life. To the extent it can do this, it can differentiate between valid forms of caring for the self and sheer lunacy, and between *parrhēsia* and *athuroglottia*. It will not turn the concept of 'care of the self' into a normative support for democratic politics *on its own*, as Myers contends was Foucault's intention, but it will normatively regulate the operation of Foucault's more political concepts, such as *governmentality*, *resistance*, *parrhēsia*, *critique*, and the like. It will also permit an understanding of the *care of the self* as constituting the educative precondition for maturity and politically effective citizenship, as Foucault did intend. A meta-ethic of life continuance will thus provide a framework to normatively regulate the arts and techniques of self-formation that Foucault charts in his genealogies of Greek and Roman antiquity in the sense that it will specify worthwhile and culturally valid techniques of self-formation as against infantile, stupid, narrowly sectarian, or fundamentalist ones. It will enable us to ask whether certain practices of the self *are* or *are not* appropriate. It can also function to regulate *parrhēsia* and provide effective normative criteria to ensure it performs a constructive and progressive role in political and social change.

As a final response to Myers, her own alternative ethics seems not that far removed from what I have always understood Foucault's ethics might involve. Instead of focusing on an ethics of the self and the other, she focuses on 'contentious and collaborative care for the world' (2013: 2). As she continues:

> The worldly ethics advocated here rests, first, on an account of democratic relations that highlights the sense in which citizens' joint action concerns something in the world ... A world-centred democratic ethos aims to incite and sustain collective care for conditions, care that is expressed in associative efforts to affect particular 'worldly things.' Moreover, this ethos is tied to an explicitly normative conception of world as both a shared human home and mediating political space. (2013: 2)

There is nothing here which Foucault could not sign up to. The 'explicitly normative conception of the world' that Myers refers to, although admittedly absent in Foucault prior to the addition of a macro-normative framework, once added, renders her approach to all extents and purposes very much compatible with his, at least in relation to political engagement in the world. Furthermore, the concepts of 'care' and 'ethos', like phrases such as 'speaking truth to power', which are now in vogue among journalists, political activists, academic writers, and the general public in large part because of Foucault, take on normative reference. Continuance can now effectively regulate and govern the use of all concepts within Foucault's *oeuvre*.

Whether Myers's own 'worldly ethics', influenced by Arendt, is not in fact a rather lame version of what today is required, and whether the absence of conceptions of *agonism, parrhēsia, governmentality, specific intellectuals, resistance, and counter-hegemony* from her work will enable her worldly ethics to face up to the real challenges that are confronting the world today, is more questionable. It seems to me that her worldly ethics lacks any tough structural analysis or understanding, as well as any realistic and viable approach to effecting change. Foucauldian insights, suitably appended to a normative architecture, can certainly strengthen Myers's 'worldly' approach.

Weak ontology and presumptive generosity

The activist character of a Foucauldian normative politics can be brought out forcefully in relation to another conception developed within the North American context. Stephen K. White's conception of a what he terms 'weak ontology' became prominent in the first decade of the twentieth century. White claims that his approach is premised on a 'subjection to mortality' as a device that can ground 'reasonableness' and 'moral compass'. The major publications outlining this approach include *Sustaining Affirmation: The Strengths of Weak Ontology in Political Theory* (2000), *The Ethos of a Late-Modern Citizen* (2009), and a special issue of *Hedgehog Review* (2005). White's conception of weak ontology, although influenced by various modernist thinkers including Jürgen Habermas and Charles Taylor, to some extent also takes up insights developed within poststructuralism. As White describes his approach:

> A 'felicitous' ontology would be one that offered a figuration of the human being in terms of at least four existential realities or universals: language, mortality or finitude, natality or the capacity for radical novelty, and the articulation of some ultimate background source. A weak ontologist recognizes that these dimensions are universal in the sense that they are constitutive of human being, but she also recognises that no one set of figurations can claim universal, self-evident truth. (2005: 17)

While many of White's comments and reflections are insightful for the life continuance approach, I have difficulty with labelling ontology as 'weak'. Concepts such attentiveness, cautiousness, uncertainty, partiality, incompleteness, inarticulacy, to name just some, seem to be the reason White adopts this label.[2] Within the approaches of writers influenced by Nietzsche and Heidegger, such as Foucault, Deleuze, Derrida, Luhmann, Morin, and others, the employment of complexity concepts was not intended to suggest tentativeness of approach, or ontological cautiousness, or uncertainty, or ontological weakness, but rather to express a *strengthened* ontology, or a *more accurate* ontology, which dictates that 'uncertainty', 'non-predictability', and so on, function as ontological postulates. For my Foucauldian-inspired continuance ethics, uncertainty, partiality, and limitations on knowledge are a result of ontological complexity, and democracy and rights are seen as indispensable for continuing life into the future within an agonistic social structure. There is no timidity or uncertainty about one's moral sources, however, as appears to be the case for White. There is both modesty and magnanimity in the face of partial, restricted knowledge, but this is something different; it is essentially an epistemological cautiousness about our ability to know the future. It is about being cautious as a result of incomplete knowledge of the future, not a timidity about one's fundamental ontological commitments.

At the same time, White suggests that certain ethical conclusions can be deduced from weak ontology, but his answers to the challenges facing humanity seem to me to lack backbone and realism. White's response to the problems facing the world today is 'presumptive generosity'. Connolly (2005a) seems to endorse this 'ethic of generosity' as a form of 'critical responsiveness to political life'. Jodi Dean (2005) argues that 'presumptive generosity' appears an unusually impotent approach to the 'trials and tribulations' that modern societies face. One is tempted to quip that a weak ontology produces a weak ethics. Dean caricatures such an approach sarcastically as comprising 'a lovely notion ... a nice, nice, approach' (2005: 57). The locus of her criticism of White, as of Judith Butler (2004) and Charles Taylor (2005), is the failure to adequately address social structures.[3] Against White she argues that generosity is unlikely to work as a response to fundamentalist or extremist politics. Weak ontology is also the wrong response in that 'it turns to acceptance and affirmation at a time when the future of hopes for equality, democracy, and a sustainable, common being-together, demand a more critical, *political* response. Critical, as opposed to affirmative theory is necessary today' (Dean, 2005: 56). White's approach, Dean says, 'divests critical theories of their oppositional political edge' (2005: 56). They appear thus as 'congenial to current power relations' and avoid engagement with the new fundamentalisms of the age – nationalistic, market-based, and religious – in what could be represented as a type of appeasement. As Dean asks: '[w]hy cultivate a tolerance or generosity toward practices and positions that are deeply wrong? Why concede ground to ruthless opponents – especially when the stakes are so very, very high?' (2005: 58). While generosity is important alongside other virtues, such as hospitality and assistance to people in need, and can be theorized as dictated by continuance itself, it cannot substitute for a social and political strategy, as White intends.

Ethics and education

Acting normatively in terms of ethics entails acting strategically, that is, utilizing power for the betterment of all in order to promote specific ends. Foucault himself, as already stated, was shy of articulating ethical principles or solutions. In this sense, continuance serves only as a meta-ethic which is regulative in only the most general sense, but for all that, it keeps the ship standing upright and steering towards the future. Within this remit, Foucault articulates a progressive politics aimed at fighting specific injustices in local sites, that would rally to the defence and protection of the marginalized and oppressed, and that would articulate strategies to remedy what is 'intolerable' in the immediate historical context. Criticism and action would take their guide therefore from problems in the present situation rather than utopian blueprints. This is what Foucault means when he says:

> If I don't ever say what must be done, it isn't because I believe that there's nothing to be done; on the contrary, it is because I think that

there are a thousand things to do, to invent, to forge, on the part of those who, recognizing the relations of power in which they're implicated, have decided to resist or escape them. From this point of view, all my investigations rest on a postulate of absolute optimism. (1991d: 174)

Foucault's activism, as Keith Gandal notes, is a political activism that is informed historically and that always takes place through 'co-optation', in terms of 'power and change'. As he states:

[Foucault] pursued struggles where the situation was 'intolerable', but also where an alteration of power relations was possible ... Those who come to Foucault's work looking for political solutions will be perpetually disappointed. Foucault's project – in both his politics and his histories – was not to lay out solutions, but rather to identify and characterize problems ... (Gandal, 1986: 122–4, 29)

In relation to the GIP for instance, the aim was not to formulate alternative solutions, but to gather information to expose what was unacceptable about prison conditions and the condition of prisoners, and to let that information do its own critical work.[4] As David Halperin says, 'the goal of struggle was not revolutionary victory so much as popular autonomy; its purpose was not to win access to state power so much as to further self-empowerment. Foucault's aim in short was not *liberation* but *resistance*' (1995: 56). It is a question of realigning or rebalancing the cultural power of legitimation and awareness. In this sense, as Halperin says, referencing Foucault's support, 'to resist is not simply a negation but a creative process' (1995: 60).[5]

Education must equip citizens with the *tekhnē* of power and politics constrained by the ethics of life continuance, which excludes hate speech, xenophobia, discrimination on the grounds of sexuality, gender, or race. In a complex structuration of the present, trial and error, problem solving (Dewey), and experimentation (Nietzsche) are all necessary as pedagogical methods. Continuance in this sense creates an 'horizon of freedom ... using Foucault to think differently about education and training' (Ball, 2019). This is the title of Stephen Ball's article, which sketches 'what a Foucauldian education might look like in practice' (2019: 132). Such an education, says Ball, would foster an orientation of 'critique and curiosity' (2019: 133). Such an education would foster an educational practice 'that encourages experimentation … [enables] the development of an awareness of one's current condition as defined and constructed by the given culture and historical moment [and encourages] an attitude of disposition to critique' (2019: 133).

This captures Foucault's emphasis on critique well and establishes education as a critical institution in problematizing the present and evacuating the ghosts and superstitions carried forth from previous times. Because one's gaze on the world is always partial, distorted, blinkered, layered, ideological, the task of education is, as Ball says, to increase the horizon, to widen the perspective. It is to perform this task that Foucault pairs critique with transgression, 'testing limits', to establish the possibilities of going beyond. This conception of testing limits, which Foucault took from Georges Bataille, endeavours to establish the boundaries of the real in a world locked behind discourse. Testing is a constant goal in various domains: it reveals, accentuates, confirms, clarifies, deepens perspective, brings to prominence, exposes, unfolds. Testing defines itself differently in different domains; in science, via empirical evidence; in political protest, via intolerability; in rational debate, via disputability; in sexuality, via eroticism. It is the task of education to simulate and inculcate the tests of life.

Experimentation, critique, testing limits, problematization, challenging power are all regulated only by a principle of life continuance with its vague and uncertain parameters in any given situation or milieu. Yet while vague and uncertain from the vantage point of the present, one can be sure that such a principle constitutes an objective parameter of life, in that although the conditions might not easily be known, leaving the sole basis for decisions in the present as tentative and uncertain, hindsight demonstrates invariably that better courses of action did in fact exist. One might not see the iceberg in the waters in which the *Titanic* sails, but in retrospect, with hindsight, one recognizes that some ways of moving forward would have been better than others. Similarly, with nutrition. While one might be unclear about the best foods to eat, one can be clear that certain foods are better for health than others. In a world of partial insight, restricted knowledge, inadequate understanding, where individuals live their lives in an ideological relationship to the lived conditions of existence, public education performs the pivotal task of 'redistributing' knowledge, of revealing hidden and concealed perspectives, of confronting received ideological conceptions, and of creating the conditions by which tolerance can take hold and bigotry and prejudice can be challenged.

Central to the complexity perspective on learning theory is its opposition to traditional empiricist and rationalist models which assume that learning is an individual matter that is linear and non-generative. The tradition of empiricism, associated with Bacon, Locke, Berkeley, and Hume, challenged Aristotle for being too unconcerned with the world and with sensory experience and too concerned with reasoning according to established and fixed principles. In Hume's *associationist* psychology, simple ideas are formed through basic sense impressions, which through associations form the basis of composite ideas. Central to all empiricist approaches, whether Hume, Locke, or John Stuart Mill, is the priority given to experience as the basis of ideas, that complex ideas can be reduced to simple ideas, that basic sensations lie at the foundation of all ideas, and that the rules of getting from simple to complex ideas and upon which predictions are made are additive. Rationalistic approaches, as sponsored by Descartes, Spinoza, and Leibniz, rejected the strong emphasis on sensory experience made by empiricism, and suggested instead that our knowledge of the world came from innate ideas, which made reliable reasoning possible. The differences between these two approaches were not as great as the similarities: both were reductionist.[6] Complexity theories, while not denying a role for experience, including sensation, differ from both empiricist and rationalist approaches in that they are non-reductionist or holistic. They emphasize that the system is more than the sum of its parts and recognize system effects through 'downward causation' and non-linear feedback loops, as well as contingent assemblages of time and place, as being central.

Learning and ethics must be seen, in this sense, as a goal-directed activity, related to the evolution and survival of life. In an open field of possibilities, living, learning, and ethics are equivalent; that is, living involves learning, which involves selections that constitute the subject as an ethical subject. Ball (2017: ix) sees education as an 'ethos of transgression and self-formation', while Jones (1990: 66) calls it a 'technology of morality'. This way of seeing ethics involves a qualitatively different type of thinking, one that recognizes uncertainty, unpredictability, novelty, openness, a balance between order and disorder, and that represents discursive elements, such as concepts and words, as conventional and historical. Due to human fallibility and limitations, the type of knowledge that complex learning results in is free of the arrogance of the Enlightenment claim to know (*aude sapere*) according to the new-found faith in reason. Exercising reason might not free one from one's tutelage. Rather, it is more modest, humble, less self-assured, recognizing 'partial knowledge', 'human error', and limited cognition. At the same time, it encompasses processes of creativity and the possibility of unexpected developments within situations.

Complex education implies, say Trueit and Doll, a view of 'education as a journey into the land of the unknown taken by ourselves but with others' (2010: 138). Trueit and Doll see the tasks of education and ethics as 'thinking complexly' (2010: 138), in the way recognized by Dewey, who explored the role and function of education in adapting to and coping with uncertainties of the environment. For Dewey (1958; 1997), education was conceptualized as 'problem solving'; that is, not as a discipline-based mode of instruction in 'the basics', but according to an interdisciplinary, 'discovery-based' curriculum, defined according to obstacles in the existing environment and based upon scientific method. As Dewey says in *Experience and Nature*, 'The world must actually be such as to generate ignorance and inquiry: doubt and hypothesis, trial and temporal conclusions' (1958: 41). Rules of living and habits of mind represent a 'quest for certainty' in an unpredictable, uncertain and dangerous world (1958: 41). For Dewey, the ability to organize experience proceeded functionally in terms of problems encountered that needed to be overcome in order to construct and navigate a future. Dewey recognized that it was skills for coping that were necessary. This was the basis of his 'problem-centred' pedagogy of learning.

While it could be seen to concentrate on transferable skills from a complexity perspective of coping with an environment, Dewey can be criticized for an overly functionalist concern with system adaptation, in the same way that structural-functionalist sociologists, such as Talcott Parsons, or contemporary systems theorists, such as Niklas Luhmann, can be. Focusing on a 'problem-centred' approach runs the risk, in other words, of neglecting the critical tasks of ideological reflexivity and criticism that are so important to the educative tasks of myth demystification and cleansing the discursive template of history from its distorted ideological elements. There is little in Dewey, for instance, that suggests any parallel with Gramsci's distinction between 'good sense' and 'folklore' as the basis of a critical pedagogy and common sense. Dewey's functionalism is further reinforced through his utilization of terms such as 'interaction' and 'growth', which run the risk of contributing to a naive Enlightenment conception of 'progress', leading inevitably to the successful resolution of both individual and societal problems and, onward and upward, to ever higher levels of experience and civilization. Yet, while Dewey runs the risk, like Hegel, of being identified with a progressive evolutionary theory of history and development, unlike Hegel, he is quite explicit about positing no end point, or resting place, or final resolution. In terms of learning theory, Dewey used the concept of 'continuity' in order to theorize the link between existing experience and the future based on the 'interdependence of all organic structures and processes with one another' (1958: 295). Learning, for Dewey, thus represented a cooperative and collaborative activity centred on experiential, creative responses to contingent sets of relations to cope with uncertainty in a never-ending quest. Foucault can well share parts of this vision, with the important proviso that, like Gramsci, he had less faith in the innocence of the existing arrangements and exercise of power. It is in this sense, however, that the processes of iteration are central for Dewey. As such, Dewey's approach conceptualizes part and whole in a dynamic interaction, posits the learner as interdependent with the environment, as always in a state of becoming, giving rise to a dynamic and forward-looking notion of agency as experiential and collaborative.

Education is necessary, then, because democracy must be *learned*. Language and rules are tools for acting in the world. Some rules we follow blindly, some require a decision, some require reflection and judgement. Education facilitates the flexible use of language and rules. Reasoning, agility, and effective problematization are the outcome of a distinctive evolutionary process that has enabled humans to surpass the limitations of the mammalian brain. In addition to Dewey (1958; 2011), writers such as Merlin Donald (1993; 2002; 2005) represent human abilities as mimetic skills emergent from social and neuronal processes in a complex evolution. In this process, mind and consciousness are represented as both emergent and irreducible. Like Dewey, Donald's mimetic approach when applied to education would also involve problem-solving activities, critical thinking, conjectures and refutations, role playing and rehearsal; the replication of skills through 'means–ends' imitation; that is, both cognitive and non-cognitive problem-solving strategies.

A possible ethical theory for a complex global society

If the world is complex and uncertain, this suggests that education is ethical and political. As Paul Cilliers (2010: viii) notes, 'complexity leads to the acknowledgement of the inevitable role played by values ...' Others, such as Gert Biesta (2010) and Richard Edwards (2010), have also noted that the educational implications of complexity are both moral and political. Edwards sees lifelong learning, although presently serving the neoliberal complexity-reduction agendas of the knowledge economy, as potentially giving rise to 'ethical orderings within which there is an inherent play of (un) predictability' (2010: 77), and raising questions pertaining to how we construct the future. Given a future horizon with problems of climate change, viral pandemics, and population increase towards ten billion, such a future may well be 'coerced' by the pressure of events.

In addition to a new global ethics, complexity posits a model of the global citizen who has knowledge of global processes, procedures, and forces, well-developed agentic skills and abilities, as well as a multidimensional global identity that is both local and global. While virtues are important for continuance ethics, the specific type of virtue that is desirable must be judged as being able to contribute to continuance. Hence, the list could change in history depending on the context. Virtues in and of themselves should therefore not be overestimated, as no list of virtues that are universally acceptable in and of themselves can be assembled. As Robert B. Louden observes:

> [P]eople have always expected ethical theory to tell them something about what they ought to do, and it seems to me that virtue ethics is structurally unable to say much of anything about this issue. If I am right, one consequence of this is that a virtue-based ethics will be particularly weak in the areas of casuistry and applied ethics. (1984: 229)

The problem of a virtue ethics approach is that virtues can result in very different courses of action unless they are themselves subordinate to a macro-normative framework or concept that is regulative. For Aristotle, *eudaimonia* served this function, although it is an open question, as Ottfried Höffe (2010) says in the title to his book on the subject, as to how to answer the question: 'Can virtue make us happy?' Simply possessing a virtue does not dictate any particular tactic, strategy, or action. Simply possessing an appropriate list of virtues might also not result in the end of happiness that Aristotle set as the good of human beings. There is also no way to reconcile differences or conflicts and there is therefore indeterminacy, unless one can specify some standard of practical wisdom. Christine Swanton (2003: 273–4), who cites Louden, also references R. Jay Wallace who notes a 'lack of convergence' among virtue ethicists by which he refers to 'the idea that the exercise of judgment enables its possessor to discern the uniquely *correct* or right thing to do, in particular circumstances of action' (1991: 491). Swanton (2003: 275) also cites Hursthouse (1999: 43), who notes that 'different virtues point us in different directions'. As Swanton summarizes the issue:

> Self-protection points towards finishing the dialogue now, perseverance points towards continuing, tolerance and openness point towards bringing into the discussion yet more affected or potentially affected parties, efficiency points towards neglecting or ignoring some of them. Caring (towards an incompetent individual) points towards giving her further chances, benevolence (towards the larger group) points towards sacking her. Small wonder, then, that different virtuous agents may recommend different courses of action. (2003: 275)

Continuance ethics resolves the problems identified and also regulates for contingency in that to ask what virtues are necessary for continuance today will produce a different list than a hundred years ago, or even ten or five years ago. In a situation of conflict, like that presented in the quotation above, the requirement to continue can introduce an element of practical wisdom. Continuance might be difficult to judge, but it is, alas, all we have. As Badiou says, one must 'keep going' (2001: 91). On some matters, such as the moral view that murder or arbitrary violence is wrong, the norms of continuance will reach consensus or near-consensus; on other issues, protracted disagreements and conflict will remain. Given this situation, democracy, which is itself necessary as guaranteeing the best strategy for continuance to succeed, becomes the only effective mechanism for the arbitration of disagreements where they persist.

Life in a complex world is both gratuitous and contingent; it has no *raison d'être*, a fact that *a priori* gives no moral justification for privilege, or hierarchy of value, or precedence. Complexity provides a cruel mathematics of existence, and yet despite this, life has value to all beings that live, at least as judged by the fact that all forms of life strive to survive and continue. According to Doubrovsky (1960: 75), this is also the message of Camus, in *L'Etranger*, where '[t]hreatened with annihilation, life gathers and concentrates its force, becomes conscious of itself and proclaims that it is the only value'. This immanent value that life affirms is the source of moral sentiment. It motivates for Camus the ethics of rebellion. As Camus states, 'il fait donc intervenir implicitement un jugement de valeur, et si peu gratuit, qu'il le maintient au milieu des périls' (Camus, 1951: 28).[7] Bataille (1991; 1993) makes a similar argument in arguing that moral sense arises from the self-consciousness of life in a system of parts and whole where the 'sovereignty of each individual' needs protection in order to survive. Morality is the protest of fairness in a limited and dangerous world. It therefore constitutes, as it were, a sentiment common to all human beings, which constitutes their humanity, a view also admirably stated by David Hume (1978: 172, 272). There is, therefore, a deontological dimension of value adhering to life itself that propels ethics, establishes right, resists perfectability and becoming should they conflict with right, and yet acts for and simultaneously with the actions of life to survive in view of becoming as the continuance of life itself. Life therefore has value that it constructs and interpolates in the course of monitoring and critically evaluating the future horizon that both enables and threatens it. In a complex world, human history can have no overall 'inner logic', or 'overall design', or 'direction', in Hegel's sense, that provides a moral justification (i.e., the end cannot justify the means); yet nevertheless, the value of life requires a context, a system, and a goal for life as a process without end. Consequences and goals are thus important although they do not override the rights of life itself. Each situation must be evaluated each time anew.

I suspect that a great deal will need to change from the liberal, modernist settlement we have lived under for many years. In fighting error, contingent events and developments such as climate change and increasing population can now be a part of the paradigm. Stephen Emmott observes how all of these matters are interconnected, all being affected by the increase in human numbers. While in 1960 there were a mere three billion inhabitants on Earth, by 2000 there were six billion, and today there are in excess of seven billion, going towards ten billion by the end of this century (Emmott, 2013: 11). The environmental crisis flows directly from the pressure of population, says Emmott. It is human numbers that accounts for our dependency on oil, coal, and gas, chemical pesticides, herbicides, and fertilizers, causing new pressures over fresh water as a depleting resource, as well as the extinction of many life forms, overfishing, unprecedented levels of pollution, and a loss of habitat for many life forms, including our own. The increasing reliance on fossil fuels accelerates climate change, damages the ecosystem, causes food shortages, and results in widespread droughts and natural calamities, an unprecedented expansion of land use by humans, the loss of tropical rainforests and woodlands, species extinction, and extreme water shortages. Climate, as Emmott notes, comprises 'the atmosphere (the air we breathe); the hydrosphere (the planet's water); the cryosphere (the ice sheets and glaciers); the biosphere (the planet's plants and animals)' (2013: 32). In *10 Billion*, he makes the case that '[human] activities have started to modify every one of these components' (2013: 33). What climate change is transforming is the earth's ecosystem, resulting in the melting of Arctic sea ice, the retreat of Arctic coastlines, the depletion of marine species, as well as an irreversible release of methane, a more potent greenhouse gas than CO_2. Yet working out what to do is difficult given the uncertainty and unpredictability of the future. Emmott writes: 'Right now, every leaf on every tree on Earth is experiencing a level of CO_2 that the planet has not experienced for millions of years. How the planet's plants will respond to this we simply don't fully understand.' Emmott continues: 'even more worryingly, there is now compelling evidence that entire global ecosystems are not only capable of suffering a catastrophic tipping point, but are already approaching such a transition' (2013: 150). Global ethics calls for action by all, at every level, in multiple sites, in order to offset a climate and ecosystem emergency of unprecedented proportions.

Freed from the myth that there are natural rights to private property prior to society or government, which surely only those vested interests that comprise middle-class affluent property owners could believe, those who are blessed with luck or good fortune, or even acumen and expertise, will need to contribute to the commonweal proportionate to their success and talent. Capitalism, in short, can provide an important role at small and medium-sized levels, in relation to a number of domains. It enables an expression of liberty or freedom. In this, it enables individuals to freely plan, and create, on their own, without impediment or interference. Capitalism also encourages creativity and initiative. It thus functions in an important sense as *educative* by allowing talent to surface and rise to public prominence. Capitalism is also generative of wealth and its dispersed mode of organization facilitates the avoidance of central planning for the entire economy. Alas, capitalism also has many negative effects, or externalities, as economists would say. As Hayek (1949: 48) increasingly accepted, the market does not self-regulate, but is prone to disequilibrium through any number of processes: the big fish quickly eat the little fish; the lubricating oil of confidence and trust, so vital to market functioning, can easily diminish and erode, as the 2008 banking crisis exposed, and as Alan Greenspan acknowledged,[8] effectively bringing market transactions to a halt. Once companies become bigger, they inevitably expand in the marketplace, both locally and globally. Traditionally, bolstered by convenient economic theories together with friendly Lockean property-rights legislation, businesses have justified profits on the grounds that they take risks in the marketplace where they also stand to fail. Yet the 2008 bailout of banks in Britain and America put paid to that argument. Suddenly the argument put forward was that these firms were 'too big' and 'too important' to be allowed to fail. It was said that their activities affected too many people's lives. In Britain, the Royal Bank of Scotland was granted substantial loans in a taxpayers' bailout. The government appointed representatives to the board of directors of the company, and conditions were set out for the repayment of public monies. Public involvement in large companies will need to become more routinely accepted and practised, even without the precipitation of a financial crisis. As companies increase in size and profitability, so public involvement and employee and government participation in business should increase. Progressive taxation should be a response to the fact that earning money from the commons is a privilege and not a private or natural right. While variations in pay and income are reasonable on the basis of rewarding and recognizing effort, talent, and initiative, and constitute an allowable difference of reward in terms of a theory of just desert, such variations must be reasonable and proportionate in relation to the public good. Progressive taxation needs to apply both to individuals and companies. In addition, essential services, such as railways, banks, energy, and water providers, should be owned and operated for the public good.

Education constitutes such a public good *par excellence*, as it is an interest shared by all. Education also influences the ability of both individuals and societies to continue life and achieve well-being. Knowledge in this sense is a shared public good, which is to say that it is indispensable for democracy. Only public action can guarantee the development of the knowledge necessary to overcome obstacles, providing security and expertise for the future. Education should be publicly provided, as well as secular, compulsory, and free. In an increasingly unstable, crowded, and dangerous world, it is especially important that major institutions serve the global common good and are not primarily vehicles to promote individual or class status and/or wealth aspirations (Youdall, 2011; Ball, 2017; 2019).

In the current horizon the issue of how to live must be critically interrogated once again. With a global viral pandemic and the world's population already past seven billion and rising,[9] issues of survival and living become critical once more. The extent to which wealth creation can and should be seen as private will need to yield to a more inclusive social conception of the good. Such a good will serve liberal principles while recognizing the important senses in which we are obliged to each other in order to survive and prosper.

Notes

1. Here Myers references Christopher Lasch, *The Culture of Narcissism: American Life in An Age of Diminishing Expectations*.
2. The concept of 'inarticulacy' is utilized by Charles Taylor, and my comments here apply to Taylor as well, for he has also sought to incorporate complexity concepts drawn from poststructuralism in order to render his own neo-Hegelian approach plausible (see Taylor, 1989; 2005).
3. For Dean's critique of Butler, see Dean (2008: 109–26).
4. See Foucault's preface to *Leurs Prisons* (Foucault, 1975; 1994d).
5. Halperin acknowledges Gallagher and Wilson (1984: 29), who make this statement to Foucault, to which he responds, 'Yes, that is the way I would put it'. See Halperin (1995: 60, 104, n. 104).
6. Descartes' reductionism can be seen in *A Discourse on Method* (1960: 15–16), where he describes his method as being 'to conduct my thoughts in such order that, by commencing with objects the simplest and easiest to know, I might ascend by little and little, and, as it were, step by step, to the knowledge of the more complex ...' Similarly, as Fritjof Capra says, 'Locke developed an atomistic view of society, describing it in terms of its basic building block, the human being' (1983: 55).
7. 'He brings in a moral judgement, so un-gratuitous, that he maintains throughout his perils.'
8. See Greenspan's acknowledgement in the film *Inside Job*, dir. Charles Fergusson, Sony Pictures, 2011.
9. The world's population is expected to increase by 2 billion persons in the next thirty years, from the current 7.7 billion to 9.7 billion in 2050, according to *The World Population Prospects 2019: Highlights*, published by the Population Division of the UN Department of Economic and Social Affairs. The study concluded that the world's population could reach its peak around the end of the current century, at a level of nearly 11 billion.

9

Ethical comportment

The importance of norms

Moral rules are socially codifiable and manifest themselves on individuals and groups as system imperatives. Although in a complex world these admit of multiple variations, they still, for the most part, in relation to day-to-day existence, are codified, to use Hume's expression, in terms of 'general rules' (Hume, 1978: 146). Such general rules express a veritable maze of norms, including laws and duties. Individuals are constantly judged in relation to such norms. As Onora O'Neill says:

> Normativity pervades our lives. We do not merely have beliefs: we claim that we and others ought to hold certain beliefs. We do not merely have desires: we claim that we and others ought to act on some of them, but not on others. We assume that what somebody believes or does may be judged reasonable or unreasonable, right or wrong, good or bad, that is answerable to standards or norms. (1996: xi)

Most people obey the law because they believe that governments frame laws, in discussion with citizens, to represent the future best interests of each and all. In an ideal sense, they assume that the laws of the land embody fair continuance norms. The fact that people do this suggests that they believe that continuance norms expressed as laws and moral duties exist over and above governments, and to which governments can be held to account, as the trials at Nuremberg demonstrated in relation to the particular actions of those who worked for the Nazi state.

In the prologue to her book *The Sources of Normativity*, Christine Korsgaard asks the question:

> Where do we get these ideas that outstrip the world we experience and seem to call it into question, to render judgment on it, to say that it does not measure up, that it is not what it ought to be? Clearly, we do not get them from experience, at least not by any simple route. (1996a: 1)

What is it that calls us out in this respect? Unlike Korsgaard, the message of this study is that it is not any Kantian-type moral law, but a norm immanent in life that manifests itself as a system requirement necessary for the ongoing reproduction of life calculated in group terms to ensure the survival of each and all. Many of these rules have remained constant for millennia, but in each age they will vary contingently according to special circumstances. In recent years, human beings have developed a greater sensitivity to environmental concerns, such as the use of plastics, the burning of fossil fuels, the wastage of water, and the like.

To say to oneself, as Korsgaard (1996a: 101) does in her neo-Kantian, constructivist account, 'I couldn't live with myself if I did that', is to accept oneself as located within a network of social rules and norms that entail standards constituted by the society within which the individual subject is interpellated and 'hailed'. Korsgaard maintains further that:

> an obligation always takes the form as a reaction against a threat of a loss of identity ... it is the conceptions of ourselves that are most important to us that give rise to unconditional obligations. For to violate them is to lose your integrity and so your identity, and to no longer be who you are. (1996a: 102).

Robert Stern notes that 'Korsgaard herself takes it that our identity as humans is more fundamental than any mere social role' (Stern, 2013: 308). Korsgaard's view is that such an identity derives from nature. In Foucault's view, the idea of a noumenal self, prior to its ends and ahistorical, is a metaphysical fiction. While Korsgaard retains Kant's individualist metaphysical system, because she has been influenced by the 'linguistic turn' as well as the poststructuralist ascendancy, incorporated through Wittgenstein, she also offers an excellent revisionist account of obligation and identity that is quite capable of a view of identities as socially and historically constituted, or that at least can be modified to accord with it.

Stern notes that writers such as T. H. Green and sociologists such as John Horton advance a similar 'social role' account of moral obligations. According to Horton:

> both the family and the political community figure prominently in our sense of who we are; our self-identity and our understanding of our place in the world ... That these kind of institutional involvement generate moral obligations, and these obligations rather than standing in need of justification may themselves be justificatory, is only to be expected. (Horton, 1992: 150–1, 157, cited in Stern, 2013: 308)

Stated in terms of continuance, normative obligations receive approval (or disapproval) for compliance (or non-compliance), and are justified on the basis of continuance norms that reside within social mores and conventions. Moral action is solely a matter of duty; it comprises acts that constitute our duty as parts of a system, that is, as citizens. Ethical actions operate in the zone of discretion, or liberty, regulating our desires according to continuance norms, permitting indefinite possibilities for action. Moral, ethical, and normative all are justified according to continuance norms within the social.[1]

Vulnerability and dependence

Foucault never denies that within social norms there may be universal rules of behaviour, but such dispositions manifest themselves variably in variable contexts, and the universal is empirically inseparable from the contingent. In Foucault's view, when we act, we do so 'not only on the ground of universal rules of behaviour but also on the specific ground of a historical rationality' (2000i: 405). Foucault articulates this point in the *Use of Pleasure*, where he asserts that 'every morality, in the broad sense, comprises the two elements ... codes of behaviour and forms of subjectivation' (1985a: 30). Codes of morality express or articulate universal norms in historically specific ways. A similar point has been made by Judith Butler when she notes that 'the problem is not with universality as such but with the operation of universality that fails to be responsive to cultural particularity and fails to undergo a reformulation of itself in response to the social and cultural conditions it includes within its scope of applicability' (2005: 6). It is in the attempted juxtaposition or resolution of 'universal rules of behaviour' with 'historical rationality' that we must search for a plausible model of the self to ground ethical comportment.

Bryan Turner in *Vulnerability and Human Rights* (2006: xv–xvi), and Richard Rorty in *Contingency, Irony, Solidarity* (1989: 87–94), appeal to the universality of vulnerability and pain in the context of making normative arguments. Turner makes a claim about the 'universality of pain', while Rorty claims that 'pain is nonlinguistic' (1989: 88, 94). Turner emphasizes vulnerability to pain because it applies to all life forms. As such, 'vulnerability defines our humanity', he says (2006: 1). Pain in this sense has implications for normativity. It is an instance of what Audi calls 'normative in upshot' as opposed to 'normative in content' (2013: 18): 'That someone is in pain is a bad thing, and thereby normatively important, but it is a natural fact, not a normative one' (2013: 19). In that pain has implications for normativity, so does vulnerability more generally. Georges Bataille, whom Foucault acknowledged as an influence, also established 'vulnerability' as an important postulate when he wrote of 'human insufficiency' as a key support for the permanent existence of communities (see Bataille 1991; 1993). The extent of insufficiency was, in Bataille's view, profoundly understated in Western liberal societies (see also MacIntyre, 1999: ch. 1).

Richard Rorty articulates a similar message in relation to the themes of security and survival. In *Contingency, Irony, Solidarity* he suggests that we ignore foundationalist arguments, and in *Truth and Progress* he advocates for what he terms a 'sentimental education' (1998: 180) on the grounds that reason doesn't suggest a unified path in ethics or morality. He rejects foundationalists who believe in an unchangeable truth of moral knowledge, in preference for what he calls 'security and sympathy' (1998: 180). Rorty defines security as 'conditions of life sufficiently risk-free as to make one's difference from others inessential to one's self-respect, one's sense of worth' (1998: 180). Sympathy refers to understanding other people in different life situations. 'Sentimental education works only for people who can relax long enough to listen', he says (1998: 180). He views Hume as better than Kant for advancing to Enlightenment. He compliments Annette Baier, whom he dubs 'the woman's moral philosopher' because she favours 'corrected sympathy' rather than reason as the fundamental moral capacity. Baier suggests that the ability to reason is centrally tied to and depends upon emotional maturity. As there is no 'true' self or 'rational' self to ground morality, we must think therefore of 'trust' and 'collaboration', rather than 'obligation to a moral law' as the fundamental moral notions. Hence, says Rorty, rather than trying to ascertain and act upon the moral law, I act in terms of what Baier (1991) calls, following Hume, 'the progress of sentiments'.[2] Such a 'sentimental education' consists, in Rorty's view, in seeing the similarities of peoples as outweighing the differences.

Beyond this, Rorty despairs of anyone who tries to provide answers of the sort Kant sought to provide. For, as he says, '[a]nyone who thinks there are ... algorithms for resolving moral dilemmas ... is still in his heart a theologian or a metaphysician. Such a metaphysician believes in an order beyond time and change which both determines the point of human existence and establishes a hierarchy of responsibilities' (1989: xv). Maybe Rorty would admonish continuance ethics on this basis, although continuance ethics doesn't apply to an order beyond time and change; quite the contrary – continuance refers to norms that permit many and varied ways of life. It supports both reason and sentiment in accounting for the fullness of life, that is, in determining how life should be lived.

Ethical motivation and reflective judgement

For Foucault, ethical comportment goes further than envisaged by either Turner or Rorty to embrace civil disobedience, political action, and speaking truth to power. The fact that Foucault is interested in challenging power suggests that he harbours a confidence that is not compatible with relativism as an attitude. One must have 'the courage of truth', as the title of Foucault's last lecture course at the Collège de France stated (Foucault, 2011a). Ethical comportment for Foucault involves not just a political engagement, but also duties and responsibilities as well as rights and entitlements, obligations to oneself, to others, and to the world. As one is imbricated to the world, so one must act. Responsibility, in this sense, is a mode of comportment compatible with continuance. Foucault can also explain motivation and commitment to ethical and political causes far more directly than liberals or social contract theorists on the grounds that, as a socially constructed subject, there is no 'hard-wiring' in terms of 'self-interest' or 'egoism'. Ethical comportment is not traded off against self-interest or mutual advantage as social contract theory renders duties or obligations. Although self-interest operates across life, in certain contexts and times it is overridden or displaced by other values or traits, such as generosity or commitment to a cause. It is therefore a possible response, but not constantly utilized, and its extent and force reflect the structuration of the environment.

It is not simply the immediate external environment that determines how the self will act, either. Even in similar contexts, individuals can react differently, and act variably, depending on any number of factors. As we saw in Chapter 3, Nietzsche gives the example of behaviour in a marketplace to illustrate the fact that there can be no basis in human nature or the world for reliably predicting human drives to be consistently the same in all times and places. Different people will respond differently depending on any number of variables, from their early upbringing to whether they had a good night's sleep. The error of social contract theorists is that to assume a subject characterized by self-interest means that explaining ethical comportment is an uphill slog all the way. Explaining political engagement on such a basis is even more difficult. Rawls speaks of reconciling the performance of obligations and moral duties on the basis of self-interest as the 'problem of congruence' (1999a: Part Three). He correctly infers from his theory that there cannot be any such thing as a 'purely conscientious act' (1999a: 418). This is a correct inference because Rawls cannot possibly explain such an act given his presuppositions as regards the subject as self-interested by nature. Indeed, he cannot account for why people would be motivated to perform moral duties at all.

Weale notes that Rawls's resolution is most inadequate. As Weale puts it, '[t]ruly moral behaviour ought to flow from the right sort of motives' (2020: 69).

Liberals criticized the social constructionist conception of the self as not allowing for authenticity, on the grounds that it failed to posit a natural basis for self. Many religious groups might also wonder what happens to the concept of soul on such a view. The Foucauldian responds that as the subject is individuated in space/time within the whole, selfhood or the person is *emergent* in the history of its development. Persons start off as arbitrary, random beings, 'thrown' into history at a time and place not of their own choosing, and become defined as the sum of their actions as well as being acted upon. For Foucault, as for Jean-Paul Sartre, 'existence precedes essence'.[3] One defines oneself and is defined by the cumulative effect of one's actions and experiences in the context of one's life. In a sense, one's character and 'soul' can be represented as emergent in the cumulative outcome or effect of one's life's actions. The ethical imperative becomes *be careful what you wish for, how you think, what words you use, as well as how you act.*

Although continuance constitutes an objective norm, because the future is difficult to predict, as documented by the postulates of complexity science, any endeavours to make judgements from the present will be inexact and experimental. While in some cases, the norm of continuance is quite clear, in others working out which policies to select and enact requires ongoing reflective judgement, deliberation, consultation, as well as arbitration and conciliation. The zone of discretion permits innumerable options and possibilities. Continuance in this sense involves not what Kant terms in *The Critique of Judgement* (2008: §§74, 75) 'determinative judgement', which reasons always from a principle, but 'reflective judgement', which starts from a particular behaviour or event and asks how and with what likely effects this might contribute to or impede continuance.[4] Kant saw 'reflective judgement' as non-authoritative and non-binding, but in a complex world, where uncertainty and non-predictability are ontological postulates, it is more apt to view it in the sense of being provisional and as requiring investigation. Hence, we might acknowledge that actions were appropriate or inappropriate in the context.

Such a 'judgement view of justice' is promulgated by Alessandro Ferrara, in his book *Justice and Judgement* (1999). Ferrara goes back to Kant's *Critique of Judgement*, where the model is universalistic and based on determinative general principles. As opposed to this, Ferrara invokes a model of 'reflective authenticity' to forge a transition from the 'early modern model of generalizing universalism based on the power of principle, laws, norms and rules [which] transcend the particularity of contexts to a new model of exemplary universalism based on an orientated reflective Judgement about self-congruity or authenticity of an identity, be it individual or collective' (1999: x). Authenticity here relates not to a primary self that is prior to history, but to congruence between the emerging self and the norms of the system within space/time. Ferrara thus claims to avoid 'both the pitfalls of modern foundationalism and the postmodernist sirens that intimate the renunciation' (1999: x).[5]

Responsibility, integrity, authenticity

Clearly a number of questions as regards ethics, agency, politics, and morality emerge as implications from Foucault's writings, which he neglected adequately to consider himself. We have already seen how continuance can justify political and moral motivation to duties and obligations directly as expressing the immanent normativity of life in its quest for survival and well-being. Socially constructed selves emerge in history and can become authentically concerned with their habitats and environment. Such a theory can also explain genuinely conscientious acts.

Judith Butler asks a series of probing questions concerning how the subject can make herself when she is already a product of the culture in which she resides; How can the subject exercise responsibility in such a socially constructed world of constraint? How does the subject craft itself using an already provided set of norms? (2005: 19–20). As she states:

> The norm does not produce the subject as its necessary effect, nor is the subject fully free to disregard the norm that inaugurates its reflexivity: one invariably struggles with conditions of one's own life

that one could not have chosen. If there is an operation of agency or, indeed, freedom in this struggle, it takes place in the context of an enabling and limiting field of constraint. This ethical agency is neither fully determined nor radically free. (2005: 19)

Butler claims further that 'the "I" has no story of its own that is not also the story of a relation – or set of relations – to a set of norms' (2005: 8). She says further that 'the social dimension of normativity precedes and conditions any didactic exchange … [t]he norms by which I recognize another, or, indeed, myself, are not mine alone' (2005: 23–4). Many critics of Foucault, she notes, claim that 'the view of the subject proffered by Foucault … undermines the capacity to conduct ethical deliberations or to ground human agency' (2005: 19). 'Does the postulation of a subject who is not self-grounding, that is, whose conditions of emergence can never be fully accounted for, undermine the possibility of responsibility and, in particular, of giving an account of oneself?' (2005: 19). Yet she argues 'otherwise by showing how a theory of subject formation that acknowledges the limits of self-knowledge can serve a conception of ethics and, indeed, responsibility' (2005: 19). The fact that the subject is 'not fully translucent and knowable to itself' (2005: 19) does not mean it can do what it likes. As Butler puts it:

> Although many contemporary critics worry that this means there is no concept of the subject that can serve as the ground for moral agency and moral accountability, that conclusion does not follow. The 'I' is always to some extent dispossessed by the social conditions of its emergence. This dispossession does not mean we have lost the subjective ground for ethics. On the contrary, it may well be the condition for moral inquiry, the condition under which morality itself emerges. (2005: 8).

It is in relation to these issues that Foucault has posed lasting questions requiring resolution concerning both liberalism and the Enlightenment. There is a distinct sense, too, given problems such as climate change and viral pandemics, that we are all morally responsible for the future in the sense that if problems are to be resolved, we must do so, even if we were not the ones who caused the problems. Looking towards the future, we are responsible irrespective of our shortcomings. Responsibility is a relational value and is not simply concerned with duty in Kant's sense. We are responsible for ourselves and for the future, which must be assessed in specific situations. As humans constitute providence according to their values, so it matters greatly as to the values that humans embrace. It is in this sense that the future transforms normativity into responsibility. This is to say, we become responsible *for* the future. The future generates conceptions of normative authority and obligation. It is 'normative in upshot', in Audi's sense. Yet, inasmuch as we are responsible, such responsibility must be exercised collectively. The model is not that of *nomos* or *kosmos*, in Hayek's sense, but of *taxis*, that is, actively constructing the future through positive state power (see Hayek, 1983: 37). Although the internal determination of the will is downplayed in Foucault, and although values are not determined by the subject, each is still free to respond or not respond to the values that are present, that is, to be responsible as permitted by the situation. Responsibility in this individual or group sense means complying with the broad arc of continuance norms as best we can. It is our partial, conditioned, 'dispossessed' selves that must act in the world, and we do so with whatever effectiveness we can muster in whatever orbit of action we inahbit. By looking to the future, the subject acts for a future that it considers it can inhabit. Foucault's analysis makes it clear that responsibility is relevant both to the extent we are implicated and aware, but also in that we are, like it or lump it, bearers or custodians of the cultural and historical traditions in terms of which we must endeavour to shape and live our lives. As Butler puts it, '[f]or Foucault, morality is inventive, requires inventiveness, and ... comes at a certain price' (2005: 18). Responsibility, she says, must be rethought based on the limitations that confront one. To the question, 'Who can I be, given the regime of truth that determines ontology for me?' is closely related the question of 'How ought I to treat another?' (2005: 25). And that question – How ought I to treat another? – is also determined by the imperatives of the future; of what it takes to move forward. It is the future that confronts and determines us, *not* human nature.

Identity as well as ethics is precariously secured because of history as well. In an open field of possibilities, every action both individuates and assimilates. Hence, particularity is established within universality, though not, of course, in Hegel's sense.[6] What this means is that no individual is equivalent to norms that predate her. Our interpellation into society at a specific time and place always differentiates the parts from each other and from the whole. Uniqueness in identity is thus assured. In 'giving an account of oneself', to use Butler's book title,[7] one can be certain that nobody else can give an account quite like yours; nobody else has experienced quite what you have experienced, a fact that accounts for one's uniqueness as well as one's likeness to others. While life will always be sought after and promoted utilizing the available assortment of historically partial and incomplete discourses to hand, there is a sense that the norms by which I live and recognize others are not mine alone, as Butler observes in the quotation provided above. In *Giving an Account of Oneself*, she draws on Foucault and others to demonstrate the limits to accountability and awareness in the context of language, finitude, and natality. This is why there is always a blind spot in our capacity to comprehend the real. The limits to giving an account of ourselves relate to the fact that we are constituted by the same norms that we employ to exercise agency. Within these normative limits, our attitudes and actions are always partial and incomplete. We never quite see ourselves as others see us. We are beings that make mistakes. We are often not in the right place at the right time. The norms one utilizes both to understand the world, exercise action, and give an account of oneself are independent of me and confront me as a facticity.

For Butler, this failure to be fully aware of ourselves translates into attitudes of patience and tolerance, humility and generosity to others, who also will not be able to live up to the model of a perfectly rational being. Ontologically, these types of moral comportment would seem to be implied and reinforced by living in a complex world. The fact is that neither we, nor others, can know ourselves fully, and this constitutes a partiality that is one source of our interdependence and interconnectedness. Drawing on Foucault, Butler says that 'the subject cannot fully furnish the grounds for its own emergence. The account he gives of himself reveals that he does not know all the reasons that operate ... on him' (2005: 116–17). As Dean puts it, 'not demanding an impossible accounting from another becomes here, for Butler, another, better version of recognition because it recognizes the desire to persist' (2005: 61). There is a sense, too, that given our own partiality and inability to account for ourselves in terms of the past, letting the future frame our ethical and moral values gives us both focus and commitment independently of who we are.

That we are socially constructed by norms that are not only our own, that belong more generally to each age, to our communities, our families, does not on such a view erase responsibility or authenticity. As Butler says: 'If the subject is opaque to itself, not fully translucent and knowable to itself, it is not thereby licenced to do what it wants or to ignore its obligations to others' (2005: 19–20). The issue as to whether we can be held responsible if we are not fully aware of ourselves raises a number of questions. It could be argued that from the point of view of assuring continuance, it is necessary to hold the individual legally or formally accountable (hence, 'responsible') even if, given a more nuanced sociological, juridical, or medical analysis, one would want to substantially qualify that assessment. This might be in the sense that, in a juridical model, judges take mitigating circumstances into account, and also speak of 'diminished responsibility'.[8] One answer is that while people might not be fully aware of themselves in a philosophical or social sense, most are sufficiently competent to comprehend and be held responsible in relation to observance of the vast majority of societal rule systems: the rules of the road, of taxation, of commerce, of international travel, the general applicability of the rule of law, etc.[9] Most also have a sense of the future, the state of the world, and what needs to be done. All of us, also, experience critical periods of doubt, anxiety, dependence, and incapacity, in response to the future, and to the obstacles, dangers, traps, and hopes that it presents. In this context, our levels of dependence and codependence will vary contingently as well. In this sense, the requirement that we learn to read the future, and become committed to goals in the future, is not only more figural as the generative source of our normativity, it is frequently of more urgent concern than our need to understand our place in the order of things.

The future as the grounds of moral responsibility

James Bernauer notes that Foucault's early lengthy introduction to the first French translation of Binswanger's *Dream and Existence* suggests that the present incorporates the future in the sense that we look from the present forwards (see Foucault, 1984–85). According to Bernauer, for Foucault, the dream posits 'the human being as a radical liberty, reveals him as fundamentally an ethical being, capable of either authentic or inauthentic choice of itself' (1990: 30). The dream links the present and the future in the sense that '[t]he movement of existence is disclosed in the dream both as spatial and as a temporal trajectory, orientated to a future ... To dream is for the future to be already in the process of making itself ... "the first moment of freedom freeing itself"' (1990: 30–1).[10] As Bernauer says, 'while authentic existence is the choice of this open trajectory toward the future, inauthentic existence is to opt for an objective determinism in which the being's original liberty totally alienates itself' (1990: 31). Such a temporal trajectory, first discussed by Binswanger, suggests for Foucault that human psychology functions not in accordance with *a priori* structures of cognition but by reflection on concrete events that orients itself by reference to a future, both lived and imagined. As is well known, in *Mental Illness and Psychology* Foucault positions psychology as subordinate to history and elevates the historical dimension in the constitution of mental illness itself. Foucault also gives the dream a contingency and relativity and sees it 'as the first condition of possibility for the imagination. The imaginary is the action that emerges in the dream as a way of seizing the reality through which and toward which the existence is moving' (Bernauer, 1990: 31). Foucault ultimately seeks to 'reverse' Binswanger – from seeing mental illness as primordial, to seeing it as a consequence of social alienation. The historical becomes the citadel for psychology.

Within this orientation to the future, says Bernauer, Foucault's ethic relates to 'a dynamic movement of relentless questioning ... to compel a desire for flight, to afflict the reader with a pressure of force' (1990: 6). Fundamentally, for Bernauer, 'thinking' means 'to interrogate the conditions that account for the appearance of a phenomenon' (1990: 35). All thinking is ethically oriented to 1) adequate knowledge, and 2) transforming the actual conditions that reflection discloses are decisive in oppressing. Thinking in this sense involves 'questioning limits' with respect to the future, and it is in this sense that the future starts from and encapsulates the present.

Foucault politicizes the present and it is through *problematization* that individuals orient themselves to the conditions of their experience. Actions are structured in power and are always political. They are weakly teleological, goal-directed movements involving selections, that is, actions that could have been otherwise, or not at all. In that they are political and invoke power, they are irreducible to the biological or psychological. To 'speak out', as opposed to 'remaining silent', in the face of patriarchal norms, for instance, implies a political *as well as* a psychological choice. Action thus implies an entire technology of power exercised over bodies.

Ethics also arbitrates the dynamic relations between living beings in a crowded space as they each demand 'justice to come' (*à-venir*).[11] Derrida's phrase well indicates how action is oriented to the future. Ethics in this sense is a discourse of 'decidability' and 'calculability'.[12] Ethics must set rules as we jostle for a place moving forwards. As such it involves creative appropriation, the testing of limits, resignifications, theatricalizations, fabrications, critical interrogations, demystification (e.g., of homophobic discourses), exposure (e.g., of injustices or disequilibria), as well as empowering (e.g., of prisoners). Such a view is also compatible with Deleuze, who represents ethics as associated with the 'selection of forces' to 'invent' criteria and solutions in an 'active way'. Ethics comes to the fore in moments of crisis and uncertainty. As Levi Bryant says, '[t]he moment of the ethical is precisely the moment of crisis ... the question of the ethical is that of how situations must be recomposed in response to the moment of crisis' (2011: 27). The future, then, confronts the individual, group, society, and globe as a series of constraints, constraints that 'coerce' the character of our normative responses.

In *Philosophy after Deleuze*, Joe Hughes quotes Deleuze, saying that we need to 'invent a principle which is adequate to the situation' (Hughes, 2012: 71). Deleuze notes how Nietzsche rejects Kant's view of morality as legislation of a universal law, in preference for an ideal that is one's own and others' as well. It is based upon creation: 'To think is to create' (Deleuze, 1983: xiv). This, of course, is Deleuze's account of Nietzsche, for whom 'thinking would then mean *discovering, inventing, new possibilities of life*' (1983: 101). Deleuze continues: 'In other words, life goes beyond the limits that knowledge fixes for it, but thought goes beyond the limits that that life fixes for it ... The thinker thus expresses the noble affinity of thought and life: life making thought active, thought making life affirmative' (1983: 101). Inventing principles to insure the future is not only a prudential concern, but constitutes the domains of politics, ethics, and morality as well. Matters such as climate change, democracy, human rights, or global contagion constitute new domains, characterized by uncertainty, risk, and danger, as new accords are developed for the twenty-first century, accords that require new types of response, new forms of knowledge, new forms of coordination and communication, new skills of agility, *tekhnē*, and comportment.

A Foucauldian ethics of the future

Being obligated and motivated is explicable directly on the basis that we are living beings for whom the state of the world is an object of concern. In this sense, our ethical responsibilities and comportment go beyond obligations to each other, narrowly defined, to include animals and the world as well. We stand in the present taking stock, appraising both our capacities and what needs to be done. In this context, continuance norms frame ethics in relation to three things: 1) one must attend to oneself and those dependent upon oneself; 2) one must avoid harming oneself, others, and the world; 3) one must facilitate and assist ongoing continuance of life as best one can in the life situation one finds oneself in. This goes beyond social contract ethics in that it recognizes responsibilities to animals, the environment, and supererogation. Duties thus go beyond 'what we owe to each other', in Scanlon's (1998) sense, to include ethical conduct beyond the call of duty. Indeed, continuance justifies non-moral virtues such as 'consideration', 'gratitude', 'politeness', or 'doing favours'.[13] Thus, if supererogation includes non-moral actions as well, then the immanent norm of continuance includes non-obligatory good actions, voluntary actions, and actions that are good both for and independent of consequences.

What we owe to the other and to ourselves

The norm of life continuance also grounds 'what we owe to each other'. In that it involves power and politics related to possible futures, it does not exclude concern as to how individuals should act in interpersonal social comportment. As Butler says, 'though Foucault does not celebrate the "lone individual" who simply makes up new norms, he would locate the practices of the subject as one site where those social conditions are worked and reworked' (2005: 133). Butler also says that 'it seems right to fault Foucault for not making more room explicitly for the other in his consideration of ethics' (2005: 23). Yet, in spite of Butler's enormously pertinent insights into Foucault's ethics and poststructuralist normativity in general, on this point I am going to defend him. A caveat should be inserted at the outset, in that Foucault's studies of Greek and Roman antiquity might be said not to represent his own views on ethics; yet that would be implausible, and writers and friends such as Paul Veyne and Pierre Hadot take the view that in these studies Foucault was searching for a possible model for Western culture as it is going to be necessary to recreate it (see Veyne, 2010: esp. chs. 3, 5, 6; Hadot, 1995: 208). As is evident from his 1982 lecture courses, *The Hermeneutics of the Subject*, the other is seen by Foucault as indispensable to the self. '[T]he care of the self ... takes shape and can only take shape by reference to the Other' (2005: 60). Further, Foucault says, '"[g]overning", "being governed", and "taking care of oneself" form a sequence, a series, whose long and complex history extends up to the development of pastoral power in the Christian Church in the third and fourth centuries' (2005: 45). The other is essential also as a check to oneself; as a provider of recognition. As he says in his 1983 lecture course, *The Government of the Self and Others*, 'one cannot attend to oneself, take care of oneself, without a relationship to another person. And the role of this other is precisely to tell the truth, to tell the whole truth' (2010: 43). The other in antiquity then functions as a *parrhēsiastes* who tells the truth to you about yourself. The other is important also in that the care of the self is characterized by ignorance in the sense that one doesn't know who one is in any total sense.

In one of his interviews, Foucault states his central interest in *The Care of the Self* as being 'how an experience is formed where the relationship to self and to others is linked' (1989b: 296). The care of the self, then, is always at the same time concerned with care for others. There is a temporal and logical order, however: 'one must not have the care for others precede the care for self. The care for the self takes moral precedence in the measure that the relationship to self takes ontological precedence' (1989b: 287). In the 1982 lecture course, in discussing the care of the self in relation to the emperor, Foucault states that 'his objective is the foundation of his action. What is his objective? It is himself ... It is in caring for himself that he will inevitably care for others' (2005: 202).[14] Far from ethical comportment being an exercise of unproblematically utilizing reason, Foucault stresses the requirements of maturity and self-development that constitute the *prior conditions* of effective agency and rational capacity. Descartes' separation of the cognitive from the affective, while being his biggest contribution to the Enlightenment, was also, for Foucault, his biggest wrong turning (see Rabinow, 1997: xxv).

Apart from presupposing others, ethical action also presupposes liberty. Liberty translates here as freedom, but does not entail or imply liberation, to the extent that this trait is intended to suggest a human basis or ground, such as an original or true nature, which has been alienated or repressed and from which the subject can be set free. Foucault is especially adamant about this in *The History of Sexuality, Volume I*, where he criticizes the repressive hypothesis associated with Freudians such as Wilhelm Reich. With regard to sexuality, it is not a matter of liberating it, or setting it free, but rather defining the sphere of its exercise and identifying the components linked together to define it as an apparatus (*dispositif*) of historically constituted elements. Freedom, in that it involves conscious choices and actions within an open future of multiple possibilities, necessarily constitutes itself as ethical. Within an open structure of possibilities, free or forced choices entail decisions that are ethical to the extent that one is conscious of options. As

Foucault says, 'for what is ethics, if not the practice of freedom, the conscious [*réfléchie*] practice of freedom?' And he continues, '[f]reedom is the ontological condition of ethics. But ethics is the considered form that freedom takes when it is informed by reflection' (1997d: 284). The processes of constructing ourselves through selecting, deciding, or choosing some actions and excluding or bypassing others constitutes us as ethical subjects of our own making. They characterize the practices and habits that constitute the care of the self, and are essential to the arts of self-formation. Although the other is thus necessary, unlike for Levinas (2004), the other does not constitute an ontological ground reinstating a form of primordial recognition, thereby constituting a transcendental ground for ethics and the self. Foucault's conception is neither that of 'dialogical ethics' or the 'ethics of alterity'.

Political obligations

Just as ethical work presupposes liberty, it also is intrinsically political. Practices of the self are political in that they constitute relations of power, they are ways of controlling and limiting, and imply different models of governance to sustain them. The care of the self thus posits a politically active subject, involving practices of the self that include governance, which entails the management of the self over time. It further involves managerial imperatives both at the level of the individual, the family, the community, and the state, including decision making, the interpretation and application of rules, gambits, risks, knowing when to act and when to hold back (*prokheiron*), or being able if necessary to attack or defend.[15] These skills require *autarkeia* (self-sufficiency) and constant 'self-testing' (*probatio*) as a preparation for life. To be successful, then, ethics in its exercise requires maturity of judgement, as well as skills of general comportment, both philosophical and practical. These qualities will depend to a large extent on experience, education, and power. Only slowly will the capacities for thought develop. Importantly, for Foucault, such skills do not exist in the individual, in advance, by nature, but must be constructed through one's engagement with the world.

Hence the care of the self does not just refer to attention to oneself in the narrow sense; nor is it concerned solely with the avoidance of mistakes and dangers; nor does it designate primarily an attitude towards one's self or a form of awareness of self. It constitutes both a principle and a constant practice: 'We may say that in all of ancient philosophy the care of the self was considered as both a duty and a technique, a basic obligation and a set of carefully worked-out procedures' (Foucault, 1997e: 95). In this sense it designates a 'regulated occupation, a work with its methods and objectives' (1997e: 95). This work is by its very nature political, and integral to it are notions concerning both the government and management of self and others. It is political also in that it constitutes a *poiesis*,[16] that is, a productive work in which the subject utilizes *tekhnē* as a mode of fabrication within a broader framework of cultural rules and guidance. McGushin (2007: xviii) calls this '*ethopoetic*' in that it emphasizes both *productiveness* as well as the *arts* of self-fashioning in the development of *ēthos*, or way of life.[17]

As well as being political, the care of the self is linked to pedagogy. It is because education is inadequate that concern for the self is indispensable. The view in Athenian society was, says Foucault, that education was always necessarily inadequate, hence care of the self is always needed. One cares because education *cannot* provide for it. One must take care of oneself to compensate for inadequate education, but beyond this one cares for oneself throughout one's life until old age because no education can completely perform this function.

The importance of critical reflection

For Foucault, Descartes turned philosophy into a methodology for arriving at truth, cut off from the body. Foucault denies the mind–body dualism and sees bodily sensation and the care of the self as important to self-creation. In *The Hermeneutics of the Subject*, Foucault asks as to 'the condition of spirituality for access to the truth' (2005: 190). He continues:

> What is the price I have to pay for access to the truth? This price is situated in the subject himself in the form of: what then is the work

I must carry out on myself, what fashioning of myself must I undertake, what modification of being must I carry out to be able to have access to the truth? (2005: 189)

For Foucault, knowledge is 'embodied' and proceeds simultaneously as care of the self, requiring 'spiritual' exercises and engagement in the world. Foucault also denies the capacity of the subject to attain truth separated from superstition and the phantoms of the past. With Descartes, 'the subject ... does not have to transform himself' (2005: 190).

In such a world where phantasms and idols circulate freely with reason, subject to hegemonic insertions and controls, the only vouchsafed method of clearing the fog is through *critical reflection* or *critique*. It is through critique that limits are tested and transgression attempted. Critique, however, is difficult, and requires practices of the self for which Foucault turned to Greek and Roman antiquity.[18] Such a spiritual training involved 'the search, practice, and experience through which the subject carries out the necessary transformations on himself in order to have access to the truth' (Foucault, 2005: 15).

Foucault's writings on critique, and on Kant, make it clear that critical reflection is both an ethical and a moral process. In his interview with Michael Bess, Foucault responds to a question by saying: 'In a sense, I am a moralist' (1988d: 11; 2016c: 127). He then articulates 'three elements to his morals' which incorporate the notion of critical reflection:

> [first,] the refusal to accept what is proposed to us as self-evident; second, the need to analyse and to know (*savoir*), because we can do nothing without reflection as well as knowledge (*connaissance*), this is the principle of curiosity; and third, the principle of innovation, that is to say, not being inspired by a pre-existing programme, but looking for what has not yet been thought, imagined, or known in elements of our reflection and the way we act. So, refusal, curiosity, innovation. (Foucault, 1988d: 11–12; 2016c: 127–8)

Critical reflection is normative in that it implicates the type of world that it is possible to inhabit at the same time that it derives from skills focused on actions in the present. As an activity, critical reflection involves thinking that derives not from the will, but 'from the nature of things, from Being itself' (Gray, 1968: xi). Thinking relates instances to norms, and is intrinsically normative.[19] It is through such critical thinking that the imperative to continue highlights a more positive or critical sense of responsibility; our responsibility *to be* ethical. Here it is possible to find in Foucault a sense of ethicality and responsibility as confronting those aspects that prevent me from living or prevent others from living.[20] In a world of overlapping interests and projects there is a responsibility to constantly instantiate the critical, in the sense of insisting on rights and obligations and just arrangements for an orderly continuance into the future. Critique, in this sense, is a part of the armature (*dispositif*) of the right in relation to the good, and in the capacity to differentiate valid norms of continuance from mere convention, folklore, or ideology. Critique is also essential for the purposes of arbitrating conflicting duties, and the relative importance of consequences versus rights in particular situations. If reason and ideology circulate together, critique becomes epistemologically mandatory and central to the democratic skills of deliberation and reflective reason. As Jodi Dean expresses this point, 'persisting in a poorly arranged world poses ethical dilemmas ... To this extent, an ethics that does not involve critique ... is itself unethical, culpable, unresponsive, as it disavows the relations of power on which it depends' (2005: 61).

Parrhēsia

Foucault's notion of *parrhēsia* links ethical action directly with power.[21] Foucault defines *parrhēsia* as truth telling, speaking truth to power, frankness in speaking the truth, or fearless speech. In his penultimate lecture course at the Collège de France, *The Government of the Self and Others* (2010), Foucault surveys the literature concerning the notion of *parrhēsia* in the Latin and Greek texts of antiquity, differentiating the notion as a particular way of telling the truth from demonstration, rhetoric, teaching, eristic, or debating. Although *parrhēsia* may use elements of demonstration, the proof of *parrhēsia* does not reside in demonstration. Similarly, it is distinct from rhetoric because it is not primarily a technique of persuasion – 'it is not essential to rhetoric that it speak the truth' (2010: 53). It is also not primarily teaching or pedagogy, although it may on occasions employ pedagogical strategies, since there is none of the progression peculiar to pedagogy, that is, there is a lack of planned sequencing of lessons calculated to achieve the aim of education as an objective. Similarly, *parrhēsia* is not a way of discussing or debating. Relatedly, *parrhēsia* is not a form of eristic. Whereas *parrhēsia* is primarily concerned with truth, with telling the truth, eristic is centrally concerned with winning the argument through the cleverness of debate. Essentially, says Foucault, what defines *parrhēsia* 'does not consist in the discourse itself and its structures' (2010: 55) but rather 'in the risk that truth-telling opens up for the speaker ... in the possible backlash on the speaker from the effect it has on the interlocutor' (2010: 56).

If risk constitutes a single aspect that defines *parrhēsia*, instances of its use nevertheless cover multiple and very different situations. In *The Government of the Self and Others*,[22] the Berkeley seminars,[23] and *The Courage of Truth*,[24] Foucault refers to a classical conception of *parrhēsia* by considering its functions in political life, specifically in relation to democracy as well as an ethical variant concerned with the care of the self and the relationship of the self and others. In the Berkeley seminar of 14 November 1983, Foucault is led to a consideration of the crisis of *parrhēsia* and democracy. This concerns the 'negative' functions of *parrhēsia*. As Foucault says:

> The problem very roughly put was the following. On the one side democracy is a *politeia*, a constitution, where the *demos*, the people exercise power, and where everybody is equal before the law. But isn't it a fact that such a constitution is condemned to give place to any kind of *parrhēsia*, even to the worst? And on the other side, since *parrhēsia* is given to the worst citizens, isn't it a fact that this *parrhēsia* becomes a danger for the city and for the democracy itself, since the overwhelming influence of bad orators leads necessarily to tyranny? (2019: 124)

This problem, or something very similar, expresses Plato's objections to democracy, which were in terms of its relationship to freedom and truth. Foucault examines Plato's *Republic* (Book VIII, 557a–b) where Socrates represents *parrhēsia* as 'anyone is allowed to do what he likes ... to suit his pleasure' (Foucault,

2019: 84).²⁵ Plato associates democracy with a lack of self-restraint and an excess of liberty on the part of people not capable of exercising it responsibly. *Parrhēsia*, for Plato, reveals the problem of democracy.

Foucault returns in *The Courage of Truth* to a study of Plato.²⁶ It is in the *Apology* that Socrates demonstrates the ethical as opposed to the political form of *parrhēsia*. The aim of ethical *parrhēsia*, says Foucault, is very different from political *parrhēsia*; the aim of ethical *parrhēsia* is to see that people take care of themselves. As Foucault says: 'What is at stake in this new form of *parrhēsia* is the foundation of *ēthos* as the principle on the basis of which conduct can be defined as rational conduct in accordance with the very being of the soul' (2011a: 86). Socrates' *parrhēsia*, then, comprises three aspects: *zētēsis, exetasis, epimeleia*: *zētēsis*, the search for veridiction; *exetasis*, the examination or test of souls; *epimeleia*, taking care of oneself and others. Socrates tests souls with the aim of encouraging individuals to take care of themselves.

If political *parrhēsia* 'consists in making use of ... true, reasonable, agonistic discourse ... in the field of the *polis*' (Foucault, 2010: 105), *parrhēsia* operates in the ethical sense as a technique in the care of the self, and in the conversion of self to self. It operates through a master, a *parrhēsiastes*, who may be a friend or someone with whom one is acquainted. The other need not always be present, or present very much. *Parrhēsia* is also employed as a technique to challenge oneself, in the function of 'self-testing', both in the presence of another directly, at a distance, or remotely without the other being present. In this sense, it functioned within an educational matrix manifesting a 'truth-telling' function. Foucault draws on Epictetus to document such a practice. In his *Discourses*, Epictetus describes various techniques of self-examination, which 'takes the form of a constant putting on trial of all of our representations' (Foucault, 2010: 160; see Epictetus, 2000: III, 12).

Foucault also refers to Philodemus,²⁷ who wrote a text 'On Frank Speaking' directly on the topic of *parrhēsia*.²⁸ Philodemus compared *parrhēsia* to the arts of medicine and to piloting a boat, both traditional metaphors in Greek culture. In the Berkeley lectures of 1983,²⁹ Foucault uses these metaphors to suggest what is an important theme in his work:

> The reason why the pilot's *technē* (sailing) and the physician's *technē* (medicine) were so often compared to each other was that in both of them ... you must take into account not only the general rules and principles that you have learned during your training, but you also must take into account some pieces of information that are specific to a given situation. (2019: 160)

Given that there is no natural basis for self, the capabilities of self, including the capability of reason, must come through training. What is important here is the 'particular circumstances', and what the Greeks call *kairos*, or the 'critical moment' to intervene. Foucault comments that *kairos*, which characterizes the 'best moment for doing something, has always had a great importance in Greek thought from an epistemological point of view, from a moral one, and from a technical one' (2019: 160–1; see also Foucault, 1985a: 57–8). *Kairos* pertains to determining the opportune time in relation to existing circumstances. It constitutes, as Foucault says in *The Use of Pleasure*, a 'politics of timeliness' (1985a: 58), and is central to the virtue of prudence in relation to 'seizing the opportunity'.

As well as timing, self-testing is important in *parrhēsia*. Foucault emphasizes *exetasis* as a distinctive feature of both *parrhēsia* and *epimeleia*. *Exetasis* is concerned with testing and examining of souls; it is a procedure of verification, or investigation, or questioning (see Foucault, 2011a: 84, 86; 2005: 430–50). The testing was a means of establishing truth both in ethics (character) and knowledge (*logos*). Socratic examination applies a *test* in the contingent circumstances of time and place as a principle that should be followed throughout life (Foucault, 2011a: 86–7). Later on, in Seneca, the *probatio* constitutes the test as a general attitude that goes throughout life, and is also a *constant attitude to life* (see Foucault, 2005: 17 March, second hour). Thus, *life, testing life*, and *attending to oneself and others* characterize both Greek and Roman *parrhēsia* in the domain of ethics.

In *The Courage of Truth*, Foucault examines the Cynic philosophers' use of *parrhēsia* in order to extend the themes of disobedience and protest. Unlike Plato, or the Stoics, or the Epicureans, the Cynics manifested *parrhēsia* mostly through their *way of life, their style of existence*. These styles of existence were 'flexible and variable' in that there could be innumerable styles of existence 'linked to one and the same metaphysics of the soul' (2011a: 164). Even though the Cynics wrote books like other philosophers, it was their way of life that marked them out in terms of their distinctive *parrhesiastic* activities. The Cynic was 'constantly characterized as a man of *parrhēsia*' (2011a: 166). It was their way of life that constituted the 'touchstone' or *basanos* of their 'relation to truth' (2019: 167; 2011a: 170).[30] While most of the Cynics after the first century BC refer to Diogenes Laertius or Antisthenes as the founders of their school, they also trace themselves back to Socrates. From the end of the first century BC to the fourth century AD the Cynics were 'very numerous', says Foucault (2019: 164). Hence, it is through their 'exemplary lives' that Foucault classifies Cynic *parrhēsia* under three major types: '(1) critical preaching; (2) scandalous behaviours; (3) ... provocative dialogue' (2019: 169).[31]

Civil liberties and civil disobedience

Foucault's own political activism has some affinities with the tradition of Cynicism, and in his own life, as we have seen, Foucault frequently spoke out on matters of concern. He manifested strong support for principles of civil liberties and civil protest and disobedience. Civil liberties are essential in the task of clarifying vital from social norms, as every perspective must be considered. Civil disobedience is a moral weapon in the fight for justice that goes well beyond what we owe to each other in a narrow social sense of duties and obligations, and involves an orientation to the world, to the environment, to animals, and to others. Civil disobedience is a weapon in the fight for justice, and justice is a necessary element of the world we inhabit. To those who say that disobedience cannot be moral, the response of *Lex iniusta non est lex* ('An unjust law is no law at all')[32] establishes the principle of disobedience as moral in Foucault's *dispositif* of the ethical in order to bring governments and leaders to face the court of world opinion.

For Foucault, the individual has both a right and a duty to resist through civil disobedience. In the same way that Henry David Thoreau exercised disobedience against the American government by refusing to pay the poll tax, an action that landed him in jail,[33] Foucault supported disobedience as a method of speaking to governments on matters of urgent social and political import. Whether on climate change, human rights, democracy, or viral pandemics, citizens have a duty today to voice their concerns to those in positions of authority. In terms of a normative Foucault, then, governments that promote or tolerate unjust practices can be seen to violate the conditions for fair and just continuance to the future. While this makes continuance norms in this sense *above the law*, such actions must be non-violent and respectful of legal outcomes, as continuance depends on non-violence and democratic processes in order to forestall anarchy and prevent 'a war of all against all'.

In relation to ethical comportment and political action, finally, continuance ethics demands an experimental approach to the problems that now beset the world. Right and wrong thus appeal to facts in the world, as it moves forward. In this sense, continuance accounts for the 'reason-giving force of facts about right and wrong' (Scanlon, 1998: 3) as we proceed into the future. This is to say that continuance provides the key regarding which reasons we should accept or reject as the basis of our normative evaluations and moral claims. It also affirms an epistemologically realist and materialist view of Foucault. Errors impede continuance in relation to risks and threats to survival. By doing so, such threats present themselves as moral duties.

Notes

1 This classification is similar to that of H. A. Prichard, the Oxford intuitionist, but unlike Prichard it does not see morality as resting on a mistake, as he claimed in his 1912 article in *Mind*, on the basis that such claims could only be directly *apprehended* (see Prichard, 1912). Rather, normative claims can be justified by appeal to continuance norms, via rational argument. The definition of moral is also similar to Kant's definition, when he says in the *Groundwork* that 'the objective necessity to act from obligation is called duty' (1959: 4, §439).
2 Baier's book on Hume is called *A Progress of Sentiments: Reflections on Hume's Treatise*.

3 This thesis is developed in Sartre's famous book *L'Existentialisme est un humanisme* (Sartre, 2007). But Foucault would not accept Sartre's radicalization and acceptance of Kant's *a priori*, of course.
4 Kant says, '[d]ogmatic procedure with a concept is then that which is conformable to law for the determinative judgement, critical procedure for the reflective judgement' (2005: §74). Determinative judgement works by asserting universal concepts dogmatically, presupposing 'the objective reality of the concept' in order to 'subsume' things under it. For 'reflective judgement', the principle is not 'determinative' and is not, therefore, constitutive, 'but merely regulative …' (§74). Determinative judgement seeks an objective subsumption of particulars under a universal principle; reflective judgement is merely regulative and open-ended (see §83). Kant further says that the 'reflective judgement must subsume under a law that which is not yet given, and is therefore in fact only a principle of reflection upon objects … [it] must serve as a mere subjective principle, for the purposive employment of our cognitive faculties, i.e., for reflecting upon a class of objects' (§69). Kant says further that '[the Understanding] is only a ground for the reflective, not the determinative judgement, and can justify absolutely no objective assertions' (§73). Continuance is 'a mere maxim of our judgement', to steal a phrase from Kant (§72). The acceptance of this epistemological distinction does not, of course, entail any commitment to Kant's conception of the *a priori* subject. And while continuance can be represented as cognitive *a priori* in a certain sense, it has real-world implications in terms of how life is lived. It can also be stated here that reflective judgement is made more relevant in a complex world, for where 'only the particular is given and the universal has to be found for it' (§69), it suggests that contextual uncertainties make judgement more relative to the situation, but still informed by a general *ēthos*. The way continuance norms are embedded in practical life contexts is therefore not empirically separable, and not amenable to deduction (in the sense of *geometrico*), although they are analytically distinct.
5 Identifying those norms that are compatible with and facilitate continuance under fair conditions for each and all is thus constructivist, not universalist.
6 The whole in complexity theory is radically open, whereas Hegel operated in conformity with the laws of mechanism, in terms of a closed conception (see Olssen and Mace, 2021).
7 Butler has taken the phrase from Foucault (2011a: 161).
8 On 'mitigating circumstances', see Horder (2007), Matravers (1998), Eastman (1999), and van Verseveld (2014). On 'diminished

responsibility', see Meynen (2016), Tøye (2017), Reed and Bohlander (2011), and Roth (2017). See also the novel by Nancy Taylor Rosenberg, *Mitigating Circumstances* (1993).
9 See Roth (2017), who develops an account of 'free will' as the capacity to respond to demands and understand them and assess responsibility in this light and to this extent. Roth concludes that one can assume responsibility in most situations, and that neuroscience does not threaten the law's commitment to responsible agency on this basis. See also van Verseveld (2014), who considers perpetrators of international crimes who were unaware that they were violating the law. Here she argues that the principle of 'no punishment without guilt' needs to apply. Clearly lack of knowledge in a global and more complicated world imposes limits on responsibility.
10 The last phrase is a citation from Foucault's first published work, *Mental Illness and Psychology* (1976: 58).
11 Derrida's (1992: 26) famous expression as used in 'Force of Law'. The issue as I am presenting it is one of reconciling differences within a finite, crowded, poorly arranged space. The issues are clearly appreciated by Derrida, when he says, for instance, that 'justice doesn't wait. It is that which must not wait.' Its presence, however, is not messianic but wholly immanent.
12 These concepts are also used by Derrida in 'Force of Law' (see Derrida, 1992: 28).
13 These are considered 'non-moral' in that they are discretionary, whereas 'moral', for me, comprises only strict duties within a system comprising mutual obligations. Although I have utilized this conception within a systems framework, the notion of morality as comprising duties, as opposed to voluntary actions, comes from Prichard (1912).
14 See Foucault (2005: 174–5), where he stipulates the ontological order or 'self first/other second' in Plato's *Alcibiades*, but that this does not mean that the other is any less fundamental to the care of the self. 'Throughout [*Alcibiades*], care of the self is therefore instrumental with regard to the care of others' (2005: 175). 'By taking care of oneself ... one makes oneself capable of taking care of others' (2005: 175). By practising *katharsis* (the art of the cathartic) I learn how to govern, for instance (my paraphrase of Foucault, 2005: 175).
15 *Prokheiron* means 'ready to hand'; 'the *logos* must be ready to hand' (in order to excel at something) (Foucault, 2005: 325). For *prokheiron*, see Foucault (2005: 325, 329n, 357, 361, 484, 499). Foucault says: 'which the Latins translated as *ad manum*. We must have it here, ready to hand. I think this is a very important notion falling within the category

of memory, no doubt fundamental in all Greek thought, but also introducing a particular inflection' (2005: 325).
16 In philosophy, *poiesis* derives from Greek origins (ποίησις). It is 'the activity in which a person brings something into being that did not exist before. Etymologically, it derives from the ancient Greek word, to make (ποιεῖν)' (Wikipedia).
17 Foucault was influenced by Hadot's conception of ancient ethics in seeing philosophy as a way of life. See Hadot (1953; 1976; 1987; 1992; 1995; 1997).
18 Such practices included ascetic exercises, fasting, testing of the self, purification, and renunciation.
19 See Heidegger (1968) and Arendt (1977; 2006). Arendt famously concluded her review of the Eichmann trial by claiming that Eichmann's failure was his 'incapacity to think' (Arendt, 1977). Foucault would be homologous to Heidegger and Arendt on this issue. Thinking always involves a possible normative reference. Thinking is thus distinct from bureaucracy (following orders), or from science (establishing truth) (see Gray, 1968: iv).
20 See chapter 3 of Butler's book, *Giving an Account of Oneself*.
21 Foucault mentioned *parrhēsia* in his lectures at Dartmouth College in 1980, in his Berkeley lectures of 1983, and several times during his lectures of 1982, published under the title *The Hermeneutics of the Subject*, especially during both the first and second hour of the lecture on 27 January (2005: 137, 164), and then again in the lecture of 10 March (2005: 382–8); and although these references are insightful, they are but fragments in a developing conception. It was during the lecture course of 1983 at the Collège de France, *The Government of the Self and Others*, that Foucault first engaged with *parrhēsia* as a theme in any major sense. Then, in the lecture course of 1984 entitled *The Courage of Truth*, *parrhēsia* continued to be a central concept of his approach to ethics.
22 1983 Lecture Course at the Collège of France (Foucault, 2010).
23 This comprises the text compiled from tape-recordings made of six lectures presented by Foucault in English at the University of California at Berkeley in the Fall term of 1983. The first lecture was on 10 October 1983, followed by 31 October, 14 November, 21 November, and 30 November. The title of the series of lectures was 'Discourse and Truth', and all of them were devoted to Foucault's studies of *parrhēsia*.
24 1984 Lecture Course at the Collège de France (Foucault, 2011a).
25 Citing Socrates talking to Adeimantus. See Plato, *Republic* (Book VIII, §557b).

26 Focusing primarily on *Apology* and *Laches*, although also on *Phaedo*, *Alcibiades* and *Crito*.
27 Foucault comments that this text is fragmentary and obscure, and he would have floundered but for the commentary provided by the Italian scholar Marcello Gigante. See Gigante, 'Philodème: Sur la liberté de parole', in Foucault (2001: 110, n. 72).
28 Philodemus, an Epicurean, is the only Greek or Greco-Roman known to have written specifically on the topic.
29 In the fifth lecture, presented on 21 November 1983, delivered in English at the University of California, Berkeley, as part of the 'Discourse and Truth' lecture series.
30 *Basanos* represented the quality of gold in a coin, being applied as a metaphor to the quality of integrity, or *gravitas*, in a person. For more on the concept of *basanos*, see Foucault (2011a: 84, 145, 153).
31 Cynics were not homogeneous as a category. While many lived as 'vagabonds' with the 'staff', such as Peregrinus, others, such as Demetrius, were philosophers and counsellors to aristocratic groups. See Foucault (2011a: 7 March, first hour, esp. 194–5). On Peregrinus, see also Lucian (1913: 13; see Foucault 2011a: 167, 181, 193, 198, 212n, 232, 254). See also Foucault (2019: lecture of 21 November).
32 Originating with St Augustine, cited by St Thomas Aquinas, and also by Martin Luther King Jr.
33 Thoreau coined the term civil disobedience in his 1848 article, 'Civil Disobedience'. The state poll tax was being levied by the American government to prosecute a war in Mexico and to enforce the Fugitive Slave Law (see Brownlie, 2017: 1).

Appendix 1

A reading list for Foucault's ethics

Foucault's writings on ethics are usually considered to denote his later writings. They include the two volumes of the history of ancient practices of the self, written after *The History of Sexuality, Volume 1: An Introduction*, which was initially published by Gallimard in 1976, and published in English in 1978. These later volumes were *The History of Sexuality, Volume 2: The Use of Pleasure* (1984/1985a), and *The History of Sexuality, Volume 3: The Care of the Self* (1984/1986a). The introduction to *Volume 2* presents an overview of Foucault's project in these three works, and a cogent summary of his views on ethics. In *Volume 3* Foucault presents an overview of Roman ethics, especially in the section 'The Cultivation of the Self' (Part Two). Throughout the latter two texts Foucault explains how material changes over time affect Greek and Roman ethics and modes of comportment, leading to an escalation in the importance of austerity concerning ethics and sexuality. Volume 4 of *The History of Sexuality*, *Les Aveux de la chair* (Confessions of the Flesh) was published posthumously in 2018, although it has not yet been translated into English.

Also noted as being particularly insightful on the topic of ethics are Foucault's interviews, 'On the Genealogy of Ethics: An Overview of Work in Progress' (1997b) and 'The Ethic of Care for the Self as a Practice of Freedom' (1997d). Many other interviews and short articles are also relevant, however. Important for me are the articles reproduced in *The Essential Works of Michel Foucault, Vol. 1: Ethics, Subjectivity and Truth* (1997a), which includes the essays 'Self-Writing' (pp. 207–22), 'Polemics, Politics, and Problematizations' (pp. 111–20), 'On the Government of the

Living' (pp. 81–6), and others. Volume II of the *Essential Works* (Foucault, 1998a) also contains many important essays, including 'Life: Experience and Science' (1998b) and 'A Preface to Transgression' (1998e). *Technologies of the Self: A Seminar with Michel Foucault* (1988) similarly contains important essays on the construction of subjectivities.

In terms of positioning Foucault philosophically, his commentaries on Kant are insightful. The article 'What is Enlightenment?' (1984c) is centrally important to the discussion on Kant. Also, the 1978 article 'What is Critique?' (1997f) is of note in that this is where Foucault first discusses Kant's essay 'What is Enlightenment?' and raises various issues of central importance for ethics conceived as self-fashioning. Also noteworthy in relation to Kant is Foucault's minor dissertation for his doctorate, entitled *Introduction to Kant's Anthropology from a Pragmatic Point of View* (2008b). It is here that he locates his own critical project firmly in relation to Kant's philosophy, albeit with certain important qualifications and exceptions, especially as regards Kant's conception of the subject.

Many of Foucault's other more general essays are important for ethics. 'The Subject and Power' (1982) provides a perspective on power that demonstrates the close relationship between power and ethics, especially in relation to how beings comport themselves in the world. The interviews in *Power/Knowledge* (1980), especially 'Truth and Power' (1980e) and 'Two Lectures on Power' (1980d), are also relevant, as are Foucault's last five courses at the Collège de France, of course. These comprise *On the Government of the Living: Lectures at the College de France 1979–1980* (2014b), *Subjectivity and Truth: Lectures at the College de France 1980–1981* (2017), *The Hermeneutics of the Subject: Lectures at the College de France 1981–1982* (2005), *The Government of the Self and Others: Lectures at the College de France 1982–1983* (2010), and *The Courage of Truth: Lectures at the Collège de France 1983–1984* (2011a). All are crucial to the development of Foucault's writings on ethics and especially *parrhēsia*, which is examined in the latter two courses that he offered. *Parrhēsia* is also a subject of focus in a volume entitled *Michel Foucault: About the Beginning of the Hermeneutic of the Self* (Foucault, 2016b), which includes the two lectures that Foucault presented initially on 20 and 21 October at the

University of California, Berkeley, and, in slightly altered form, at Dartmouth College on 17 and 24 November of the same year, entitled 'Subjectivity and Truth' and 'Christianity and Confession'. Also included in this book is the transcript of the discussion of 'Truth and Subjectivity' that took place two days after the second of the lectures at Berkeley, on 23 October 1980, plus the brief interview conducted in French by Michael Bess on 3 November 1980 (see Foucault, 1988d; 2016c). Also important is the lecture on *parrhēsia* presented by Foucault at the University of Grenoble in May 1982, later published in *Anabases* 16 (1982). The following year, from October to November 1983 at the University of California, Berkeley, Foucault presented six lectures in English entitled 'Discourse and Truth' (Foucault, 2019), a group of lectures also edited by Joseph Pearson in a book entitled *Fearless Speech* (Foucault, 2001).

Before he visited America, in 1981 Foucault presented a course of lectures at the Catholic University of Louvain, entitled *Mal faire, dire vrai: Function de l'aveu en justice*, translated as *Wrong-Doing, Truth-Telling: The Function of Avowal in Justice* (Foucault, 2014a). The editors of the volume, Fabienne Brion and Bernard E. Harcourt, note that the reference to *dire vrai* in the title reflects Foucault's 'incipient interest in *parrhēsia*' (2014a: 1), and also constitutes 'the most common English translation of Nietzsche's concept of *Wahrsagen*' (2014a: 1), which Foucault frequently refers to in his writings, especially when defining *dire vrai* in the inaugural lecture at Louvain. Finally, from among his very early writings and radio broadcasts on literature, specifically on Sade, Genet, Joyce, Jakobson, Bataille, and Raymond Roussel, Foucault elaborates his complex ontology in a way that is highly relevant to ethical actions in the world. It was these early radio broadcasts and seminars, such as the essay on Sade's *La Nouvelle Justine*, that pre-shadow Foucault's philosophical mindset as simultaneously 'critical, complex and strategic' (2015: x), in a way that reveals a deeper continuity of philosophical intention throughout his academic career, leading us ultimately to a formulation of what a Foucauldian ethics could possibly entail.

Although this list of works is not in any sense definitive, it does give some idea of my own reading, at least in terms of the major works that have guided me for this study.

Appendix 2

The Anglo-American and Continental traditions on Nietzsche scholarship, a note

In drawing upon writers such as Brian Leiter, Christopher Janaway, Richard Schacht, Christa Davis Acampora, Maudemarie Clark, and David Dudrick, I am conscious of mixing the views of different traditions in philosophy, namely the Anglo-American approach and the Continental tradition, with which Foucault and Nietzsche interpreters such as Gilles Deleuze have their home. Just as both traditions stem from different readings of Kant's philosophy, so, too, both offer readings of Nietzsche that are different in certain respects. In an attempt to engage with both traditions, I have included representatives of the Anglo-American approach who have written on naturalism in a very interesting and competent way. In this, I have followed Foucault, who sought to engage with Anglo-American philosophy at various times in his career. Having said this, it is not possible to do justice to the issue of the divide between these two traditions of philosophy, except to make a few pertinent comments.

The first is that this divide between Anglo-American and Continental approaches itself attests to the way that power operates in and through professional philosophy. As this chasm has been very marked over my time as a professional academic in England, it constitutes an unhealthy situation and subverts the arguments of both sides to claim to be motivated by reason.

The second relates to the fact that Anglo-American philosophers on Nietzsche have seemingly been more interested in offering both critical and what I will term individualist and foundationalist readings of Nietzsche. The individualist reading of Nietzsche interprets him through the lens of Western liberalism as concerned to represent life as a merciless and competitive struggle of all against all. The foundationalist trope posits fixed psycho-instinctual drives which anchor and structure human interaction. Although this situation is changing rapidly, historically I think it accurate to register that those who have interpreted Nietzsche in these ways have invariably been on the Anglo-American side.

The third comment is that it is important to separate Nietzsche the philosopher from his demonization in Western culture generally. Popular cultural representations have traded on both individualist and foundationalist representations of Nietzsche. Films such as Alfred Hitchcock's *Rope* misrepresent Nietzsche as the author of a vicious morality, 'beyond good and evil', in order that two youths can justify lynching and killing another youth, freed from all moral constraints. In *Cape Fear*, Robert de Niro plays a murderous psychopath influenced by Nietzsche, whom he reads avidly. The British-Irish television series *The Fall*, with Gillian Anderson as the police detective, represents a serial killer as motivated and informed by Nietzsche. The killer articulates a view of Nietzsche as proselytizing for a non-morality driven by the 'will to power', which manifests 'a desire to control everything and everyone', while 'living and breathing moral relativism', thereby being 'freed from conventional values of right and wrong'. The serial killer represents the sense of freedom as 'exhilarating'.

One can only obtain such a misreading of Nietzsche if one interprets him through the lens of Western liberal individualism and systematically ignores the collective, social, and historical idioms in his texts. Often associated with such a view is that Nietzsche sees the Overman as a Superman, championing the interests of the 'higher types' in developing what is seen as a thoroughly elitist and individualist view in order to provide strength and vigour and aggression over the qualities of the herd. Yet it is not clear how this view squares with Nietzsche's anti-essentialism, his view that humans are historically constituted. It could mean, of course, that Nietzsche is advocating a type of social Darwinist ethic of the 'survival of the fittest', where all are pitted against all in an endless struggle, and that the strongest win out. All I can say here is that while I have found some evidence that Nietzsche is elitist, it is not in the sense of the illustrations just given, but rather in the sense that he accepts the view that *cultures* based on folklore, superstition, religion, and so on, are less fit to survive than cultures based on strong values, reason, clear thinking, and so on. In this sense, Nietzsche could be elitist in a more 'structuralist' sense, of preferring higher types of culture over lower, 'herd' cultures. What certainly appears the case is that he lacked a language in which to express himself unambiguously. Heidegger (1991) wrote his four-volume study *Nietzsche*, as Derrida (1989) notes, to challenge the biological, zoological, and individualist interpretations of Nietzsche. Deleuze notes that *Übermensch* translates, not as Superman, but Overman, and that the Overman in Nietzsche, as Deleuze (1983) interprets him, represents more of an affirmative ethical response than a self-aggrandizing individualist trying to advance the interests of the stronger. In this sense, the Overman might also be seen as a type of 'specific intellectual', who fights for justice on behalf of specific groups. In some of his works, Nietzsche limits the wealth and possessions of the Overman; Zarathustra 'walks the other way' when others act unethically or inappropriately.

It is pointless disputing certain Anglo-American characterizations of Nietzsche, however, for there are clearly senses in which he does harbour aristocratic or elitist attitudes. He also shows a marked preference for certain character traits and values, and disdain for others. Let me just say that to the extent that Nietzsche was an elitist, he fails to develop a meaningful conception of the future. If he is represented as *not* being elitist, or if his personal attitudes are disregarded, then there is a distinctive philosophical thesis within his *oeuvre*, a thesis that is different to all other major contenders within the Western philosophical tradition. The crucial, fourth point here is that Foucault, at any rate, is not interested in an elitist view of Nietzsche. To the extent that there are unacceptable attitudes in Nietzsche, they are tangential, not central, and it is possible, in Nietzsche's own parlance, 'to walk the other way'. Foucault harnesses Heidegger's philosophy of the future to augment Nietzsche's powerful historical ontological thesis. For Foucault, it is Nietzsche and Heidegger together that are centrally illuminating. Both together constitute a *dispositif* that can be worked with productively, even though neither can be taken up in their entirety.

References

Works by Foucault

(1970). *The Order of Things*. London: Tavistock/Routledge.
(1972). 'The Discourse on Language', in *The Archaeology of Knowledge and the Discourse on Language*, trans. A. M. Sheridan Smith. New York: Pantheon, pp. 215–37 [translated by Rupert Swyer from Foucault's inaugural lecture at the Collège de France, given on 2 December 1970, and published in French as 'L'Ordre du Discours' (Paris: Gallimard, 1971)].
(1975). 'Preface', in B. Jackson (ed.), *Leurs Prisons: Autobiographies de prisonniers et d'ex-deténus américains*. Paris: Plon, pp. i–vi. See also Foucault, 1994d.
(1976). *Mental Illness and Psychology*, trans. A. Sheridan. New York: Harper and Row.
(1977a). *Discipline and Punish*, trans. A. Sheridan. New York: Pantheon.
(1977b). 'La grande colère des faits', *Le Nouvel Observateur*, 9 May, pp. 84–6. See also Foucault, 2016a.
(1977c). *Language, Counter-Memory, Practice: Selected Essays and Interviews*, ed. D. F. Bouchard, trans. D. F. Bouchard and S. Simon. Ithaca, NY: Cornell University Press.
(1977d). 'Nietzsche, Genealogy, History', in *Language, Counter-Memory, Practice: Selected Essays and Interviews*, ed. D. F. Bouchard, trans. D. F. Bouchard and S. Simon. Ithaca, NY: Cornell University Press, pp. 139–64.
(1978a). 'Politics and the Study of Discourse', trans. C. Gordon, *Ideology and Consciousness*, 3, pp. 7–26.
(1978b). 'Introduction', in G. Canguilhem, *On the Normal and the Pathological*, trans. C. Fawcett with R. S. Cohen. Dordrecht: Reidel, pp. 7–24.
(1980a). *Power/Knowledge*, ed. C. Gordon. New York: Pantheon.
(1980b). 'George Canguilhem: Philosopher of Error', trans. G. Burchell, *Ideology and Consciousness*, 7, pp. 51–62.

(1980c). *The History of Sexuality, Vol. 1: An Introduction*, trans. R. Hurley. New York: Vintage.
(1980d). 'Two Lectures on Power', in *Power/Knowledge: Selected Interviews and Other Writings, 1972–1977*, ed. C. Gordon. Brighton: Harvester Press, pp. 78–108.
(1980e). 'Truth and Power', in *Power/Knowledge: Selected Interviews and Other Writings 1972–1977*, ed. C. Gordon. Brighton: Harvester Press, pp. 109–33.
(1981a). 'The Order of Discourse', trans. I. McLeod, in R. Young (ed.), *Untying the Text: A Post-Structuralist Reader*. London: Routledge and Kegan Paul, pp. 51–78.
(1981b). 'Questions of Method: An Interview with Michel Foucault', trans. C. Gordon, *Ideology and Consciousness*, 8, pp. 3–14.
(1982). 'The Subject and Power', in H. L. Dreyfus and P. Rabinow (eds), *Michel Foucault: Beyond Structuralism and Hermeneutics*. Chicago: University of Chicago Press, pp. 208–26.
(1983). 'Preface', in G. Deleuze and F. Guattari, *Anti-Oedipus: Capitalism and Schizophrenia*, trans. R. Hurley, M. Seem, and H. R. Lane. Minneapolis, MN: University of Minesota Press, pp. xi–xiv.
(1984a). 'Preface to the *History of Sexuality, Volume II*', in *The Foucault Reader: An Introduction to Foucault's Thought*, ed. P. Rabinow. New York: Pantheon, pp. 333–9.
(1984b). 'On the Genealogy of Ethics: An Overview of Work in Progress', in *The Foucault Reader: An Introduction to Foucault's Thought*, ed. P. Rabinow. New York: Pantheon, pp. 340–72.
(1984c). 'What is Enlightenment?', in *The Foucault Reader: An Introduction to Foucault's Thought*, ed. P. Rabinow. New York: Pantheon, pp. 32–50.
(1984d). 'Le source de la vérité: interview with François Ewald', *Magazine litteraire*, 270 (May); repr. in Foucault, 1994a: vol. 4, 668–78.
(1984e). 'Politics and Ethics: An Interview', in *The Foucault Reader: An Introduction to Foucault's Thought*, ed. P. Rabinow. New York: Pantheon, pp. 373–80.
(1984–85). 'Dream, Imagination and Existence', trans. F. Williams, *Review of Existential Psychology and Psychiatry*, XIX, 1, pp. 29–78.
(1985a). *The Use of Pleasure: History of Sexuality, Vol. 2*, trans. R. Hurley. New York: Pantheon [orig. pub., *Histoire de la sexualité II: L'Usage des plaisirs* (Paris: Gallimard, 1984)].
(1985b). 'Georges Canguilhem: Philosopher of Error', *Revue de métaphysique et de morale*, 90.1, pp. 3–14.
(1986a). *The Care of the Self: History of Sexuality, Vol. 3*, trans. R. Hurley. New York: Pantheon [orig. pub., *Histoire de la sexualité III: Le Sourci de soi* (Paris: Gallimard, 1984)].

(1986b). *Death at the Labyrinth: The World of Raymond Roussel*, trans. C. Ruas. New York: Doubleday.
(1987). 'Questions of Method', in K. Baynes, J. Bonman, and T. McCarthy (eds), *After Philosophy: End or Transformation?* Cambridge, MA: MIT Press, pp. 100–17.
(1988a). *Politics, Philosophy, Culture: Interviews and Other Writings, 1977–1984*, ed. L. D. Kritzman. New York: Routledge.
(1988b). 'The Return to Morality', in Foucault, 1988a: 242–54.
(1988c). *Technologies of the Self: A Seminar with Michel Foucault*, ed. L. H. Martin, H. Gutman, and P. H. Hutton. Amherst, MA: University of Massachusetts Press.
(1988d). 'Power, Moral Values, and the Intellectual', *History of the Present*, 4.1–2, pp. 11–13 [interview with Michael Bess conducted on 3 November 1980, republished online as 'In a Sense I Am a Moralist', http://www.critical-theory.com/read-me-foucault-interview-in-a-sense-i-am-moralist (accessed 7 November 2018)]. See also Foucault, 2016c.
(1988e). 'Critical Theory/Intellectual History', in Foucault, 1988a: 17–46.
(1989a). 'Friendship as a Way of Life', trans. J. Johnston, in *Foucault Live: Interviews, 1966–1984*, ed. S. Lotringer. New York: Semiotext(e), pp. 203–10.
(1989b). 'The Concern for Truth', in *Foucault Live: Interviews, 1966–1984*, ed. S. Lotringer. New York: Semiotext(e), pp. 455–65.
(1991a). 'The Ethic of Care for the Self as a Practice of Freedom: An Interview', trans. J. D. Gauthier, in *The Final Foucault*, ed. J. Bernauer and D. Rasmussen. Cambridge, MA: MIT Press, pp. 1–20.
(1991b). 'Governmentality', in G. Burchell, C. Gordon, and P. Miller (eds), *The Foucault Effect: Studies in Governmentality*. Chicago: University of Chicago Press, pp. 87–104.
(1991c). 'Introduction', in G. Canguilhem, *The Normal and the Pathological*, trans. C. Fawcett with R. Cohen. New York: Zone Books, pp. 7–24.
(1991d). *Remarks on Marx: Conversations with Duccio Trombadori*, trans. R. J. Coleman and J. Cascaito. New York: Semiotext(e).
(1994a). *Dits et écrits: 1954–1988*, ed. D. Defert and F. Ewald with J. Lagrange, 4 vols. Paris: Gallimard.
(1994b). 'Linguistique et sciences sociales', in Foucault, 1994a: vol. 1, 821–42.
(1994c). 'La philosophie analytique de la politique', in Foucault, 1994a: vol. 3, 534–51.
(1994d). 'Sur les prisons' [1971], in Foucault, 1994a: vol. 1, 1043–4.
(1994e). 'Croître et multiplier', in Foucault, 1994a: vol. 1, 967–72 [orig. pub. in *Le Monde*, 15–16 November 1970, 13].

(1997a). *The Essential Works of Michel Foucault, 1954–1984, Vol. 1: Ethics, Subjectivity and Truth*, ed. P. Rabinow, trans. R. Hurley. London: Allen Lane, The Penguin Press.
(1997b). 'On the Genealogy of Ethics: An Overview of Work in Progress', in Foucault, 1997a: 253–80.
(1997c). 'Self-Writing', in Foucault, 1997a: 207–22.
(1997d). 'The Ethic of Care for the Self as a Practice of Freedom: An Interview', in Foucault, 1997a: 281–302.
(1997e). 'The Hermeneutic of the Subject', in Foucault, 1997a: 95–108.
(1997f). 'What is Critique?', in *The Politics of Truth*, ed. S. Lotringer and L. Hochroth, trans. L. Hochroth. New York: Semiotext(e), pp. 23–82.
(1998a). *The Essential Works of Michel Foucault, 1954–1984, Vol. 2: Aesthetics, Method and Epistemology*, ed. J. D. Faubion. London: Allen Lane, The Penguin Press.
(1998b). 'Life: Experience and Science', in Foucault, 1998a: 465–78.
(1998c). 'On the Archaeology of the Sciences: Response to the Epistemology Circle', in Foucault, 1998a: 297–333.
(1998d). 'Speaking and Seeing in Raymond Roussel', in Foucault, 1998a: 21–32.
(1998e). 'A Preface to Transgression', in Foucault, 1998a: 69–87.
(1998f). 'Theatrum Philosophicum', in Foucault, 1998a: 343–68.
(1998g). 'The Thought of the Outside', in Foucault, 1998a: 147–69.
(1998h). 'What is an Author?', trans. J. V. Harari, in Foucault, 1998a: 205–22.
(2000a). *The Essential Works of Michel Foucault, 1954–1984, Vol. 3: Power*, ed. J. D. Faubion. London: Allen Lane, The Penguin Press.
(2000b). 'Is It Useless to Revolt?', in Foucault, 2000a: 449–454.
(2000c). 'Confronting Governments: Human Rights', in Foucault, 2000a: 474–5.
(2000d). 'Interview with Michel Foucault', in Foucault, 2000a: 239–97.
(2000e). 'An Ethic of Discomfort', in Foucault, 2000a: 443–8.
(2000f). 'Open Letter to Mehdi Bazargan', in Foucault, 2000a: 439–42.
(2000g). 'Interview with *Actes*', in Foucault, 2000a: 394–402.
(2000h). 'The Risks of Security', in Foucault, 2000a: 365–81.
(2000i). 'The Political Technology of Individuals', in Foucault, 2000a: 403–17.
(2001). *Fearless Speech*, ed. J. Pearson. Los Angeles: Semiotext(e).
(2004). *Sécurité, territoire, population. Cours au Collège de France (1977–78)*. Paris: Gallimard/Seuil.
(2005). *The Hermeneutics of the Subject: Lectures at the College de France, 1981–1982*, trans. G. Burchell. New York: Palgrave Macmillan.
(2008a). *The Birth of Biopolitics: Lectures at the Collège de France,*

1978–1979, ed. M. Senellart, trans. G. Burchell. New York: Palgrave Macmillan.
(2008b). *Introduction to Kant's Anthropology from a Pragmatic Point of View*, trans. R. Nigro and K. Biggs. Los Angeles: Semiotext(e).
(2010). *The Government of Self and Others. Lectures at the Collège de France, 1982–1983*, ed. F. Gros, trans. G. Burchell. New York: Palgrave Macmillan.
(2011a). *The Courage of Truth: The Government of the Self and Others, II. Lectures at the Collège de France, 1983–1984*, ed. F. Gros, trans. G. Burchell. New York: Palgrave Macmillan.
(2011b). *Speech Begins after Death: In Conversation with Claude Bonnefoy*, ed. P. Artières, trans. R. Bononno. Minneapolis, MN: University of Minnesota Press.
(2013). *Lectures on the Will to Know. Lectures at the Collège de France, 1970–1971*, ed. D. Defert, trans. G. Burchell. New York: Palgrave Macmillan.
(2014a). *Wrong-Doing/Truth-Telling: The Functions of Avowal in Justice*, ed. F. Brion and B. E. Harcourt, trans. S. W. Sawyer. Chicago: University of Chicago Press.
(2014b). *On the Government of the Living: Lectures at the Collège de France, 1979–1980*, ed. M. Senellart, trans. G. Burchell. New York: Palgrave Macmillan.
(2015). *Language, Madness and Desire: On Literature*, ed. P. Artières, J.-F. Bert, M. Potte-Bonneville, and J. Revel, trans. R. Bononno. Minneapolis, MN: University of Minesota Press.
(2016a). 'The Great Rage of Facts', trans. M. S. Christofferson, in D. Zamora and M. C. Behrent (eds), *Foucault and Neoliberalism*. Cambridge: Polity, pp. 170–5.
(2016b). *About the Beginning of the Hermeneutics of the Self: Lectures at Dartmouth College, 1980*, ed. H.-P. Fruchaud and D. Lorenzini, trans. G. Burchell. Chicago: University of Chicago Press.
(2016c). 'Interview with Michel Foucault' (3 November 1980 with Michael Bess), in Foucault, 2016b: 127–38.
(2017). *Subjectivity and Truth: Lectures at the Collège de France, 1980–1981*, ed. F. Gros, trans. G. Burchell. New York: Palgrave Macmillan.
(2019). *Michel Foucault: Discourse and Truth & Parrēsia*, ed. H.-P. Fruchaud and D. Lorenzini. Chicago: University of Chicago Press.

Secondary works

Aczel, A. (2000). *The Mystery of the Aleph*. New York: Pocket Books.
Agamben, G. (1998). *Homo Sacer: Sovereign Power and Bare Life*. Stanford, CA: Stanford University Press.

— (2009). *What Is an Apparatus? And Other Essays*, trans. D. Kishik and S. Pedatella. Stanford, CA: Stanford University Press.
Althusser, L. (1969). *For Marx*, trans. B. Brewster. London: Penguin.
— (1971). 'Ideology and the Ideological State Apparatuses', in Althusser, *Lenin and Philosophy and Other Essays*. London: New Left Books.
— (1982). *Montesquieu, Rousseau, Marx*. London: Verso.
Ameriks, K. (2000). *Kant and the Fate of Autonomy: Problems in the Appropriation of the Critical Philosophy*. Cambridge: Cambridge University Press.
Anscombe, G. E. M. (1979). 'Under a Description', *Nous*, 13.2, pp. 219–33.
Ansell-Pearson, K. (1994). *Introduction to Nietzsche as Political Thinker*. Cambridge: Cambridge University Press.
— (1997). *Viroid Life: Perspectives on Nietzsche and the Transhuman Condition*. London: Routledge.
Aquinas, Thomas (1993). *Selected Philosophical Writings*, trans. T. McDermott. Oxford: Oxford University Press.
Arendt, H. (1957). *The Human Condition*. Chicago: University of Chicago Press.
— (1977). 'Thinking – I', *New Yorker*, 21 November, p. 65 (followed by 'Thinking – II', 28 November, p. 114; and 'Thinking – III', 5 December, p. 135).
— (2000). 'The Public and the Private Realm, Part I, The Vita Activa', in *The Portable Hannah Arendt*, ed. P. Baehr. London: Penguin, pp. 182–230.
— (2006). *Eichmann in Jerusalem: A Report on the Banality of Evil*. London: Penguin.
Aristotle (1905). *Politics*, trans. B. Jowett. Oxford: Oxford University Press.
— (1946). *The Politics*, trans. E. Barker. Oxford: Clarendon.
— (2001a). 'De Interpretatione' ('On Interpretation'), in *The Basic Works of Aristotle*, ed. R. McKeon. New York: Random House, pp. 40–61.
— (2001b). *The Nicomachean Ethics*, in *The Basic Works of Aristotle*, ed. R. McKeon. New York: Random House, pp. 935–1112.
Audi, R. (2013). 'The Nature of Normativity and the Project of Naturalizing the Normative', in J. Stelmach, B. Brożek, and M. Hohol (eds), *The Many Faces of Normativity*. Kraków: Copernicus Center Press, pp. 15–50.
Ayer, A. J. (1946). *Language, Truth and Logic*, 2nd edn. London: Victor Gollancz.
Bachelard, G. (1928). *Essai sur la connaissance approchée*. Paris: Vrin [Essay on Approximate Knowledge].
— (1934). *Le nouvel esprit scientifique*. Paris: PUF [The New Scientific Mind].

— (1938). *La formation de l'esprit scientifique: contribution à une psychoanalyse de la connaissance objective*. Paris: Vrin [The Formation of the Scientific Mind: A Contribution to a Psychoanalysis of Objective Knowledge].
— (1940). *La philosophie du non*. Paris: PUF [The Philosophy of No].
— (1949). *Le rationalisme appliqué*. Paris: PUF [Applied Rationalism].
Badiou, A. (1999). *The Clamor of Being*, trans. L. Burchill. Minneapolis, MN: University of Minnesota Press.
— (2001) [1993]. *Ethics: An Essay on the Understanding of Evil*, trans. P. Hallward. London: Verso.
— (2005) [1988]. *Being and Event*, trans. O. Feltham and Ray Brassier. New York: Continuum.
— (2009). *Logic of Worlds: Being and Event II*. New York: Continuum.
Bagnoli, C. (2013). 'Introduction', in C. Bagnoli (ed.), *Constructivism in Ethics*. Cambridge: Cambridge University Press, pp. 1–5.
Baier, A. (1991). *A Progress of Sentiments: Reflections on Hume's Treatise*. Cambridge, MA: Harvard University Press.
Ball, S. (2017). *Foucault as Educator*. Cham, Switzerland: Springer.
— (2019). 'A Horizon of Freedom: Using Foucault to Think Differently about Education and Learning', *Power and Education*, 11.2, pp. 132–44.
Barry, B. (1965). *Political Argument*. London: Routledge and Kegan Paul.
— (1989). *Theories of Justice*. London: Harvester Wheatsheaf.
— (1990) [1965]. *Political Argument. A Reissue with a New Introduction*. London: Harvester Wheatsheaf.
Bataille, G. (1980). *Inner Experience*, trans. L. A. Boltd. Albany, NY: SUNY Press.
— (1991). *The Accursed Share: An Essay on General Economy. Volume 1, Consumption*. New York: Zone Books.
— (1993). *The Accursed Share: An Essay on General Economy, Volume II, The History of Eroticism & Volume III, Sovereignty*. New York: Zone Books.
— (2004). *On Nietzsche*, trans. B. Boone. London: Continuum.
Becker, G. (1962). 'Investment in Human Capital: A Theoretical Analysis', *Journal of Political Economy*, 70.5, 2nd part, pp. 9–49.
— (1993) [1964]. *Human Capital: A Theoretical and Empirical Analysis with Special Reference to Education*, 3rd edn. Chicago: University of Chicago Press.
Bentham, J. (1960) [1789]. *An Introduction to the Principles of Morals and Legislation*, ed. W. Harrison. Oxford: Oxford University Press.
Berlin, I. (1958). *Two Concepts of Liberty*. Oxford: Clarendon.
Bernauer, J. W. (1990). *Michel Foucault's Force of Flight: Towards an Ethics for Thought*. Atlantic Highlands, NJ: Humanities Press.

Biesta, G. (2010). 'Five Theses of Complexity Reduction and its Politics', in D. Osberg and G. Biesta (eds), *Complexity Theory and the Politics of Education*. Rotterdam: Sense Publishers, pp. 5–14.

Birkhoff, G. D. (1913). 'Proof of Poincaré's Geometric Theorem', *Transactions of the American Mathematical Society*, 14, pp. 14–22; repr. in *Collected Mathematical Papers*, Providence, RI: American Mathematical Society, 1950, I, pp. 673–81.

— (1931). 'Proof of the Ergodic Theorem', *Proceedings of the National Academy of Sciences of the United States of America*, 17.12, pp. 656–60.

Blackburn, S. (1993). *Essays on Quasi-Realism*. Oxford: Clarendon.

— (1998). *Ruling Passions: A Theory of Practical Reason*. Oxford: Clarendon.

Brewer, T. (2009). *The Retrieval of Ethics*. Oxford: Oxford University Press.

Brink, D. O. (2003). *Perfectionism and the Common Good: Themes from the Philosophy of T. H. Green*. Oxford: Oxford University Press.

Broadie, A. (2001). *The Scottish Enlightenment: The Historical Age of the Historical Nation*. Edinburgh: Barlinn.

Brown, P., Lauder, H., and Cheung, S. Y. (2020). *The Death of Human Capital: Its Failed Promise and How to Repair it in an Age of Disruption*. Oxford: Oxford University Press.

Brownlie, K. (2017). 'Civil Disobedience', in *The Stanford Encyclopedia of Philosophy*, autumn 2017 edition, ed. E. N. Zalta, http://plato.stanford.edu/archives/fall2017/entries/civil-disobedience/.

Brożek, B. (2013). 'The Normativity of Meaning', in J. Stelmach, B. Brożek, and M. Hohol (eds), *The Many Faces of Normativity*. Kraków: Copernicus Center Press, pp. 147–76.

Bryant, L. R. (2011). 'The Ethics of the Event: Deleuze and Ethics without Arché', in D. Smith and N. Jun (eds), *Deleuze and Ethics*. Edinburgh: Edinburgh University Press, pp. 21–43.

Buchanan J., and Tullock, G. (1962). *The Calculus of Consent*. Ann Arbor, MI: University of Michigan Press.

Butler, J. (2004). *Precarious Life: The Powers of Mourning and Violence*. London: Verso.

— (2005). *Giving an Account of Oneself*. New York: Fordham University Press.

Camus, A. (1951). *L'Homme revolté*. Paris: Gallimard.

— (1975) [1942]. *The Myth of Sisyphus*, trans. J. O'Brien. London: Penguin.

Canguilhem, G. (1952). *La connaissance de la vie*. Paris: Hachette. (2nd rev. edn, Paris: Vrin, 1965.)

— (1975). *Le normale et le pathologique*. Paris: PUF.

— (1989). *Writings on Medicine*. New York: Fordham University Press.

— (1991). *The Normal and the Pathological*, trans. C. Fawcett with R. Cohen. New York: Zone Books.
— (1994). *A Vital Rationalist: Selected Writings from Georges Canguilhem*, ed. F. Delaporte. New York: Zone Books.
— (2008). *Knowledge of Life*, ed. P. Marrati and T. Meyers, trans. S. Geroulanos and D. Ginsburg. New York: Fordham University Press.
Canguilhem, G., and Foucault, M. (2013). 'Jean Hyppolite (1907–68)', trans. F. Chouraqui and R. Lambert, *Pli: The Warwick Journal of Philosophy*, 24, pp. 1–9 [orig. pub. in *Revue de Métaphysique et de Morale*, April–June 1969].
Capra, F. (1983). *The Turning Point: Science, Society and the Rising Culture*. London: Fontana.
— (1996). *The Web of Life: A New Synthesis of Mind and Matter*. London: HarperCollins.
Carver, T., and Chambers, S. A. (2008). *Judith Butler's Precarious Politics*. London: Routledge.
Cavarero, A. (2000). *Relating Narratives: Storytelling and Selfhood*, trans. P. A. Kottmman. London: Routledge.
Cilliers, P. (2010). 'Foreword', in D. Osberg and G. Biesta (eds), *Complexity Theory and the Politics of Education*. Rotterdam: Sense Publishers, pp. vii–viii.
Clark, M., and Dudrick, D. (2007). 'Nietzsche and Moral Objectivity: The Development of Nietzsche's Metaethics', in B. Leiter and N. Sinhababu (eds), *Nietzsche and Morality*. Oxford: Clarendon, pp. 192–226.
Clegg, B. (2003). *A Brief History of Infinity: The Quest to Think the Unthinkable*. London: Robinson.
Coleman, J. (1989). 'Rationality and the Justification of Democracy', in G. Brennan and L. E. Lomasky (eds), *Politics and Process: New Essays in Democratic Thought*. Cambridge: Cambridge University Press, pp. 194–220.
Connolly, W. E. (1995). *The Ethos of Pluralization*. Minneapolis, MN: University of Minnesota Press.
— (1999). *Why I am Not a Securalist*. Minneapolis, MN: University of Minnesota Press.
— (2005a). 'White Noise', *The Hedgehog Review: Critical Reflections on Contemporary Culture*, 7.2, pp. 26–34.
— (2005b). *Pluralism*. Durham, NC: Duke University Press.
Cooper, M. (2008). *Life as Surplus*. Seattle, WA: University of Washington Press.
Cranston, M. (1986). *Philosophers and Pamphleteers*. Oxford: Oxford University Press.
Dagognet, F. (1977). *Georges Canguilhem: Philosophie de la vie*. Paris: Les Empêcheurs de Penser en Rond.

Daly, C. B. (1996). *Moral Philosophy in Britain: From Bradley to Wittgenstein*. Blackrock: Four Courts Press.
Danto, A. C. (1965). *Analytical Philosophy of History*. Cambridge: Cambridge University Press.
Davidson, A. (1994). 'Ethics as Ascetics: Foucault, the History of Ethics, and Ancient Thought', in J. Goldstein (ed.), *Foucault and the Writing of History*. Oxford: Blackwell, pp. 63–80.
— (1997). *Foucault and His Interlocutors*. Chicago: University of Chicago Press.
Davis Acampora, C. (2006). 'Naturalism and Nietzsche's Moral Psychology', in K. Ansell-Pearson (ed.), *A Companion to Nietzsche*. Oxford: Blackwell, pp. 314–33.
Dean, J. (2005). 'The Politics of Avoidance: The Limits of Weak Ontology', *The Hedgehog Review: Critical Reflections on Contemporary Culture*, 7.2, pp. 55–65, special issue, 'Commitments in a Post-Foundationalist World: Exploring the Possibilities of Weak Ontology'.
— (2008). 'Change of Address', in T. Carvier and A. Chambers (eds), *Judith Butler's Precarious Politics*. London: Routledge, pp. 109–26.
Dean, M., and Villadsen, K. (2016). *State Phobia and Civil Society*. Stanford, CA: Stanford University Press.
Deleuze, G. (1983). *Nietzsche and Philosophy*, trans. H. Tomlinson. New York: Columbia University Press.
— (1990). *The Logic of Sense*, ed. C. V. Bourdas, trans. M. Lester with C. Stivale. New York: Columbia University Press.
— (1992). 'What is a Dispositif?', in T. J. Armstrong (ed.), *Michel Foucault: Philosopher*. London: Harvester Wheatsheaf, pp. 159–68.
— (1994a). *Difference and Repetition*, trans. P. Patton. London: Continuum.
— (1994b). *Pure Immanence: Essays on a Life*. New York: Zone Books.
Deleuze, G., and Guattari, F. (1987). *A Thousand Plateaus: Capitalism and Schizophrenia*, trans. B. Massumi. London: Continuum.
Derrida, J. (1989) [1987]. *Of Spirit: Heidegger and the Question*, trans. G. Bennington and R. Bowlby. Chicago: University of Chicago Press.
— (1991). '"Eating Well", or the Calculation of the Subject: An Interview with Jacques Derrida', in E. Cadava, P. Connor, and J.-L. Nancy (eds), *Who Comes After the Subject?* London: Routledge, pp. 1–14.
— (1992). 'Force of Law: The Mystical Foundations of Authority', in D. Cornell, M. Rosenfield, and D. G. Carlson (eds), *Deconstruction and the Possibility of Justice*. New York: Routledge, pp. 1–65.
— (1997). *Adieu à Emmanuel Lévinas*. Paris: Galilée.
Descartes, R. (1960) [1637]. *A Discourse on Method*, trans. J. Veitch. London: J. M. Dent.
— (2013) [1641]. *Meditations on First Philosophy*, trans. and ed. J. Cottingham. Cambridge: Cambridge University Press.

Dewey, J. (1958) [1925]. *Experience and Nature*. Mineola, NY: Dover Publications.
— (1997) [1910]. *How We Think*. Mineola, NY: Dover Publications.
— (2011). *Democracy and Education: An Introduction to the Philosophy of Education*. New York: Simon and Brown.
Donald, M. (1993). *Origins of the Modern Mind: Three Stages in the Evolution of Culture and Cognition*. Cambridge, MA: Harvard University Press.
— (2002). *A Mind So Rare: The Evolution of Human Consciousness*. New York: W. W. Norton.
— (2005). 'Imitation and Mimesis', in S. Hurley and N. Chater (eds), *Perspectives on Imitation, Vol. 2: Imitation, Human Development and Culture*. Cambridge, MA: MIT Press, pp. 283–300.
Doubrovsky, S. (1960). 'The Ethics of Albert Camus', in G. Bree (ed.), *Camus: A Collection of Critical Essays*. Upper Saddle River, NJ: Prentice Hall, 1962, pp. 16–19.
Duplantier, B., Nonnenmacher, S., and Rivasseau, V. (eds.) (2010). *Chaos: Poincaré Seminar 2010*. Berlin: Birkhäuser.
Dworkin, R. (2000). *Sovereign Virtue: The Theory and Practice of Equality*. Cambridge, MA: Harvard University Press.
Eastman, N. (1999). *Law Without Enforcement: Integrity, Mental Health and Justice*. Oxford: Hart Publishing.
Edwards, R. (2010). 'Complex Global Problems, Simple Lifelong Learning Solutions: Discuss', in D. Osberg and G. Biesta (eds), *Complexity Theory and the Politics of Education*. Rotterdam: Sense Publishers, pp. 69–78.
Eisenmann, C. (1933). 'L'esprit des lois et la séparation des pouvoirs', in *Mélanges R. Carré de Malberg*. Paris: L. R. Sirey, pp. 163–92.
— (1952). 'The Constitutional Thought of Montesquieu', in B. Mirkine-Guetzevitch and H. Puget (eds), *Sirey Collection of the Bicentenary of the Spirit of the Laws, 1748–1948: Political Thought and Constitutional Thesis of Montesquieu*. Paris: PUF, pp. 133–60.
Eldon, S. (2016). *Foucault's Last Decade*. Cambridge: Polity.
Emmott, S. (2013). *10 Billion*. London: Penguin.
Epictetus (2000). *The Discourses as reported by Arian*, vol. II, trans. W. A. Oldfather. Cambridge, MA: Harvard University Press.
Érdi, P. (2008). *Complexity Explained*. Berlin: Springer-Verlag.
Eribon, D. (1991). *Michel Foucault: A Biography*, trans. B. Wing. Cambridge, MA: Harvard University Press.
Esposito, R. (2008). *Bios: Biopolitics and Philosophy*, trans. T. Campbell. Minneapolis, MN: University of Minnesota Press.
Ewing, A. C. (1953). *Ethics*. London: English Universities Press.
Farrell Krell, D. (1991). 'Introduction to the Paperback Edition', in

M. Heidegger, *Nietzsche*, 4 vols. San Francisco: Harper Collins, vol. I, pp. ix–xxvii.

Ferrara, A. (1999). *Justice and Judgment: The Rise and the Prospect of the Judgment Model in Contemporary Political Philosophy*. London: Sage.

Flynn, T. (2005). 'Philosophy as a Way of Life: Foucault and Hadot', *Philosophy and Social Criticism*, 31.5–6, pp. 609–22.

Foot, P. (2001). *Natural Goodness*. Oxford: Clarendon.

Fraser, N. (1989). *Unruly Practices: Power, Discourse and Gender in Contemporary Social Theory*. Cambridge: Polity.

Gallagher, B., and Wilson, A. (1984). 'Michel Foucault. An Interview: Sex, Power and the Politics of Identity', *The Advocate*, 400, 7 August, pp. 26–30.

Gandal, K. (1986). 'Michel Foucault: Intellectual Work and Politics', *Telos*, 67, pp. 121–34.

Gauthier, D. (1963). *Practical Reasoning: The Structure and Foundations of Prudential and Moral Arguments and their Exemplification in Discourse*. Oxford: Clarendon.

— (1969). *The Logic of Leviathan: The Moral and Political Theory of Thomas Hobbes*. Oxford: Clarendon.

Gayon, J. (1998). 'The Concept of Individuality in Canguilhem's Philosophy of Biology', *Journal of the History of Biology*, 31, pp. 305–25.

Gibbard, A. (1990). *Wise Choices, Apt Feelings*. Cambridge, MA: Harvard University Press.

— (2003). *Thinking How to Live*. Cambridge, MA: Harvard University Press.

Ginsborg, H. (2015). *The Normativity of Nature: Essays on Kant's Critique of Judgment*. Oxford: Oxford University Press.

Glucksmann, A. (1975). 'De la violence: entretien avec André Glucksmann', *Actuel*, 54, 17 May.

— (1977). *Les Maîtres Penseurs*. Paris: Grasset.

Goldstein, K. (1995) [1934]. *The Organism: A Holistic Approach to Biology Derived from Pathological Data in Man*. New York: Zone Books.

Gordon, C. (1998). 'Canguilhem: Life, Health and Death', *Economy and Society*, 27.2–3, pp. 182–9.

— (2016). Paper summarized in a report from the American University of Paris of the 'Foucault and Neoliberalism 13/13' conference, 25–26 March 2016, http://blogs.law.columbia.edu/foucault1313/2016/03/28/foucault-813-epilogue-foucault-and-neoliberalism-conference-report/ (accessed 15 August 2020).

Gramsci, A. (1971). *Selections from Prison Notebooks*, ed. and trans. Q. Hoare and G. Nowell Smith. London: Lawrence and Wishart.

Gray, J. G. (1968). 'Introduction', in M. Heidegger, *What Is Called Thinking*, trans. J. G. Gray. New York: Harper and Row, pp. vi–xvi.
Green, T. H. (1885–88). 'Lectures on the Philosophy of Kant', ed. R. L. Nettleship, in *The Works of T. H. Green*. London: Longmans Green, vol. II, pp. 1–157.
— (1986). 'On Different Senses of "Freedom" as Applied to Will and to the Moral Progress of Man', in *T. H. Green: Lectures on the Principles of Political Obligation and Other Writings*, ed. P. Harris and J. Morrow. Cambridge: Cambridge University Press, pp. 228–49.
— (2003) [1883]. *Prolegomena to Ethics*, ed. A. C. Bradley. Oxford: Oxford University Press.
Grice, R. (1967). *The Grounds of Moral Judgement*. Cambridge: Cambridge University Press.
— (1977). 'The Contract Ground: A Reply to Jesse Kalin', *Philosophical Studies*, 32.3, pp. 269–82.
Gros, F. (2010). 'Course Context', in M. Foucault, *The Government of Self and Others. Lectures at the Collège de France, 1982–1983*, ed. F. Gros, trans. G. Burchell. New York: Palgrave Macmillan, pp. 377–91.
— (2011). 'Course Context', in M. Foucault, *The Courage of Truth: The Government of the Self and Others, II. Lectures at the Collège de France, 1983–1984*, ed. F. Gros, trans. G. Burchell. New York: Palgrave Macmillan, pp. 343–58.
Grumley, J. E. (1989). *History and Totality: Radical Historicism from Hegel to Foucault*. London: Routledge.
Gutting, G. (2011). *Thinking the Impossible: French Philosophy since 1960*. Oxford: Oxford University Press.
Habermas, J. (1984). *Theory of Communicative Action, Vol. 1: Reason and the Rationalization of Society*, trans. T. McCarthy. Boston: Beacon Press.
— (1986). 'Taking Aim at the Heart of the Present', in D. C. Hoy (ed.), *Foucault: A Critical Reader*. Oxford: Blackwell, pp. 103–8.
— (1987). *The Philosophical Discourses of Modernity*, trans. F. Lawrence. Cambridge, MA: MIT Press.
Hacking, I. (1975). *The Emergence of Probability: A Philosophical Study of Early Ideas About Probability, Induction, and Statistical Inference*. Cambridge: Cambridge University Press.
— (1990). *The Taming of Chance*. Cambridge: Cambridge University Press.
Hadot, P. (1953). '*Epistrophē* and *metanoia*', in *Actes du XI congrès international de Philosophie, Bruxelles, 20–26 août 1953*. Louvain-Amsterdam: Nauwelaerts, vol. XII, pp. 31–6.
— (1976). 'Exercices spirituels', *École pratique des hautes études, Section des sciences religieuses. Annuaire*, 84, pp. 25–70.

— (1987). *Exercices spirituels et philosophie antique*, 2nd edn. Paris: Etudes Augustiniennes.
— (1992). 'Reflections on the Notion of "The Culturation of the Self"', in T. J. Armstrong (ed.), *Michel Foucault: Philosopher*. London: Harvester Wheatsheaf, pp. 225–32.
— (1995). *Philosophy as a Way of Life*, ed. A. I. Davidson, trans. M. Chase. Oxford: Blackwell.
— (1997). 'Forms of Life and Forms of Discourse in Ancient Philosophy', trans. A. I. Davidson and P. Wissing, in A. I. Davidson (ed.), *Foucault and his Interlocutors*. Chicago: University of Chicago Press, pp. 203–24.
Hage, J. (2013). 'The Deontic Furniture of the World: An Analysis of the Basic Concepts that Embody Normativity', in J. Stelmach, B. Brożek, and M. Hohol (eds), *The Many Faces of Normativity*. Kraków: Copernicus Center Press, pp. 74–114.
Hallward, P. (2001). 'Translator's Introduction', in A. Badiou, *Ethics: An Essay in the Understanding of Evil*. London: Verso, pp. vii–xlvii.
Halperin, D. (1995). *Saint=Foucault: Towards a Gay Hagiography*. Oxford: Oxford University Press.
Hamann, J. G. (1967). 'Metakritik: Über den Purismum der Vernunft', in *Schriften zur Sprache*, ed. Josef Simon. Frankfurt: Suhrkamp, pp. 219–27 [Eng. trans. in R. G. Smith, *J. G. Hamann: A Study in Christian Existence*. London: Collins, 1960, pp. 213–21].
Hampton, J. (1986). *Hobbes and the Social Contract Tradition*. Cambridge: Cambridge University Press.
Hardin, G. (1968). 'The Tragedy of the Commons', *Science*, 162, pp. 1243–8.
Hardt, M., and Negri, A. (2005). *Multitude: War and Democracy in the Age of Empire*. London: Hamish Hamilton.
Harman, G. (1977). *The Nature of Morality*. New York: Oxford University Press.
Harsanyi, J. C. (1953). 'Cardinal Utility in Welfare Economics and in the Theory of Risk-Taking', *Journal of Political Economy*, 61.5, pp. 434–5.
— (1955). 'Cardinal Welfare, Individualistic Ethics, and Interpersonal Comparisons of Utility', *Journal of Political Economy*, 63.4, pp. 309–21.
— (1976). *Essays on Ethics, Social Behaviour, and Scientific Explanation*. Dordrecht: Reidel.
Hart, H. L. A. (1979). 'Between Utility and Rights', *Columbia Law Review*, 79.5, pp. 828–46.
Hartmann, K. (1972). 'Hegel: A Non-Metaphysical View', in A. MacIntyre (ed.), *Hegel: A Collection of Critical Essays*. Garden City, NY: Anchor Books, pp. 101–24.
Hartmann, N. (2007). *Ethics: Moral Phenomena*, vol. I, trans. S. Coit. London: Routledge.

Hayek, F. A. (1944). *The Road to Serfdom*. London: Routledge and Kegan Paul.
— (1949). 'Economics and Knowledge', in Hayek, *Individualism and Economic Order*. London: Routledge and Kegan Paul, pp. 33–56.
— (1983). *Law, Legislation and Liberty, Vol. I: Rules and Order*. Chicago: University of Chicago Press.
Hayles, N. K. (1999). *How We Became Post-Human: Virtual Bodies in Cybernetics, Literature, and Informatics*. Chicago: University of Chicago Press.
Hegel, G. W. F. (1942) [1821]. *Hegel's Philosophy of Right*, trans. T. M. Know. Oxford: Clarendon.
— (1948). 'The Spirit of Christianity and its Fate', in *Werke*, vol. I, *Early Theological Writings*. Philadelphia: University of Pennsylvania Press, pp. 182–301.
— (1953) [1824]. *Reason in History: A General Introduction to the Philosophy of History*. New York: Liberal Arts Press.
— (1956) [1924]. *The Philosophy of History*. New York: Dover Publications.
— (1975) [1857]. *Lectures on the Philosophy of World History*, trans. H. B. Nisbet. Cambridge: Cambridge University Press.
— (1977) [1807]. *The Phenomenology of Spirit*, ed. J. N. Findlay, trans. A. V. Miller. Oxford: Clarendon.
Heidegger, M. (1962) [1927]. *Being and Time*. Oxford: Blackwell.
— (1968) [1954]. *What Is Called Thinking?*, trans. J. G. Gray. New York: Harper and Row.
— (1971) [1959]. 'The Nature of Language', in Heidegger, *On the Way to Language*. New York: Harper and Row, pp. 57–136.
— (1991) [1961]. *Nietzsche*, trans. D. Farrell Krell. San Francisco: Harper Collins.
— (1993). 'The Question Concerning Technology', in *Basic Writings*, ed. D. Farell Krell, rev. edn. London: Routledge, pp. 307–42.
Herman, B. (1993a). *The Practice of Moral Judgement*. Cambridge, MA: Harvard University Press.
— (1993b). 'Leaving Deontology Behind', in Herman, 1993a: 208–40.
— (1993c). 'On the Value of Acting from the Motive of Duty', in Herman, 1993a: 1–22.
— (2007a). *Moral Literacy*. Cambridge, MA: Harvard University Press.
— (2007b). 'Making Room for Character', in Herman, *Moral Literacy*. Cambridge, MA: Harvard University Press, pp. 1–28.
Hobbes, T. (1840) [1642]. *The English Works of Thomas Hobbes*, ed. W. Molesworth. Vol. II: *De Cive* or *The Philosophical Rudiments Concerning Government and Society*. London: John Bohn.
— (1968) [1651]. *Leviathan*, ed. C. B. Macpherson. London: Penguin.

Höffe, O. (2010). *Can Virtue Make Us Happy? The Art of Living and Morality*. Evanston, IL: Northwestern University Press.
Hollingdale, R. J. (1973). *Nietzsche*. London: Routledge and Kegan Paul.
Horder, J. (2007). *Excusing Crime*. Oxford: Oxford University Press.
Horton, J. (1992). *Political Obligation*. Basingstoke: Macmillan.
Houlgate, S. (2009) [1986]. *Hegel, Nietzsche and the Criticism of Metaphysics*. Cambridge: Cambridge University Press.
Hughes, J. (2012). *Philosophy after Deleuze*. New York: Continuum.
Hume, D. (1975a) [1748]. Enquiry Concerning Human Understanding, in Hume, *Enquiries Concerning Human Understanding and Concerning the Principles of Morals*, 3rd edn, ed. L. A. Selby Bigge and P. H. Nidditch. Oxford: Clarendon, pp. 5–165.
— (1975b) [1751]. Enquiry Concerning the Principles of Morals, in Hume, *Enquiries Concerning Human Understanding and Concerning the Principles of Morals*, 3rd edn, ed. L. A. Selby Bigge and P. H. Nidditch. Oxford: Clarendon, pp. 169–284.
— (1978) [1777]. *A Treatise on Human Nature*, 2nd edn, ed. P. H. Nidditch. Oxford: Clarendon.
Hunt, L. H. (1991). *Nietzsche and the Origin of Virtue*. London: Routledge.
Hursthouse, R. (1999). *On Virtue Ethics*. Oxford: Oxford University Press.
Hutchings, K. (2003). *International Political Theory: Rethinking Ethics in a Global Era*. London: Sage.
Hyppolite, J. (1968) [1955]. *Studies of Marx and Hegel*, trans. J. O'Neill. London: Heinemann.
— (1996) [1948]. *Introduction to Hegel's Philosophy of History*. Gainesville, FL: University Press of Florida.
— (1997) [1953]. *Logic and Existence*, trans. L. Lawler and A. Sen. Albany, NY: SUNY Press.
Ignatieff, M. (2005). *Human Rights as Politics and Idolatory*. Princeton, NJ: Princeton University Press.
Irigaray, L. (1991). *Irigaray Reader*, ed. M. Whitford. Oxford: Blackwell.
Irrera, O. (2010). 'Pleasure and Transcendence of the Self: Notes on "A Dialogue Too Soon Interrupted" between Michel Foucault and Pierre Hadot', *Philosophy and Social Criticism*, 36.9, pp. 995–1017.
Irwin, T. H. (1984). 'Morality and Personality: Kant and Green', in A. W. Wood (ed.), *Self and Nature in Kant's Philosophy*. Ithaca, NY: Cornell University Press, pp. 31–56.
Jablonka, E., and Lamb, M. J. (2014). *Evolution in Four Dimensions: Genetic, Epigenetic, Behavioural, and Symbolic Variation in the History of Life*, rev. edn. Cambridge, MA: MIT Press.
Jackson, B. (ed.) (1975). *Leurs Prisons: Autobiographies de prisonniers et d'ex-deténus américains*. Paris: Plon.

Jacob, F. (1973) [1970]. *The Logic of Life: A History of Heredity*, trans. Betty E. Spillmann. Princeton, NJ: Princeton University Press.
Janaway, C. (2007). 'Naturalism and Genealogy', in K. Ansell-Pearson (ed.), *The Blackwell Companion to Nietzsche*. Oxford: Blackwell, pp. 337–52.
— (2012). *Nietzsche, Naturalism and Normativity*. Oxford: Oxford University Press.
Johnson, J. (1997). 'Communication, Criticism, and the Postmodern Consensus: An Unfashionable Interpretation of Michel Foucault', *Political Theory*, 25.4, pp. 559–83.
Johnson, M. R. (2005). *Aristotle on Teleology*. Oxford: Oxford University Press.
Jonas, H. (1984). *The Imperative of Responsibility: In Search of an Ethics for the Technological Age*, trans. H. Jonas with the collaboration of D. Herr. Chicago: University of Chicago Press.
Jones, D. (1990). 'The Genealogy of the Urban Schoolteacher', in S. J. Ball (ed.), *Foucault and Education: Disciplines and Knowledge*. London: Routledge, pp. 57–76.
Kant, I. (1902). *Gesammelte Schriften*. Berlin: Akademie-Ausgabe.
— (1928) [1781]. *Critique of Pure Reason*, trans. N. K. Smith. London: Macmillan.
— (1959) [1785]. *Groundwork of the Metaphysics of Morals*, trans. L. W. Beck (as *Foundations of the Metaphysics of Morals*). Indianapolis: Bobbs-Merrill, Library of Liberal Arts.
— (1974). *Logic*, trans. R. Hartman and W. Swartz. Indianapolis: Bobbs-Merrill.
— (1991) [1784]. 'Idea for a Universal History with a Cosmopolitan Purpose', in Kant, *Political Writings*, trans. H. B. Nisbet, ed. H. Reiss, 2nd edn. Cambridge: Cambridge University Press, pp. 41–53.
— (2004) [1788]. *Critique of Practical Reason*, trans. T. K. Abbott. New York: Dover Publications.
— (2006) [1795]. 'Toward Perpetual Peace: A Philosophical Sketch', in Kant, *Toward Perpetual Peace and Other Writings on Politics, Peace, and History*, ed. P. Kleingeld, trans. D. L. Colclasure. New Haven, CT: Yale University Press, pp. 67–109.
— (2008) [1790] *Critique of Judgement*. Oxford: Oxford University Press.
Kauffman, S. A. (2008). *Reinventing the Sacred*. New York: Basic Books.
Kelly, M. (2018). *For Foucault*. Albany, NY: SUNY Press.
Korsgaard, C. M. (1996a). *The Sources of Normativity*, ed. O. O'Neill with G. A. Cohen, R. Guess, T. Nagel, and B. Williams. Cambridge: Cambridge University Press.
— (1996b). *Creating the Kingdom of Ends*. Cambridge: Cambridge University Press.

— (1996c). 'An Introduction to the Ethical, Political and Religious Thought of Kant', in Korsgaard, 1996b, pp. 3–42.
— (1996d). 'Kant's Analysis of Obligation: The Argument of Groundwork I', in Korsgaard, 1996b, pp. 43–76.
— (1996e). 'Kant's Formula of Universal Law', in Korsgaard, 1996b, pp. 77–105.
— (2009). *Self-Constitution: Agency, Identity and Integrity*. Oxford: Oxford University Press.
Koyré, A. (1965) [1950]. 'The Significance of the Newtonian Synthesis', in *Newtonian Studies*. London, pp. 3–24 [orig. pub. in *Archives Internationales d'Histoire des Sciences*, 3, pp. 291–311].
— (1968). *From the Closed World to the Infinite Universe*. Baltimore: Johns Hopkins University Press.
Kraut, R. (2007). *What is Good and Why?* Cambridge, MA: Harvard University Press.
Kripke, S. (1984). *Wittgenstein on Rules and Private Language*. Cambridge, MA: Harvard University Press.
Lasch, C. (1991). *The Culture of Narcissism: American Life in An Age of Diminishing Expectations*. New York: W. W. Norton.
Lasota, A., and Mackey, M. (1998). *Chaos, Fractals, and Noise: Stochastic Aspects of Dynamics*, 2nd edn. New York: Springer.
Lecourt, D. (1975). *Marxism and Epistemology*. London: New Left Books.
— (2008). *Georges Canguilhem*. Paris: PUF.
Leibniz, G. W. (2008) [1898]. *The Monadology*, trans. R. Latta. New York: Forgotten Books.
— (2009) [1898]. *Principles of Nature and Grace*, trans. R. Latta. Ithaca, NY: Cornell University Press.
Leiter, B. (2002). *Nietzsche on Morality*. London: Routledge.
— (2008). 'Nietzsche's Naturalism Reconsidered', University of Chicago Public Law and Legal Theory Working Paper no. 235, September.
Lemke, T. (2011). *Biopolitics: An Advanced Introduction*. New York: New York University Press.
Levinas, E. (2004) [1961]. *Totality and Infinity*. Pittsburgh, PA: Duquesne University Press.
Locke. J. (1994) [1690]. *Essay Concerning Human Understanding*. London: Penguin.
Long, A. A. (2001). *Stoic Studies*. Berkeley, CA: University of California Press.
Louden, R. B. (1984). 'On Some Vices of Virtue Ethics', *American Philosophical Quarterly*, 21, pp. 227–36.
Lovibond, S. (2002). *Ethical Formation*. Cambridge, MA: Harvard University Press.

Lucian (1913). *The Passing of Peregrinus*, in *The Works of Lucian*, two vols, trans. A. M. Harmon. Cambridge, MA: Harvard University Press.

Macey, D. (1993). *The Lives of Michel Foucault: A Biography*. New York: Pantheon.

Macherey, P. (1998). *In A Materialist Way*. London: Verso.

— (2009). *De Canguilhem à Foucault: la force des norms*. Paris: La Fabrique.

MacIntyre, A. (1999). *Dependent Rational Animals*. Notre Dame, IN: University of Notre Dame Press.

Mackie, J. L. (1977). *Ethics: Inventing Right and Wrong*. New York: Penguin.

Magun, A. (2013a). 'Introduction', in Magun (ed.), *Politics of the One: Concepts of the One and the Many in Contemporary Thought*. London: Bloomsbury, pp. xi–xxii.

— (2013b). 'Unity and Solitude', in Magun (ed.), *Politics of the One: Concepts of the One and the Many in Contemporary Thought*. London: Bloomsbury, pp. 23–50.

Maker, W. (1994). *Philosophy without Foundations: Rethinking Hegel*. Albany, NY: SUNY Press.

Mander, W. J. (2016). *Idealist Ethics*. Oxford: Oxford University Press.

Markell, P. (2003). *Bound by Recognition*. Princeton, NJ: Princeton University Press.

Markovits, J. (2017). 'On What it is to Matter', in S. Kirchin (ed.), *Reading Parfit: On What Matters*. London: Routledge, pp. 54–81.

Marrati, P., and Meyers, T. (2008). 'Foreword: Life, as Such', in G. Canguilhem, *Knowledge of Life*. New York: Fordham University Press, pp. vii–xii.

Marschak, J. (1950). 'Rational Behaviour, Uncertain Prospects, and Measurable Utility', *Econometrica*, 18.2, pp. 111–41.

Masterman, R. (2011). *The Separation of Powers in the Contemporary Constitution: Judicial Competence and Independence in the United Kingdom*. Cambridge: Cambridge University Press.

Matravers, M. (1998). *Punishment and Political Theory*. Oxford: Hart Publishing.

May, S. (1999). *Nietzsche's Ethics and his War on 'Morality'*. Oxford: Clarendon.

May, T. (1997). *Reconsidering Difference: Nancy, Derrida, Levinas, and Deleuze*. University Park, PA: Pennsylvania State University Press.

McCumber, J. (2014). *Understanding Hegel's Mature Critique of Kant*. Stanford, CA: Stanford University Press.

McDowell, J. (1994). *Mind and World*. Cambridge, MA: Harvard University Press.

McGushin, E. F. (2007). *Foucault's Askesis: An Introduction to the Philosophical Life*. Evanston, IL: Northwestern University Press.

Meynen, G. (2016). *Legal Insanity: Explorations in Psychiatry, Law and Ethics*. Dordrecht: Springer.

Mill, J. S. (1910) [1871]. 'Utilitarianism', in *Utilitarianism, On Liberty, and Representative Government*. London: J. M. Dent, pp. 1–60.

— (1956) [1859]. *On Liberty*, ed. C. V. Shield. Indianapolis, IN: Bobbs-Merrill Library of Liberal Arts.

— (1998) [1871]. *Utilitarianism*, ed. R. Crisp. Oxford: Oxford University Press.

Miller, J. (1994). *The Passion of Michel Foucault*. London: Flamingo.

Mills, C. (2005). 'Biopolitics and the Concept of Life', in V. W. Cisney and N. Morar (eds), *Biopower: Foucault and Beyond*. Chicago: University of Chicago Press, pp. 82–101.

Mitchell, M. (2009). *Complexity: A Guided Tour*. New York: Oxford University Press.

Mollers, C. (2013). *The Three Branches: A Comparative Model of the Separation of Powers*. Oxford: Oxford University Press.

Montesquieu, C.-L. de (1964). *Œuvres complètes*, ed. D. Oster. Paris: Seuil.

— (2015). *The Spirit of Laws*. Alexandria, Egypt.

Moore, G. E. (1903). *Principia Ethica*. Cambridge: Cambridge University Press.

— (1922a). 'The Refutation of Idealism', in Moore, *Philosophical Studies*. London: Routledge and Kegan Paul, pp. 1–30 [orig. pub. in *Mind*, 12.48, pp. 433–53].

— (1922b). 'The Nature of Moral Philosophy', in Moore, *Philosophical Studies*. London: Routledge and Kegan Paul, pp. 310–33.

Morgan, A. (2007). *Adorno's Concept of Life*. London: Continuum.

Morin, E. (1992) [1977]. *Method. Towards a Study of Humankind. Vol. 1: The Nature of Nature*. New York: Peter Lang.

— (1999). 'Organization and Complexity', *Annals of the New York Academy of Sciences*, 879.1, pp. 115–21.

— (2007). 'Restricted Complexity, General Complexity', in C. Gershenson, D. Aerts, and B. Edmonds (eds), *Worldviews, Science and Us: Philosophy and Complexity*. Singapore: World Scientific, pp. 5–29.

— (2008). *On Complexity*, trans. R. Postel. Cresskill, NJ: Hampton Press.

Muirhead, J. H. (1924). 'Recent Criticism of the Idealist Theory of the General Will (I)', *Mind, New Series*, 33.130, pp. 166–75.

Myers, E. (2008). 'Resisting Foucauldian Ethics: Associative Politics and the Limits of the Care of the Self', *Contemporary Political Theory*, 7.2, pp. 125–46.

— (2013). *Worldly Ethics: Democratic Politics and Care for the World*. Durham, NC: Duke University Press.

Nagel, T. (1978). 'Ruthlessness in Public Life', in S. Hampshire (ed.), *Public and Private Morality*. Cambridge: Cambridge University Press, pp. 75–92.
— (1989). *The View from Nowhere*. Oxford: Oxford University Press.
Nancy, J.-L. (ed.) (1991). *Who Comes After the Subject?* London: Routledge.
— (2000). *Being Singular Plural*, trans. R. Richardson and A. O'Byrne. Stanford, CA: Stanford University Press.
Nehemas, A. (2001). 'How One Becomes What One Is', in J. Richardson and B. Leiter (eds), *Nietzsche*. Oxford: Oxford University Press, pp. 255–80.
Nelson, W. (2010). *On Justifying Democracy*. Abingdon: Routledge.
Nicholson, P. (1990). *The Political Philosophy of the British Idealists: Selected Studies*. Cambridge: Cambridge University Press.
— (1995). 'T. H. Green's Doubts About Hegel's Political Philosophy', *Bulletin of the Hegel Society of Great Britain*, 31, pp. 61–72.
Nicolis, G., and Prigogine, I. (1989). *Exploring Complexity*. New York: W. H. Freeman.
Nielsen, K. (1996). *Naturalism Without Foundations*. New York: Prometheus.
Nietzsche, F. (1966) [1886]. *Beyond Good and Evil*, trans. W. Kaufmann. New York: Random House.
— (1968a). *The Will to Power*, ed. W. Kaufmann, trans. W. Kaufmann and R. J. Hollingdale. New York: Vintage.
— (1968b) [1888]. *Twilight of the Idols*, trans. R. J. Hollingdale. London: Penguin.
— (1968c) [1888]. *The Anti-Christ*, trans. R. J. Hollingdale. London: Penguin.
— (1969). *La Livre du Philosophe*, trans. A. Kremer-Marietti. Paris: Aubier-Flammarion.
— (1974) [1882]. *The Gay Science*, trans. W. Kaufmann. New York: Vintage.
— (1983/1997). *Untimely Meditations*, trans. R. J. Hollingdale. Cambridge: Cambridge University Press.
— (1986) [1878]. *Human, All Too Human*, trans. R. J. Hollingdale. Cambridge: Cambridge University Press.
— (1992) [1908]. *Ecco Homo*, trans. R. J. Hollingdale. London: Penguin.
— (1996) [1887]. *On the Genealogy of Morals*, trans. D. Smith. Oxford: Oxford University Press.
— (1998) [1881]. *Daybreak: Thoughts on the Prejudices of Morality*, ed. M. Clark and B. Leiter. Cambridge: Cambridge University Press.
— (2003) [1883]. *Thus Spoke Zarathustra: A Book for Everyone and No One*, trans. R. J. Hollingdale. London: Penguin.

Nussbaum, M., and Sen, A. (eds) (1993). *The Quality of Life*. Oxford: Oxford University Press.

O'Hagan, T. (1987). 'On Hegel's Critique of Kant's Moral and Political Philosophy', in S. Priest (ed.), *Hegel's Critique of Kant*. Oxford: Clarendon, pp. 135–60.

O'Leary, T. (2002). *Foucault and the Art of Ethics*. London: Continuum.

Olssen, M. (1993). 'Science and Individualism in Educational Psychology: Problems for Practice and Points of Departure', *Educational Psychology: An International Journal of Experimental Educational Psychology*, 13.2, pp. 155–72.

— (1996). 'Michel Foucault's Historical Materialism: An Account and Assessment', in M. Peters, J. Marshall, W. Hope, and S. Webster (eds), *Critical Theory, Poststructuralism and the Social Context*. Palmerston North: Dunmore Press, pp. 82–105.

— (1999). *Michel Foucault: Materialism and Education*. London: Bergin and Garvey.

— (2005). 'Foucault and Marx: Re-writing the History of Historical Materialism', *Policy Futures in Education*, 2.3, pp. 453–80.

— (2006). *Michel Foucault: Materialism and Education*, rev. edn. Boulder, CO: Paradigm Publishers.

— (2008). 'Foucault as Complexity Theorist: Overcoming the Problems of Classical Philosophical Analysis', in M. Mason (ed.), *Complexity Theory and the Philosophy of Education*. Oxford: Wiley–Blackwell, pp. 91–111.

— (2009). *Toward a Global Thin Community: Nietzsche, Foucault and the Cosmopolitan Commitment*. Boulder, CO: Paradigm Publishers.

— (2010). *Liberalism, Neoliberalism, Social Democracy: Thin Communitarian Perspectives on Political Philosophy and Education*. London: Routledge.

— (2015). 'Ascertaining the Normative Implications of Complexity Thinking for Politics: Beyond Agent-Based Modeling', in E. Kavalski (ed.), *World Politics at the Edge of Chaos: Reflections on Complexity and Global Life*. Albany, NY: SUNY Press, pp. 139–66.

— (2017a) 'Wittgenstein and Foucault: The Limits and Possibilities of Constructivism', in M. A. Peters and J. Stickney (eds), *A Companion to Wittgenstein on Education: Pedagogical Investigations*. Singapore: Springer, pp. 305–20.

— (2017b). 'Complexity and Learning: Implications for Teacher Education', in M. A. Peters, B. Cowie, and I. Mentor (eds), *A Companion to Research in Teacher Education*. Singapore: Springer Nature, pp. 507–20.

— (2019). 'Foucault and Neoliberalism: A Response to Critics and a New Resolution', *Materiali Foucaultiani*, V.12–13, pp. 28–55.

— (2021). 'The Rehabilitation of the Concept of Public Good: Reappraising the Attacks from Liberalism and Neo-Liberalism from a

Poststructuralist Perspective', *Review of Contemporary Philosophy*, 20, pp. 7–52.

Olssen, M., and Mace, W. (2021). 'British Idealism, Complexity Theory and Society: The Political Usefulness of T. H. Green in a Revised Conception of Social Democracy', *Linguistic and Philosophical Investigations*, 20.1, pp. 7–34.

O'Neill, O. (1996). 'Introduction', in C. M. Korsgaard, *The Sources of Normativity*, ed. O. O'Neill with G. A. Cohen, R. Guess, T. Nagel, and B. Williams. Cambridge: Cambridge University Press, pp. xi–xv.

Packard, M. C. (ed.) (2002). *The Separation of Powers Doctrine: Rationale, Applications and Bibliography*. New York: Novinka Publishing.

Papineau, D. (1993). *Philosophical Naturalism*. Oxford: Oxford University Press.

— (1999). 'Normativity and Judgement', *Aristotelian Society Supplementary Volume*, 73.1, pp. 16–43.

Parekh, B. (2005). 'Principles of a Global Ethic', in J. Eade and D. O'Byrne (eds), *Ethics and Global Politics*. Aldershot: Ashgate, pp. 15–34.

Parfit, D. (1986). *Reasons and Persons*. Oxford: Oxford University Press.

— (2011a). *On What Matters*, vol. 1. Oxford: Oxford University Press.

— (2011b). *On What Matters*, vol. 2. Oxford: Oxford University Press.

— (2017). *On What Matters*, vol. 3. Oxford: Oxford University Press.

Pateman, C. (1988). *The Sexual Contract*. Cambridge: Polity.

Patton, P. (1989). 'Taylor and Foucault on Power and Freedom', *Political Studies*, XXXVII, pp. 260–76.

— (1993). 'Politics and the Concept of Power in Hobbes and Nietzsche', in Patton (ed.), *Nietzsche, Feminism & Political Theory*. London: Routledge, pp. 144–61.

— (1998). 'Foucault's Subject of Power', in J. Moss (ed.), *The Later Foucault*. London: Sage, pp. 64–77.

— (2004). 'Power and Right in Nietzsche and Foucault', *International Studies in Philosophy*, XXXVI.3, pp. 43–61.

— (2005). 'Foucault, Critique and Rights', *Critical Horizons*, 6.1, pp. 267–87.

— (2010). 'Foucault and Normative Political Philosophy', in T. O'Leary and C. Falzon (eds), *Foucault and Philosophy*. Oxford: Blackwell, pp. 204–21.

Peirce, C. S. (1955). 'The Scientific Attitude and Fallibilism', in *Philosophical Writings of Peirce*, ed. J. Buchler. New York: Dover Publications, pp. 42–59.

Petersen, K. (1990). *Ergodic Theory*. Cambridge: Cambridge University Press.

Philodemus (1914). *On Plain Speaking* (Περὶ παρρησίας), ed. A. Olivera. Leipzig: Teubner.

Pinkard, T. P. (1988). *Hegel's Dialectic: The Explanation of Possibility*. Philadelphia, PA: Temple University Press.
— (2002). *German Philosophy, 1760–1860: The Legacy of Idealism*. Cambridge: Cambridge University Press.
— (2012). *Hegel's Naturalism*. Oxford: Oxford University Press.
Pippin, R. (1989). *Hegel's Idealism: The Satisfactions of Self-Consciousness*. Cambridge: Cambridge University Press.
— (2008). *Hegel's Practical Philosophy: Rational Agency as Ethical Life*. Cambridge: Cambridge University Press.
Plant, R. (1973). *Hegel*. London: Allen and Unwin.
Plato (1997a). *Meno*, in *Plato: Complete Works*, ed. J. M. Cooper, trans. G. M. A. Grube. Indianapolis: Hackett Publishing, pp. 870–97.
— (1997b). *Protagoras*, in *Plato: Complete Works*, ed. J. M. Cooper, trans. S. Lombardo and K. Bell. Indianapolis: Hackett Publishing, pp. 746–90.
— (1997c). *Republic*, in *Plato: Complete Works*, ed. J. M. Cooper, trans. S. Lombardo and K. Bell. Indianapolis: Hackett Publishing, pp. 971–1223.
Plotnitsky, A. (1996). 'Foreword: Reading and Rereading Hyppolite and Hegel', in J. Hyppolite, *Introduction to Hegel's Philosophy of History*, trans. B. Harris and J. B. Spurlock. Gainesville, FL: University Press of Florida, pp. vii–xix.
Poincaré, H. (1890). 'Sur le problème des trois corps et les équations de la dynamique', *Acta Mathematica*, 13, pp. 1–270.
— (1891). 'Le problème des trois corps', *Revue générale des sciences pures et appliquées*, 2, pp. 1–5.
— (1907). *The Value of Science*, trans. G. B. Halsted. New York: Science Press.
— (1908). *Science et methode*. Paris: Flammarion.
— (1909). 'La Logique de l'Infini', *Revue de Métaphysique et de Morale*, 17.4, pp. 461–82.
— (1913). *The Foundations of Science: Science and Hypothesis, The Value of Science, Science and Method*, trans. G. B. Halsted. New York: Science Press.
Popper, K. R. (1945). *The Open Society and its Enemies*. London: Routledge and Kegan Paul.
— (1959). *The Logic of Scientific Discovery*. London: Routledge.
— (1961). *The Poverty of Historicism*. London: Routledge and Kegan Paul.
— (1992). *The Lesson of This Century* (interviewed by G. Bosetti). London: Routledge.
Poster, M. (1975). *Existential Marxism in Post-War France: From Sartre to Althusser*. Princeton, NJ: Princeton University Press.
Prichard, H. A. (1912). 'Does Moral Philosophy Rest on a Mistake?', *Mind*, 81, pp. 21–37.

Prigogine, I. (1980). *From Being to Becoming*. San Francisco: W. H. Freeman.
— (1997). *The End of Certainty: Time, Chaos and the New Laws of Nature*. London: Free Press.
— (2003). *Is Future Given?* Hackensack, NJ: World Scientific.
Prigogine, I., and Stengers, I. (1984). *Order Out of Chaos*. New York: Bantam.
Protevi, J. (2006). 'Deleuze, Guattari and Emergence', *Paragraph*, 29.2, pp. 19–39.
Provenzano, L. (2016). 'Foucault 8/13 Epilogue: Foucault and Neoliberalism Conference Report', a report from the American University of Paris of the 'Foucault and Neoliberalism 13/13' conference, 25–26 March, http://blogs.law.columbia.edu/foucault1313/2016/03/28/foucault-813-epilogue-foucault-and-neoliberalism-conference-report/ (accessed 15 August 2020).
Quine, W. V. O. (1990). *The Pursuit of Truth*. Cambridge, MA: Harvard University Press.
Raaper, R., and Olssen, M. (2017). 'In Conversation with Mark Olssen: On Foucault with Marx and Hegel', *Open Review of Educational Research*, 4.1, pp. 96–117.
Rabinow, P. (1994). 'Introduction: A Vital Rationalist', in G. Canguilhem, *A Vital Rationalist: Selected Writings of Georges Canguilhem*, ed. F. Delaporte. New York: Zone Books, pp. 11–22.
— (1997). 'Introduction: The History of Systems of Thought', in *The Essential Works of Michel Foucault, 1954–1984, Vol. 1: Ethics, Subjectivity and Truth*, ed. P. Rabinow, trans. R. Hurley. London: Allen Lane, The Penguin Press, pp. xi–xlii.
— (1998). 'French Enlightenment: Truth and Life', *Economy & Society*, 27.2&3, pp. 193–201.
— (2003). *Anthropos Today: Reflections on Modern Equipment*. Princeton, NJ: Princeton University Press.
Rabinow, P., and Rose, N. (2006). 'Biopower Today', *Biosciences*, 1, pp. 197–204.
Rae, A. (2009). *Quantum Physics: Illusion or Reality?*, 2nd edn. Cambridge: Cambridge University Press.
Rae, D. W. (1975). 'The Limits of Consensual Decision', *The American Political Science Review*, 69.4, pp. 1270–94.
Raunig, G. (2013). 'Dividuum and Condividuality', in A. Magun (ed.), *Politics of the One: Concepts of the One and the Many in Contemporary Thought*. London: Bloomsbury, pp. 131–46.
Rawls, J. (1971). *A Theory of Justice*. Cambridge, MA: Harvard University Press.
— (1980). 'Kantian Constructivism in Moral Theory', *Journal of Philosophy*, 77, pp. 515–72.

— (1987). 'The Idea of an Overlapping Consensus', *Oxford Journal of Legal Studies*, 7.1, pp. 1–25.
— (1999a). *A Theory of Justice: Revised Edition*. Oxford: Oxford University Press.
— (1999b). 'An Outline of a Decision-Procedure for Ethics', in *John Rawls: Collected Papers*, ed. S. Freeman. Cambridge, MA: Harvard University Press, pp. 1–34 [orig. pub. in *Philosophical Review*, 64 (1951), pp. 177–97].
— (2005). *Political Liberalism*. New York: Columbia University Press.
Reed, A., and Bohlander, M. (eds) (2011). *Loss of Control and Diminished Responsibility: Domestic, Comparative, International Perspectives*. London: Routledge.
Reginster, B. (2006). *The Affirmation of Life: Nietzsche on Overcoming Nihilism*. Cambridge, MA: Harvard University Press.
Rescher, N. (1998). *Complexity: A Philosophical Overview*. New Brunswick, NJ: Transaction Publishers.
Rorty, R. (1989). *Contingency, Irony, Solidarity*. Cambridge: Cambridge University Press.
— (1998). 'Human Rights, Rationality and Sentimentality', in *Philosophical Papers, Vol. 3: Truth and Progress*. Cambridge: Cambridge University Press, pp. 167–85.
Rose, G. (1981). *Hegel Contra Sociology*. London: Athlone.
Rose, N. (2007). *The Problems of Life Itself*. Princeton, NJ: Princeton University Press.
Rosenberg, N. T. (1993). *Mitigating Circumstances*. London: Orion.
Ross, J. (2009). 'Should Kantians Be Consequentialists?', in J. Suikkanen and J. Cottingham (eds), *Essays on Derek Parfit's On What Matters*. Oxford: Wiley-Blackwell, pp. 144–53.
Ross, W. D. (2002) [1930]. *The Right and the Good*, ed. P. Stratton-Lake. Oxford: Oxford University Press.
Roth, M. (2017). *Philosophical Foundations of Neurolaw*. Lanham, MD: Lexington Books.
Ryle, G. (1970) [1928]. 'Review of Heidegger's *Sein und Zeit*', *Journal of the British Society of Phenomenology*, 1.3, pp. 3–13.
— (2009) [1953]. 'Thinking', in *Collected Essays*, ed. J. Tanney, vol. II. Oxford: Routledge, pp. 307–13.
Sagan, C. (2009). *Pale Blue Dot: A Vision of the Human Future in Space*. New York: Random House.
Sallis, J. (1995). *Delimitations: Phenomenology and the End of Metaphysics*, 2nd edn. Bloomington, IN: Indiana University Press.
Sartre, J.-P. (2007). *Existentialism is a Humanism*, ed. J. Kulka, trans. C. McComber. New Haven, CT: Yale University Press.
Scanlon, T. M. (1978). 'Rights, Goals, and Fairness', in S. Hampshire (ed.),

Public and Private Morality. Cambridge: Cambridge University Press, pp. 93–113.
— (1982). 'Contractualism and Utilitarianism', in A. Sen and B. Williams (eds), *Utilitarianism and Beyond*. Cambridge: Cambridge University Press, pp. 101–28.
— (1998). *What We Owe to Each Other*. Cambridge, MA: Harvard University Press.
— (2008). *Moral Dimension*. Cambridge, MA: Belknap Press of Harvard University Press.
— (2014). *Being Realistic About Reasons*. Oxford: Oxford University Press.
Schacht, R. (2001). 'Nietzschean Normativity', in Schacht (ed.), *Nietzsche's Postmoralism: Essays on Nietzsche's Prelude to the Future*. Cambridge: Cambridge University Press, pp. 149–80.
Schatzki, T. R. (2010). *The Timespace of Human Activity: On Performance, Society, and History as Indeterminate Teleological Events*. Lanham, MD: Lexington Books.
Schnädelbach, H. (1984). *Philosophy in Germany: 1831–1937*, trans. E. Matthews. Cambridge: Cambridge University Press.
Schopenhauer, A. (2010) [1841]. *The Two Fundamental Problems of Ethics*, trans. D. E. Cartwright and E. E. Erdmann. Oxford: Oxford University Press.
Schumpeter, J. (1976) [1943]. *Capitalism, Socialism, Democracy*. London: Routledge.
Sedgwick, S. (2000a). 'Metaphysics and Morality in Kant and Hegel', in Sedgwick, *The Reception of Kant's Critical Philosophy*. Cambridge: Cambridge University Press, pp. 306–23.
— (2000b). *The Reception of Kant's Critical Philosophy*. Cambridge: Cambridge University Press.
— (2012). *Hegel's Criticism of Kant: From Dichotomy to Identity*. Oxford: Oxford University Press.
Sembou, E. (2015). *Hegel's Phenomenology and Foucault's Genealogy*. Farnham: Ashgate.
— (2018). 'Comments on Yirmiyahu Yovel's "Hegel's Preface to the Phenomenology of Spirit"', www.academia.edu (accessed 14 November 2018) [comments made at the annual conference of the Hegel Society of Great Britain, Oxford, 10–12 September, 2007].
Sen, A. (1992). *Inequality Re-Examined*. Oxford: Oxford University Press.
Seneca (1989). *The Epistles of Seneca*, 3 vols, trans. R. M. Gunmore. Cambridge, MA: Harvard University Press.
Seth, J. (1897). *A Study of Ethical Principles*, 8th rev. edn. Edinburgh: Blackwood.

Shackleton, R. (1961). *Montesquieu: A Critical Biography*. Oxford: Oxford University Press.
Shapiro, I. (1990). 'Three Fallacies Concerning Majorities, Minorities, and Democratic Politics', in J. W. Chapman and A. Wertheimer (eds), *Majorities and Minorities*. New York: New York University Press, pp. 79–125.
Sidgwick, H. (1874). *The Method of Ethics*. London: Macmillan.
— (1902). *Lectures on the Ethics of T. H. Green, Mr. Herbert Spencer and J. Martineau*. London: Macmillan.
Simons, H. (1982). *Models of Bounded Rationality*. Cambridge, MA: MIT Press.
— (1983). *Reason in Human Affairs*. Stanford, CA: Stanford University Press.
Small, R. (2007). 'Nietzsche's Evolutionary Ethics', in G. von Tevenar (ed.), *Nietzsche and Ethics*. Oxford: Peter Lang, pp. 119–35.
Smith, A. (1976a) [1759]. *The Theory of Moral Sentiments*, ed. D. D. Raphael and L. Macfie. Oxford: Clarendon.
— (1976b) [1776]. *An Inquiry into the Nature and Causes of the Wealth of Nations*, ed. R. H. Campbell and A. S. Skinner. Oxford: Clarendon.
Soniewicka, M. (2013). 'A Command without a Commander: From the Paradigm of Normativity to the Paradigm of Responsibility', in J. Stelmach, B. Brożek, and M. Hohol (eds), *The Many Faces of Normativity*. Kraków: Copernicus Center Press, pp. 257–88.
Sorabji, R. (2000). *Emotion and Peace of Mind: From Stoic Agitation to Christian Temptation*. Oxford: Oxford University Press.
Spinoza, B. (1993). *Ethics and Treatise on the Correction of the Intellect*. London: J. M. Dent.
Spivak, G. C. (1996). *The Spivak Reader*, ed. D. Landry and G. Maclean. London: Routledge.
Stark, W. (1943). *The Ideal Foundations of Economic Thought*. London: Kegan Paul, Trench, Trubner & Co.
Starobinski, J. (1953). *Montesquieu par lui-même*. Paris: Seuil.
Stelmach, J. (2013). 'The Naturalistic and Antinaturalistic Fallacies in Normative Discourse', in J. Stelmach, B. Brożek, and M. Hohol (eds), *The Many Faces of Normativity*. Kraków: Copernicus Center Press, pp. 137–44.
Stern, R. A. (2013). '"My Station and its Duties": Social Role Accounts of Obligation in Green and Bradley', in K. Ameriks (ed.), *The Impact of Idealism: Volume 1, Philosophy and Natural Sciences*. Cambridge: Cambridge University Press, pp. 299–322.
Suikkanen, J. (2009). 'Introduction', in J. Suikkanen and J. Cottingham (eds), *Essays on Derek Parfit's On What Matters*. Oxford: Wiley-Blackwell, pp. 1–20.

Swanton, C. (2003). *Virtue Ethics: A Pluralistic View*. Oxford: Oxford University Press.
— (2015). *The Virtue Ethics of Hume and Nietzsche*. Oxford: Wiley–Blackwell.
Talcott, S. (2014). 'Errant Life, Molecular Biology, and the Conceptualization of Biopower: Georges Canguilhem, Francois Jacob, and Michel Foucault', *History and Philosophy of the Life Sciences*, 36.2, pp. 254–79.
— (2019). *Georges Canguilhem and the Problem of Error*. Cham, Switzerland: Palgrave Macmillan.
Taylor, C. (1977). *Hegel*. Cambridge: Cambridge University Press.
— (1979). *Hegel and Modern Society*. Cambridge: Cambridge University Press.
— (1984). 'Foucault on Freedom and Truth', *Political Theory*, 12.2, pp. 152–83.
— (1989). *Sources of the Self*. Cambridge: Cambridge University Press.
— (1994). 'The Politics of Recognition', in A. Gutmann (ed.), *Multiculturalism: Examining the Politics of Recognition*. Princeton, NJ: Princeton University Press, pp. 25–73.
— (1997). 'The Importance of Herder', in Taylor, *Philosophical Arguments*. Cambridge, MA: Harvard University Press, pp. 79–99.
— (2005). 'The "Weak Ontology" Thesis', *The Hedgehog Review: Critical Reflections on Contemporary Culture*, 7.2, pp. 35–41.
Temkin, L. S. (2017). 'Has Parfit's Life Been Wasted? Some Reflections on Part Six of *On What Matters*', in P. Singer (ed.), *Does Anything Really Matter? Essays on Parfit on Objectivity*. Oxford: Oxford University Press, pp. 1–34.
Thiem, A. (2008). *Unbecoming Subjects: Judith Butler, Moral Philosophy, and Critical Responsibility*. New York: Fordham University Press.
Thompson, M. (2008). *Life and Action*. Cambridge, MA: Harvard University Press.
Timmerman, J. (2005). 'Good But Not Required: Assessing the Demands of Kantian Ethics', *Journal of Moral Philosophy*, 2, pp. 9–27.
Tøye, G. (2017). *Diminished Responsibility*. London: Endeavour Media.
Trueit, D., and Doll, W. E. (2010). 'Thinking Complexly', in D. Osberg and G. Biesta (eds), *Complexity Theory and the Politics of Education*. Rotterdam: Sense Publishers, pp. 135–52.
Turner, B. S. (2006). *Vulnerability and Human Rights: Essays on Human Rights*. University Park, PA: Pennsylvania State University Press.
Turner, F. (1997). 'Foreword: Chaos and Social Science', in R. A. Eve, S. Horsfall, and M. E. Lee (eds), *Chaos, Complexity and Sociology: Myths, Models and Theories*. Thousand Oaks, CA: Sage, pp. xi–xxvii.

van Verseveld, A. (2014). *Mistake of Law: Excusing Perpetrators of International Crimes.* The Hague: T. M. C. Asser.
Veyne, P. (1997). 'The Final Foucault and his Ethics', in A. Davidson (ed.), *Foucault and his Interlocutors.* Chicago: University of Chicago Press, pp. 225–33.
— (2010). *Foucault: His Thought, his Character.* Cambridge: Polity.
Vico, G. (1965). *On the Study Methods of Our Time.* New York: Bobbs-Merrill Library of Liberal Arts.
von Neumann, J. (1932). 'Proof of the Quasi-Ergodic Hypothesis', *Proceedings of the National Academy of Sciences of the United States of America*, 18.1, pp. 70–82.
von Wright, G. H. (1963). *Norm and Action: A Logical Enquiry.* London: Routledge and Kegan Paul.
— (1978). 'On So-Called Practical Inference', in J. Raz (ed.), *Practical Reasoning.* Oxford: Oxford University Press, pp. 46–62.
Waldron, J. (2005a). *God, Locke and Equality: Christian Foundations in Locke's Political Thought.* Cambridge: Cambridge University Press.
— (2005b). 'Response to Critics', *Review of Politics*, 76, pp. 495–513.
Wallace, R. J. (1991). 'Virtue, Reason, and Principle', *Canadian Journal of Philosophy*, 21, pp. 469–95.
Walters, P. (1982). *An Introduction to Ergodic Theory.* New York: Springer.
Weale, A. (2020). *Modern Social Contract Theory.* Oxford: Oxford University Press.
Wedgwood, R. (2007). *The Nature of Normativity.* Oxford: Clarendon.
Wempe, B. (2004). *T. H. Green's Theory of Positive Freedom: From Metaphysics to Political Theory.* Charlottesville, VA: Imprint Academic.
Westphal, K. (1989). *Hegel's Epistemological Realism.* Dordrecht: Kluwer.
Westphal, M. (1979). *History and Truth in Hegel's Phenomenology.* Atlantic Highlands, NJ: Humanities Press International.
White, S. K. (2000). *Sustaining Affirmation: The Strengths of Weak Ontology in Political Theory.* Princeton, NJ: Princeton University Press.
— (2005). 'Weak Ontology: Genealogy and Critical Issues', *The Hedgehog Review: Critical Reflections on Contemporary Culture*, 7.2, pp. 11–25.
— (2009). *The Ethos of a Late-Modern Citizen.* Cambridge, MA: Harvard University Press.
Williams, B. (1971). 'Morality and Emotions', in J. Cassey (ed.), *Morality and Moral Reasoning.* London: Methuen, pp. 1–24.
— (1997). 'Stoic Philosophy and the Emotions: Reply to Richard Sorabji', in R. Sorabji (ed.), *Aristotle and After (Bulletin of the Institute of Classical Studies*, suppl. Vol. 68), pp. 211–13.
Williams, E. (2016). *The Ways We Think: From the Straits of Reason to the Possibilities of Thought.* Oxford: Wiley–Blackwell.

Wittgenstein, L. (1953). *Philosophical Investigations*, trans. G. E. M. Anscombe. Oxford: Blackwell.
— (1967). *Remarks on the Foundations of Mathematics*. Cambridge, MA: MIT Press.
Wood, A. (1990). *Hegel's Ethical Thought*. Cambridge: Cambridge University Press.
— (2005). *Kant*. Oxford: Blackwell.
Worrall, J. (1989). 'Structural Realism: The Best of Both Worlds', *Dialectica*, 43.1–2, pp. 99–124.
Wright, C. (1992). *Truth and Objectivity*. Cambridge, MA: Harvard University Press.
Youdell, D. (2011). *School Trouble: Identity, Power and Politics in Education*. Abingdon: Routledge.
Yovel, Y. (2005). *Hegel's Preface to the Phenomenology of Spirit*. Princeton, NJ: Princeton University Press.
Žižek, S. (1999). *The Ticklish Subject: The Absent Centre of Political Ontology*. London: Verso.
Zund, J. D. (2002). 'George David Birkhoff and John von Neumann: A Question of Priority and the Ergodic Theorems, 1931–1932', *Historia Mathematica*, 29.2, pp. 138–56.
Zurn, P., and Dilts, A. (eds) (2016). *Active Intolerance: Michel Foucault, the Prisons Information Group, and the Future of Abolition*. Basingstoke: Palgrave Macmillan.

Index

action
  as individuating 174
  as normative 33, 36, 38, 38, 39, 40, 41, 42, 78
  as under a description 78
agnosticism 35, 152, 202–3
agonism 172, 195, 211, 212, 213, 235, 238, 247, 284
Anglo-American philosophy 19, 22–3, 25, 26, 43, 54, 79, 85, 91, 112, 127, 158, 216, 295–8
analytic philosophy 22–3, 32, 35, 52, 119, 121
animals 79, 109, 140, 149, 150, 156, 187, 189, 194, 209, 258, 276, 286, 316
  ethical obligations towards 140, 209, 276
  humans as custodians of the earth 156, 187
anthropocentrism 149, 194
anthropology 14, 163, 165, 293, 302
a priori structures of cognition 119, 130, 257, 274, 288
Aristotle ix, 3, 8, 9, 11, 23, 69, 70, 79, 83, 118, 156, 168, 170, 175, 177, 185, 191, 215, 226, 240, 252, 256, 303, 314, 327

atheism 163, 202
authenticity 6, 27, 58, 64, 268, 269, 273, 274

Barthez, P.-J. 70
becoming 25, 100, 101, 102, 153, 167, 168, 254, 257, 322
Bentham, J. ix, 23, 119, 146, 152, 214, 219, 304
  Bentham's dictum 214
Bergson, H. 57
Berkeley, G. 252
Binswanger, L. 274
biology 9, 13, 14, 59, 64, 66–9, 70, 71, 72, 76, 82, 87, 88, 109, 115, 201, 275, 297, 309, 326
biosphere 73, 140, 258
Boltzmann, L. 29
Boyle, R. 167
Bradley, F. H. 176, 177
Breton, A. 182
Buchanan, J., and Tullock, G. 156, 186, 208, 209, 216, 217, 305
Butler, J. vi, 4, 27, 28, 248, 261, 265, 269, 270, 271, 272, 273, 277, 288, 290, 305, 306, 307

Camus, A. 26, 201, 357, 305
Canguilhem, G. 1, 2, 24–5, 56–84, 126, 158, 219, 298, 299, 300, 305, 306, 309, 315, 316, 322, 326
Cantor, G. 16
capabilities/capability 50, 199, 215, 285
capitalism 169, 259, 299, 307, 324
Char, R. 80, 84, 239
circumstance (Hume) 39, 42, 198
citizens 36, 155, 173, 179, 200, 217, 222, 227, 228, 238, 244, 246, 250, 262, 264, 283, 287
citizenship 173, 179, 200
civil disobedience 266, 286–7, 291
civil society 170, 213, 223, 224, 225, 226, 227, 228, 229, 231, 233, 241, 307
  alternative models of 226
  as a governmental technology 227, 229
  as an 'historical-natural constant' 241
  as non-statist 228–9
Clark, M., and Dudrick, D. 24, 90, 91, 92, 93, 94, 95, 96, 97, 112, 113, 295, 306
climate change 74, 99, 120, 140, 179, 180, 200, 255, 258, 270, 276, 287
closed universe 8, 15, 166, 288
collective 8, 14, 17, 39, 43, 71, 80, 97, 103, 106, 119, 124, 125, 126, 143, 144, 145, 146, 147, 148, 149, 151, 169, 179, 180, 181, 192, 211, 212, 214, 238, 244, 246, 269, 296
  deliberation/decision-making 151, 179
  dimension to personhood 71, 144, 146, 179, 210
  and individual 69, 97, 146

complexity
  accidents 9, 42, 60, 65, 130
  bifurcation 11–13, 39, 52, 75, 111–12 (*see also* Prigogine)
  causation 7, 8, 28, 30, 70, 105, 124
  chance/chance occurrences 8, 11, 12, 13, 15, 20, 22, 23, 59, 60, 68, 71, 161, 182, 185, 310
  chaos/chaos theory x, 10, 16, 30, 197, 308, 315, 319, 322, 326
  complex adaptive or dynamical systems/system interactions 8, 11, 14, 29, 30, 70, 102, 194
  contingencies/contingency 9, 11, 16, 19, 21, 23, 28, 30, 42, 59, 60, 61, 63, 74, 76, 105–6, 110, 115, 121, 136, 140, 142, 147, 155, 174, 177, 179, 185, 193, 194, 195, 205, 209, 252, 254, 256, 257, 258, 263, 264, 274, 323
  creative/creativity 5, 25, 62, 63, 64, 65, 68, 80, 95, 101, 242, 250, 253, 254, 259, 275–6
  determinism/deterministic (causation) 7, 8, 10, 11, 12, 22, 28, 29, 86, 109, 159, 274
  downward causation 8, 28, 30, 252
  emergent/emergence 9, 11, 13–15, 21, 22, 70, 73, 114, 121, 125, 144, 145, 151, 167, 174, 179, 194, 195, 222, 240, 255, 268, 270, 272, 310
  'feedback loops' 30, 185, 252
  holism/wholes 3, 8, 11, 15, 30, 50, 82, 90, 97, 103, 120, 125, 129, 135, 144, 156, 158, 159, 167, 170, 173, 182, 187, 188, 196, 227, 230, 240, 252, 254, 257, 268, 272, 288, 309

Index

indeterminism 8, 9, 10, 11, 12, 16, 22, 30, 71, 256
interconnectedness/interrelatedness 14, 76, 143, 159, 180, 196, 201, 258, 272
inventing/inventiveness 67, 84, 106, 143, 271, 276, 316
irreversible/irreversibility 9, 10, 11, 16, 29, 66, 112, 167, 170, 201, 258–9
linear/non-linear 8, 9, 11–12, 14, 15, 21–2, 30, 60, 70, 139, 159, 184, 185, 252
'logical relations' 21–2
mechanism/mechanical system 10, 21, 29, 30, 40, 61, 68, 69, 70, 102, 131, 139, 159, 160, 166, 167, 170, 179, 189, 190, 220, 225, 252, 257, 288
'multi-referentiality' (Morin) 14
non-reductionism/reductionism ix, 8, 37, 38, 41, 42, 43, 53, 61, 64, 65, 68, 69, 114, 125, 143, 144, 170, 252, 255, 261, 275
novelty 8, 14, 16, 71, 247, 253
perturbations 11, 12, 15
physics 7, 10, 11, 29, 167, 322
principle of ergodicity 10, 29, 305, 320, 327, 328
probability 22, 214, 310
quantum/post-quantum theory 10, 11, 19, 30, 322
'restricted' and 'general' approaches to (Morin) 8
self-organization 9, 13–15
stratification 14–15
'strong mixing' (Prigogine) 30
thermodynamics 9, 13
uncertainty viii, 8, 9, 15, 16, 25, 61, 71, 77, 96, 108, 117, 120, 142, 150, 170, 173, 185, 194, 195, 215, 239, 248, 253, 254, 255, 259, 268, 275, 276, 288
unintended consequences 9, 32, 77, 185
uniqueness 8, 11, 80, 105, 139, 170, 174, 194, 256, 272
unknown/unknowability 13, 14, 106, 107, 163, 253
unpredictability 8, 9, 11, 30, 60, 68, 69, 71, 77, 173, 175, 194, 248, 253, 255, 259, 268
community ix, 50, 71, 110, 140, 160, 161, 165, 173, 226, 227, 228, 232, 264, 279, 319
conatus 88, 109
conceptualization/concepts viii, 2, 3, 9, 10, 16, 18, 19, 36, 37, 38, 40, 42, 45, 46, 53, 56, 59, 61–3, 66, 67, 75, 81, 84, 107, 119, 163, 165, 167, 176, 183, 184, 197, 222, 236, 245, 248, 253, 261, 288, 289, 304, 311, 316, 322, 326
  as emergent from life 61–2, 66
  as normative 61–3
Connolly, W. 27, 220, 237, 244, 248, 306
conscientious acts 209, 267–8, 269
consent/compliance 175, 209–10, 218, 238, 264
consequences/consequentialism 129, 135, 138, 140, 141, 142, 144, 146, 147, 148, 155, 169, 194, 205, 214, 216, 258, 277, 282
constructivism 2, 7, 37, 38, 39, 61, 71, 76, 90, 94, 109, 112, 113, 114, 122, 128, 143, 167, 168, 178, 192, 204, 205–6, 215, 216, 251, 263, 267, 269, 273, 275, 279, 288, 322, 304
Continental philosophy 7, 23, 42, 85, 112, 137, 295–8

convention/conventionalism 18, 31, 81, 88, 93, 98, 100, 117, 121, 126, 176, 179, 215, 253, 264, 282, 296
convergence/accord 80, 85, 96, 97, 99, 156, 172, 203, 209, 239, 256
corruption 118, 213, 228, 231, 237, 238
Crick, F., and Watson, J. 66, 67
crisis/crises 60, 82, 97, 146, 160, 258, 259, 260, 275, 283
critique 23, 36, 77, 181, 182, 183, 194, 222, 236, 237, 243, 245, 246, 250, 251, 280–2
  critical reflection/interrogation 183, 237, 239, 280–1, 282
  critical refection as normative 77, 281
  as essential to democracy 282
Cynics 236, 238, 285–6, 291

danger 74, 83, 96, 97, 98, 99, 108, 117, 142, 147, 148, 166, 179, 180, 195, 198, 200, 211, 220, 235, 260, 273, 276, 280, 283
Daniel, J. 180–1
Darwin, C. 57, 66, 69, 79, 88, 100–1, 102, 104, 113, 307
Dasein 83
Deleuze, G. 10, 12, 19, 30, 56, 58, 70, 76, 85, 100, 102, 104, 112, 113, 114, 124, 167, 185, 211, 221, 248, 249, 275, 295, 297, 307
  and Guattari, F. 19, 102, 307
democracy x, 26–7, 43, 57, 71, 80, 146, 147–8, 156, 169, 183, 184, 192, 195, 201, 202, 205, 210, 211, 212, 213, 214, 215, 218, 220, 222, 223, 225, 228, 229, 236, 238, 240, 241, 243–61, 276, 283, 284, 287, 306, 308, 311, 318, 319, 320, 324
  accountability 147, 213, 270, 272, 273
  best method 147, 148, 179, 201, 205, 212, 213, 214–15, 220, 257
  checks and balances 156, 211, 212, 213, 223, 225, 228, 229
  concordance principle 141–2, 212, 215, 236, 240, 241
  constitutional safeguards 195, 208, 211, 224, 308
  contestation 120, 151, 172, 174, 174, 175, 211, 212, 213, 225, 230–31
  deliberation 117, 142, 151, 213, 232, 268
  democratic justice 214, 232, 234, 241
  free press 195
  global demos 26, 53, 99, 128, 140, 146, 179, 180, 189, 211, 222, 223, 225, 233, 238, 255, 259, 260, 276, 289, 308, 313, 319, 320
  processes of appeal 212
  public engagement 233–5
  thesis of ascending concentric circles (Stoics) 211
  transparency 44, 83, 147, 165, 213
deontology 119, 132, 134, 141, 142, 144, 147, 168, 169, 170, 205, 257
  and consequences 129, 135, 141, 142, 144
deontic dimension to action/life 125, 135, 142, 205, 257
and teleology 169, 205

Derrida, J. 6, 51, 54, 72, 126, 248, 275, 289, 307
Descartes, R. 52, 73, 89, 165, 167, 176, 210, 218, 252, 261, 278, 307
Dewey, J. 82, 253, 254, 255, 308
dialectics 8, 159, 160, 161, 162, 163, 166, 172, 173, 174, 178, 184, 321
  Absolute, the 62, 159, 161, 162, 172, 178, 184
difference ix, 6, 76, 117, 170, 173, 174, 214, 220, 236, 307, 316
  rule of 117, 131–2, 138–9, 141
discontinuity 68, 84
  see also chance
discourse 2, 6, 18, 19, 22, 36, 37, 38, 41, 42, 43, 44, 50, 53, 63, 83, 94, 114, 124, 153, 161, 206, 213, 251, 275, 284, 288, 290, 298, 299, 302, 309, 311, 325
  see also Foucault
disputability, principle of 74, 251
duties 110, 133, 135, 138, 144, 145, 147, 148, 154, 169, 177, 182, 204, 205, 213, 232, 262, 267, 269, 276, 282, 286, 287, 289
  conflicting 135, 138–9, 142, 144–8, 169, 205, 214, 216, 258, 282
  ethical 140, 264
  of governments 232, 233–4
  moral 140, 264
  non-moral 276, 289
  'what is not reasonable to reject' (Scanlon) 218
  'what we owe to each other' (Scanlon) 209, 218, 276, 277
  what we owe to ourselves 277

education x, 1, 24, 27, 53, 63, 94, 113, 231, 237, 243–61, 280, 283, 284, 304, 305, 306, 308, 314, 319, 322, 326, 328
  as concerned with experimentation 63
  as a critical institution 251, 254
  as problem-solving pedagogy 253–5
Eichmann Trial 197, 290
Einstein, A. 10, 29
Eisenmann, C. 26, 223, 224, 308
Enlightenment 8, 73, 88, 149, 166, 167, 181, 210, 213, 218, 226, 227, 235, 236, 253, 254, 266, 270, 278, 293, 299, 305, 322
  arrogance of 149
  Enlightenment I and II 213, 218
  rationalism 73, 88, 252, 254, 278
  Scottish 226, 227
equality 26, 38, 46, 81, 146, 157, 188, 197, 198, 199, 200, 230, 249, 308, 327
  among humans 188, 197–203
  basic inequalities justified 200–1
  life continuance justification 200–1
  Locke's justifications of equality 199
essentialism/essence 7, 11, 16, 20, 21, 37, 57, 67, 89, 101, 104, 107, 114, 123, 159, 165, 166, 168, 170, 191, 221, 226, 240, 268, 296
  ahistorical 13, 25, 57, 89, 119, 134, 137, 173, 191, 192, 203, 263
  ousia 11, 67, 69, 170
  substance 5, 8, 11, 57, 67, 89, 123, 124, 159, 170
ethical comportment/engagement 27, 78, 171, 265, 266, 267, 272, 277

ethics of equal consideration 187, 213, 214
ethics of life continuance ix, 4–7, 25, 90–3, 105–12, 116–18, 120–1, 122, 125, 126, 127, 128, 140–51, 202–3, 205, 214–15, 276–87
  as meta-ethical 213, 249
  method of ethics 213
  non-moral virtues 276–7
  obligations 182, 276, 277
  supererogation 209, 276
ethical/meta-ethical
  immanent non-metaphysical objectivity in ethics 42, 60, 90–100, 109, 110, 113, 116, 117, 118, 120–1, 122, 125, 126, 140, 150, 152, 205, 214, 215, 251
  objectivism in ethics (metaphysical) 25, 26, 39, 60–1, 90–100, 110, 112, 116, 118, 119, 121, 122, 127, 152
  objectivity as convergence on the future 96–100, 140
  objectivity as widening perspectives 90–6
  subjectivism in ethics 25, 38, 100, 113, 118, 121, 122, 127–8, 145, 152
  types of objectivity in ethics 91–4, 96–100, 110, 121–2, 125
ethics of presumptive generosity 27, 248
ethical perspectives
  alterity, ethics of ix, 6, 279
  Badiou's ethics ix, 6, 15–19, 20, 242, 257, 304, 311
  dialogical ethics 46, 279
  ethics/politics of difference ix, 6, 117
  global ethics 27, 179, 243–61, 255–61

intuitionism in ethics 57, 118, 119–26, 127, 144, 151, 152, 153, 155, 159, 184, 204, 208, 216, 287
multiculturalism ix, 6
poststructuralist ethics 3, 4, 5, 20, 24, 53, 179
self-realization, ethic of 26, 176–80, 185
virtue ethics 27, 255–7
ethnic cleansing/genocide 161, 197, 211
evolution 12, 13, 30, 59, 63, 66, 67, 68, 69, 100, 101, 102, 113, 114, 151, 159, 180, 184, 194, 201, 252, 254, 255, 308, 313, 325
  adaptation, concept of 100, 101, 102
  complex 102, 255
  natural selection 66, 79, 100
  as shaped by external circumstances (Darwin) 66, 69, 100–4
  Spencer and evolution theory 113, 114
  von Nageli's theory of (orthogenesis) 101–2
existentialism 162, 163, 247, 299, 321, 323
experimentation viii, 8, 12, 63, 68, 69, 71, 90, 101, 102, 126, 156, 215, 250, 251, 268, 276, 287
Ewing, J. C. 144, 145, 154, 155, 308

fallibilism 88, 112
falsification (Popper) 83, 156, 222
Farrell Krell, D. 108, 308–9
'felicific calculus' (Bentham) 146
Ferguson, A. 27, 225–30, 232, 241

Fichte, J. G. 159, 184
finitude 51, 62, 82, 131, 132, 156, 158, 173, 192, 202, 247, 272
form/s of life 57, 76, 88, 108–10, 122, 187, 257, 311
Foucault
  'advice-giving'/'telling people what to do' 31, 34, 36
  anti-humanism 7, 16, 20, 165, 194, 323, 327
  as 'anti-normative' 31–6, 47
  care of the self 51, 52, 75, 76, 243–7, 277–8, 279, 280, 281, 283, 284, 285, 289, 292, 317
  criticism of socialism 228
  'death of man' thesis 20, 30
  discourse, conception of 42, 43, 53, 164
  dispositif (apparatus, assemblage, ensemble) ix, 7, 21, 42, 75, 79, 278, 286
  event/eventalization 16, 19, 20, 21, 89
  genealogy 3, 21, 32, 45, 60, 61
  governmental technology 227, 229
  governmentality 19, 73, 226, 227, 228, 229, 245, 247
  intellectuals/specific intellectuals 31, 247
  limit/limit-experience 20, 63, 76, 118, 145, 183, 222, 232, 251
  as normative 1, 31–56, 181–2, 233–4
  other, the 6, 28, 277–9, 289
  other as *parrhēsiastes* 277–8, 284
  political activism/politics/prison reform (GIP) 174, 222, 225, 234–5, 249–50
  problematization 82, 251, 255, 275
  regime of truth 88
  resistance 36, 78, 221, 222, 225, 231, 246, 247, 250
  structural linguistics 21–2
  tactics/strategies – deploying power 165, 231
  transgression 20, 251
  writing on writing viii–ix
Foucault's conception of power 19–21, 23, 221, 230–2
  biopower 71, 75, 83, 179, 221
  equalities/equalization of power 45–7
  fixity/congealment of power relations 46, 230
  power as a check on power 222–3, 225, 231, 251, 266
  power as dangerous/perilous 232, 235
  power, disciplinary 45, 75, 162, 221
  power, as productive 20–1, 221, 225
  power, as repressive 20–1, 221, 225, 230, 231
  power, as ubiquitous 19, 221, 223, 225, 230
  reciprocities of power 45–6, 56, 230–1, 232
  states of domination/subjugating power 36, 46–7, 212
  symmetries/asymmetries of power 45–7, 56, 230–1
Foucault's ethics
  curiosity 250–1, 281
  'ethics of discomfort' 181–2
  innovation 281
  moralism 281
  questioning 237, 238, 274, 275, 285
  refusal 281
  speaking truth to power 78, 246, 266, 282

Foucault's ethics (*cont.*)
  writings on ethics 1, 5, 6, 28, 279, 281, 292–4
Foucault's sceptical suspicion 212, 218
Foucault and truth telling
  access to truth 271, 277, 278, 280–1
  'courage of truth' 1, 75, 266, 283, 284, 285, 290, 293, 302, 310
  ethical *parrhēsia* 283, 284
  parrhēsia (truth-telling) 36, 78, 150, 234, 237, 238, 245, 246, 247, 282–6, 290
  parrhēsiastes 277–8, 284, 286
  political *parrhēsia* and democracy 283, 284
foundationalism/anti- or non-foundationalism 9, 16, 21, 85, 86–7, 88, 112, 164, 185, 189, 192, 193, 206–7, 265, 269, 295–6
  Archimedean points 88
  biological foundationalism 86–7
  foundationalist readings of Nietzsche 295–6
  historical constants/laws 9, 10, 22, 30, 36, 70, 88, 89, 130, 137, 154, 167, 189, 190, 192, 212, 226, 229, 269, 288, 322
  postfoundationalism 244
freedom/liberty 28, 45, 46, 47, 100, 103, 137, 146, 149, 165, 186, 188, 195, 202, 223, 228, 229, 239, 242, 259, 264, 270, 274, 278–9, 284, 289, 304, 312, 317
fundamentalism 27, 237–8, 249
future 97–100, 109, 139, 140–2, 163, 167, 182, 195, 221, 228, 239, 255, 270, 271, 274–6
  acting for the 97, 271, 276
  as collective idiom 99
  and life continuance 97, 99, 182
  obligations to the future 141–2
  as ontological ground of justice and ethics 98, 275
  responsibility/authenticity and the future 182, 274

games 23, 44, 46, 54, 80, 110, 111, 117
generosity 27, 192, 247, 248, 249, 267, 272
genetics 66, 67, 68, 69, 102, 156, 313
  epigenetics approaches 156
Ginsborg, H. 40–1, 43, 45, 53, 121, 134, 185, 309
God 26, 70, 86, 88, 89, 90, 97, 102, 103, 117, 118, 120, 139, 152, 161, 163, 176, 178, 184, 187, 189, 191, 193, 195, 197, 199, 200, 201, 202, 203, 205, 207, 209, 211, 213, 215, 217, 219, 227, 237, 239
  religion 26, 37, 122, 145, 157, 163, 168, 178, 181, 185, 188, 197, 199, 201, 238, 249, 268, 297, 315
Golden Rule 120, 152
good, the, x, 6, 31, 37, 38, 47, 49, 79, 88, 95, 103, 108, 113, 114, 117, 118, 119, 120, 123, 129, 130, 131, 132, 135, 138, 142, 143–8, 168–9, 175, 176, 177, 178, 188, 203, 204, 205, 210, 214, 235, 239, 240, 254, 256, 260, 261, 277, 282, 296
  claims against 205, 210
  classical doctrine of 169, 175, 178
  'the greatest happiness for the greatest number' (Bentham) 119

Index

as multiple and constructed 178
the right and 144–8, 169, 210, 282
Gulag Archipelago (Solzhenitsyn) 161, 166, 180

hailing (Althusser) 185, 263
Hampshire, S. 90
Hampton, J. 191, 311
happiness 129, 132, 145
harm principle 76, 128, 141, 146, 154, 155, 276
health 34, 39, 57, 58, 64, 65, 66, 79, 160, 251, 308
Hegel, G. W. F. ix, x, 6, 7, 10, 15, 20, 22, 23, 26, 70, 72, 73, 110, 115, 131, 132, 133, 134, 135, 136, 154, 155, 156, 157–86, 226, 236, 254, 258, 272, 288, 310, 311, 312, 313, 316, 318, 319, 321, 322, 323, 324, 326, 327, 328
  British Hegelians 176–80
  Foucault's criticisms of 158–9, 162–5
  Hegelian/ism 26, 35, 45, 46, 107, 137, 157, 161, 163, 164, 170, 171, 173, 174, 176, 177, 178, 180, 186, 224, 232, 236
Heidegger, M. ix, 1, 6, 7, 8, 16, 22, 51, 56, 58, 59, 72, 83, 103–4, 108, 111, 112, 160, 182, 183, 248, 290, 297, 307, 309, 310, 312, 323
historicity 3, 9, 13, 16, 19, 73, 104, 105, 107, 160, 163, 164, 239
Hobbes, T. 26, 83, 88, 151, 187, 187–219, 203, 206, 213, 215, 216, 217, 219, 226, 309, 311, 312
Hölderlin, F. 159, 184
homo economicus 227, 230

Human Capital Theory (Gary Becker) 211, 218, 304, 305
humanism 7, 16, 140, 165, 187, 237, 323
humanity 52, 89, 98, 99, 132, 140, 141, 148, 149, 152, 180, 195, 248, 257, 265
Hume, D. 56, 58, 91, 121, 127, 168, 193, 196, 198, 216, 252, 257, 262, 266, 287, 304, 313, 326
Hutcheson, F. 152, 153
Hyppolite, J. 26, 82, 162, 163, 164, 166, 306, 313, 321

idealism x, 72, 84, 119, 136, 158, 169–70, 176–80, 184, 317, 318, 320, 321, 325
identity/identities ix, 6, 67, 71, 125, 144, 170, 172, 173, 174, 175, 176–7, 181, 203, 237, 240, 255, 263, 264, 269, 271, 272, 309, 315, 324, 328
  as emergent and irreducible 125, 144
  as fixed/deriving from nature 172, 263
  as provisional/precarious/frail 172, 271, 272, 181
  as socially and historically constructed 165, 172, 264
ideologies/ideology 5, 35, 57, 58, 74, 78, 83–4, 122, 151, 153, 165, 179, 201, 210, 211, 213, 238, 251–2, 282, 297, 298, 299, 303
'impartial spectator' (Smith) 228
infinity 8, 15, 17, 18, 77, 98, 147, 164, 166–7, 170, 188, 232, 306, 315
institutions 10, 17, 31, 39, 45, 51, 60, 74, 79, 117, 142, 148, 150, 177, 178, 202, 214, 223, 234, 238, 240, 244, 260

institutions (cont.)
  institutionalization 78–9, 80,
    140, 147, 150, 196, 214, 231,
    264
  integrity 27, 125, 148, 205, 215,
    223, 263, 269, 291, 308,
    315
  intentionality 24, 37, 38, 49, 135,
    141, 167, 185
  interpellation 263, 272
  intolerability/intolerance 17, 74,
    76–7, 222, 232, 249, 250,
    251, 328

Jacob, F. 24, 56, 58, 66–9, 81, 314
Jonas, H. 140–2, 314
judgement 2, 19, 38, 39, 40, 41,
    44, 54, 58, 64, 76, 79, 87, 90,
    92, 96, 108, 114, 117, 139,
    142, 144, 145, 150, 151, 152,
    156, 169, 182, 198, 205, 206,
    214, 216, 232, 233, 254, 256,
    261, 266, 268, 279, 288, 309,
    314
  as considered 90, 145, 150,
    151, 152, 156, 216, 254, 266,
    279
  'determinative judgement' (Kant)
    268, 288
  as inexact and experimental 268
  'judgement view of justice' 268,
    269
  as normative 38, 39, 40, 41,
    108, 114, 198, 206
  proportionality 205
  'reflective judgement' (Kant)
    232, 254, 266, 268–9, 288
justice 38, 45, 98, 99, 116, 126,
    135, 146, 151, 152, 157, 183,
    203–6, 207, 208, 209, 215,
    216, 218, 232, 241, 269, 275,
    286, 289, 294, 297, 302, 304,
    307, 309, 322, 334

Kant, I. 40–1, 89–90, 116–56
  categorical imperatives 31, 129,
    130, 132, 133, 134, 135, 138,
    139, 140, 141, 148, 152, 155,
    177
  concept of the 'moral law' 119,
    129, 131, 135, 137, 138, 263,
    266
  conception of the will 131,
    136–7, 154, 155, 178
  consequences 123, 129, 135–6,
    138, 140, 141, 142, 144, 145,
    147, 155
  criticisms of Kant's conception of
    will 136–7, 178
  criticisms of universalization
    principle 131, 135, 138–9,
    140–2, 155, 156, 177, 266
  Foucault's criticism of Kant's *a
    priori* 274, 288
  immanence, conception of 114
  individualism of Kant's moral
    theory 128, 135–7, 138, 140,
    141, 149–50, 156, 178, 263
  moral autonomy/freedom 129,
    137, 149, 150, 152, 154, 156,
    178, 303
  promise-keeping, lying, theft, etc.
    130, 131–2, 134, 136, 138,
    222
  rejection of knowledge of the
    noumenal 89
  revisionist views of 132–3,
    140–1
  universalization rule 116, 119,
    120, 129, 130, 131, 135, 138,
    140, 141, 142, 152, 155, 263,
    266
keep going 17, 188
Kelly, M. 23–4, 31–6, 45, 47, 53,
    314
knowledge 9, 18, 61–3, 84, 161,
    227, 252, 255–6, 276

Index

absolute/perfect 6, 20, 62, 68, 69, 82, 144, 158, 159, 161, 162, 171, 172, 178, 184, 220, 235, 237, 250
  'embodied' 213, 281
  and ideology 58, 74, 78, 83–4, 151, 165, 210, 211, 213, 281, 282
  partial 9, 91, 163, 171, 172, 210–11, 212, 228, 248, 251, 253, 269–73
Kojève, A. 162

language 15, 18, 21, 22–3, 54, 83, 134, 163, 165, 173, 189, 191, 212, 215, 254, 297, 298, 302, 312, 315
law 148, 189, 197, 212, 216, 222, 223, 224, 228, 231, 232, 262, 286, 287, 308, 317
legal aid 147, 155
Leibniz, G. W. 159–60, 167, 252, 315
Leurs prisons (book) 261
liberalism x, 127, 147, 153, 156, 171, 173, 179, 183, 192, 194, 199, 210, 226, 229, 230, 233, 236, 237, 239, 241, 258, 261, 265, 267, 268, 270, 295, 319, 323
  liberal individualism 71, 149, 156, 173, 192, 296
  liberal-modernist settlement/ liberal Enlightenment 73, 149, 210, 253, 254, 258
life continuance ix, 4, 25, 26, 113–14, 116–19, 140–51
  arguments for 120, 148–9, 187–8
  continuance agendas 142
  as codifying common sense 116, 120
  as collective and individual 97, 117, 118, 140
  and consequences 140, 142, 144, 146, 205, 214, 216
  as constructivist 37, 76, 112, 114, 128, 143, 167, 178, 192, 205–6, 215, 216, 288
  and conventionalism 117, 126
  and democracy 148–9, 205
  as equal for all 197–203, 214
  as establishing limits 118, 220
  as extra-moral source for ethical values 108, 113
  and the future 97, 106–8, 120, 142, 182, 214
  and the good 117, 142, 143–8, 205
  as hypothetical imperative 203
  and the law 148, 287
  as meta-ethical and normative 213–14
  and the naturalistic fallacy 113–14
  as objective norm 19, 42, 60, 90–100, 109, 110, 113, 116, 117, 118, 120–2, 125, 126, 142, 150, 205, 214, 215, 251, 268
  'permanent continuation of life' 141
  and practical judgement 142, 205, 287
  and relativism/pluralism 110, 220
  as theory of obligations 205, 209, 264, 269
  and unanimity 148–9
  and utilitarianism 146–7, 205
  see also ethics of life continuance
life philosophy 1, 4, 24, 26, 52, 53, 56–84, 85–115, 188, 219
  bios 75–6, 83
  'commodious living' 189, 192
  concept of life 61, 74, 75

life philosophy (*cont.*)
  élan vital (Bergson) 57
  error/errancy 2, 24, 59, 60, 61, 63, 74, 78, 56–81, 82, 83–4, 94, 126, 128, 151, 161, 212, 219, 253, 258, 298, 299, 326
  forms of 57–8
  'fullness of life' 138, 266
  irreducibility of life 61, 64, 65, 68
  life as emergent 15, 70, 268, 269
  life as immanent normativity 17, 25, 41, 43, 48, 51, 52, 58, 63, 64, 65, 74, 76, 79, 81, 91, 93, 100, 101, 108–12, 114, 116, 117, 118, 126, 128, 140, 148, 149–50, 184, 189, 192, 197, 201, 209, 214, 239, 240, 245, 257, 263, 269, 277, 289, 307
  'living system' (*système vivant*) 67, 68, 83
  'permanence of life' 141
  'way of life'/ways of life 52, 63, 266, 280, 285, 290
Locke, J. 6, 151, 156, 189, 190, 192, 194, 195, 199, 203, 206, 215, 216, 226, 252, 259, 261, 315
logic 18, 130
logos 66, 67, 69
Lucian 291, 316
Luhmann, N. 248, 254
Lwoff, A. M. 66, 67

Mackie, J. L. 126, 127, 153, 316
markets 88, 226–7, 228, 229–30
Marx, K. ix, 7, 9, 89, 157–86
Marxism/neo-Marxism 9, 32, 89, 157–86, 242
  Foucault's criticisms of 158–9, 180–3, 221, 242
materialism x, 28, 58, 72, 112, 124–5, 287, 319

historical 9, 28, 87, 319
'incorporeal' 124–5
vital 42, 53, 70, 102, 103
mathematics 16, 18, 29, 129, 130, 257
maturity 18, 74, 137, 191, 246, 266, 278, 279
  of judgement 266, 278, 279
  as a precondition for reason 279
  of science 18, 74, 266, 278
meta-ethics 3, 47, 56, 91, 213
metaphysics
  of exteriority 25, 50, 51, 57, 62–63, 87, 88–9, 90, 110, 117, 118, 119, 121–6, 152
  immanent non-metaphysics of interiority 25, 41, 43, 51, 52, 63, 74, 76, 79, 81, 91, 109, 114, 121–6, 152, 153, 154, 192, 214, 239, 263
  immanent non-metaphysical interiority as objective norm 38, 42, 60, 63, 90–100, 109, 110, 113, 116, 117, 118, 120–2, 125, 126, 140, 150, 152, 214, 205, 214, 215, 251
  Kant's 'thing-in-itself' 92, 100, 110, 139
  Plato's external world of Forms 88, 110, 118, 125
  queerness 126, 153–4
mind/consciousness 15, 17, 18, 49, 50, 53, 54, 57, 88, 106, 122, 125, 136, 142, 150, 158, 159, 163–4, 165, 171, 172, 176, 178, 179, 184, 194, 195, 197, 198, 234, 253, 255, 280, 308
  as emergent and irreducible 15, 255
  product of a complex evolution 14–15, 255
mitigating circumstances 288–9
monarchy 223–4

Monod, J. 66, 67
Montesquieu, C.-L. de 26–7, 220–5, 228, 239, 241, 317
Moore, G. E. 113, 144, 156, 176, 216, 217, 317
Morin, E. 8, 14–15, 28, 248, 317
motives/motivation 125, 129, 266–8, 269, 276
Myers, E. 27, 243, 261, 317
  critique of Foucault 243–7

Nageli, C. von 101, 102
natural selection (Darwin) 66, 79, 100
naturalism 24, 37, 53, 73, 79, 84–90, 91, 92, 108, 112, 114, 122, 124, 151, 166, 171, 187, 189, 190, 191, 192, 194, 209, 226, 295, 307, 314, 315, 318, 320
  beyond nature/getting rid of nature 26, 86, 192
  laws of nature/empire of nature 62–3, 88, 89, 129, 189, 190, 192, 322
  m-naturalism (Leiter) 86
  nature as metaphysical ground 62–3, 78, 86, 88–9, 112, 119, 134, 167, 190, 191, 192, 194, 206, 263
  s-naturalism (Leiter) 86, 112
  spare naturalism 86
  state of nature 88, 190, 191–2, 203
  supernaturalism 86, 87, 88, 112, 124
naturalistic fallacy 113–14, 156, 216–17
Nazis, Nazism 144, 161, 197, 220, 262
neoliberalism 229–30
needs 213
  see also survival

Newton, I. 7, 10, 28, 150, 159, 166, 167
Newtonian 10, 28, 150, 166, 315
Nietzsche, F. xiii, ix, 1, 3, 4, 5, 6, 7, 8, 21, 22, 24, 25, 45, 56, 58, 59, 60, 63, 79, 85–115, 121, 127, 137, 139, 150, 160, 162, 163, 167, 168, 184, 189, 192, 193, 202, 215, 235, 267, 275, 294, 295, 296, 297, 306, 307, 315, 316, 318, 324, 325
  concept of valuation 90, 103–4, 107
  concept of will to power viii, 24, 25, 72, 76, 85, 99, 100, 101, 102, 103, 104, 106, 107, 108, 109, 193, 296, 318
Nietzsche studies 115, 295–8
nihilism 18, 201
nominalism 9, 44, 114, 139, 158, 170, 230
nomos/kosmos (Hayek) 271
non-Marxist culture of the Left 180
norms/normativity
  benefits of being normative 35–6
  as a byword for prescription 32, 35, 53
  causal impact of normative values 122–3
  choices, decisions, and selections as normative 33, 34, 39, 62–6, 111–12, 275
  intentional action as normative 37–8, 167, 185
  irreducibility of the normative 38–9, 41, 42, 43, 53, 65
  non-normativity 31–6, 47, 53
  normal 61, 64, 65, 66
  normalization/normalizing society 61, 75, 239

norms/normativity (*cont.*)
  'normative in content' (Audi) 97, 265
  normative domain 41–2, 142
  normative facts 37, 123–5
  normative 'internalism' 38
  normative/ethical 'turn' 32, 33, 43, 44
  'normative in upshot' (Audi) 97, 265, 271
  normativity as collective 39, 43, 71, 80, 97, 99, 102, 103, 106, 119, 124, 125, 126
  normativity and health 64–6
  pervasiveness of normativity 32–3, 34, 36–42, 39, 45, 47, 262
  rules of formation of discourse as normative 37, 43–4
  Ur-source of normativity 108, 109
  vital and social norms 74, 117, 286
  von Wright's definition 36
  as what ought to be 32, 36, 37, 38
nuclear power/annihilation 99, 179
Nuremberg Trials 197, 262

objectivity 19, 26, 93–100, 100–4, 102, 103, 112, 113, 114, 119–26, 127, 128, 142, 153, 164, 204, 214
  in knowledge/science 18–19, 140
  objectively better ways to live 60, 117, 118, 126
  as queer 127–8, 153
obligation/obligations 98, 129, 134, 135, 136, 138, 139, 141, 144, 145, 149, 176, 177, 182, 199, 204, 209, 213, 216, 217, 219, 234, 238, 263, 264, 266, 267, 271, 273, 276, 277, 279–80, 282, 286, 287, 289

altruism 209, 267–8, 269
  to animals 209, 276
  to the future 98, 141, 145, 182, 267, 269, 282
  moral 219, 234, 264, 289
  non-moral 276–7, 289
  non-obligatory good actions 276–7
  political 279–80
  social role account 76, 263, 264
  supererogation 209, 276–7
one and the many 180, 196, 204, 215
ontology 7, 8, 9, 11, 13, 15, 16, 17, 19, 27, 63, 68, 99, 103, 109, 114, 115, 124, 126, 137, 144, 153, 157, 158, 167, 169, 170, 175, 178, 190, 191, 197, 213, 230, 235, 236, 241, 247, 248, 249, 268, 271, 279, 294, 307, 326, 327, 328
  complex systems ontology 7, 8, 9, 15, 63, 68, 294
  of the event 16–19
  historical 7, 16, 18, 19, 20, 68, 115, 126, 297
  individualist/subjective 137, 178, 190, 191
  ontological uniqueness 11, 170
  'weak ontology' 27, 247–9, 307, 326
open/openness 8, 13, 15, 16, 19, 21, 45, 46, 60, 63, 64, 65, 66, 98, 126, 161, 166–7, 168, 170, 173, 174, 175, 179, 183, 194, 211, 212, 213, 231, 232, 239, 253, 256, 271, 274, 278, 288
  contra teleology 15, 166–7, 168, 170, 173, 175
  to the future 8, 16, 60, 98, 126, 168, 173, 179, 194, 253, 271, 278

Index

'original position' (Rawls) 203, 212
overdetermination 105, 106
overlapping consensus 216
overpopulation 99, 179, 180, 196, 200, 255, 258, 260–1

pain ix, 28, 97, 265
Parfit, D. 120, 121, 122, 123, 124, 125, 126, 152, 154, 210, 320
partiality/partialities 9, 61, 91, 163, 171, 172, 174, 212, 228, 248, 251, 253, 271, 272–3, 248, 272, 273
   as justification for democracy 248
   partial control and power 61, 172, 271
   partial knowledge/awareness 9, 91, 172, 212, 228, 253, 272
   as source of interdependence and vulnerabilities 61, 172, 272
Peirce, C. S. 112, 320
perspectivism, method of 90, 91, 93, 95, 96, 97, 99, 251
plans 39, 80, 117, 271
plants 79, 140
Plato/Platonism 7, 75–6, 88, 110, 118, 121, 125, 194, 200, 216, 283, 284, 289, 290, 291, 321
pleasure 49, 54, 129, 132, 145, 204
   joy 49, 54
pluralism 26, 27, 162, 174, 175, 188, 220–42
poiesis 280, 290
Poincaré, H. 10, 18, 19, 29, 30, 321
'politics of timeliness' (*kairos*) 285
Popper, K. 83, 112, 158, 186, 321
possibility/possibilities 8, 15, 65, 67, 68, 126, 142, 168, 194, 195, 202, 268, 276, 278
   as multiple futures 15, 16, 22, 39, 44, 58, 61, 76, 80, 105, 111, 142, 148, 178, 209, 240, 259, 262, 276, 277, 278
   related to choosing/selecting 34, 38, 39, 112, 275, 278, 279
   related to individuation and uniqueness 144, 271, 268
post-human (Hayles) 26, 193–7
postmodern/ism 45, 51, 55, 78, 269
poststructuralism 4, 41, 53, 54, 84, 92, 111, 134, 137, 175, 176, 178, 179, 185, 186, 204, 216
   poststructuralist innovation to Hegel 173–4
   poststructuralization of Western philosophy 41, 54, 172, 175–6, 185, 186, 261, 263
power (non-Foucauldian) 45, 46, 77, 111, 193, 221–5, 230–1
practices of self 1, 36, 46, 48–9, 50, 51, 52, 138, 171, 241, 255, 279, 280, 285, 290
   autarkeia (self-sufficiency) 279
   basanos 286, 291
   ēthos/cthos 46, 112, 200, 244, 245, 246, 252, 284, 288, 327
   exetasis (testing of souls) 284, 285
   kairos (timeliness) 285
   parrhēsiastic activities 282–6, 290
   piloting/fasting, etc. 284, 290
   probatio (self-testing) 279, 285
   prokheiron 279, 289
   purification/renunciation 235, 290
   self-fashioning/self-examination 13, 48, 138, 280, 284, 290, 293
   skills 61, 71, 255, 279, 285
   tekhnē/technē 108, 237, 241, 250, 276, 280, 285

practices of self (*cont.*)
  zētēsis (search for veridiction) 284
pragmatism, philosophical 18, 74, 82
prescriptive/prescription 1, 3, 24, 32, 35, 53, 140
Prichard, H. A. 155, 204, 216, 217, 287, 289, 321
Prigogine, I. 10, 11, 12, 15, 16, 19, 167, 322
prima facie duty (Ross) 144
problem-solving 150, 156, 252, 253, 254, 255
progressive taxation 260
Provenzano, L. 228, 322
providence 80, 271
prudence/prudential 276, 285
punishment 209–10, 235, 241, 289

Quine, W. V. O. 54, 322

Rawls, J. 6, 16, 26, 32, 90, 116, 128, 151, 152, 156, 186, 203, 204, 206, 207, 208, 212–13, 215, 216, 217, 267, 322–3
  problem of congruence 267–8
  purely conscientious acts 267–8
realism/anti-realism 18, 19, 25, 91, 100, 121, 151, 171, 248, 287
  metaphysical realism 96
  in Nietzsche's ethics 90, 91, 92, 93, 96–100, 112
  social/historical realism 96, 117, 126, 171
reason/reasoning 58, 156, 158, 183, 196–7, 199, 202, 210, 254, 287
  collective 211, 212
  Hobbes's normative conception of 196–7
  Hume's instrumental view of 196–7, 212–13
  and ideology 78, 151, 210, 213, 281, 282
  as normative 38, 42, 211, 287
  reasoning capacities of subject 137, 149, 156, 210–11, 212–13, 269–73
  as dependent upon maturity 137, 246, 266, 278, 279
recognition theory, politics of recognition, culture of recognition 6, 26, 171–6, 185–6, 210, 273, 277–9, 284, 289, 316, 326
'red thread' (Foucault) 64, 214, 219
reflective equilibrium 90, 93, 150, 151, 156, 201, 203, 216
  considered judgements 90, 116, 145, 150–1, 156, 212, 216
relativism
  Berlin's relativism 220, 240
  'bridgeheads' 63, 110, 122
  criticisms of Foucault as relativist 220, 243–7, 266
  moral, ethical relativism 2, 3, 6, 16, 17, 18, 20, 34, 36, 48, 51, 53, 59, 78, 80, 81, 109, 110, 188, 266, 296
  relativity of norms/historical relativity 20, 80, 235
repetition, theory of ix, 6, 67, 170, 271, 307
  emergent individuation 144, 170
  individuating and assimilating 144, 170, 205, 268, 271–2
responsibility 27, 54, 140–2, 182, 233, 266, 267, 269–76, 277, 282, 289, 314, 323, 325, 326
  to animals, the environment, and the world 140, 209, 276, 286
  and continuance to future 182, 267, 270–1, 274–6

diminished 273, 288–9
'giving an account of oneself'
    270, 272
of governments 232, 233–5
imperative to 140–2
limits on 140–2, 289
ressentiment 81, 199, 215, 240
revolution 231, 232
right, concept of 38, 143–8, 282
rights, human 6, 26, 27, 77, 81,
    169, 187–9, 208, 231, 232,
    231, 259, 265, 267
  equal right not to be disposed
    of 214
  'unrestricted rights' (Foucault)
    77, 231
risk/risks 111, 179, 276, 283
Romantics 70, 71, 184
Ross, W. D. 144, 155, 216, 323
Rousseau, J. J. 151, 156, 160, 184,
    189, 192, 203, 216, 226
rules 7, 8, 14, 31, 36, 37, 39, 40,
    43–4, 46, 53, 54, 79, 80, 110,
    111, 116–19, 120, 123, 125,
    133, 134, 135, 137–9, 140,
    141, 145–6, 148, 177, 195,
    208, 214, 215, 229, 232, 234,
    238, 252, 253, 254, 262, 263,
    264, 265, 269, 273, 275, 279,
    280, 285, 312, 315
  of the game 23, 54, 79, 80, 110,
    111, 117
  general rules (Hume) 262, 285
  life continuance ground rules
    116–19
  as prescriptive/normative/moral
    36, 37, 39, 40, 44, 53, 120,
    162
  of right 145–6, 148, 229
Russell, B. 18, 115, 176

Sartre, J.-P. 162, 163, 268, 288,
    323

Scanlon, T. 41–2, 43, 45, 54,
    150–1, 153, 156, 206, 209,
    216, 218, 276, 287, 323–4
Schacht, R. 107, 110, 115, 295,
    314, 324
Schelling, F. W. J. 159, 160, 184
Schnädelbach, H. 57–8, 81, 324
Schopenhauer, A. 160, 189, 324
Schumpeter, J. 169, 324
science/scientific theories 7, 8, 9,
    10, 18, 19, 21, 22, 30, 41, 59,
    60, 61, 68, 70, 71, 73, 82, 84,
    86, 89, 90, 92, 106, 112, 123,
    145, 146, 153, 166–8, 185,
    208, 227, 236, 251, 268, 290,
    301, 306, 318, 319, 321
  as concerned with elimination of
    error 60, 82, 83–4
  as infused with ideology 19, 73,
    78, 83–4, 210, 211, 213, 282
  as infused with norms of life 19,
    60, 61, 70, 77, 83–4
  and objectivity 18–19, 84
  and teleology 166–8
security 179, 180, 195, 214, 222,
    265
self-satisfaction 177, 178
Seneca 49, 50, 54, 324
sentiments 257, 266
  'progress of sentiments' (Baier)
    266
separateness of persons thesis 170,
    204
separation of powers 26, 195, 223
  distribution/balance of powers
    221, 223, 224, 225
  reputation of the powers 223
set theory 16–18, 20, 242
shared interests/shared world 98,
    117, 118, 143, 169, 180, 205,
    239–40, 266
shared objective values 98, 99,
    125–6

social construction/ism 214, 268, 273
social contract theory 26, 76, 151, 156, 187–93, 194, 203–11, 215, 216, 267
   Foucault's objections to 206–11
social democracy 228, 229, 233–4, 242
socialism 208, 228
Socrates 4, 52, 238, 284, 286, 290
Solzhenitsyn, A. 161
Sorabji, R. 52, 55, 325
soul 69, 75–6, 139, 215, 268, 286
specificity/specific situations 16, 17, 19, 20, 132, 142, 144, 174, 205
   see also difference
Spencer, H. 100, 113, 114
Stalinism 161
state/State 159, 170, 222, 228–9, 233, 241
   governmentalization of 228–9
   negative role of 179, 186
   positive role for 178, 179
Steuart, J. 160, 184
Stevenson, C. L. 127
Stoics 49, 50, 109, 120, 211
strategies/strategic 23, 60, 61, 111, 174, 231
subject, the 11, 20, 27, 35, 39, 48, 50, 51, 63, 67, 72, 119, 165, 170, 206, 211, 212, 252, 206, 241, 270, 271, 272, 273, 279, 280–1, 288, 290, 293, 299, 301, 307, 318, 320, 328
   ahistorical/essentialized conception of 20, 69, 71–2, 112, 119, 165, 191, 194, 226, 263
   as emergent in history 15, 70, 268, 269
   motley beings (not hard-wired) 76, 81, 267

   normativity of 24, 39, 48, 49, 50
   as not fully knowable to itself 210, 212, 269–73
   self-interest/self-interested subjects 209, 216, 218, 207, 267
   social/historical conception of 51, 67, 71, 163–4, 165, 170, 194, 226, 241, 268, 269
   uniqueness of 11, 268
suicide 78, 201, 203
supererogation 209, 276
survival 9, 38, 41, 43, 52, 66, 72, 76, 79, 80, 81, 83, 97, 98, 100, 102, 108, 109, 110, 111, 116, 121, 122, 124, 125, 126, 137, 142, 153, 172, 175, 188, 189, 190, 192, 195–6, 199, 200, 201, 203, 209, 210, 214, 252, 257, 261, 263, 265, 269, 287, 296, 297
   concept of survival defined 196, 209
   as consensual norm 196, 200, 203
   as hypothetical imperative 196, 203
   as immanent quest of life 41, 66, 81, 100, 110, 124, 172, 200, 214, 269
   as non-metaphysical 153, 190, 192
   as source of normative objectivity 44, 98, 111, 121, 125
   as source of normativity in general 38, 79, 126, 189, 200, 252, 287
   as source of rules and order 111, 142, 195, 196, 263
   survive and prosper 108, 109, 110, 116, 121, 122, 126, 188, 201, 209, 214, 261

survival and well-being 76, 80, 81, 83, 110, 126, 137, 142, 214, 269
sustainability 104
sympathy 265–6

technologies/technology 7, 75, 140, 183, 188, 192, 211, 221, 222, 227, 229, 253, 275, 293, 300, 301, 312
teleology 6, 7, 40, 56, 58, 76, 78, 86, 109, 143, 157, 161, 166–9, 172, 181, 178, 181, 182, 183, 185, 188, 194, 205, 240, 255, 314
  ends 7, 40, 78, 109, 127, 140, 142, 143, 147, 166, 168, 169, 177, 178, 185, 197, 198, 207, 242, 249, 263, 275, 314
  ends justifying means 181, 255, 258
  final causes 78, 166, 167
  goals/goal-directed 78, 97, 109, 140, 142, 143, 159, 168, 173, 187, 196, 197, 240, 252, 258, 273, 275, 323
  perfection/ism 58, 167, 168, 178, 257, 305
  purposes, teleological 78, 80, 78, 80, 94, 95, 120, 142, 166, 168, 169, 179, 240, 246
  'strong teleology' 167–8, 181, 183
  teleological dimension to action 40, 78, 144, 205
  telos 48, 51, 168
  'weak' teleology 56, 143, 168, 275
testing 51, 52, 74, 76, 77, 251, 275, 281, 284, 285, 290
  as practice of the self 51, 52, 76, 281, 284, 285, 290

test of relevance/tests of life 52, 74, 76, 96, 102, 141, 155, 285
testing limits 77, 251, 275
thinking 4, 7, 9, 11, 14, 18, 31, 32, 38, 41, 67, 68, 103, 120, 140, 150, 151, 156, 162, 165, 167, 168, 169, 194, 211, 213, 237, 253, 255, 274–5, 276, 281, 282, 290, 297, 303, 309, 310, 312, 319, 323, 326
  as challenging prejudice/ interrogating 31, 140, 162, 213, 255, 274–5, 282
  as necessary to knowledge 14, 18, 38, 67, 68, 120, 140, 253, 275, 282, 290
  as normative 32, 38, 275, 282, 290
Thoreau, H. D. 286–7, 291
totalitarianism 71, 158, 161, 179, 211
totality/totalization 15, 22, 50, 72, 158, 159, 160, 161, 164, 172, 183, 232, 310, 315
trust/collaboration 259, 266

unanimity/unanimity rule 148, 155, 208, 209, 217
unity/plurality 43, 44, 75, 80, 160, 161, 163, 169–70, 171, 172, 173, 188, 236, 239–40, 316
  excessive unity 159–60, 161, 163, 169–70, 171, 172, 184, 223, 228
  necessary concordance of difference within unity 188, 220, 236, 240, 271–2, 188
universalism 3, 50, 56, 57, 62, 65, 68, 73, 99, 116, 117, 232, 135, 140, 187, 207, 208, 264–5, 268, 275–6

universalism (*cont.*)
  criticisms of universal rule-type moralities 3, 6, 56–7, 106, 107, 116, 117, 119, 129–35, 137–9, 140–2, 194, 207, 275–6
  universal rights 77, 187–8, 231, 232
  universal values/historical rationalities 50, 57, 62, 65, 68, 73, 99, 140, 154, 197, 264–5
  universality of pain 265
utilitarianism 6, 119, 135, 145, 146, 147, 151, 152, 156, 204, 214, 238, 311, 316, 317, 324
  greatest happiness principle 119, 204–5
  majority principle/averaging strategy 145, 146, 147, 204–5, 208–9, 214
  maximization principle 119, 144–5, 146, 204–5, 207, 209, 214
utopia/utopianism 35, 159, 166, 181, 182, 249

'veil of ignorance' (Rawls) 203, 211, 216, 218

viral pandemics 74, 179, 255, 260, 275
vitalism/vitalist biology 42, 53, 57, 58, 65, 66, 67, 69–72, 74, 76, 83, 101, 102, 103, 117, 168, 286, 306, 322
vulnerability 72, 97, 144, 172, 174, 175, 185, 264–6, 326
  dependence/interdependency 9, 146, 170, 178, 187, 254, 264–6, 273
  human insufficiency (Bataille) 9, 172, 178, 264–266
  to pain 97, 265
  to unpredictability of life 72, 172, 175, 273

Wedgwood, R. 37, 38, 39, 43, 45, 327
Whewell, W. 153
White, S. K. 27, 247, 327
Whitehead, A. N. 16
Wittgenstein, L. 34, 41, 44, 54, 109, 115, 134, 154, 185, 194, 263, 328
worldly ethics (Myers) 243–7

Zermelo, E. 18
zone of freedom/discretion 118, 239, 264, 268

EU authorised representative for GPSR:
Easy Access System Europe, Mustamäe tee 50,
10621 Tallinn, Estonia
gpsr.requests@easproject.com

www.ingramcontent.com/pod-product-compliance
Lightning Source LLC
Chambersburg PA
CBHW050200240426
43671CB00013B/2193